UNIX System Security Tools

McGraw-Hill Unix Series Titles:

Maxwell	UNIX Network Management Tools	0-07-913782-2
Medinets	UNIX Shell Programming Tools	0-07-913790-3
Carasik	UNIX Secure Shell	0-07-134933-2
Ross	UNIX System Security Tools	0-07-913788-1

To order or receive additional information on these or any other McGraw-Hill titles, in the United States please call 1-800-722-4726, or visit us at www.computing.mcgraw-hill.com. In other countries, contact your McGraw-Hill representative.

UNIX System Security Tools

Seth T. Ross

McGraw-Hill

New York • San Francisco • Washington, D.C. • Auckland • Bogotá • Caracas
Lisbon • London • Madrid • Mexico City • Milan • Montreal • New Delhi
San Juan • Singapore • Sydney • Tokyo • Toronto

Library of Congress Cataloging-in-Publication Data

Ross, Seth.
    UNIX system security tools / Seth Ross.
            p.   cm.
    ISBN 0-07-913788-1
    1. Computer security. 2. UNIX (Computer file) I. Title.
QA76.9.A25R665 1999
005.8—dc21   99-33668
                                                                      CIP

McGraw-Hill

A Division of The McGraw·Hill Companies

1 2 3 4 5 6 7 8 9 0   AGM/AGM   9 0 4 3 2 1 0 9

P/N 0-07-054054-3

Part of ISBN 0-07-913788-1

*The sponsoring editor for this book was Simon Yates, and the production supervisor
was Clare Stanley. It was set in Sabon by TIPS Technical Publishing.*

Printed and bound by Quebecor/Martinsburg.

Throughout this book, trademarked names are used. Rather than put a trademark
symbol after every occurrence of a trademarked name, we use names in an editorial
fashion only, and to the benefit of the trademark owner, with no intention of infringement of the trademark. Where such designations appear in this book, they have been
printed with initial caps.

This book is printed on recycled, acid-free paper containing a minimum of
50% recycled, de-inked fiber.

To Dylan

Contents

Foreword

How do you make a UNIX computer that is secure? It's easy... really. Just put the computer in a steel room, turn it off, and lock the door as you leave. Unfortunately, while this strategy leaves you with a computer that is fairly secure, it also leaves you with a machine that is completely unusable.

Many people believe that it is impossible to build a computer system that is both usable and secure. They see security as something that gets in the way, rather than as a tool that makes it possible to get the job done. But in fact, security and usability go hand-in-hand. Security measures that are too difficult to properly implement are not likely to be used at all—making them not terribly secure. On the other hand, there is nothing "usable" about a computer that has had its disk wiped clean by a teenage attacker from Argentina. Both security and usability are proper goals of any competent system administrator or clued-in user.

But if security and usability are the twin goals, then what is the best way to proceed? The days are long gone when you could simply purchase a UNIX workstation with the operating system pre-installed, and then download patches over the Internet as they became available by the vendor. One reason is that the majority of computers running the UNIX operating system are running "free" versions of the operating system that are not necessarily supported, or for which support costs extra. An even bigger reason is the fact that the best computer security tools are not bundled with operating systems in the first place. Instead, you need to research and find the tools on the Internet and install them yourself.

The world of UNIX system security tools is vast, constantly changing, and largely undocumented. There is a lot of good software available on the Internet today—but little of it is accompanied by good documentation. User guides and README files only go so far. Even the programs that have well-written manuals do not include overview documents explaining general security postures or planning. And no README file will tell you how to frame together many publicly available tools into an overall security framework.

That's why this book is so important. In this volume, Seth Ross has gathered together, in one place, concrete information on dozens of different state-of-the-art tools, including scanners, vulnerability assessment tools, and network programs. He's combined installation and running information with tips on why you should be running the programs in the first place. And he's also written an engaging primer on UNIX for people who are new to the security game, or who are simply too busy to keep up with all of the required reading. This book and the tools it covers can help you attain both security and usability, along with some peace of mind.

—Simson L. Garfinkel
Author, *Practical UNIX and Internet Security*

Preface

The UNIX operating system is a critical part of our civilization's infrastructure. Many tens of millions of people utilize services provided by UNIX machines each and every day, usually without realizing it. While UNIX has been deployed in commercial and academic settings for decades, its importance has been greatly amplified by the rise of the Internet as a mass medium. While UNIX and the Internet are logically distinct entities, in the real world the two are intricately intertwined. Most critical Internet services were first developed and deployed on UNIX boxes, and despite the rise of interloping operating systems like Windows NT, UNIX continues to be the mainstay of the communications revolution initiated by the Internet.

There is an irony here: UNIX was never intended to be a secure computing platform. From its start in AT&T's Bell Laboratories thirty years ago, UNIX was designed to be a multi-user, multitasking operating system that featured ease-of-programming and functionality over security. So it's not surprising that as UNIX has become an increasingly important part of the worldwide information milieu, it has come under unrelenting attack from the curious and malevolent alike. While no one knows how many UNIX and UNIX-like systems are in use, let alone how many are attacked in a given year, one can infer that many tens of thousands are probed, and hundreds compromised each and every day.

The purpose of this book is to provide UNIX system administrators with tools and techniques that can help provide a given UNIX system with a baseline of security. The UNIX security community has produced an amazing assortment of add-on security tools in the past decade. Using security archives like COAST as reference points, I evaluated over three dozen tools in the course of my research. I chose half a dozen to cover in-depth, selecting some that represented a certain kind of tool (e.g., Crack is an archetypal password checker) and some that demonstrate overall excellence (e.g., Tripwire measures up well to the criteria I recommend in "Evaluating Security Tools" on page 15). Others I cover in survey form.

While I did not intend this book to be a general primer on UNIX system security, much of the material is aimed at the technically astute individual who, by virtue of running a departmental server or home machine, has been thrust into the role of a security administrator. I assume that most UNIX installations, large or small, share a common set of policy objectives: that continued operation is important; that user accounts and data should not be compromised; that important system events should be logged and monitored; and that systems need to be usable as well as secure.

No tool or collection of tools can secure an operating system, nor can any book account for the amazing variety of ways that a system can be compromised by malevolence, incompetence, or the entropy of the universe. If you deploy the tools and techniques discussed herein, however, you can achieve a security baseline that in most circumstances would be considered both practical and reasonably diligent. Of course, "most circumstances" doesn't include top secret military installations, nuclear power plants, aviation control systems, banking systems, and the like. While nothing in this book is likely to harm the security of these types of important systems, reasonable diligence requires a far more thorough approach than can be presented in these scant pages.

You should observe additional provisos when using this book and the tools it covers. Although this text refers to "UNIX," there is really no such thing. UNIX was developed by AT&T and subsequently released in large part to the public domain. There are dozens of different kinds of UNIX today, produced by different vendors, universities, organizations, and individuals (see Table 1.1 on page 6). While I've taken steps to try to ensure that the commands, tools, and techniques will run on common UNIX implementations, there's absolutely no guarantee that anything in this book will work as described on any particular UNIX system. The reference platform for most of the examples in this book is Red Hat Linux 5.0. I also used a system running HP-UX 10.20 and various BSD-based systems. These systems were deployed in a test network that was broken down once the book was finished.

The world of UNIX is extremely dynamic. Even as I write this, all three reference platforms have been replaced by newer versions (Red Hat Linux 6.0, HP-UX 11, etc.). The world of computer security tools is also extremely dynamic. Most likely, some of the tools described herein have also been replaced by newer versions. I've provided URLs for most of the tools and many of the methods I describe in this book as well as a list of Internet resources (page 345). I strongly recommend that you seek out online information both before and while you work with any of these tools. If you have questions about the tools or UNIX security in general, I highly recommend the Usenet newsgroup `comp.security.unix` as a helpful resource.

You can find additional information about the topics covered in this book as well as errata, information about future editions, and links to reviews at the URL

`http://www.albion.com/usst/`

A note on vocabulary: as dedicated computer lovers and tinkerers have been pointing out for years, "hackers"—problem-solvers who enjoy exploring the details of how systems work—are not "crackers"—malevolent persons who break into systems for fun and profit. The distinction has been lost by mainstream reporters, popular culture, and by criminals themselves, who like to call themselves "hackers" rather than trespassers, thieves, spies, extortionists, vandals, etc. I prefer to reserve the term "hacker" to describe the really smart people whose tinkering created everything from the World Wide Web to Linux. In this text, I refer to the unauthorized persons who break into systems as "crackers," "attackers," or "intruders."

A note on typography: commands that appear in the text are set in `bold`. Command line examples, sample output, code listings, and URLs are set in a `fixed-pitch` font. In command examples, elements that the user needs to type are set in `bold` (text that isn't displayed on screen—like passwords—takes the ~~strikethrough~~ style). Filenames, system calls, and system libraries are set in *italics*. Words as words are quoted.

I'd like to thank Simon Yates at McGraw-Hill for having the vision to launch a UNIX series, my agents Neil Salkind and David Rogelberg at Studio B, Lynanne Fowle, Sandra Henry-Stocker, Robert Kern, Todd Knorr, and the rest of the editorial and production team, Hal Miller for allowing me to use his text on sysadmin ethics, Brian Cunnie for his UNIX wizardry, Simson Garfinkel for his feedback, John Perry Barlow for trying to set me on the right path seven years ago, Steve Jobs for creating the NeXT, and my wife Catherine. Without her love and support, this all would be for naught.

—Seth T. Ross
San Francisco

Introduction

This chapter starts off with a practical definition of UNIX, a quick UNIX history, and a snapshot of the different UNIX variants. It presents a taxonomy of computer security and related concepts. It introduces the world of UNIX security tools and cites criteria for evaluating security tools. This chapter also discusses the security implications of open-source software and makes an argument for a full-disclosure approach to security. It concludes with an overview of several important rules to think about when planning for and implementing system security.

UNIX: A Practical Definition

There's no such thing as UNIX. I realize this is a strange statement to make at the beginning of a book purporting to be about "UNIX System Security." UNIX has been around for a long time —over 30 years as of this writing. During these decades, it has been metamorphosed millions of times, if not billions of times, by many thousands of individuals and companies implementing thousands of variants or "flavors," and by millions of system administrators installing it on everything from tiny embedded devices to supercomputers. Arguably, no two instances of the UNIX operating system are exactly the same.

Some of the drift in the meaning of UNIX is due to legal quandaries; some of it is the result of various commercial "UNIX wars" that have been waged over the years; some of it results from battles of wit and mind, with superior but unorthodox technologies winning over inferior authorized ones.

Given the polymorphous essence of UNIX, I'll start with a few different ways of looking at it and then shed some additional light by reviewing UNIX history. Here are several working definitions of UNIX:

- Legal—While there may be no such thing as "UNIX," the term is a trademark owned by the Open Group, an international consortium that demands the mark receive proper attribution.[1] Repeat after me: "UNIX is a registered trademark of The Open Group." You'll sometimes see AT&T, Bell Labs, Novell, or X/Open Company Ltd. listed as the trademark holders—it's been passed off time and again. Arguably, the mark has been diluted to the point of meaninglessness. Nonetheless, the Open Group promulgates "The Single UNIX® Specification" which can be viewed at `http://www.UNIX-systems.org/online.html`

- Technical—According to the UNIX FAQ, UNIX is "an operating system typically written in C, with a hierarchical file system and integration of file and device I/O, whose system call interface includes services such as *fork()* and *pipe()*, and whose user

---

1. See `http://www.opengroup.org/trademarks.htm`

interface includes tools such as cc, troff, grep, awk, and a choice of shell."[2] I might add that UNIX provides a consistent approach to multitasking, with built-in operations for the creation, synchronization, and termination of processes. It is intrinsically portable between different kinds of computers.

- Linguistic—The name "Unix" was intended as a pun on the name Multics and was written "Unics" at first, for UNiplexed Information and Computing System. Both "Unix" and "UNIX" are in wide use today. At one point, Dennis Ritchie tried to promulgate the lower-case version, since "UNIX" isn't an acronym. In deference to the trademark, this text uses "UNIX."

- Social—Many people who run UNIX-like systems such as Linux think they're running UNIX. Official UNIX systems and unofficial UNIX systems are commonly treated as belonging to a single category—in books, in media coverage, on the net, and by general social consensus.

A Quick History of UNIX

In order to define UNIX, it helps to look at its history. In 1969, Ken Thompson, Dennis Ritchie and others started work on what was to become UNIX on a "little-used PDP-7 in a corner" at AT&T Bell Labs. For ten years, the development of UNIX proceeded at AT&T in numbered versions. V4 (1974) was re-written in C—a major milestone for the operating system's portability among different systems. V6 (1975) was the first to become available outside Bell Labs—it became the basis of the first version of UNIX developed at the University of California Berkeley.

Bell Labs continued work on UNIX into the 1980s, culminating in the release of System V (as in "five," not the letter) in 1983 and System V, Release 4 (abbreviated SVR4) in 1989. Meanwhile, programmers at the University of California hacked mightily on the source code AT&T had released, leading to many a master thesis. The Berkeley Standard Distribution (BSD) became a second major variant of "UNIX." It was widely deployed in both university and

---

2. See http://www.faqs.org/faqs/unix-faq/faq/contents/

corporate computing environments starting with the release of BSD 4.2 in 1984. Some of its features were incorporated into SVR4.

As the 1990s opened, AT&T's source code licensing had created a flourishing market for hundreds of UNIX variants by different manufacturers. AT&T sold its UNIX business to Novell in 1993, and Novell sold it to the Santa Cruz Operation two years later. In the meantime, the UNIX trademark had been passed to the X/Open consortium, which eventually merged to form The Open Group.[3]

While the stewardship of UNIX was passing from entity to entity, several long-running development efforts started bearing fruit. Traditionally, in order to get a BSD system working, you needed a source code license from AT&T. But by the early 1990s, Berkeley hackers had done so much work on BSD that most of the original AT&T source code was long gone. A succession of programmers, starting with William and Lynne Jolitz, started work on the Net distribution of BSD, leading to the release of 386BSD version 0.1 on Bastille Day, 1992. This original "free source" BSD was spun out into three major distributions, each of which has a dedicated following: NetBSD, FreeBSD, and OpenBSD, all of which are based on BSD 4.4.[4]

BSD wasn't the first attempt at a "free" UNIX. In 1984, programmer Richard Stallman started work on a free UNIX clone known as GNU (GNU's Not UNIX). By the early 1990s, the GNU Project had achieved several programming milestones, including the release of the GNU C library and the Bourne Again SHell (bash). The whole system was basically finished, except for one critical element: a working kernel.

Enter Linus Torvalds, a student at the University of Helsinki in Finland. Linus looked at a small UNIX system called Minix and decided he could do better. In the fall of 1991, he released the source code for a freeware kernel called "Linux"—a combination

---

3. This version of events is captured by the History & Timeline that can be found at http://www.UNIX-systems.org/what_is_unix/ history_timeline.html
4. For more information about the *BSD family, see the FAQ at http://www.faqs.org/faqs/386bsd-faq/part1/

of his first name and Minux, pronounced lynn-nucks.[5] By 1994, Linus and a far-flung team of kernel hackers were able to release version 1.0 of Linux. Linus and friends had a free kernel; Stallman and friends had the rest of a free UNIX clone system: People could then put the Linux kernel together with GNU to make a complete free system. This system is known as "Linux," though Stallman prefers the appellation "GNU/Linux system."[6] There are several distinct GNU/Linux distributions: some are available with commercial support from companies like Red Hat, Caldera Systems, and S.U.S.E.; others, like Debian GNU/Linux, are more closely aligned with the original free software concept.

The spread of Linux, now up to kernel version 2.2, has been a startling phenomenon. Linux runs on several different chip architectures and has been adopted or supported to varying extents by several old-line UNIX vendors like Hewlett-Packard, Silicon Graphics, and Sun Microsystems, by PC vendors like Compaq and Dell, and by major software vendors like Oracle and IBM. Perhaps the most delicious irony has been the response of Microsoft, which acknowledges the competitive threat of ubiquitous free software but seems unwilling or unable to respond with open-source software of its own.[7]

Microsoft has, however, struck blows with Windows NT (Windows 2000). During the late 1990s, vendor after vendor has abandoned the UNIX server platform in favor of Windows NT or wavered in their support. Silicon Graphics Inc., for example, has decided that Intel hardware and NT is the graphics platform of the future.

A Practical Definition

The phenomenon of old-line UNIX vendors jumping ship and the concurrent rush to Linux by vendors large and small brings us back to the question at the top of this section: What is UNIX?

---

5. Linux is a trademark of Linus Torvalds. See "Linux Trademark dispute resolved, Linus Torvalds is owner!" at
http://www.linuxmall.com/Allann/lxtm.001.html
6. See http://www.gnu.org/gnu/linux-and-gnu.html
7. See The Halloween Documents at
http://www.opensource.org/halloween.html

While one can abide by the legal definition as embodied in the trademark, I believe that this does a major disservice to the industry. As the base software of the Internet, UNIX technology is one the significant achievements of 20th century civilization. To restrict it to a narrow legal or technical definition—as formulated by some of the vendors now abandoning it—is to deny its ongoing relevance and importance, which is most evident in the amazing popularity and strength of UNIX-like clones such as GNU/Linux and BSD.

For the purposes of the book, I define UNIX as

> A set of enabling technologies first developed at AT&T that have been incorporated into several legally distinct but closely related operating systems, each of which can be considered to be a "UNIX system." If it looks like UNIX, operates like UNIX, runs common UNIX utilities and programs, and is developed with UNIX as a model, it's UNIX.

The Many Flavors of UNIX

Table 1.1 summarizes some of the common UNIX variants and clones. While the table lists about forty different variants, the UNIX world isn't nearly as diverse as it used to be. Some of them are defunct and are listed for historical purposes. Others are on their way out. In some cases, vendors have defected to Microsoft technology. In others, mergers and acquisitions have led to the consolidation of different UNIX implementations. A list of "dead" UNIX implementations would be substantial indeed, consisting of hundreds of variations on the letters "U," "I," and "X" (CLIX, CX/UX, MV/UX, SINIX, VENIX, etc.).

Table 1.1 *UNIX Variants and Clones*

UNIX Variant	Company/Org.	For More Info
A/UX	Apple Computer, Inc.	defunct
AIX	IBM	http://www.rs6000.ibm.com/ software/
AT&T System V	AT&T	defunct

Table 1.1 *UNIX Variants and Clones (Cont'd)*

UNIX Variant	Company/Org.	For More Info
BS2000/OSD-BC	Siemens AG	http://www.siemens.com/servers/bs2osd/
BSD/OS	Berkeley Software Design, Inc.	http://www.bsdi.com
CLIX	Intergraph Corp.	http://www.intergraph.com
Debian GNU/Hurd	Software in the Public Interest, Inc.	http://www.gnu.org/software/hurd/debian-gnu-hurd.html
Debian GNU/Linux	Software in the Public Interest, Inc.	http://www.debian.org
DG/UX	Data General Corp.	http://www.dg.com/products/html/dg_ux.html
Digital Unix	Compaq Computer Corporation	http://www.unix.digital.com/
DYNIX/ptx	Sequent Computer Systems, Inc.	http://www.sequent.com/products/software/operatingsys/dynix.html
Esix UNIX	Esix Systems	http://www.esix.com/
FreeBSD	FreeBSD group	http://www.freebsd.org
GNU Herd	GNU organization	http://www.gnu.org
HAL SPARC64/OS	HAL Computer Systems, Inc.	http://www.hal.com
HP-UX	Hewlett-Packard Company	http://www.hp.com/unixwork/hpux/
Irix	Silicon Graphics, Inc.	http://www.sgi.com/software/irix6.5/
Linux	several	http://www.linux.org
LynxOS	Lynx Real-Time Systems, Inc.	http://www.lynx.com/products/lynxos.html

Table 1.1 *UNIX Variants and Clones (Cont'd)*

UNIX Variant	Company/Org.	For More Info
MachTen	Tenon Intersystems	`http://www.tenon.com/` `products/machten/`
Mac OS X Server	Apple Computer, Inc.	`http://www.apple.com/macosx/`
Minix	none	`http://www.cs.vu.nl/~ast/` `minix.html`
MkLinux	Apple Computer, Inc.	`http://www.mklinux.apple.com`
NCR UNIX SVR4 MP-RAS	NCR Corporation	`http://www3.ncr.com/` `product/integrated/` `software/p2.unix.html`
NetBSD	NetBSD group	`http://www.netbsd.org`
NeXTSTEP	NeXT Computer Inc.	defunct, see `http://www.apple.com/` `enterprise/`
NonStop-UX	Compaq Computer Corporation	`http://www.tandem.com`
OpenBSD	OpenBSD group	`http://www.openbsd.org`
OpenLinux	Caldera Systems, Inc.	`http://www.calderasystems.com`
Openstep	Apple Computer, Inc.	`http://www.apple.com/` `enterprise/`
QNX Realtime OS	QNX Software Systems Ltd.	`http://www.qnx.com/` `products/os/qnxrtos.html`
Red Hat Linux	Red Hat Software, Inc.	`http://www.redhat.com/`
Reliant UNIX	Siemens AG	`http://www.siemens.com/` `servers/rm/`
Solaris	Sun Microsystems	`http://www.sun.com/` `software/solaris/`

Table 1.1 *UNIX Variants and Clones (Cont'd)*

UNIX Variant	Company/Org.	For More Info
SunOS	Sun Microsystems	defunct
SuSE	S.u.S.E., Inc.	http://www.suse.com
UNICOS	Silicon Graphics, Inc.	http://www.sgi.com/software/unicos/
UnixWare	SCO—The Santa Cruz Operation Inc.	http://www.sco.com/unix/
UTS	Amdahl Corporation	http://www.amdahl.com/uts/

Computer Security: A Practical Definition

Defining "computer security" is not trivial. The difficulty lies in developing a definition that is broad enough to be valid regardless of the system being described, yet specific enough to describe what security really is. In a generic sense, security is "freedom from risk or danger." In the context of computer science, security is the prevention of, or protection against,

- access to information by unauthorized recipients, and

- intentional but unauthorized destruction or alteration of that information[8]

This can be re-stated: "Security is the ability of a system to protect information and system resources with respect to confidentiality and integrity." Note that the scope of this second definition includes system resources, which include CPUs, disks, and programs, in addition to information.

---

8. *Dictionary of Computing*, Fourth Ed. (Oxford: Oxford University Press, 1996).

A Taxonomy of Computer Security

Computer security is frequently associated with three core areas, which can be conveniently summarized by the acronym "CIA":

- Confidentiality—Ensuring that information is not accessed by unauthorized persons

- Integrity—Ensuring that information is not altered by unauthorized persons in a way that is not detectable by authorized users

- Authentication—Ensuring that users are the persons they claim to be

A strong security protocol addresses all three of these areas. Take, for example, Netscape's SSL (Secure Sockets Layer) protocol. It has enabled an explosion in ecommerce which is really about trust (or more precisely, about the lack of trust). SSL overcomes the lack of trust between transacting parties by ensuring confidentiality through encryption, integrity through checksums, and authentication via server certificates (see "Protecting Against Transmission Risks" on page 317).

Computer security is not restricted to these three broad concepts. Additional ideas that are often considered part of the taxonomy of computer security include:

- Access control—Ensuring that users access only those resources and services that they are entitled to access and that qualified users are not denied access to services that they legitimately expect to receive

- Nonrepudiation—Ensuring that the originators of messages cannot deny that they in fact sent the messages[9]

- Availability—Ensuring that a system is operational and functional at a given moment, usually provided through redundancy; loss of availability is often referred to as "denial-of-service"

---

9. Bryan Pfaffenberger, *Webster's New World Dictionary of Computing Terms,* Sixth Ed. (New York: Simon and Schuster, 1997).

- Privacy—Ensuring that individuals maintain the right to control what information is collected about them, how it is used, who has used it, who maintains it, and what purpose it is used for

These additional elements don't neatly integrate into a singular definition. From one perspective, the concepts of privacy, confidentiality, and security are quite distinct and possess different attributes. Privacy is a property of individuals; confidentiality is a property of data; and security is a property assigned to computer hardware and software systems. From a practical perspective, the concepts are interwoven. A system that does not maintain data confidentiality or individual privacy could be theoretically or even mathematically "secure," but it probably wouldn't be wise to deploy anywhere in the real world.

A Functional View

Computer security can also be analyzed by function. It can be broken into five distinct functional areas:[10]

- Risk avoidance— A security fundamental that starts with questions like: Does my organization or business engage in activities that are too risky? Do we really need an unrestricted Internet connection? Do we really need to computerize that secure business process? Should we really standardize on a desktop operating system with no access control intrinsics?

- Deterrence—Reduces the threat to information assets through fear. Can consist of communication strategies designed to impress potential attackers of the likelihood of getting caught. See "Rule 5: The Fear of Getting Caught is the Beginning of Wisdom" on page 23.

- Prevention—The traditional core of computer security. Consists of implementing safeguards like the tools covered in this book. Absolute prevention is theoretical, since there's a vanishing point where additional preventative measures are no longer cost-effective.

---

10. Donn B. Parker, *Computer Security Management* (Reston, VA: Reston Publishing Company Inc., 1981).

- Detection—Works best in conjunction with preventative measures. When prevention fails, detection should kick in, preferably while there's still time to prevent damage. Includes log-keeping and auditing activities

- Recovery—When all else fails, be prepared to pull out backup media and restore from scratch, or cut to backup servers and net connections, or fall back on a disaster recovery facility. Arguably, this function should be attended to before the others

Analyzing security by function can be a valuable part of the security planning process; a strong security policy will address all five areas, starting with recovery. This book, however, is primarily concerned with prevention and detection.

Security Domains

Computer security is also frequently defined in terms of several interdependent domains that roughly map to specific departments and job titles:

- Physical security—Controlling the comings and goings of people and materials; protection against the elements and natural disasters

- Operational/procedural security—Covering everything from managerial policy decisions to reporting hierarchies

- Personnel security—Hiring employees, background screening, training, security briefings, monitoring, and handling departures

- System security—User access and authentication controls, assignment of privilege, maintaining file and filesystem integrity, backups, monitoring processes, log-keeping, and auditing

- Network security—Protecting network and telecommunications equipment, protecting network servers and transmissions, combatting eavesdropping, controlling access from untrusted networks, firewalls, and detecting intrusions

This text is solely concerned with the latter two. System and network security are difficult, if not impossible, to separate in a UNIX system. Nearly every UNIX distribution in the past fifteen years has included a TCP/IP protocol implementation as well as numerous network services such as FTP, Telnet, DNS, and, more recently, HTTP.

A Practical Definition

In the spirit of practicality, I like the straightforward definition promulgated by Simson Garfinkel and Gene Spafford in Practical UNIX & Internet Security: "A computer is secure if you can depend on it and its software to behave as you expect."[11] In essence, a computer is secure if you can trust it. Data entered today will still be there tomorrow in unaltered form. If you made services x, y, and z available yesterday, they're still available today.

I also like the practical definition offered by Tomas Olovsson, which is narrowed a bit: "A secure system is a system on which enough trust can be put to use it together with sensitive information."[12]

Intrinsically, a secure system should be hard for unauthorized persons to break into—i.e., the value of the work necessary for an unauthorized person to break in should exceed the value of the protected data. Increasing attacker workload and the risks of detection are critical elements of computer security.

For the purposes of this book, I define "system security" as:

> The ongoing and redundant implementation of protections for the confidentiality and integrity of information and system resources so that an unauthorized user has to spend an unacceptable amount of time or money or absorb too much risk in order to defeat it, with the ultimate goal that the system can be trusted with sensitive information.

The World of UNIX Security Tools

The history of UNIX security is the stuff of lore. Since its humble beginnings as a Bell Laboratories project lead by Dennis Ritchie

---

11. Simson Garfinkel and Gene Spafford, *Practical UNIX & Internet Security*, Ed. 2 (Sebastopol, CA: O'Reilly, 1996), 6. Highly recommended.
12. Tomas Olovsson, "A Structured Approach to Computer Security," Technical Report No. 122, 1992. See http://www.ce.chalmers.se/~ulfl/webmdemo/wmwork/www/security_122_1.html

and Ken Thompson in the late 1960s, the UNIX operating system has been programmed and hacked by successive generations of systems programmers.

In November 1988, Robert Tappan Morris released the infamous "Internet worm" that corrupted thousands of net-connected machines overnight.[13] Morris, son of a top US security official, brought issues of UNIX security to the forefront of the nation's attention. The worm exposed a Pandora's Box of vulnerabilities in UNIX, including bugs in the venerable sendmail and finger programs. It also exploited the concept of "trusted hosts" in UNIX—a mechanism developed as part of the Berkeley networking software that enabled users to execute commands from remote machines. Beyond it's immediate impact on infected systems, the worm called into question the "open lab" approach to UNIX security, which maximizes resource-sharing and trusting cooperation at the expense of formal security controls. It represented a turning point—from the worm on, many UNIX installations have had to reconsider their security standing.

In the wake of Morris' worm attack, the UNIX community expended considerable energy to beef up security. Several leading organizations formed CERT (Center for Emergency Response Teams), which to this day is the number one source of information regarding security problems in UNIX systems.[14] Vendors patched holes and increased their efforts to make sure updates were adopted by their customers. Perhaps most significantly, UNIX programmers developed an arsenal of new security tools and made them freely available on the Internet.

As a result, every UNIX sysadmin now has a toolbox of security tools at his or her disposal. Many of these tools and capabilities are built into modern UNIX implementations. Indeed, there is a major trend toward incorporating and bundling security tools in both

---

13. For detailed accounts of the worm, see the papers by Donn Seely ("A Tour of the Worm"), Mark W. Eichin and Jon A. Rochlis ("With Microscope and Tweezers"), and Eugene H. Spafford ("The Internet Worm Program: An Analysis") collected at ftp://ftp.cs.sunyit.edu/pub/FTP/ISI/worm.papers/ and a follow-up by Spafford at http://www.cs.purdue.edu/homes/spaf/tech-reps/933.ps
14. See http://www.cert.org

commercial and free UNIX implementations. In many cases, however, UNIX systems need to be hardened—either a needed capability is not included or it is insufficient. Older systems in particular may be lacking in security protections. In other circumstances, even a modern UNIX box may need additional security functionality. Whether you're running a bit-rotten NeXT box designed with nominal security protection or a spanking new Solaris 7 box with the latest security programs, your system's security standing needs to be closely tailored to the security vulnerabilities it might face. Add-on security tools can help.

Note that many UNIX security tools are "free" both in the sense of not costing money and in the sense that you're free to deploy them without strict licensing or other restrictions. Be forewarned: none of them are "free" in terms of the time needed to find, understand, implement, and run them. To paraphrase Richard Stallman: think "free speech" rather than "free beer."

The "free tool" trend has greatly accelerated in the past few years with the advent of the "open source" movement. The Internet has fostered a vast gift economy in which value—from free content to free programs—is freely exchanged. The Internet has facilitated the formation of virtual teams of programmers developing everything from operating systems (Linux) to server software (the Apache web server) to sophisticated end-user applications (the Mozilla web browser).

Evaluating Security Tools

There's no stock answer to the question of whether or not a sysadmin should install and run a given security tool. It is advisable, as one certification firm suggests, to "Choose Your Weapons Wisely."[15] While evaluating various tools for coverage in this book, I kept the following attributes in mind:

- Is source code available for this tool?
  There's no way to audit or thoroughly evaluate a security tool without source code. While there are many fine commercial tools that don't provide source, I eliminated them from cover-

---

15. See http://www.icsa.net/services/product_cert/
products.shtml

age in these pages. Closed proprietary products require a high level of trust in the supplier. Without access to source code, there's no way to know for sure that holes aren't introduced by the product and that the product doesn't contain back doors. For more discussion of this issue, see "The Benefits of Open Source" on page 18. In general, security safeguards—from door locks and safes to a cryptographic method—shouldn't rely on design and implementation secrecy.

- Is this tool easy to install?
  The concept of "easy" is tricky in this context because none of the tools in the entire UNIX security corpus are no-brainers to install. They all require some forethought and effort. In many cases, tools that I thought might be very useful would not install at all on my reference machines. In other cases, tools were very elegantly designed and implemented—installation was painless enough that I could devote time and mental energy to configuration and use rather than compiler errors and such.

- Can this tool be configured to specific circumstances?
  No two UNIX systems are identical in every way. A good tool is flexible—the designers considered the various environments the tool would be used in and provided for customization.

- Is this tool reliable?
  An unreliable security tool can be worse than no security tool at all since it may provide a sysadmin with a false sense of security.

- Is this tool reasonably easy to use?
  The regular operation of a tool should be a relatively simple matter. Human nature resists using complex or overly difficult tools—a tool that is too cumbersome won't get used and thus won't provide needed protection. Also, the tool should produce readable output. Succinct reports are preferable to voluminous ones since the data reduction capabilities of any one person are limited. The Crack tool is a good example of a tool that provides relevant output: account so-and-so has a weak password, here it is. This question illustrates the general principle that security safeguards must be accepted in order to be effective.

- Is this tool cost effective?

  Both time and money are valuable. Every tool provides some
  sort of benefit. The benefit needs to be weighed against the cost
  of implementing and running the tool. In some cases, a tool
  might degrade performance to an unacceptable extent. This is a
  common problem, for example, with some firewall
  implementations.

- Is this tool maintained?

  There are a number of tools available that for one reason or
  another are no longer maintained by the original authors. In
  general, security safeguards should be sustainable over time—
  an old tool that's been "orphaned" may not be a good fit in a
  global security environment that's constantly in flux. On the
  other hand, sometimes old tools can be very useful, particularly
  on old systems—Dan Farmer's COPS tool was first written in
  1990 but I was still able to use it to find several holes in one of
  my vintage 1990 NeXT cubes. Occasionally, old tools are
  picked up and improved by new maintainers. An example is the
  SATAN network probing tool, which was written by Dan
  Farmer and Wietse Venema and then updated by programmers
  at an outfit called World Wide Digital Security, Inc. (and re-
  christened "SAINT").

- Does this tool depend on other (possibly insecure) programs?

  The UNIX way is to combine different programs to achieve a
  desired result. This can backfire when a security tool depends
  on complex UNIX programs that were not designed for security purposes. Wietse Venema tells the story of setting a booby
  trap for an intruder that was breaking into and deleting systems
  at Eindhoven University of Technology.[16] The trap relied on fin-
  gering the host the attacker was using and mailing the result to
  root. Later, Wietse realized that relying on the `finger` and `mail`
  programs (neither of which was designed for security) could
  open up security holes. The attacker could have included shell
  escapes in his *.plan* file which could have been picked up by the

---

16. See "Murphy's law and computer security" at
`http://www.fish.com/security/murphy.html`

booby trap and sent on for execution by root. The moral of the story: good security tools either stand alone or minimize their trust when relying on other programs.

- Is this tool portable across different UNIX implementations?
  Many sites run a variety of UNIX systems. A cleanly coded tool should be portable across systems. If written for platform A, it should be possible to port it to platform B. Of course, there are fine platform-specific tools, so this is only a general rule.

- Does this tool do any harm?
  This should go without saying. "Do no harm" should be operating assumption number one for any security professional. A number of security tools have recently come to market that feature "strikeback" provisions. Modeled after Department of Defense systems, they can detect an intrusion attempt and then automatically launch a denial-of-service counter-attack. I believe the widespread deployment of this kind of harmful tool is a bad idea. It will be all too easy for one of these systems to attack an innocent party. In fact, it opens new lines of attack for crackers. A cracker on system C could masquerade as system B and then attack system A, knowing that A will automatically retaliate against B. This is known as "killing two systems with one packet."

The Benefits of Open Source

The widespread availability of source code for UNIX operating systems and programs has been a boon for security administrators. Providing source code for programs is an old tradition in computing; recently, with the increasing popularity of open source operating systems like Linux and programs like Apache, the tradition has been formalized. A group of free software evangelists lead by Eric S. Raymond have formed a non-profit organization that, among other things, has trademarked the term "Open Source" (see http://www.opensource.org/[17]).

---

17. See also Tim O'Reilly's engaging overview of the open-source movement in Esther Dyson's Release 1.0 newsletter—
http://www.edventure.com/release1/1198.html

Almost all of the security tools covered in this book are open source, as is the Red Hat Linux reference platform I'm using. The benefits of open source security software are numerous. In a process similar to peer review in the scientific community, open source code can be analyzed, audited, and vetted by dozens, hundreds, or even thousands of concerned practitioners. Bugs and other aberrations can be quickly discovered and patched, creating a substantial disincentive for programmers to place back doors, Trojan Horses, and other kinds of malicious code in their programs. In this way, open source software can be more trustworthy than proprietary software, illustrating what Raymond calls "Linus's Law" (after Linux inventor Linus Torvalds): "Given enough eyeballs, all bugs are shallow."[18] Given open source, security problems can be characterized quickly and the fix will be obvious to someone.

In January 1999, attackers were able to plant a Trojan Horse version of the TCP/Wrappers tool on a well-known FTP site—since source code is available, the back door was quickly noticed and removed. Contrast this with a monolithic operating system like Windows 2000, which has tens of millions of lines of secret, bug-ridden code. Without access to the source code, customers are 100% reliant on the good will and competence of the Microsoft Corporation, an entity with a well-documented record of dubious behavior.[19]

Naturally, just because a program's source is available doesn't necessarily means it's secure—what I'll call "security through disclosure" isn't foolproof (though it's usually stronger than "security through obscurity" [see page 21]). It's theoretically possibly for a programmer to create clean source code that nonetheless includes a Trojan Horse (see "Rule 10: Trust is a Relative Concept" on page 28). In general, source code needs to be widely distributed, reviewed, and fixed in order for its openness to be a security benefit. There have been cases in which popular UNIX utilities with available source have stumbled along for years with significant vul-

---

18. See Raymond's seminal "The Cathedral and the Bazaar" essay about open source at http://www.tuxedo.org/~esr/writings/cathedral-bazaar/
19. An extensive rap sheet has been compiled by the US Department of Justice at http://www.usdoj.gov/atr/cases/ms_index.htm

nerabilities[20] —perhaps people assume that a program that's been around for a while must be safe, or perhaps people were just too lazy or busy to fix it. Conversely, some of the most secure programs are probably deployed by national security organizations, with top-secret source code.

In some ways, open source can make it easier for the "bad guys" to find security holes in the first place, creating an ongoing "cat-and-mouse" game in which cooperating developers attempt to find and patch holes before they can be exploited. This is where the "sunshine effect" comes into play. Karsten M. Self describes this:[21]

> There's still what I call the sunshine effect—the good guys can act overtly, the bad guys must act covertly. Everyone—good guy or bad—has an interest in seeing that their own systems are secure. Hacks will happen, but both alerts and fixes will be communicated rapidly. While crackers operate behind pseudonyms, anonymous remailers, owned systems, and IRC, legitimate operators can communicate openly and to authoritative information channels (e.g.: CERT).

Community plays a large role in open source software. As Self points out, every UNIX operator has an interest in security. This communal interest gets played out in the open source community space, where good will and the free exchange of ideas and code benefits everyone. If you have a problem with an open source tool, you have a good shot at finding a solution online.

There are additional benefits of open source security tools. Most of them are more or less "free"; the solutions are available to anyone with the time and need to install them. This helps put the "little guys" on the same footing as large corporations, security-wise. An open source tool puts the system administrator in control of the level of risk assumed in deploying the tool. Perhaps you don't trust the open source developer any more than the proprietary vendor. Then you can audit the code yourself, or hire someone to do it for you. Finally, open source solutions are by their nature dynamic. Perhaps a tool doesn't do exactly what you need—you can break open the code and fix it yourself. Open

---

20. For an example of this phenomena, see "The Risks of FTP" on page 278.
21. In `comp.security.unix`, December 29, 1998.

source provides a flexibility not available in closed products. Hopefully, if you do make improvements to an open tool you'll offer them back to the original developer and community at large. The give-and-take of the gift economy benefits everyone.

Ten General Security Rules

Before we roll up our sleeves and get into the devilish details of planning and implementing UNIX system security, I'd like to posit ten general rules or themes that I'll return to again and again in this book.

Rule 1: Security Through Obscurity Doesn't Work

As they say in the movies, you can run but you can't hide. You may think that you're running an obscure UNIX-based web server that no one would dream of breaking into, but your obscurity is no protection in an era when thousands of malicious little punks have access to powerful network scanning tools which may discover your system and its vulnerabilities. You may think that you're hiding critical data by burying it several directories deep, but you'd be wrong given the powerful search facilities built into UNIX. A software or hardware vendor might realize that a hole exists in their offering but ship it anyway, thinking that no one will find it. These kinds of holes are discovered all the time.

At best, security through obscurity can provide temporary protection. But never be lulled by it—with modest effort and time, secrets can be discovered. As Deep Throat points out on X-Files: "There's always someone watching."

Rule 2: Full Disclosure of Bugs and Holes Benefits Security

As cited above, some vendors may feel comfortable shipping software with security holes with the expectation that the software is so complex and proprietary that no one will find them—the tree hasn't fallen if no one was there to hear it fall. Some security professionals feel uncomfortable with the publicity that security holes and problems receive. They worry that announcing security exploits can give the "bad guys" ideas about how to attack systems. On the other hand, the security community on the Internet has committed itself to sharing knowledge about holes and possible exploits: numerous mailing lists like bugtraq and newsgroups like `comp.security.unix` maintain open discussions intended to identify and then close holes. It's somewhat paradoxical, but the routine public disclosure of security problems benefits the overall security of the Internet and the systems on it. Security through disclosure works. Note: This doesn't mean you should widely publicize a security hole as soon as you find it. Protocol requires that you contact the system vendor or authors of the affected program first, thus giving them a chance to develop a fix. It's good when security holes are announced. It's best if they're announced along with fixes.

Rule 3: System Security Degrades in Direct Proportion to Use

This is Farmer's Law (promulgated by computer security researcher Dan Farmer): "The Security of a Computer System Degrades in Direct Proportion to the Amount of Use the System Receives."[22]

Ignoring availability for a moment, a computer that's powered down is more secure than one that's powered up. A computer that's powered down, in a locked cage, in a subterranean bomb shelter, with armed guards might be secure. Once one person is using a system, risk increases. Once two or more are using a system, risk increases even more. Put the system on the Internet and provide some services ... I'm sure you get the idea. As Dan says, "Ignorant or malicious users do more damage to system security than any other factors."[23]

The trade-off between security and usefulness/functionality is the classic computer security dilemma. Many Linux distributions are built for maximum functionality and thus ship with massive collections of programs and wide-open security settings. On the other end of the continuum are bastion hosts set up as part of a firewall design. Many of these do one thing (i.e., filter packets between network A and network B) and one thing only. Analyze

---

22. Farmer admits that he probably wasn't the first to state it but since he calls it "Farmer's Law," I will too.
23. Dan Farmer, `http://www.trouble.org/survey/conclusions.html`

where you need to be along the security versus functionality continuum and plan appropriately.

Rule 4: Do It Right Before Someone Does It Wrong For You

Computer security can never be implemented in a vacuum. Simply establishing security mechanisms doesn't guarantee that they will work as planned. Security policies and mechanisms must account for the legitimate needs of users: i.e., they must be done right. An organization can decree that no users will have Internet access only to find that savvy users can buy cheap modems to circumvent this policy, thus greatly increasing the organization's vulnerability. It would be better to set more realistic policies and provide for monitored, controlled access to the net in the first place. A firewall administrator may decide to implement a fascist firewall that only allows HTTP/web access via port 80, leaving users that need Telnet access to the outside out of luck. Alternately, these users may discover that it's possible to encapsulate forbidden protocols in HTTP packets. The administrator would be better off providing for legitimate needs rather than encouraging workarounds that can create substantial and unknown risks. It's better to set things up properly yourself than to wait for someone to do it wrong for you.

Rule 5: The Fear of Getting Caught is the Beginning of Wisdom

Don't underestimate the value of deterrence. Many potential attacks can be prevented by instilling fear in the potential attackers.[24] Deterrence can be particularly effective against the amateur white-collar criminal or insider. The goal is to prevent the attacker's intent from reaching the critical point of action. There are many kinds of safeguards that can deter an attack, ranging from login banner warnings such as "WARNING! Use of this system constitutes consent to security monitoring and testing. All activity is logged with your host name and IP address."[25] to written reminders of computer-related laws, background checks, security briefings, and audits. Of course, these safeguards may not phase the hardened computer criminal, but even a pro will think twice after surveying a newly-cracked system and finding that a monitor-

---

24. "Fear of the Lord is the beginning of wisdom" (Psalms 111:10)
25. Warning text from `http://ciac.llnl.gov/ciac/`

ing tool like Tripwire has been configured to write daily filesystem integrity reports to read-only media.

Rule 6: There's Always Someone Out There Smarter, More Knowledgeable, or Better-Equipped Than You

Be careful about the assumptions you make concerning the threats your systems face. Even redundant security mechanisms and careful monitoring won't necessarily protect you against the uebercracker. Consider this excerpt from Dan Farmer's and Wietse Venema's article, "Improving the Security of Your Site by Breaking Into It":[26]

> Why "uebercracker"? The idea is stolen, obviously, from Nietzsche's *uebermensch*, or, literally translated into English, "over man." Nietzsche used the term not to refer to a comic book superman, but instead a man who had gone beyond the incompetence, pettiness, and weakness of the everyday man. The uebercracker is therefore the system cracker who has gone beyond simple cookbook methods of breaking into systems. An uebercracker is not usually motivated to perform random acts of violence. Targets are not arbitrary—there is a purpose, whether it be personal monetary gain, a hit and run raid for information, or a challenge to strike a major or prestigious site or net.personality. An uebercracker is hard to detect, harder to stop, and hardest to keep out of your site for good.

Many security threat models assume than the bad guy will be a one-dimensional loner or a script kiddie probing systems for fun. While redundant security mechanisms and careful monitoring might protect against these threat models, they may fail against a determined, hardened, and skilled professional—an uebercracker.

An even more serious threat than the uebercracker is the attack cell—a group of complex individuals who work together to attack systems in order to further a common goal. While an organization prepares for the lone cracker, an attack may be executed by professionals with extensive financial and technical resources. An attack cell might include a social engineering expert who's just been hired into Marketing, a systems expert who can model your network "UNIX box by bloody UNIX box," a security program-

---

26. See `http://www.fish.com/security/admin-guide-to-cracking.html`

mer who's spent years developing custom tools, and a phone
phreak specializing in moving information via intermediaries. It
might have significant research and development capabilities or
even the backing of a government organization.[27] All the tools and
techniques discussed in this book (or any book!) will only be mar-
ginally effective in this scenario. If your UNIX systems (or any of
your systems) contain commercially or politically valuable secrets,
be prepared to make substantial investments in security management, physical security, personnel security, and a significant inves-
tigative capability in addition to system and network security.

Rule 7: There Are No Turnkey Security Solutions

Businesses have been rushing to connect to the Internet with the
expectation that they can buy complete turnkey security. While
security vendors may disagree, I don't believe turnkey solutions are
even possible. There are too many variables to account for. There
are too many variations in security policies, threat models, system
configurations, and connectivity. You want to avoid the Maginot
Line syndrome: i.e., relying on a singular safeguard like a firewall
that can be systematically sidestepped. Security is not something
you buy, invent or do as a one-time event; it's a continual process
that requires ongoing planning, monitoring, and refinement.

A corollary to this rule: There's no checklist that will account
for all vulnerabilities. Security checklists are a venerable way to
check for errors and omissions, but don't be lulled by them. The
checklist method of security will fail against an intelligent attacker,
who has already seen the published checklists and works to devise
attacks not covered by them.

Rule 8: Good and Evil Blend into Gray

All definitions of computer security contain an implicit conceit:
that there are "good guys" and "bad guys" out there, or "white
hats" and "black hats." Virtually every popular book and movie
on the topic indulges in this conceit, from Clifford Stoll's *The
Cuckoo's Egg*, where the wily Berkeley hacker hunts down interna-

---

27. For an extension of this kind of scenario, see Fred Cohen's article
"Anatomy of a Successful Sophisticated Attack" at
http://all.net/journal/netsec/9901.html

tional spies, to *The Net,* in which Sandra Bullock plays a system administrator stripped by identity thieves. In some ways, the adversarial nature of computer security reduces it to a kind of game. Unfortunately for the security practitioner, this game of judgement is "played against unknown adversaries plotting unknown harm at unknown times and places."[28] As someone concerned about the security of your systems, you might think of yourself as playing a part in grand drama, and this book and accompanying tools as props that can help you defend against nameless attackers who might be everywhere or nowhere at all.

I advise you not to fall into this conceit. You may be giving yourself too much credit and assigning too little to your "opponents." Don't overlook the fact that most security violations are perpetuated by company insiders. Your perpetrators might look a lot more like the suburban wallflowers that sit together in the lunch room than the techno-pop-addled ravers in the movies. Never forget that between every white hat and black hat actor, there are hundreds that wear gray.

The computer security profession includes a wide variety of practitioners, including highly-credentialed academics, retired military personnel, snake-oil salespeople from commercial vendors, and reformed crackers who have now seen the light. There is no central certifying body overseeing the development of the skills necessary for computer security professionals, nor is there an accepted canon of ethics. In this way, the profession resembles that of its opponents: the extended, multi-national, multi-cultural cracking community, from those who develop complex "exploits" to the "script kiddies" who learn at a tender age that computer crime is as easy as a double-click.

Rather than make a dichotomous break between those who protect systems and those that compromise them, consider how intimately intertwined the two are and the large numbers of people who fall into the gray areas in between. Consider the case of the "tiger team"—computer security professionals who are hired to

---

28. Walter A. Kleinschrod, as quoted by Charles F. Hemphill, Jr. and John M. Hemphill, *Security Procedures for Computer Systems* (Homewood, IL: Dow-Jones Irwin, 1973), 1.

test the security of systems by attacking them. In some cases, these teams are composed of reformed system crackers whose former malevolence is generously rewarded. Even IBM advertises the services of its "ethical hackers." On the other hand, many a cracker has resorted to the educational defense—claiming that, by cracking into systems, he is actually doing the victim a favor. Conversely, there are most likely more than a few professionals on the inside of almost any organization who have discovered that crime does pay.

Just as there is no clear line between the "white hats" and "black hats" in the computer security culture—between the "ethical hackers" who find holes and the crackers who find holes—there's no clear line between tools for improving security and tools that break it. A tool is just that. Any of the security tools discussed in this book can be used for good or evil just as a hammer can be used to build a house or break into one. A password-cracking program can be used to find weak passwords before an attacker does or it can be used by the attacker to gain entry. A security auditing program can help either a sysadmin or a system cracker to find holes.

Even tools and measures that appear to be purely defensive, like firewalls, are implemented by crackers in order to bolster their attacks. Only the most naive attacker doesn't account for the contingency that the victim may counter-attack. The most sophisticated crackers build sophisticated defenses to provide cover for their activities. Conversely, some organizations are adopting "strike-back" capabilities in order to bolster their defenses through deterrence.

Rule 9: Think Like the Enemy

This rules follows naturally from the dichotomous nature of computer security—where good and evil blur into gray, the "game theory" of computer security cited above, and the "There Are No Turnkey Security Solutions" rule. If computer security is a game, then the enemy makes the rules. This is why checklists and stock solutions like firewalls, which derive from set defensive rules, can prove to be ineffective against smart opponents. Assume that the other side has maximum capabilities, in accordance with the notion that "There's Always Someone Out There Smarter, More

Knowledgeable, or Better-Equipped Than You." Identify those that could pose a threat to your systems and model their motives, capabilities, and worldviews. Surf to "hacker" sites that contain articles and tools for breaking into systems. Develop scenarios based on the threat model you face; if you were a UNIX systems programmer from a competing organization, how would you breach your organization's security?[29]

Rule 10: Trust is a Relative Concept

For the purpose of achieving the strongest possible computer security, "trust no one" is the strongest policy. Any piece of software or hardware could deliver a Trojan Horse or other malicious features. Of course, unless you're able to build your own hardware and code all your software, you're going to have to trust someone. Most computer and software companies are relatively trustworthy, even if they don't operate in full disclosure mode by publishing source code or exhaustive hardware specs. Most open source programs are relatively trustworthy as well. Even published source code, however, cannot provide complete protection from malicious code.

In a famous speech, Ken Thompson, one of the creators of UNIX, told of a frightening pair of bugs he was able to code.[30] He planted a Trojan Horse in the source of a C compiler that would find and miscompile the UNIX `login` command in such a way that it would accept either the correct password or one known to him. Once installed in binary, this C compiler would create a `login` command that enabled him to log into the system as any user. That's a security hole! Now, Thompson knew that another programmer looking at the source would likely see this gaping hole. So he created a second Trojan Horse aimed at the C compiler. He compiled the Trojaned source with the regular C compiler to produce a Trojaned binary and made this the official C compiler. Voila, Thompson could then remove the bugs from the source, knowing that the new (Trojaned compiler) binary would reinsert

---

29. This approach is championed in Donn B. Parker, *Computer Security Management* (Reston, VA: Reston Publishing Company Inc., 1981), 158–161. Also see Fred Cohen's site, http://all.net/
30. *Communication of the ACM*, Vol. 27, No. 8, August 1984, pp. 761–763. See http://www.acm.org/classics/sep95/

the bugs whenever it was compiled. Thus, the `login` command was Trojaned with no trace in the source code. Thompson pointed out the clear moral of the story: "You can't trust code that you did not totally create yourself." On the other hand, not many of us are Ken Thompson, with resume items like "Invented UNIX operating system." Perhaps a better moral would be: "Trust no one completely."

## 02

Security Planning

Sound security management starts with a reasoned plan. This chapter covers the essential steps in security planning. It helps you to identify the information and system assets that need protection, size up the threats those assets face, perform a cost-benefit analysis, and develop a security policy that you'll need before you can start implementing security measures. In order to provide additional context for planning, I present a UNIX security model for defense-in-depth. This chapter also touches on key people topics such as user education and system administration ethics.

Security is a process that starts with planning. While it may be possible to manage UNIX system security without a plan in place, such a nonchalant course is likely to lead to a disaster sooner or later. Good security planning formalizes a defensive strategy, which, in turn, forms the basis for a security policy. Think of a security plan and an accompanying security policy as the roots of all other security efforts.

A security plan can be specified in a formal document, drafted by a committee, or expressed as a simple set of strategies that you base your security tactics on. If you work for a large organization, some form of plan is almost certainly already in place. If you work for a start-up or an organization connecting to the Internet for the first time, you may need to develop a security plan and policy from scratch.

The first step in developing a security policy and plan is to conduct a security review that focuses on analyzing the threats a site or installation faces. A security review should include a risk assessment that answers questions like: What are the system and information resources that need to be protected? How much are the data on your systems and system uptime worth? What are the threats that confront your systems? How probable are they? How expensive are the time and tools required to adequately defend the systems?

A risk assessment provides fodder for a cost-benefit analysis. Perfect security is theoretically possible, but carries a price that no one can pay. In the real world, the potential costs of insecurity are weighed against the costs of security safeguards and procedures. Once an organization has performed a risk assessment and cost analysis, it can begin to formulate both security policy and a plan for implementing security based on the policy.

Risk Assessment

Risk assessment requires that you determine four things: 1) what you need to protect, 2) what it's worth, 3) what you need to protect it from, and 4) how it can be protected. You need to identify your assets, identify the threats, and identify the resources needed to minimize the threat in a cost effective manner.

Asset Identification

Draft a list of all the assets within your security domain. This will include all your systems, including hardware and software, all the data living on your systems, and your people (time is money). Think hardware, software, and wetware. You'll also need to account for intangibles such as good will and reputation.

A complete inventory includes hardware items such as CPUs, motherboards, RAM, disk drives, display monitors, printers, telephone lines, modems, network cabling plants, routers, and switches. Software assets include operating system binaries, operating system source code, application programs, utilities, security software, and diagnostic programs.

How valuable is all the data within your security domain? Account for and classify proprietary or confidential data, from customer databases to patent applications. Then throw in more routine data. Include databases, documents, backups, system logs, and offline data.

As for people, they are the users that depend on your systems. Their time is valuable. If they're working in a mission-critical setting, their time may be extremely valuable. The health and safety of your personnel may be on the line as well. There are administrators, IT support staff, and even customers and vendors to consider as well.

Finally, it would be wise to identify intangible assets such as your organization's public image and reputation and the goodwill of customers. In the case of a bank, for example, its reputation for integrity and reliability is essential to operations.

Asset Valuation

Determining the value of assets can be daunting. For the purposes of a security review, asset valuation need not be precise. Most assets can be evaluated on a monetary basis. Some, such as software packages, hardware, and mailing lists, have an obvious market value. Others can be measured in terms of business interruption. A trading firm, for example, knows that a certain dollar volume of business will be lost if its web servers are down for an extended period of time.

It may be possible to value assets in a relative fashion, as a percentage of total budget, assets, or the worth of the firm as a whole. The IT assets of a highly-valued Internet company may be worth far more than their simple market value.

Asset valuation can be complicated by the fact that an asset may have a different value for the owner than for those who covet it. A list of personnel and contact information may have nominal replacement value for the HR department, but it would be far more valuable for a head-hunting firm acting on behalf of a competitor. Consider developing as many as four estimated values: the average expected loss for the owner, the maximum expected loss for the owner, the average gain for an attacker, and the maximum gain for an attacker.

Naturally, the process of identifying and valuating assets is more complex for a large organization than a small one. In a large company, it may be necessary to convene a committee for this purpose with members drawn from various line units as well as the IT department. If an organization has a great deal of sensitive data, it may be necessary to proceed on a need-to-know basis, with each part of an organization reporting and discovering only those assets within its domain.

Identifying Threats

Given the assets you need to protect, what are the threats to these assets? In this era of the Internet, the system cracker or intruder is a popular figure depicted in more than a few Hollywood movies. Judging from the popular media, the crackers seem to be everywhere and nowhere at once, tweaking unclassified Department of Defense systems here, and changing a home page there. While network security is a serious concern for any system connected to the Internet, a more serious threat often comes from within the organization. Insiders, from disgruntled employees to contractors, consistently rank high in corporate security risk assessments.

Malevolent intruders and insiders aside, there are dozens of threats to the security and availability of any computer system: from software bugs to hardware failures; from the cup of coffee spilled into the keyboard to the backhoe that cuts off ten million phone lines.

Below is a partial taxonomy of computer threats.

- Internal failure—hardware bugs, software bugs, hardware failure

- Environmental—fire, flood, lightning strike, wind/tornado, earthquake, explosions, structural building failure, dust, dirt, smoke, strong electromagnetic radiation

- Personnel—illness or death of key personnel; resignation or termination of key personnel; user error; professional incompetence; information leaks via the Internet; sabotage, fraud and embezzlement; labor unrest

- Outsiders—theft or disclosure of confidential information; theft of hardware, software, disks, tape; riots; terrorism; eavesdropping; social engineering; random hackers

A large organization that's been running computers for an extended period has likely already experienced losses from some of these threats. If so, a list or file of loss experiences may be available and could prove to be an invaluable aid in identifying potential future threats. In addition, there are several additional sources for identifying the range of potential threats, including security literature, web sites, mailing lists, and organizations like the Computer Security Institute.[1]

Identifying Safeguards

Once you've identified the threats, you need to identify safeguards that can minimize them. Some of the safeguards will be based on software tools (see "Evaluating Security Tools" on page 15 for a description of how to evaluate them). Some safeguards may require hardware—from door locks to smartcards. Others may be procedural or operational in nature: thorough employee background checks, posting guards at entrances, and buying insurance.

Some safeguards will be as obvious as assigning passwords to all user accounts. Others will be disqualified for obvious reasons; i.e., your organization probably can't afford to attach biometric scanning systems to every workstation. Safeguards should be

---

1. See http://www.gocsi.com

planned to provide defense-in-depth, paying attention to all the
key functions of computer security including prevention, deterrence, detection, and recovery. Avoid the Maginot Line syndrome
of depending on a single safeguard—such as a firewall—to protect
the security of networked machines. A networked UNIX system
should have safeguards for account security, filesystem security,
process security, and network security. We'll examine each of these
types of security (see "A UNIX Security Model" on page 39).

Cost-Benefit Analysis

A complete consideration of cost-benefit risk analysis is beyond the
scope of this book. In brief, there are four steps for evaluating the
costs and benefits of security measures.

The first two key off a simple risk formula: $R = L \times P$, where R is
the risk of expected loss, L is the potential loss, and P is the probability or expected frequency of loss. Keeping this formula in mind,
the first two steps are:

- Quantifying the Threats (P)—Given the threats that face your
  systems, what is the probability of each causing a loss in a given
  time frame (i.e., a year)

- Quantifying the Cost of Loss (L)—Includes the cost of repairing
  or replacing an item, the cost of system downtime, the cost to
  an organization's reputation, and the cost to clients

Once you've established the level of risk (R), there are two more
steps:

- Quantifying the Cost of Prevention—The cost of preventing
  each kind of loss. This may include the cost of hardware, such
  as uninterruptable power supplies or card access systems; the
  cost of software, such as a commercial intruder detection system; and the cost of personnel such as new hires, training, etc.

- Calculate the Bottom Line—For each loss, compare the calculated risk with the cost of avoiding or preventing the loss

For example, the probability that a critical server will fail may
be relatively high due to the age of the system. If there's a 2%

chance of complete system failure within a year, and the loss would cost $2 million in lost business, the annual risk factor would be approximately $40,000. A fallback server would cost $20,000 to deploy, a sum that would pay for itself in six months.

Weighing the potential cost of security violations against the cost of enhancing security can be tricky. In most circumstances, the cost of enhancing security greatly increases as the level of theoretical security approaches 100%. At the same time, the cost of potential violations decrease as the level of security increases. The graph below illustrates this conundrum. As you attempt to calculate the bottom line, consider the sweet spot in the middle where the cost of violations meets the cost of security.

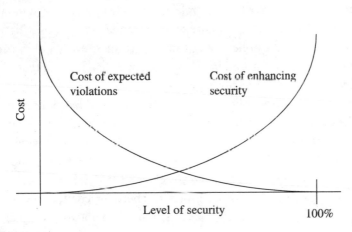

Figure 2.1 *The Security Cost Function*

A security review consisting of a thorough risk assessment and a rigorous cost-benefit analysis can become either the basis for formal security policies or a benchmark for evaluating the effectiveness and appropriateness of existing policy. Alternatively, such a review can serve to reinforce the status quo or decisions that have already been made. For example, management may already have budgeted $500,000 for IT security. It's always possible to work backwards to a budget stipulation. If you're forced to do this, consider taking a blue-sky approach. Calculate the cost of every single safeguard or procedure you'd like to put in place. Then work backwards. Starting with those with high cost or low impact, eliminate safeguard by safeguard until you make your budget.

Security Policies

RFC 2196 offers this lucid definition of security policy: "a formal statement of the rules by which people who are given access to an organization's technology and information assets must abide."[2]

Why Have a Security Policy?

The primary purpose of any security policy is to provide a baseline for acquiring, configuring, managing, and auditing computer resources. While a security policy can be developed on an entirely informal basis (it may be as simple as "no one touches my standalone home box"), any UNIX site with more than two users will need to commit the policy to writing. A written security policy can be a good tool for informing users, staff, and managers of their obligation to protect technology assets.

A strong security policy is a pre-condition for the rational and successful deployment of security tools. If a site doesn't have a clear set of rules and goals, the process of setting up, deploying, and running security tools is unlikely to be effective. For example, a security administrator can run Crack against a system's passwords but, unless a password policy has been articulated, the admin is likely to waste time discovering the obvious—users pick bad passwords.

Qualities of a Good Security Policy

Security policies should be clear and unambiguous. Brevity is a benefit. A strong security policy establishes ownership and provides clear lines of responsibility. Without citing specific names, it establishes who within the organization has primary responsibility for maintaining key aspects of system security. It should have the buy-in of all important constituencies within the organization: the security or system administrators, IT technical staff, line managers, and legal counsel. Naturally, a good security policy is one that can

---

2. B. Fraser, Ed., "Site Security Handbook", RFC 2196. See
`http://www.faqs.org/rfcs/rfc2196.html`

actually be implemented! It's one thing to establish a rule, and quite another to enforce it. Thus, the importance of good security tools. Systems fortified with appropriate tools should be able to prevent policy breaches when feasible. If a breach cannot be prevented, it should be detectable with sanctions in place for violators.

A strong security policy will also provide for contingencies such as handling intruders once they are detected. The worse time to formulate a response to an attacker is during an attack! You could be losing data by the minute. Your critical systems could be unavailable, damaging either your organization's finances or reputation (or both). You need to be able to ensure that your organization, along with its owners, employees, and customers, is protected by permitting the organization to resume operations within a minimum time period after a disruption or disaster.

A UNIX Security Model

Security is a very old science that has been studied for centuries. The principles of computer security are derived from the traditional principles of defense.

There are three traditional approaches to the defense of systems: dispersion, designed to minimize losses; redundancy, designed to ensure the system operates despite damage to an individual part; and defense in depth, designed to make the attacker overcome a series of barriers before he can damage a vital part of the system.[3]

Dispersion can be an effective defense against both accidental and deliberate damage. When dispersion is effectively implemented, total destruction requires coordinated, multiple attacks— no single attack can destroy the entire system. The design of the Internet is a classic example of defense by dispersion. In the early 1960s, a series of incidents disrupted military communications. Researcher Paul Baran proposed that military command-and-control communications be dispersed throughout a distributed communications network so that the failure of any single relay or site

---

3. Adrian R.D. Norman, *Computer Insecurity* (New York: Chapman and Hall, 1983), 247.

could be isolated and routed around.[4] Many corporations have adopted similar strategies: many critical computing resources are internetworked among geographically dispersed sites. Even if a central system goes down, the distributed machines can continue to provide local service.

Redundancy provides for backup systems that can take the place of a critical but downed system. A classic example of this strategy is the use of RAID disk arrays. Disk drives are mirrored and as soon as a primary drive fails, a second disk takes over.

Defense in depth is an age-old way to secure either a central system or dispersed individual systems. Successive rings of defense increase the effort an attacker has to undertake. By increasing the work factor of getting inside, defense in depth discourages the attacker. Medieval castles were built with concentric rings or keeps, ramparts, and moats. As attackers penetrate the outer walls, defenders fall back on increasingly well-protected defenses like a keep or bailey. Once through the outer wall, attackers must defeat a keep with only one access route: a ladder to a door high in the wall.

As with the Medieval castle, so with UNIX. Figure 2.2 provides a model for how to look at the security of a UNIX system.

In a given computing system, the first line of defense is physical security. If your systems are open to the public and unsupervised, you effectively have no security whatsoever. The root account can be compromised by an intruder who might open the computer's case and pull the non-volatile ROM chip that stores a hardware password. Or the attacker could simply rip out a hard drive, take it home, and attach it to another computer.

Assuming that your systems are protected from physical access by mechanisms such as locked doors or pass cards, the next layer of defense is account security. Here, the username and password combination is critical. Can an attacker create an account, access a legitimate user's account, or in the worse case scenario, access the root account? If so, your system is obviously at great risk.

---

4. Paul Baran et al. *On Distributed Communications*. RAND Report Series, August 1964.

Figure 2.2 *A UNIX Defense Model*

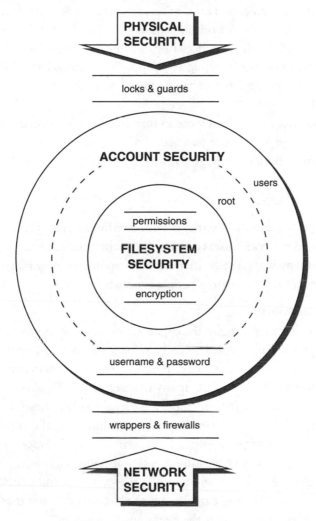

The innermost wall is filesystem security: the ability to protect your information even in the event that an account or accounts have been breached. The UNIX permissions mechanism is critical here. If an attacker compromises an account, key files can still be protected by permissions, the limited access assigned to that account. Another important aspect of file security is encryption. If important files are encrypted, an attacker can breach an account and even defeat the permissions system without being able to use or exploit the encrypted data.

At the outermost perimeter is network security: maintaining the security of communications and ensuring that only permitted traffic reaches the system. A firewall is a canonical perimeter defense. The security of standard services like FTP and Telnet can be bolstered by invoking them through "wrapper" programs like TCP Wrappers. Perimeter defenses can be tested by scanning programs like SATAN.

This book covers each of these in turn (see "Account Security Basics" on page 49, "Filesystem Security" on page 111, and "Network Security Basics" on page 251).

User Education

Even the most elaborate security plan and enforcement will fail if a system's or a network's users are not savvy about basic security issues. In many ways, the entire field of computer security represents a technical solution to a people problem.

Promulgate Policy

Make sure that every user in the organization is made accountable for the security policy. Policies can be publicized via traditional corporate communications techniques, ranging from email distributions to reminders in the company newsletter. Ideally, maintaining security should be part of employee performance reviews.

Security briefings can be effective in communicating the importance of maintaining an organization's security profile. Since security breaches may occur infrequently, a briefing can reiterate the consequences of losses and describe relevant laws and policies. Regular security briefings can also act as a deterrent, in so far as "the fear of getting caught is the beginning of wisdom."

Beware of Social Engineering

All computer users should be aware of the cracker technique known as "social engineering." Social engineering is a cracking method that relies on deceit or trickery to overcome impediments posed by information security measures. A master of deception can neutralize even the most hardened system security with a few quick phone calls.

UNIX security guru Peter Galvin provides a canonical test of your organization's ability to repel a social engineering attack.[5] Suppose one of your users, say Bob, receives a message like this:

> Hi Bob, I'm doing a survey of computer accounts and user names. Can you send me a copy of the password file? Simply issue the command cat /etc/passwd | mail me@example.com.
>
> Thanks!

What would he do? Have Bob and the other users been informed about basic security procedure? Has he been exposed to the concept of social engineering or does he trust everyone?

Susan Thunder was a famous social engineer who hung out with Kevin Mitnick and other crackers in Los Angeles. In the book *Cyberpunk*, she recounts to the authors how she was once invited to Washington to demonstrate her cracking skills to the military.[6] She was placed in a room with a computer and phone, handed a sealed envelope with the name of a military computer system, and invited to break into the system by any and all means. Without missing a beat, she looked the system up and found out where it was located. She called the base and found out who the commanding officer was. She was chatty and "kittenish." She also found out who the officer's secretary was. Then she called the data center, claimed to be the officer's secretary, calling on his behalf: "He's trying to access his account on this system and hasn't been able to get through and he'd like to know why." When the operator balked, she demanded his name, rank, and serial number. Within minutes, she had classified data scrolling on her terminal.

This is a canonical social engineering attack, which relies on selecting a target, gathering as much information as possible from directory listings, Usenet posts, web pages, etc., and then initiating verbal contact with a set alter ego in place.

Since social engineering attacks rely on publicly available information, you need to evaluate everything your organization makes

---

5. See `http://www.sun.com:80/sunworldonline/ swol-07-1995/swol-07-security.html`
6. Katie Hefner and John Markoff, *Cyberpunk* (New York: Simon & Schuster, 1991), 60-61.

public. In an article called "Case study: the devil you know", John Ceraolo makes the following suggestions:[7]

- Develop an acceptable usage policy for Internet access. Restrict what Internet groups can be posted to. How much is too much to post in a Usenet message?

- Search on postings from your own company's domain, just like an attacker would.[8]

- Do you need contact names on your Web page? Do you need your phone directory on your Web page? Do your voice mail messages disclose employees' itineraries?

- Make your receptionist a member of the security team. The person who has the most information about your company's employees is your receptionist.

- Decline to respond to marketing surveys that ask questions about your information systems—particularly those that are done over the phone.

- Your staff should know to report any and all suspicious activities. You will receive numerous trivial reports, but the handful that require your attention will make it worth your while to review each of them.

- Implement a strong physical access policy: visitor sign-in sheets, badges, escorted access, special care for former employees. Do not accept cold calls or walk-ins.

- Communicate suspicions to all shifts, especially terminations or resignations of employees.

- Make it a specific policy bullet point that "no one, from any department, will ever need your password."

- Change your modem ring count to higher than three.

---

7. From the March 1998 issue (#180) of Computer Security Institute's monthly newsletter, *Computer Security Alert*. See
`http://www.gocsi.com/devil.htm`
8. You can use Deja News for this at `http://www.dejanews.com`

As always, the best prevention is awareness.

Ethics

As our society grows increasingly dependent on computer systems, the role of the system administrator has been increasingly pivotal. Sysadmins often hold significant power. They handle all kinds of sensitive data, from bank transactions to medical records. They manage machines connected to networks which, in turn, connect to other networks. With these powers come responsibility.

These responsibilities exist whether the administrator recognizes them or not. Sometimes those who operate home systems don't view themselves as "system administrators" per se. Perhaps they've converted some old Windows PCs to Linux boxes and built small home LANs. Perhaps they come from the PC world, where your responsibility doesn't extend beyond the system you're sitting at. All this is fine, until those systems get connected to the Internet, where thousands of script kiddies running port scanning software prowl. An operator may think that no one will be interested in a humble home LAN but he or she would be wrong. All of a sudden, that innocent Linux box gets "root-kitted" and is set up as a base to attack other systems on the net. This happens everyday, as evidenced by the plaintive cries for help on `comp.security.unix` and other newsgroups: "My Linux box got cracked! What do I do?"

If you run a UNIX system connected to the Internet, whether it's a massive corporate LAN or a box in a basement, you're ethically responsible for maintaining security.

The SAGE Code of Ethics

The Systems Administrators Guild (SAGE) promulgates a Code of Ethics that is relevant to anyone who administers systems, handles sensitive information, or manages security. Drafted by Hal Miller, the code is divided into six canons. The code is neither prescriptive nor all-encompassing; still, it represents a valuable slice of insight into the ethical issues that operate "behind the scenes."

Here is the Code, as presented on the SAGE web site.[9]

---

9. See `http://www.usenix.org/sage/publications/code_of_ethics.html`

- Canon 1—The integrity of a system administrator must be beyond reproach. A system administrator may come into contact with privileged information on a regular basis and thus has a duty to the owners of such information to both keep confidential and to protect the confidentiality of all such information. Protecting the integrity of information includes ensuring that neither system administrators nor unauthorized users unnecessarily access, make any changes to, or divulge data not belonging to them. It includes all appropriate effort, in accordance with industry-accepted practices, by the system administrator to enforce security measures to protect the computers and the data contained on them. System administrators must uphold the law and policies as established for the systems and networks they manage, and make all efforts to require the same adherence from their users. Where the law is not clear, or appears to be in conflict with their ethical standards, system administrators must exercise sound judgment, and are also obliged to take steps to have the law upgraded or corrected as is possible within their jurisdiction.

- Canon 2—A system administrator shall not unnecessarily infringe upon the rights of users. System administrators shall not act with, nor tolerate from others, discrimination between authorized users based on any commonly recognized grounds (e.g., age, gender, religion, etc.), except where such discrimination (e.g., with respect to unauthorized users as a class) is a necessary part of their job, and then only to the extent that such treatment is required in dealing with the issue at hand. System administrators will not exercise their special powers to access any private information other than when necessary to their role as system managers, and then only to the degree necessary to perform that role, while remaining within established site policies. Regardless of how it was obtained, system administrators will maintain the confidentiality of all private information.

- Canon 3—Communications of system administrators with all whom they may come in contact shall be kept to the highest standards of professional behavior. System administrators must keep users informed about computing matters that might affect

them, such as conditions of acceptable use, sharing and availability of common resources, maintenance of security, occurrence of system monitoring, and any applicable legal
obligations. It is incumbent upon the system administrator to
ensure that such information is presented in a manner calculated to ensure user awareness and understanding. Honesty and
timeliness are keys to ensuring accurate communication to
users. A system administrator shall, when advice is sought, give
it impartially, accompanied by any necessary statement of the
limitations of personal knowledge or bias. Any potential conflicts of interest must be fully and immediately declared.

- Canon 4—The continuance of professional education is critical
  to maintaining currency as a system administrator. Since technology in computing continues to make significant strides, a
  system administrator must take an appropriate level of action
  to update and enhance personal technical knowledge. Reading,
  study, acquiring training, and sharing knowledge and experience are requirements to maintaining currency and ensuring the
  customer base of the advantages and security of advances in the
  field.

- Canon 5—A system administrator must maintain an exemplary
  work ethic. System administrators must be tireless in their
  effort to maintain high levels of quality in their work. Day-to-
  day operation in the field of system administration requires significant energy and resiliency. The system administrator is
  placed in a position of such significant impact upon the business of the organization that the required level of trust can only
  be maintained by exemplary behavior.

- Canon 6—At all times system administrators must display pro-
  fessionalism in the performance of their duties. All manner of
  behavior must reflect highly upon the profession as a whole.
  Dealing with recalcitrant users, upper management, vendors or
  other system administrators calls for the utmost in patience and
  care to ensure that mutual respect is never at risk. Actions that
  enhance the image of the profession are encouraged. Actions
  that enlarge the understanding of the social and legal issues in

computing are part of the role. System administrators are obligated to assist the community at large in areas that are fundamental to the advancement and integrity of local, national, and international computing resources.

## 03

Account Security Basics

Breaking into a user account is often the easiest
way for an attacker to gain access to a system.
Throughout the brief history of computing, users
have been notorious for picking easy-to-guess passwords. This chapter contains a short guide to
choosing secure passwords. It covers the traditional, *crypt()*-based UNIX password mechanism
and its intrinsic vulnerability. Many systems have
inactive accounts, misconfigured system accounts,
or other problematic accounts. This chapter discusses managing UNIX accounts, including protecting the root account and setting up restricted
environments.

Why Account Security?

Each individual that uses a UNIX system should have an account on that system. Each account is associated with a unique username and a secret password. These two items represent a vital UNIX security mechanism: a username (also known as an "account name" or "login name") identifies who is using the system, while passwords authenticate that the user is who he or she claims to be. Without authentication, it's impossible to hold individuals accountable for their actions or to implement basic security controls.

Account security is one of the "outer rings" of UNIX system security. A canonical line of attack targets the username/password authentication safeguard. Accounts that belong to regular users and system users can be cracked open, sometimes by mere password guessing, sometimes by systematic dictionary attacks, and sometimes due to negligence. If a system is connected to a network, its account security will be vulnerable to probes by snoopers, crackers, and other entities with malevolent intent. Once on the "inside," they can use a user account to impersonate a legitimate user, abuse system resources, launch attacks on other networked systems, or attempt to gain a higher level of privilege. Once the root account is compromised, the system is "owned" by the attacker. He can change any file or operating parameter, insert malicious code, add bogus users for future attacks, and then erase the evidence by altering log files.

Choosing Secure Passwords: A User Guide

Passwords are a simple form of authentication. They represent a shared secret between the computer and a user. By presenting a password, the user proves to the computer that he or she is who he or she claims.

Bad passwords can severely compromise the security of a UNIX system. It's trivial for an attacker to use a hit list of common passwords to feed one after another to a system until they're in. Even a modest home computer with a good password cracking program can generate thousands of guesses in just a few hours.

In theory, the most secure passwords consist of completely random combinations of letters, both upper and lower case, numbers, punctuation marks, and special characters. Unfortunately such passwords are difficult to memorize, and passwords that can't be memorized need to be written down. Writing down passwords can, however, be risky (see "Writing Down Passwords" on page 52).

The password you select needs to be protected against two lines of attack: 1) guesses that another person might make based on information gathered about you personally, and 2) guesses that a password-guessing program might make.

Password No-no's

Here's a list of things you should not do when selecting a password:

- Don't choose a password that could by found in any dictionary of any language. Password-guessing programs can be configured with massive multi-lingual word lists that are widely available on the Internet.

- Don't choose a password consisting of a simple sequence of letters (for example, "qwerty" or "abcdef").

- Don't choose a password that contains any identifiable information about you (for example, your birthday, your first or last name, your spouse's name, the names of your children, telephone numbers, Social Security numbers, the brand of car you drive, car license plate numbers, the name of the street you live on, etc.).

- Don't choose a new password that's similar to one you're replacing.

- Don't choose a password that contains your username or any variant of it.

- Don't choose a password shorter than six characters or one that contains only alphabetic characters or only digits.

- Don't choose a password that contains all lower-case or upper-case letters.

• Don't choose a password that you've seen published as a password example.

Good Passwords

Here's a list of things you should do when selecting a password:

• Choose a password that's at least six characters long.

• Choose a password that contains non-alphabetic characters including numbers and special characters like `~`!@$%^&*()_-+={}[]|\:;'"<>,.?/<space>`.

• Choose a password that's easy to remember so you don't have to write it down.

• Choose a password that you can type quickly without looking at the keyboard so that someone looking over your shoulder can't tell what it is.

Writing Down Passwords

As a general rule, passwords should not be written down. A password written on a legal pad, Post-It note, etc. can be discovered. A password committed to memory is the most secure.

Even experts sometimes trip up by writing down their passwords. For several months, Cliff Stoll, author of *The Cuckoo's Egg*, hosted TV segments for the computer show "The Site" at his Oakland home. In one segment, Cliff admitted that he had committed a security blunder: he had his password written down on a Post-It note attached to his monitor, the same monitor that could be clearly seen by millions during the "over the air" segments. Needless to say, Cliff changed his password.

If it's absolutely necessary to write a password, consider the following precautions:

• Write the password on a folded piece of paper and place in a lockbox or safe.

• Write the password on something kept in your wallet. This is preferable to having this critical information right by your system. It raises the bar for a potential intruder—to get to the password, they have to get to you first. It should go without saying, but if you do keep your password in your wallet, make sure your wallet is secure at all times. In *Cyberpunks*, John Markoff and Katie Hafner describe how a wily cracker named Susan Thunder would pick up military officers at bars outside bases and go home with them. In the wee hours, she'd rifle through the officer's personal affects searching for logins and passwords.

- If you must record passwords, never write down username and password combinations, or associate either with a specific system or telephone number.

- If you must record a password, garble it in a way you can remember. Add extra characters, invert the order of characters, or truncate it.

- Never attach a password to any piece of computer hardware, especially monitors (and especially if you're hosting nationally broadcasted TV segments).

The Password Mechanism

On many UNIX systems, passwords and other user information are stored in the */etc/passwd* file. The passwords displayed in this file are encoded using a one-way hash function—an algorithm that is easy to compute in one direction but computationally expensive to compute in the reverse direction.

In a landmark paper, Robert Morris and Ken Thompson described how this "elaborate and strange design" evolved over the course of several years. Early UNIX systems stored user passwords in a flat readable "password file" that could be intercepted and exploited without a sysadmin noticing. It was also subject to happenstance.

Morris and Thompson tell of an embarrassing lapse on an early time-sharing system, when one system administrator was

> ... editing the password and another system adminstrator was editing the daily message that is printed on everyone's terminal at login. Due to a software design error, the temporary editor files of the two users were interchanged and thus, for a time, the password file was printed on every terminal when it was logged in.[1]

Starting with Version 6 of AT&T UNIX, Thompson et al decided to take a different approach: UNIX passwords were encoded using a rotor-based algorithm modeled after the US Army's M-209 cipher machine. This fast algorithm proved vulnerable to exhaustive plaintext searches and was replaced by a more advanced *crypt()* library that first appeared in Version 7 AT&T UNIX.

Caution   The *crypt()* library should not be confused with the `crypt` encryption command, which is based on the German Enigma machine. The `crypt` command (also known as `enigma`) provides only nominal security—it can be defeated by the Crypt Breaker's Workbench (CBW), a collection of tools released by Robert W. Baldwin in 1986 (see page 148).

The crypt () Algorithm

At the heart of the UNIX password encoding mechanism is a derivation of DES (Data Encryption Standard), which usually uses a 56-bit key (eight 7-bit characters) to encrypt 64-bit blocks of clear text. The traditional UNIX *crypt()* function takes the user's password, pads it out to eight characters, and then uses seven bits of each character to form a 56-bit DES key. This key is used to encrypt a 64-bit block of zeros (00000000). The product of this encryption is encrypted again with the key—this process is

---

1.   Robert Morris and Ken Thompson, "Password security: A Case History." In Unix Programmer's Supplementary Documentation. AT&T, November 1979. See `ftp://coast.cs.purdue.edu/pub/doc/passwords/morris.password_security_case_study.ps.Z`

repeated 25 times. The final output of the process is written into a string of 11 characters and stored in the */etc/passwd* file.

It is practically impossible to reverse this process, to take an encrypted password and work back to the plaintext version. This method of encoding is, however, vulnerable to a dictionary attack. A large corpus of words can be encrypted, stored, and then compared to the encoded passwords found in */etc/passwd*.

In order to make the DES-based scheme stronger and more resistant to dictionary attack, the designers of the traditional UNIX password mechanism added "salt"—a 12-bit number, between 0 and 4095. The salt is used to perturb the DES algorithm so that each of the 4096 possible salt values causes a given plaintext password to encode to a different value.

When a user picks or changes a password, the /bin/passwd program selects a salt based on the time of day, converts it into a two-character string, and stores that string as the first two characters of the encoded entry in */etc/passwd*. Thus, a complete encoded password entry consists of 13 characters: two for the salt, followed by 11 for the coded password.

Figure 3.1 illustrates the UNIX password mechanism.

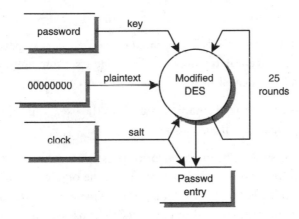

Figure 3.1 *UNIX Password Encoding*

The encoded entry in */etc/passwd* is often described as the **Tip** "encrypted password." But as described above, the plaintext password is used as the key for encrypting a block of zeros—it has been encoded, but it's actually the block of zeros that's been encrypted.

When a user supplies a plaintext password to the /bin/login program, the salt is retrieved from the encoded password entry. Then, the supplied password is used as the key to encrypt a block of zeros, using the salt value as a seed. This is then compared with the encoded password. If there is a match, then the user is authenticated.

Salt makes attacks against encoded passwords using pre-compiled dictionaries more expensive. Instead of doing a single encoding run on each word in a dictionary, the attacker now has to encode and store 4096 permutations of each word in the dictionary. While this was a substantial resource barrier when salt was introduced over twenty years ago, a 12-bit salt can no longer be considered an effective safeguard (see "Password Vulnerabilities" on page 58).

Tip

> You can find out more about how passwords are encoded in the */etc/passwd* file by consulting your system's man page for crypt (3).

Anatomy of the Passwd File

Each entry in the passwd file looks something like the following:

```
name:coded-passwd:UID:GID:user-info:home-directory:shell
```

Each of the seven fields is separated by a colon. Blank spaces are not allowed, except in the user-info field. Here's a summary of what each field means:

* name—This is the username assigned to the user. Typically, this is not proprietary information.

* coded-passwd—The user's encoded passwd. If a sysadmin needs to prevent a user from logging in, he or she will often replace this field with an asterisk (:*:). In general, this field isn't edited manually. Users should change their passwords using the passwd command. It is important to note that many recent UNIX implementations rely on "shadow passwords"—passwords that are not stored in */etc/passwd* (see "Managing Accounts" on page 61).

- UID—The user's unique identification number. By convention, UIDs smaller than 100 are reserved for system accounts.

- GID—The user's primary group membership. Usually, this will determine the group ownership of the files the user creates. Under Red Hat Linux, each user account is assigned its own unique group by default.

- user-info—By convention, this contains the user's full name. Mail systems and utilities like finger traditionally use the information in this field. This field is also known as the GECOS field.

- home-directory—This field specifies the user's home directory, the initial working directory when the user logs in.

- shell—This field specifies a path to the command interpreter that will be executed when the user logs in. There are several popular shells, including the Bourne shell (*/bin/sh*), the C shell (*/bin/csh*), the Korn shell (*/bin/ksh*), and the Bash shell (*/bin/bash*). Note that it's possible to assign a value of /bin/false to this field for users to prevent them from logging in.

So, the following */etc/passwd* entry:

```
jrandom:Npge08pfz4wuk:513:100:J. Random Hacker:/home/
jrandom:/bin/csh
```

indicates that the user J. Random Hacker has the username jrandom, UID 513, GID 100, a home directory */home/jrandom*, the C shell as a default, and a salted password. Note that the salt is contained in the first two characters of the coded-password field. In the example above, "Np" is the salt and "ge08pfz4wuk" is the encoded password. The encoded salt/password combination could just as easily have been "kbeMVnZM0oL7I": these two strings result from excrypting the same password. The example password in this case is "password"—don't use this example![2]

---

2. This example comes from Michael H. Jackson's Linux Shadow-Password-HOWTO, http://metalab.unc.edu/LDP/HOWTO/Shadow-Password-HOWTO-2.html

The fact that the same password encodes two (actually 4096!) different ways highlights a significant security feature of salt—even if two users have the same exact password, it will encode differently. This prevents an easy line of attack whereby a user notices another user has the same password and can thus abuse or subvert the other user's account.

Password Vulnerabilities

There are two fundamental problems with the traditional UNIX password system: guessable passwords and the inevitable march of progress.

Some of the leading minds in computer security have been analyzing the problem of guessable passwords for decades. While the number of eight-character combinations of letters and digits is huge, human psychology falls back on a relatively small space of memorable dictionary words and derivatives. Morris and Thompson found that of 3,289 passwords they analyzed, 86% contain one or more signifcant weaknesses. It took them five minutes of dictionary searching to guess a third of them.[3] One researcher compiled over 15,000 password entries and was able to crack 21% within a week, using late 1980s hardware.[4] The human tendency toward guessable passwords leaves the password system, and, thus, account security, very vulnerable to dictionary attack.

Time has not been kind to the security of the UNIX password mechanism. The DES-based encoding system was designed to be slow, and for many years it protected against this kind of attacks by increasing the work factor. At the same time, what was computationally-expensive for an attacker using late 1970s hardware is now computationally trivial.

A canonical dictionary attack abuses password guessability by encoding words from a dictionary (or many dictionaries) as well as permutations of those words and comparing the results to the encoded password entries—see the chapter "Crack" on page 99 for a detailed description of how this is done.

---

3. See footnote 1 on page 54.
4. Daniel V. Klein, "Foiling the Cracker: A Survey of, and Improvements to, Password Security," USENIX Security Workshop Proceedings (Portland, 1990). See http://www.raptor.com/lib/klein.pdf

A related but more forceful approach is to pre-compute, sort, and store the encoding of all the words in a dictionary (or many dictionaries). Once the professional computer criminal has compiled an encrypted dictionary, user passwords are just a simple look-up away. This approach is brutally fast but, of course, takes more storage space. Salt, in particular, makes this kind of pre-computation more expensive—instead of doing a single encoding run on each word in a dictionary, the attacker now has to encode 4096 permutations of each word in the dictionary. But this added complexity does not provide adequate protection against determined crackers. A pre-computed dictionary of 500,000 common words, names, passwords, and simple variations might fit on a pair of 16 GB hard drives. While 32 GB was a nearly impossible resource barrier when salt was introduced over twenty years ago, this much disk space now costs only a few hundred dollars—well within the means of most system crackers.

Even without lots of drive space, Crack can usually break at least a couple of passwords on a system with several dozen users (assuming the users of the system are allowed to pick their own passwords). While it may be not possible to successfully match any particular password, the law of averages favors attackers.

You can use a relatively simple formula to evaluate the vulnerability of the UNIX password mechanism: $K \times C \gg E \times T$, where

- K is the absolute size of the password space. This is the space the attacker needs to search in order to break into a particular user's account.

- C is a constant that captures the amount of effort the attacker must expend per user for a specific system. In the UNIX scheme, this constant is 4096—the number of salt permutations.

- E represents the number of encryptions/second for the DES-based password scheme.

- T is the maximum time in seconds the attacker can spend on the attack. Time is of the essence in a dictionary attack. The attacker has a limited window to crack a password, since passwords change, the purpose of the attack becomes moot, victims go out of business, etc.[5]

As long as the product of the password space (K) and the constant (C) exceeds the product of the encryption speed (E) and the maximum time allowed (T), the system is theoretically secure enough. While this formula may be useful in evaluating security, it is not infallible. The effective password space is eroded by guessable passwords. You may also want to factor in the number of users—as this increases, the probability that the attacker will be able to match a single encoded password increases. In any case, the formula exposes a sad truth about UNIX passwords: while K and C have remained the same for twenty years, E dramatically increases every year due to faster CPUs and other system components. Even worse, improvements in storage technology allow attackers to compile exhaustive encoded dictionaries in advance, thus diminishing the time needed for a successful brute-force attack.

There are at least three general ways that system designers and administrators can address the vulnerability of the traditional UNIX password mechanism to brute-force attack. One can:

- Enhance password security by preventing or detecting weak passwords. There are several different ways to do this. This works by increasing the effective password space (K). Protect the encoded passwords by hiding them—setting up a shadow password file exemplifies this popular approach. When in doubt, conceal your vulnerabilities. An attacker can't break what he can't find (see "Shadow Password Files" on page 76, and "Managing Accounts" on page 61).

- Protect against password cracking with improvements to the password encoding mechanism—it's possible to increase the constant (C) with bigger salts or to increase the number of DES encryption rounds (thus decreasing the number of encryptions per second or E). Some newer versions of UNIX support

---

5. The formula is derived from Ravi Ganesan and Chris Davies, "A New Attack on Random Pronounceable Password Generators." See http://www.raptor.com/lib/attack.pdf

alternatives to DES which decrease E, and longer password lengths that increase the password space (see "Algorithm Improvements" on page 78).

The next chapter covers each of these strategies in turn. None of these measures is fool-proof. Arguably, they represent workarounds designed to address weaknesses in a subsystem that wasn't designed for strong security. Some systems support alternative authentication mechanisms designed to increase security. Solaris and Linux, for example, support PAM (Pluggable Authentication Modules), a flexible mechanism for systematically improving UNIX authentication (see "PAM" on page 84). There are also authentication mechanisms designed to increase the security of passwords as they travel across networks. One-time passwords do this quite effectively—if a password is only used once, it doesn't matter if it's intercepted or guessable (see "One-Time Passwords" on page 81). Kerberos is another network authentication solution (see "Kerberos" on page 94).

Managing Accounts

Maintaining account security requires careful management of both system and user accounts. In addition to the password security measures discussed above, you need to consider how usernames are set up. Some accounts require special handling, including default accounts included with the system (root in particular) and shared accounts. In some situations, it may be desirable to set up special account controls or restricted environments.

Usernames

Usernames consist of between one and eight letters and numbers. Most sites require usernames longer than three characters since short usernames can cause confusion. Some versions of UNIX have difficulty with usernames that contain punctuation or control characters: use of punctuation in usernames is often discouraged.

Usernames are important because of their many uses. A username is not only an identifier used to access a specific system. It's also a public persona, doubling as an email address and printed on business cards, etc. Many large sites use a consistent scheme for generating usernames from the proper names of their employees. For example, using first initials plus last names to form usernames is fairly common. Josephine Hacker becomes jhacker. This is a convenient and memorable system. If you know someone's name and where they work, you can guess that John Random at Example Corp. has the email address jrandom@example.com.

The downside to memorable username assignments is that they are so easy to discover. An outsider can easily obtain someone's name by calling your organization's switchboard or doing a web search, and, thus, guess valid usernames. Once they have a username, only the password prevents them from accessing a system.

Tip

> You can use the mail aliases file (usually */etc/sendmail/aliases*) to provide users with appropriate email identities—like John_Random@example.com—that don't map to or reveal usernames.

Default Accounts

All UNIX systems ship with default accounts; sometimes these accounts have standard passwords or no password at all. Thus, they are a UNIX cracker's best friend.

Early versions of UNIX came without passwords for any account. As UNIX became commercialized, the tradition of password-less accounts, unfortunately, survived for some time. Most modern UNIX systems don't install with password-less accounts; still, some UNIX systems arrive at a customer's door with no root password. The root account, or "superuser," is the most important account and the one most coveted by crackers—root has unrestricted access to all aspects of the system. The first thing any sysadmin should do with a new UNIX box is set a root password. Vendors should set up their systems so that the sysadmin is prompted for the root password during the installation process or the very first time the system is booted.

In addition to the root account, many systems have "pseudo-user" accounts such as bin, daemon, mail, and uucp. These accounts are usually never logged into, but are basically placeholders for process and file ownership.

Many systems also support accounts that run a single command like date, finger, halt, etc.

You should review all pseudo-user and single-command accounts on your system. Check */etc/passwd* for these accounts and make sure that there's a "*" in the password field (rather than a blank entry). By and large, these default accounts don't represent security holes, although bugs and misconfiguration can make them dangerous. For example, NeXT systems used to ship with a default account "me." The me account was innocuous in and of itself, but the system designers put it in the privileged "wheel" group—thus, someone using the me account could use the su command to access the root account. While this problem was the subject of a CERT advisory and was fixed in later versions of NeXTSTEP, it illustrates the potential dangers of default accounts.[6]

Become familiar with the accounts your systems ship with. Table 3.1 summarizes common default accounts.

Table 3.1 *Common Default Accounts*

Username	Function
adm	Owns accounting files; home directory */var/adm* often contains log files
bin	Owns the executable files for user commands
daemon	Used to execute system processes
finger	Executes the finger command
games	For playing games
halt	Executes the halt command
lp (or lpd)	Owns the printer (line printer) spool files
mail	Owns mail-related processes and files
news	Owns USENET-related processes and files

---

6. See http://www.cert.org/advisories/CA-91.06.NeXTstep.vulnerability.html

Table 3.1 *Common Default Accounts (Cont'd)*

Username	Function
nobody	Used by NFS (Network File System)
shutdown	Executes the shutdown command
sync	Executes the sync command
sys	Owns system files
uucp	Owns the uucp utilities and files

Shared Accounts

Every user of a UNIX system should have his or her own account. If users are allowed to share accounts, then accountability—the ability to determine who did what when—and thus account security is breached.

Some systems provide accounts for guests or visitors that do not require passwords. This is a bad idea. With names like guest, they give an attacker an easy way into a system. Once innocuously logged in as guest, they can probe for greater security lapses.

If a system must provide for a guest account, set a password that is changed daily. Even better, consider providing guests—and other untrusted users—with a restricted shell (see "Restricted Environments" on page 67).

If a system must provide for a group account so that team members can work on a project together, you should, at the very least, stipulate that these users use the su (substitute user) command in order to access it. The su command enables a user to assume the effective user ID of another user—su attempts are logged to the file */var/log/messages* (or to the *sulog* file in the */usr/adm* directory, on older systems). A much better alternative is to create a new group in the file */etc/group* and add each team member to the group.

Disabling or Removing Accounts

Inactive accounts are a favorite target for intruders and thus represent a significant risk for system security. Systems with a large number of users will inevitably experience account turnover. When users move on, it's important to methodically remove their accounts. If an employee quits or gets fired under cloudy circumstances, the wise sysadmin makes sure the account is immediately disabled and then removed.

> A quick way to disable an account is to add an asterisk (*) to the **Tip**
> beginning of the user's encoded password in */etc/passwd* or the
> shadow password file. The user will no longer be able to log in.

Most UNIX systems make provision for commands that remove users. Under Solaris and a shadow-enabled Linux, the following should work:

```
# userdel jrandom
```

Be thorough when removing an account. Among the steps you may need to take, you might have to:

- Kill any processes or print jobs owned by the user.

- Check the user's home directory and make a backup of anything that needs to be saved.

- Remove the user's home directory and its contents.

- Remove the user's mail file (from */var/spool/mail*).

- Remove the user from the mail aliases file (*/usr/lib/aliases* or */etc/sendmail/aliases*).[7]

If you know in advance that user accounts will expire on a certain date, consider setting the password and account expiration fields in */etc/shadow* (see "Anatomy of /etc/shadow" on page 76).

Protecting Root
The following common sense rules should guide the sysadmin while operating as root or the super-user.

- Avoid logging in as the super-user unless it's necessary.

---

7. This list is based on one from Aeleen Frisch, *Essential Security Administration,* 2nd ed. (Sebastopol, CA: O'Reilly & Associates, Inc., 1995), 190.

- If you must operate as root, first log in as yourself and then use /bin/su - to become root.

- Never leave a root shell on your terminal unattended.

- Change the root password regularly. Choose a strong password for root.

- Never give the root password to someone you don't trust or to someone who doesn't have a demonstrated need for it.

- If someone has a demonstrated need to run commands as root, consider installing and using a facility like sudo, which enables regular users to run individual commands as root and maintains a log.[8]

- Never place the current directory (".") in the root account's search path. Never place a regular user's bin directories in root's search path. You don't want anyone running as superuser to inadvertently execute a Trojan Horse program.

- Never run another user's or an unfamiliar program as root.

- When using the su command to become the super-user, always invoke it with the full path name, /bin/su, instead of su in order to thwart a Trojan Horse su program designed to steal the root password. Better yet, use the form "/bin/su -"; the extra "-" ensures that you are acquiring root's environment along with the switch in effective userid.

Additional Account Controls

Some UNIX implementations support additional controls for securing user accounts. Depending on the version you're running, consider setting up:

- automatic account locking—you can specify the maximum number of failed login attempts; once this number is reached, the account is locked

---

8. For more information on sudo, see
http://www.courtesan.com/sudo/sudo.html

- day and time restrictions—you can specify when during a week or during a day a user's account can be used; this is handy for protecting against late-night hackers

- automatic log-out—you can specify the automatic termination of idle user sessions that have been running for a long period time; this is risky since there may be a legitimate reason why a session seems inactive (the user is running X Windows, for example).

Note that these controls (and many others) can be set up via Pluggable Authentication Modules (see "PAM" on page 84 or the modules listed on page 90).

Restricted Environments

If a system needs to host guest accounts or other untrusted accounts, it makes sense to set up those accounts with limited functionality. There are two main ways to set up a restricted account: through the *rsh* (Restricted Shell) mechanism, or by creating a chroot jail.

The *rsh* mechanism is available on many System V-based systems—it should not be confused with the rsh (remote shell) command used in Berkeley UNIX for issuing remote commands. Typically, a restricted account is set up by invoking */bin/rsh* in the password file. An individual using *rsh* cannot:

- Change the working directory with the cd command—the user cannot view the contents of other directories

- Change the PATH environment variables—the user cannot execute random commands, since the PATH variable for finding programs is set to a single directory (*usr/rbin*) that contains only secure commands selected by the sysadmin

- Execute a command name that contains a "/"—the user cannot specify a path to a protected command (like ../../bin/chmod)

- Redirect output with ">" and ">>"—the user cannot use shell commands to create new files

When set-up properly, *rsh* can provide the user with a general-purpose but limited environment. It is not trivial to do it right—a single configuration mistake can lead to a breach. Shell scripts provide another potential line-of-attack, since *rsh* lifts restrictions while executing them. As a general rule, a determined and knowledgeable user may be able to break out. While it may be an appropriate solution in some circumstances, don't rely on *rsh* as a fail-safe measure for system security.

The "change root" facility provides a more secure way to set up a restricted environment. The *chroot()* system call changes a process' notion of where the root (/) directory is—it makes a specified directory appear as the root directory to users of the affected accounts. For example, a file might be accessed by the path */usr/restricted/yourfile*. After the *chroot()* call `chroot` (`"/usr/restricted"`), *yourfile* will be accessible by the pathname */yourfile*.

The chroot facility creates a restricted area sometimes known as a "chroot jail." It is sometimes used to limit FTP users and others that only need to run a few commands. Only root can execute *chroot()*. Generally, setting up a chroot jail is non-trivial—many programs expect files and directories to be in a specific place.[9] There is, however, a chroot module for PAM which may simplify the process on systems that are PAM-aware (see page 84). Breaking out of a chroot jail is difficult but possible, especially if the jail includes directory hard links, memory device files, or compilers. It can provide more security than *rsh* but, like many security measures it can be defeated by a determined opponent with UNIX system programming skills.

---

9. For detailed examples of how to set up a *chroot* environment, see David Ferbrache, Gavin Shearer, *UNIX Installation Security and Integrity* (Englewood Cliffs, NJ: PTR Prentice Hall, 1993), 55, Appendix I.

04

Hardening Account Security

This chapter covers a variety of tools and methods that can help harden the security of UNIX accounts. User education can help as can various tools that check for weak passwords or assign strong ones. This chapter covers the shadow password system, which protects weak passwords by hiding them, as well as structural improvements to the password mechanism that make password cracking more difficult. It also covers one-time passwords and Pluggable Authentication Modules (PAM)—a flexible system for controlling account access. It concludes with a survey of account security tools.

Enhancing Password Security

Given the persistent problem of guessable passwords described in the last chapter (see "Password Vulnerabilities" on page 58), there are five major ways that system administrators can enhance or enforce password security:

- User education—Spreading the word via a formal password policy

- Reactive password checking—Running a password-checking program in order to find weak passwords

- Assigning passwords—Providing passwords for users, thus denying them the opportunity to select weak ones

- Proactive password checking—Disallowing the choice of poor passwords in the first place

- Password Aging—Forcing users to change their passwords with some frequency

Additionally, threats to password security can be mitigated by the following measures:

- Shadow passwords—Storing passwords in a protected "shadow" file instead of */etc/passwd*

- One-time passwords—Providing each user with a list of passwords that work once and once only

Each of these methods has pros and cons. Some of them are built into base UNIX implementations; others need to be added. They can be provided by the tools listed in the "Account Security Tools Survey" on page 93. The following subsections discuss each of them in turn.

To help you decide which to implement on your systems, these measures are covered in some depth starting on page 89.

Spreading the Word

A strong, well-articulated password policy is critical for large installations with many users. While password policies can, for the most part, be enforced by software, there is no effective replacement for extensive and consistent user education. If your organization does not distribute a document describing password policies, consider creating one. Emphasize the moral responsibility each user has for protecting the entire community: even an "unimportant" account can be a beachhead for an attack on other users.

> **Tip**
>
> You can find several model policies on the Internet that can help in formulating the right things to say. CERN, the high-energy physics lab, promulgates one that can be found at
>
> `http://consult.cern.ch/writeup/security/security_3.html#SEC7`

While user education is an important element of any password security plan, it is not, in itself, sufficient protection. It may, for example, prove to be ineffective in an environment with high turnover. When even "expert" users may not appreciate how insecure their password choices are, educating an ever-changing population of novices may be too great a challenge. In the end, the sysadmin has a greater stake in strong passwords than any individual user. Strictly speaking, education is not an "enforcement" measure. Software safeguards will provide stronger protection.

> **Caution**
>
> Be careful when giving advice in any password policy document. Any algorithm you suggest can be used to reduce the number of guesses needed to break passwords. The following advice, for example, makes it easier for an attacker to set up a cracking program: "Take two short words and separate them with a special character or a number as in these examples: Robot4my, eye-con or kid?goat."

Reactive Password Checking

An age-old UNIX password security method is to run a program that checks the guessability of passwords after they've been chosen by users. Alec Muffett's Crack program runs a variety of password guessing routines, from iterations of the username to full-blown multi-dictionary match attempts. It reports successfully guessed passwords to the sysadmin and can be set to mail "nastygrams" to the owners of these "cracked" passwords (see "Crack" on page 99). Another program called "John the Ripper" has similar features. Both of these programs provide security through detection.

A traditional downside to reactive password checking is the amount of computational resources (CPU time, disk space) the guessing program requires, especially when working on large sets of passwords. Today's fast cheap hardware, however, makes this less of a barrier than it used to be. A more intrinsic problem is the vulnerability "window" that exists between the time a user picks a weak password and the time the password-checking program detects it. Crack can be set to run on a regular basis, but will always leave a window of opportunity for an attacker.

Another weakness of this approach is this: your Crack runs produce negative reports, but your attacker may have far more computing power and a much larger corpus of dictionary words. He or she may, in fact, already "own" the accounts you're checking (see "Rule 6: There's Always Someone Out There Smarter, More Knowledgeable, or Better-Equipped Than You" on page 24).

Even worse, an attacker could run your password checking program or intercept the results. Even if protected, its mere presence on your system increases your risk. Finally, there's no guarantee your users will cooperate when notified that their passwords are broken; the warning mail sent by Crack can be easily disregarded.

If you run Crack, you may want to let users know that their passwords are being checked. This notice may act as a deterrent, particularly if repeat offenders risk losing their accounts. Here's a sample policy statement:[1]

> As a security measure, we run a program on our server called 'Crack'. This program periodically tries to break into (or crack) passwords. If the program is able to break into your account, you will receive an email message informing you that you need to change to a different password. If your password is 'cracked' more than three times, you will lose your account on our system.

---

1. From http://joules.swvgs.k12.va.us/public/password.html

Generating Random Passwords

Many UNIX implementations can be configured with a password generating program that presents a choice of several random character strings and asks the user to choose one. UNIX systems also can be configured to prescriptively assign such passwords to users. Examples of generated passwords include:

- a random 32-bit word converted to characters

- a passphrase composed of random dictionary words

- a password composed of consonant-vowel-consonant groups

This solution may not be as easy or as satisfactory as it seems at first glance. For starters, the password generator must be truly random; otherwise, an attacker will be able to analyze its output. Morris and Thompson describe a random password system built around a random number generator. Since it only had 2^{15} possible starting values, it didn't stand up to a cracker who was able to break in using one minute of machine time.[2] David Ferbrache and Gavin Shearer describe what happened to a university system that implemented a password generator.[3] It used:

> ... a machine-generated password as the initial password for all new undergraduates. This password was unfortunately based solely on the user's name and his/her class details. This led to an attack by an older student who managed to determine the algorithm (presumably by discovering a selection of the allocated passwords). This student was then able to extrapolate the password of the entire year's intake and to compromise many of the student accounts.

Generated passwords which are not sufficiently random can open up huge holes in your security posture. At the same time, passwords which are sufficiently random are almost always very hard to remember. Users end up writing them down, thus defeating security (see "Writing Down Passwords" on page 52). Think like the enemy: why run a complex program when you can walk down

---

2. Robert Morris and Ken Thompson. See footnote on page 54.
3. David Ferbrache, Gavin Shearer, UNIX Installation Security and Integrity (Englewood Cliffs, NJ: PTR Prentice Hall, 1993), 66.

the hall and find dozens of passwords on Post-It notes attached to the edges of monitors?

Passphrases can be somewhat easier to remember. The ppgen tool automatically generates evocative phrases like "blackout stipend's entrenching lordier video"—try to crack that! It uses a relatively small dictionary of memorable words and a random number generator. While this kind of phrase may not be suitable for everyday use, it can be particularly effective when used in conjunction with improved algorithms (like FreeBSD's MD5 or OpenBSD's Blowfish), with Kerberos, or for highly sensitive items like a PGP keyring (see "ppgen" on page 97).

Password Aging

Time is a critical factor in maintaining the confidentiality of passwords. The longer a password is in use, the greater the likelihood that it will be compromised (see "Rule 1: Security Through Obscurity Doesn't Work" on page 21 and the equation on page 59). Many UNIX implementations (and System V Release 4-based systems in particular) support password aging—the ability to expire passwords after a set interval time. This feature is often enabled in the *etc/shadow* file (see "Anatomy of /etc/shadow" on page 76). Typically, users are warned in advance that their passwords are about to expire.

Military-grade security mandates the deployment of password aging. According to the Department of Defense's "Password Management Guideline":[4]

> There should be a maximum lifetime for all passwords. To protect against unknown threats, it is recommended that the maximum lifetime of a password be no greater than 1 year. The presence of known threats may indicate a need for a shorter maximum lifetime.

In addition to a maximum lifetime, some systems assign a minimum lifetime—this prevents users from changing their passwords when they expire and then immediately changing them back.

---

4. National Computer Security Center, Department of Defense Password Management Guideline. Report N. CSC-STD-002-85. See
http://www.radium.ncsc.mil/tpep/library/rainbow/
CSC-STD-002-85.html

While password aging doesn't prevent or detect weak passwords, it mitigates the associated risk. An attacker can spend time and energy defeating the */etc/passwd* file, only to find that the passwords on several successfully cracked accounts have subsequently changed. On the other hand, aging is far from foolproof. Users can defeat it by switching back and forth between stock passwords. Even when this is prevented, users may still pick an easy sequence of weak passwords (pwlastmonth, pwthismonth, pwnextmonth, etc.). Password aging can even increase the risk that a user will choose a weak password. Consider the outcome of this scenario: J. Random's password has just expired and he must select a new one right now, under time pressure.

Proactive Password Checking

The best way to avoid weak passwords is to prevent users from selecting them in the first place. A proactive password checker either replaces the standard password changing program (passwd)—or wraps around it—and evaluates each user-selected password before associating it with an account. For the most part, it works like a reactive password checker—checking the just-entered password against iterations of username, first name, and last name, as well as against dictionaries. It typically can be configured on a per-machine basis, allowing the sysadmin to establish an appropriate level of password security. Some programs provide users with feedback about their rejected choices ("You may not use your last name," etc.) though this mechanism can be exploited by an attacker to reduce the keyspace for password cracking.

Several proactive password checkers have been implemented, including passwd+ , npasswd , and epasswd (all three are detailed later in this chapter). None of these is trivial to install and configure. Some modern UNIX implementations include a built-in password checker. Red Hat Linux, for example, uses Alex Muffett's CrackLib to check user-selected passwords. Red Hat and Solaris both implement PAM, which provides great flexibility in setting up alternative authentication mechanisms in general and proactive password checking in particular (see "PAM" on page 84 or the listing for the CrackLib module on page 94).

Shadow Password Files

Traditionally, the *letc/passwd* file is world-readable since many programs need to use it to translate UIDs to usernames. The ls -l command, for example, would display numeric UIDs instead of usernames if it couldn't access *letc/passwd*. Unfortunately, given the availability of password-guessing programs, the world-readable *letc/passwd* file with encoded passwords presents a major security risk. Most recent UNIX implementations support a workaround: shadow password files.

The shadow password system essentially splits the password file into two parts: *letc/passwd* and the shadow password file. The shadow password file stores the encoded passwords; the coded-password fields in *letc/passwd* are all set to "x" or another place-holder. The shadow password file can only be read by root or set-uid programs like passwd that legitimately need access while all non-privileged users are denied access. By convention, the shadow password file is stored as *letc/shadow,* though some systems use alternate paths and filenames. BSD systems, for example, store the encoded passwords in *letc/master.passwd.*

Anatomy of /etc/shadow

The *letc/shadow* file contains fields for the username and the encoded password as well as the following:

- Date password was last changed expressed as the number of days since Jan 1, 1970

- Minimum days between password changes. Days after which password must be changed

- Days before password is to expire that user is warned

- Days after password expires that account is disabled

- Days since Jan 1, 1970, that account is disabled

- A reserved field

Here's an example of an *letc/shadow* file taken from a Red Hat Linux system:

```
root:mGqQwuvdF41bc:10612:0:99999:7:::
bin:*:10612:0:99999:7:::
daemon:*:10612:0:99999:7:::
adm:*:10612:0:99999:7:::
lp:*:10612:0:99999:7:::
sync:*:10612:0:99999:7:::
shutdown:*:10612:0:99999:7:::
halt:*:10612:0:99999:7:::
mail:*:10612:0:99999:7:::
news:*:10612:0:99999:7:::
uucp:*:10612:0:99999:7:::
operator:*:10612:0:99999:7:::
games:*:10612:0:99999:7:::
gopher:*:10612:0:99999:7:::
ftp:*:10612:0:99999:7:::
nobody:*:10612:0:99999:7:::
postgres:!!:10612:0:99999:7:::
alice:BP4x8kkiH8Vn2:10619:0:99999:7:::
bob:VHrvqML2pbrlY:10612:0:99999:7:::
carol:JKACdvAGtot.I:10612:0:99999:7:::
eve:uKlkD2PzXTzkk:10612:0:99999:7:::
mallory:zLY1VG7gBuz2U:10612:0:99999:7:::
trent:ZMDQwveTzWl/w:10612:0:99999:7:::
```

By default, password aging is not turned on. There is no minimum number of days before the password can be changed and, essentially, there is no date at which they must be changed. The specification that passwords must be changed before day 99999 is hardly significant; this is almost 250 years from now. The specification that the user will be warned seven days before the password expires has no effect unless you elect to use password aging. While not specified in this example, it's also possible to set up a grace period between the time a password expires and the account is disabled.

The benefits and risks of password aging is discussed in "Password Aging" on page 74.

Setting Up Shadow Passwords

On systems where the shadow password feature is optional, a single relatively-simple command sets up and updates the shadow password file: pwconv. This command creates a shadow password file if none exists. If a shadow file is already in place, pwconv adds new users in */etc/passwd* to */etc/shadow*, removes users not in

/etc/passwd from the shadow file, and moves passwords from */etc/passwd* to the shadow file.

Under Red Hat Linux, pwconv writes the new */etc/passwd* file to a file named *npasswd* and the new shadow file to *nshadow*. These new files then need to be renamed or copied by hand.

You can return to a non-shadowed scheme by the pwunconv command, which merges information from the shadow file back into the traditional password file.

Tip

> Early Linux distributions did not include support for shadow passwords. This capability could be added via the Shadow Suite—see the Shadow Password HOWTO that can be found at `http://metalab.unc.edu/LDP/HOWTO/Shadow-Password-HOWTO.html` Other UNIX systems can use the shadow program by John F. Haugh, II (see "shadow" on page 98).

Algorithm Improvements

If the traditional UNIX password-encoding algorithm is subject to easy dictionary attack, why not improve the algorithm to make it more resistant? As outlined above, this has worked in the past, with the introduction of encoded passwords, DES, and salt. Unfortunately, the installed base of systems that use the traditional password mechanism is substantial and re-engineering production systems can be a daunting prospect. If you have access to the source code for *crypt()*, programming knowledge, and time, there are several improvements that you can make to even the most tool-limited systems. Alternatively, many newer UNIX variants allow you to set the password mechanism so that it's harder to crack.

Common tactics for hardening the *crypt()* mechanism include:

- Increasing the number of encryption rounds—Boost the number of rounds (the iteration count) beyond 25. This will slow the encryption process and thus the cracking process. It also will make it more difficult for an attacker that steals the */etc/passwd* file and tries to crack it on another machine.

- Increasing the amount of salt—Use four characters of salt (24 bits) instead of the traditional two characters (12 bits). This perturbs the DES algorithm in one of 16,777,216 ways instead of 4096 ways. The attacker who uses a pre-compiled crack dictionary with 4096 permutations will have to start from scratch.

Extended Crypt

NetBSD and OpenBSD implement the above tactics. Both of these free systems support an "extended crypt" that allows for larger salt values and an increased number of rounds—these can be specified in the *passwd.conf* file.[5] Under this scheme, the plaintext password (which can be longer than eight characters) is divided into groups of eight characters (a short final group is padded with zeros). Seven bits of each character (56 bits per group) are used to form DES keys. The first group of 56 bits becomes the initial DES key, which is encrypted with itself. The next group's bits are XOR'ed against the encrypted initial key—the resulting value becomes the next DES key. This process is repeated for each additional group. The final DES key is then used to perform cumulative rounds of encryptions on a 64-bit constant.

This *crypt()* variant creates a 20 character password entry which is composed of two parts: the "setting" and the encoded password. The setting is a 9-character array consisting of an underscore ("_") followed by 4 bytes of iteration count (specifying the number of rounds) and 4 bytes of salt. Each byte is encoded as a 6-bit printable character for a total of 48 bits for both count and salt.

> **Increasing the number of rounds provides some protection against cracking, but only in situations in which the cracker doesn't know how many rounds were used. If attackers know you use 50 rounds instead of 25, they can easily adjust their password cracking program to account for this. It may take more time, but it's still do-able.**   **Caution**

Alternative Algorithms

While a variant of DES has long been the stalwart of UNIX password encryption, other algorithms can be used instead of DES.

5. See the man pages for crypt. For NetBSD, see `http://www.flame.org/cgi-bin/uncgi/hman`. For OpenBSD, see `http://www.openbsd.org/cgi-bin/man.cgi`

Again, modern BSD systems provide examples of how additional algorithms can be implemented. By default, FreeBSD uses a *crypt()* function built around the MD-5 one-way hash function (i.e., a function that operates on an arbitrary-length message and returns a fixed-length hash value). As part of a "dual-track" strategy intended to leave the core distribution free of crypto export restrictions, FreeBSD can be retrofitted with a separate add-on library supporting the DES-based password hash.[6]

OpenBSD goes even further. The group that develops it is based in Canada and thus is not subject to US export restrictions. Open-BSD can be configured to use the traditional UNIX crypt(), the "extended crypt" described above, MD5, or Blowfish.

MD5 was developed by Ronald L. Rivest—it's described in RFC 1321.[7] The MD5-based *crypt()* in FreeBSD and OpenBSD produces a password entry that includes the version number, salt, and the hashed password, separated from each other by the "$" character. An MD5 password entry might look like:

```
$1$caeiHQwX$hsKqOjrFRRN6K32OWkCBf1
```

where "$1" indicates MD5, and "caeiHQwX" is the salt.[8]

Blowfish was developed by Bruce Schneier in 1993 as a fast, compact, simple, and free replacement for DES.[9] While Schneier states that Blowfish is not suitable for generating one-way hashes, OpenBSD uses it for just that purpose.[10] The Blowfish version of *crypt()* uses 128 bits of salt—enough to slow down even the most persistent crackers. Pre-compiling a dictionary with all possible salt values would be very expensive indeed. The maximum password length is 72 characters.

---

6. Garrett Wollman, "FreeBSD Handbook,"
http://www.freebsd.org/handbook/handbook68.html#146
7. See http://www.faqs.org/rfcs/rfc1321.html
8. The example is from the OpenBSD *crypt(3)* man page.
9. Bruce Schneier, "Description of a New Variable-Length Key, 64-Bit Block Cipher (Blowfish)," Fast Software Encryption, Cambridge Security Workshop Proceedings (December 1993), Springer-Verlag, 1994, 191–204. See http://www.counterpane.com/bfsverlag.html
10. Bruce Schneier, *Applied Cryptography,* 2nd Ed. (New York, NY: John Wiley & Sons, 1996), 336.

The Blowfish algorithm is initialized with a fixed string consisting of the hexadecimal digits of pi. The initial Blowfish state is then expanded with the salt and the password—this process is repeated a variable number of rounds (the number is encoded in the password string). The final Blowfish password entry is created by encrypting the string "OrpheanBeholderScryDoubt" with the Blowfish state 64 times.

The encoded password entry contains the Blowfish version number, the logarithm of the number of rounds, and the concatenation of salt and hashed password—each separated by the "$" character. An encoded "8" would specify 256 rounds. A valid Blowfish password might look like:

```
$2a$12$eIAq8PR8sIUnJ1HaohxX209x9Q1m2vK97LJ5dsXdmB.eXF42qjchC
```

In this example, the initial expansion proceeded for 4096 rounds. Given the large number of rounds and long passwords, Blowfish-encoded passwords are far more difficult to crack than those encoded with the traditional DES-based mechanism. Given the added security provided by these kinds of algorithmic improvements, it should only be a matter of time before they're implemented in other UNIX systems.

One-Time Passwords

All the methods above are effective in a local environment, but what happens when those proactively-checked properly-aged passwords are sent over a network (i.e., in plain text)? An attacker can use a password sniffer tool that monitors LAN traffic and records username/password combinations. The username/password combination is also vulnerable every time someone logs in via an untrusted network like the Internet.

An elegant solution to the threat of password interception is to use a password once and then throw it away. Essentially, you concede that there is no way to protect a password in transit. Instead of trying to prevent the threat of eavesdropping, an authentication system based on one-time passwords neutralizes the benefits of interception, a classic example of strong security through risk avoidance. Capturing passwords that can't be re-used is a truly futile line-of-attack.

One-time passwords represent one of the most effective and elegant solutions in the entire canon of security tools and techniques. They can be implemented with hardware like a token card or with software and (gasp) paper. All one-time password schemes are conceptually based on the one-time pad, a perfect encryption method developed in 1917 by Major Joseph Mauborgne. A classic one-time pad consists of a large set of non-repeating key letters written on paper and glued together into a pad or codebook. The message sender uses each key letter in turn to encrypt one plaintext character—the encryption routine adds (modulo 26) the message character and the one-time key letter. The receiver uses an identical pad to decrypt the message character by character. Once the pads are used, they are destroyed.

As long as the eavesdropper can't get access to the pad, this scheme is perfectly secure—even the most determined opponent can't deduce anything since any given encrypted text can correspond to any plaintext message of the same size. Supposedly, the cold-war era hotline between the United States and the old Soviet Union was protected by a one-time pad system. As Bruce Schneier points out,[11]

> These are still secure today and will remain that way forever. It doesn't matter how long the supercomputers work on the problem. Even after the aliens from Andromeda land with their massive spaceships and undreamed-of computing power, they will not be able to read the Soviet spy messages encrypted with one-time pads (unless they go back in time and get the one-time pads).

The strength of the one-time pad has been incorporated in various one-time password (OTP) schemes that rely on a code book. A code book of passwords is generated using a shared secret (typically a pass phrase). When a user needs to log in, he or she looks up the next available password in the code book, uses it to gain access, and then crosses it out. Assuming the code book is not defeated, this performs an almost perfect authentication.

---

11. Ibid., 17.

This method of protecting password security was first proposed by Leslie Lamport in 1981 and first implemented on a wide-scale by the S/Key system developed by Phil Karn at Bellcore (see "S/Key" on page 97).[12] S/Key is the basis of several related one-time password systems such as OPIE (see "OPIE" on page 96) and the otp library (see "otp" on page 96). Unfortunately, these related but different one-time password systems are largely incompatible—the overall deployment of the technology has been slowed by implementation differences.

In recent years, there's been an effort to develop standards for OTP systems. RFC 1938 by Neil Haller and Craig Metz describes a generic architecture for OTP.[13] It specifies two key pieces of an OTP system: a password-generator that produces one-time user passwords based on a secret passphrase, and a server that verifies the received passwords and stores the last valid one that was used.

OpenBSD 2.4 includes an exemplary implementation of S/Key. The OpenBSD login utility will accept either regular passwords or the password "s/key," in which case S/Key authentication is performed. The `skeyinit` command initializes the system and asks the user enter a secret passphrase consisting of several words. The `skeyinfo` command can be used to print out sets of one-time passwords. OpenBSD's implementation provides maximum flexibility. A user working from an office console can use his or her regular password. When the same user is on the road using untrusted Internet facilities, he or she can avoid risk by using the one-time passwords from a code book.

In the future, more and more UNIX vendors are likely to implement the OTP standard. While OTP provides strong protection to passwords, it doesn't address the confidentiality of the actual user session. In the long run, the need for special password security may decrease as network transmissions are routinely encrypted using emerging standards such as Transport Layer Security (see "TLS" on page 318) or Secure Shell (SSH).

---

12. S/Key is a trademark of Bellcore.
13. "A One-Time Password System," 1996. See
`http://www.faqs.org/rfcs/rfc1938.html`

PAM

PAM (Pluggable Authentication Modules) is a suite of shared
libraries that provides sysadmins with a wide variety of precise
controls over how applications authenticate users. While PAM is
not a tool per se, it establishes a flexible framework for implementing site security policies.

PAM represents an elegant solution to a persistent problem.
Most UNIX programs that require user authentication rely on
/etc/passwd and the traditional UNIX authentication scheme. As
discussed in the previous chapter, a variety of factors have diminished the security of this system. Not only is it inherently vulnerable to cracking, but systems that used to stand alone are now
deployed on networks where many more individuals may have
access to their login prompts.

In response, several new authentication schemes have been
developed over the years, including complex replacements for
/etc/passwd like shadow and one-time passwords, those that utilize
a challenge-response scheme, and those that depend on hardware
(i.e., smart-card systems). While these new schemes improve security, they have been problematic to implement. Since many UNIX
applications (login, telnet, ftp, su etc.) depend on */etc/passwd,* all
those applications have to be re-written before a new authentication scheme can be deployed.

In order to solve this development bottleneck, several engineers
at Sun Microsystems developed PAM—a general solution that sep-
arates the development of privilege-granting software from the
development of secure authentication schemes. PAM provides a
front-end library of functions—an Application Programming
Interface (API)—that an application may use to authenticate a user.
The PAM library is configured by either a single file, */etc/pam.conf,*
or a series of configuration files located in */etc/pam.d/* which allow
user requests for access ("let me log in") to be transparently hon-
ored by locally-available back-end authentication modules, in
accordance with local security needs.

Making things easy for users is a core goal of PAM. In order for
security safeguards to be useful, they must be easy to use. Given the
proliferation of different authentication schemes, users could get

caught having to type multiple passwords. PAM can be configured to provide a "unified" or "integrated" login so that users can enter a single password to access multiple services.

> PAM is described by Open Software Foundation RFC 86.0: "Unified **Tip**
> Login with Pluggable Authentication Modules" by Vipin Samar and
> Roland J. Schemers III. See
> `http://www.osf.org/tech/rfc/rfc86.0.html`

By abstracting authentication functions in a "plug-and-play" fashion, PAM gives sysadmins great flexibility in securing their systems. Figure 4.1 illustrates the relationship between privilege-granting applications, the PAM API (as controlled by *pam.conf*), and potential authentication mechanisms.

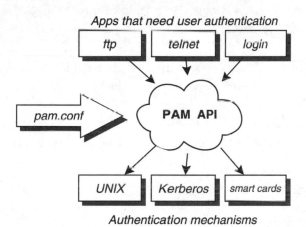

Figure 4.1 *The Basic PAM Architecture*[14]

For example, traditionally the FTP application relies on the UNIX */etc/passwd* mechanism to authenticate a user who wishes to start an FTP session. As the diagram illustrates, a system configured with PAM sends the ftp authentication request to the PAM API, which relies on rules set out in the *pam.conf* or related files. The sysadmin can set up PAM so that one or more authentication mechanisms are "plugged into" the PAM API. Perhaps the system

---

14. The diagram is roughly based on one that appears in the RFC. See
`http://www.osf.org/tech/rfc/rfc86.0.html`

uses the traditional */etc/passwd* mechanisms, or perhaps the system uses a more secure system like Kerberos along with retinal scans. Perhaps */etc/passwd* is fine for local logins, but one-time passwords should be used to open telnet sessions. The beauty of PAM is its flexibility—sysadmins can fine-tune the overall authentication scheme on the fly without having to worry about breaking applications.

Tip

PAM was developed by Sun Microsystems. Thus, it has been implemented in Solaris, starting with version 2.3. Engineers at Red Hat Software implemented an open source version (Linux-PAM) that first appeared in Red Hat Linux version 3.0.4 (for a colorful explanation of PAM on Red Hat, see `http://www.redhat.com/linux-info/pam/`). Other Linux distributions have followed, including Caldera OpenLinux and Debian GNU/Linux. FreeBSD added PAM support with release 3.1.

PAM's essential code is contained in a library (Linux-PAM in the Linux environment) that consults the PAM configuration file and then loads one or more of a variety of loadable object files, or "modules," that perform the various authentication tasks for an application. Linux-PAM is capable of four separate types of management tasks:

- authentication management

- account management

- session management, and

- password management.

The PAM configuration file contains entries that associate a management task with the appropriate module, which then performs the actual work.

Tip

For more information on Linux-PAM, including documentation and source code, see the primary distribution site at `http://www.kernel.org/pub/linux/libs/pam/index.html`

PAM Configuration Files

PAM configuration information can be held in either a single file *letc/pam.conf* or in the directory *letc/pam.d/*. The PAM library can be compiled in one of two modes—one which uses either a single *letc/pam.conf* file or a *letc/pam.d/* directory but not both, and a second which allows both configuration set-ups, with *letc/pam.d/* overriding the settings of *letc/pam.conf*.

In general, the directory format is easier to configure and maintain. It's also a bit faster—only a short file needs to be parsed each time PAM is invoked, rather than a longer, singular configuration file. Since Red Hat Linux systems typically utilize the directory format, I'll use this set-up in my examples.

> The Linux-PAM System Administrators' Guide by Andrew G. Morgan **Tip**
> is an excellent guide to setting up PAM. See `http://www.`
> `kernel.org/pub/linux/libs/pam/Linux-PAM-html/pam.html`

Each of the files in *letc/pam.d/* controls a specific "service" or application. The file *letc/pam.d/login,* for examples, governs the parameters of the login application.

The syntax of each file in *letc/pam.d/* consists of lines of the following form:

```
module type   control-flag   module-path   arguments
```

I'll cover each of these in turn.

There are four types of modules, each of which corresponds to a management task outlined above.

- `auth`—Establishes that users are who they claim to be by instructing the application to prompt the user for a password (or another means of identification). Can also grant group membership or other privileges through its credential granting properties.

- `account`—Performs various account management tasks. Can be used to restrict or permit access to an application based on a variety of parameters such as the time of day, available system resources, or the location of the user (console vs. tty).

- `session`—Controls what needs to happen either before or after a user is authenticated. Can be used to mount directories, etc.

- `password`—Updates the authentication token associated with the user. Typically, there is one module for each "challenge/response" authentication module.

The control-flag entry determines how PAM reacts to the success or failure of a module. Modules can be stacked so that modules of the same type execute in series, one after another. The control-flags also determine the relative importance of each module. Note that applications are not made aware of the success or failure of stacked modules—they only receive a summary response from PAM.

The control-flag is set via a simple syntax composed of a single keyword that indicates how important the success or failure of a specific module may be. There are four keywords:

- `required`—Indicates that the success of the module is necessary for the module-type to succeed. Failure will not be apparent to the user until all of the remaining modules are executed.

- `requisite`—Similar to `required`, except that control is directly returned to the application in the event of failure. The return value is that associated with the first required or requisite module to fail. Note that this flag can be used to prevent a user from entering a password over an unsafe medium. Unfortunately, this behavior could reveal valid accounts to an attacker.

- `sufficient`—The success of this module is deemed "sufficient" to satisfy the Linux-PAM library that this module-type has succeeded in its purpose. In the event that no previous required module has failed, no more stacked modules of this type are invoked (Note: in this case, subsequent required modules are not invoked). A failure of this module is not deemed as fatal to satisfying the application that this module-type has succeeded.

- `optional`—Marks the module as not being critical to the success or failure of the user's application for service. However, in the absence of any successes of previous or subsequent stacked modules, this module will determine the nature of the response to the application.

> The control-flag syntax outlined here can be augmented with a   **Tip**
> newer, more complex syntax that is much more specific and gives
> sysadmins very granular control over authentication. While this syn-
> tax is beyond the scope of this chapter, it may be helpful to know
> that it delimits a series of value=action tokens in square brackets:
> [value1=action1 value2=action2 ...]

The "Module-path" is the path-name to the pluggable module. If the first character of the module path is "/", it is assumed to be a complete path. If this is not the case, the given module path is appended to the default module path.

> PAM modules might be located in the either */usr/lib/security/*, or in   **Tip**
> the case of Red Hat Linux, */lib/security*.

Finally, shell-like arguments can be passed to the module when it's invoked. This field (called "options" in the original PAM proposal) can be used by a sysadmin to fine-tune the behavior of PAM modules. Arguments are usually optional and specific to a given module. Here are some common arguments that can be specified:

- debug—Use the *syslog(3)* call to log debugging information to the system log files.

- no_warn—Instruct module to not give warning messages to the application.

- use_first_pass—The module should not prompt the user for a password. Instead, it should obtain the previously-typed password (from the preceding auth module) and use that. If that doesn't work, the user will not be authenticated.

- try_first_pass—The module should attempt authentication with the previously-typed password (from the preceding auth module). If that doesn't work, the user is prompted for a password.

- `use_mapped_pass`—The use_mapped_pass argument instructs the module to take the plaintext authentication token entered by a previous module and use it to generate an encryption/decryption key with which to safely store/retrieve the authentication token required for this module. In this way the user can enter a single authentication token and be quietly authenticated by a number of stacked modules. Note that his argument is not currently supported by any of the modules in the Linux-PAM distribution due to US encryption export restrictions. This argument is intended for the auth and password module types only.

Tip

An incorrectly formatted line in any one of the configuration files will cause the authentication process to fail. A corresponding error is written to the system log files via *syslog*. Invalid arguments are also written to the syslog.

Caution

It's possible to totally hose your system with PAM. Deleting your configuration files could lock you out of your system. The PAM System Administrators' Guide contains detailed instructions on how to recover from this kind of problem—see `http://www.kernel.org/pub/linux/libs/pam/Linux-PAM-html/pam-5.html`

Modules

A wide variety of modules can be configured as part of a PAM installation and many new ones are in active development. The following are included in the standard Linux-PAM distribution. This list is not exhaustive though it provides a taste of what PAM can do.

Tip

You can discover additional modules, including those that support Netware, SAMBA, LDAP, and more, at `http://www.kenel.org/pub/linux/libs/pam/modules.html`

- Chroot Module—By setting up this module, you can lock users into an ersatz system environment with access to a limited set of programs (say, ls, cp, rm). Their "root directory" will actually be somewhere else. They won't be able to see other users' files.

- Cracklib Password Checker—This module implements a regime that checks the strength of new user passwords according to rules established by the sysadmin. It requires the system library *libcrack* and a system dictionary: */usr/lib/cracklib_dict*. Traditional UNIX passwords can be replaced with strong MD5 encoding using this module. When a user requests a new password, he or she is presented with the following prompt: "New UNIX password:". The new password is then confirmed at the "Retype UNIX password:" prompt. A new password is checked against the *cracklib* routine, which can be set to reject short passwords, those without digits, etc. If it passes, additional checks are run that compare the new password against the old one. The password checker evaluates whether a new password is the same string in reverse, whether only the case has been changed, whether many characters are similar, whether the new one is too simple, or whether the new one is a rotated version of the old one.

- The Locking-out Module—Can be used to prevent users from changing passwords, running default applications, or from logging in at all.

- Anon Access Module—Supports various anonymous FTP settings. Anonymous access can be limited or granted to a comma-delimited list of users.

- Kerberos 4 Module—Provides an interface for doing Kerberos verification of a user's password, handling Kerberos tickets, and changing a Kerberos password.

- Last Login Module—Provides a "Last login on ..." message; using information from the */var/log/wtmp* file.

- Resource Limits Module—Can limit anything from a user's maximum file size to the number of processes a user can run.

- List-file Module—Provides a way to deny or allow services to users listed in an arbitrary file.

- Mail Module—Delivers the "You have new mail" message to the user.

- No-login Module—If the file */etc/nologin* exists, this module allows only root to log in; other users are turned away with an error message.

- Promiscuous Module—Effectively allows anyone to log in (dangerous!).

- Time Control Module —Restricts access to users based on their name, the time of day, the day of week, the service they are applying for, and their terminal.

- The Wheel Module—Restricts root access to members of the wheel (gid=0) group.

Single Sign-on

PAM was originally designed to provide users with a unified or integrated login across various applications while using a single system. The original concept has been extended to provide a "single sign-on"—the ability to log in once and then transparently access various applications and services across an entire enterprise. In general, this is a good idea. It can become difficult to get work done when one has to enter one password to log into a primary workstation, a second to access a corporate database, another to run a distributed client-server application, yet another to start an FTP session, and so on. In this kind of environment, the impulse to write down passwords on Post-It notes attached to a monitor can become irresistible. With a single sign-on, the user can establish trust with a single authentication.

In environments where security is mission-critical, a single sign-on system can be dangerous—a single breach on a single workstation can give an attacker access to an entire enterprise network. In some situations, the security of applications and services is preserved by distinct and separate authentication schemes. The issue is moot to some extent, since single sign-on remains a design concept rather than a widely-implemented feature. It does, however, seem likely that the idea of a single sign-on will gain currency, especially as network and distributed computing environments become more complex and offer more and more privilege-granting applications and services.

The Open Group has taken the lead in establishing a single sign-on **Tip** standard built around PAM. You can find out more by surfing to the overview page at http://www.opengroup.org/security/ sso/index.htm or by reviewing the preliminary specification "X/Open Single Sign-on Service (XSSO)—Pluggable Authentication Modules" at
http://www.opengroup.org/onlinepubs/8329799/toc.htm

Account Security Tools Survey

There are a wide variety of authentication and password-related tools available on the net. In most cases, I provide URLs for more information and for downloading. In some cases, the descriptions are derived from documents included with the tools.

anlpasswd

A proactive password checker from Argonne National Laboratory that prevents users from choosing weak passwords.

For more information:
ftp://coast.cs.purdue.edu/pub/tools/unix/anlpasswd/

Crack

A password-guessing program by Alex Muffett that is designed to quickly locate insecure passwords by scanning the contents of a password file, looking for users who have chosen a weak login password. This program is covered in depth in the next chapter (see "Crack" on page 99). Crack is available on the accompanying CD-ROM.

For more information:
http://www.users.dircon.co.uk/~crypto/

To download:

`http://www.users.dircon.co.uk/~crypto/`

`ftp://ftp.cert.org/pub/tools/crack/`

`ftp://ftp.cert.dfn.de/pub/tools/password/Crack/`

`ftp://ftp.win.tue.nl/pub/security/`

`ftp://coast.cs.purdue.edu/pub/tools/unix/crack/`

CrackLib

CrackLib is a library of functions (as opposed to a freestanding tool) that can be called from passwd-like programs in order to prevent users from choosing passwords that Crack would be able to guess. This offshoot of Crack can be configured to filter out weak passwords at the source. If you want to set up a proactive password-checking mechanism (as opposed to a reactive one like Crack), this is where you should start. CrackLib has been worked up as a PAM module (see page 84).

To download:

`http://www.users.dircon.co.uk/~crypto/`

`ftp://coast.cs.purdue.edu/pub/tools/unix/cracklib/`

epasswd

This application by Eric Allen Davis replaces the standard UNIX passwd program. Epasswd supports both shadow passwords and password aging. It enforces strict password construction requirements which include a minimum number of numeric, special, lower, and upper case characters as well as the minimum and maximum password length.

For more information:

`http://science.nas.nasa.gov/Groups/Security/epasswd/index.html`

Kerberos

Kerberos is a network authentication protocol for physically insecure networks, based on the key distribution model presented by Needham and Schroeder. It is designed to provide strong authentication for client/server applications by using secret-key cryptography. The protocol uses strong cryptography so that a client can prove its identity to a server (and vice versa) across an insecure network connection. After a client and server have used Kerberos to prove their identities, they can also encrypt all of their communications to assure privacy and data integrity as they go about their business. A free implementation of this protocol is available from the Massachusetts Institute of Technology. There are many commercial products that also use Kerberos.

For more information:
```
http://web.mit.edu/kerberos/www/
```
```
http://gost.isi.edu/info/Kerberos/
```

John the Ripper

This is a password-guessing program similar to Crack.

To download:
```
http://www.false.com/security/john/index.html
```
```
ftp://coast.cs.purdue.edu/pub/tools/unix/john/
```

npasswd

This application replaces the passwd command. Written by Clyde Hoover, it subjects user passwords to stringent guessability checks in order to prevent users from choosing weak passwords. The first version of the program was written in 1989 in the wake of the Morris Internet Worm. According to the author: "Configuring npasswd requires some thought on the part of the administrator. It's not a 'plug and play' process. There are configuration options to select, and there is policy in the code that may not meet your needs."

For more information:
```
ftp://ftp.cc.utexas.edu/people/clyde/npasswd/doc/index.html
```

To download:
```
ftp://ftp.cc.utexas.edu/pub/npasswd/
```
```
ftp://coast.cs.purdue.edu/pub/tools/unix/password/
```

obvious-pw

This is a function by John Nagle that depends upon a subtle property of English—less than one-third of the possible "triples," sequences of three letters, are used in English words. This property makes it possible to distinguish random letter strings from strings that look like English words. The idea is to reject passwords that resemble English words.

To download:

```
http://www.leo.org/pub/comp/usenet/comp.sources.unix/
obvious-pw/index.html

ftp://isgate.is/pub/unix/sec7/obvious-pw.tar.Z

http://ftp.sunet.se/ftp/pub/usenet/ftp.uu.net/
comp.sources.unix/volume16/
```

OPIE

OPIE (One Time Passwords in Everything) is an S/Key derivative (the name was changed to avoid trademark infringement) developed by the US Naval Research Laboratory (NRL) and other institutions over the past few years. Per the README file included with the distribution: "OPIE is derived in part from the BSD UNIX software developed at UC Berkeley, in part from the S/Key (TM) software developed at Bell Communications Research (Bellcore), and also includes enhancements developed at NRL." OPIE implements the IETF One-Time Passwords (OTP) standard as per RFC 1938[15] and runs out of the box on most versions of UNIX. OPIE supports MD5 in addition to MD4 and has a number of other security enhancements when compared with the original Bellcore S/Key.

For more information:
```
http://inner.net/opie
```

To download:
```
ftp://ftp.inner.net/pub/opie/
```

otp

Otp is a C program that generates one-time key pads or password lists. Modeled after the one-time pad system used by Swiss banks, otp creates key and password lists for verification and security purposes in a variety of formats.

For more information:
```
http://www.fourmilab.ch/onetime/otpgen.html
```

passwd+

A proactive password checker by Matt Bishop that is driven by a configuration file to determine what types of passwords are and are

---

15. See `http://info.internet.isi.edu:80/`
`in-notes/rfc/files/rfc1938.txt`

not allowed. The configuration file allows the use of regular expressions, the comparison of passwords against the contents of files (e.g., dictionaries) and the calling of external programs to examine the password.

For more information:

`ftp://ftp.dartmouth.edu/pub/security/`

pidentd

This daemon by Peter Eriksson implements an RFC 1413 identification server that can be used to query a remote host for the identification of the user making a TCP connection request.

To download:

`ftp://coast.cs.purdue.edu/pub/tools/unix/ident/servers/`

`ftp://ftp.csc.ncsu.edu/pub/security/`

`ftp://ftp.lysator.liu.se/pub/ident/servers/`

ppgen

This random passphrase generator by Michael Shields can be used with programs that accept long passwords (like MD5-based FreeBSD, Blowfish-based OpenBSD, Kerberos, PGP). It can use various dictionaries and sources of randomness. It can work as a free-standing tool or it can be integrated with `passwd` and other programs to choose passphrases for users. Ppgen is available on the accompanying CD-ROM.

To download:

`ftp://coast.cs.purdue.edu/pub/tools/unix/ppgen/`

S/Key

This one-time password system from Bellcore provides authentication over insecure networks. It's designed to defeat eavesdroppers "listening" for username and password transmittals. The user's secret password never crosses the network during login or when executing other commands requiring authentication such as the UNIX passwd or su commands. No secret information is stored anywhere, including the host being protected, and the underlying algorithm is public knowledge. The remote end of this system can run on any locally available computer, including PC's and Mac's. RFC 1938[16] is based on the S/KEY implementation. OpenBSD includes a built-in S/Key implementation. S/Key can also be implemented via PAM on PAM-aware systems. Note that OPIE is intended to be a replacement for S/Key with additional security enhancements.

For more information:
`ftp://thumper.bellcore.com/pub/nmh/docs/skey.txt`

To download:
`ftp://thumper.bellcore.com/pub/nmh/`

`ftp://coast.cs.purdue.edu/pub/tools/unix/skey/`

shadow

The shadow program by John F. Haugh, II replaces login and `passwd` in order to enable any system to use shadow password files. Shadow includes support for shadow password files, shadow group files, DBM password files, double-length passwords, and password aging.

For more information:
`ftp://ftp.std.com/src/freeunix/shadow.tar.Z`

SRA

Secure RPC Authentication (SRA) is part of the TAMU tool set that provides drop in replacements for telnet and ftp client and server programs. These replacements use Secure RPC code to provide encrypted authentication across the network so that plaintext passwords are not used. The clients and servers negotiate the availability of SRA so that they work with unmodified versions. The programs require no external keyserver or ticket server, and work equally well for local or internet wide connections. Full sources as well as binaries for Solaris and Linux are available.

For more information:
`ftp://coast.cs.purdue.edu/pub/tools/unix/TAMU/sra.README`

To download:
`ftp://coast.cs.purdue.edu/pub/tools/unix/TAMU/`

---

16. See `http://info.internet.isi.edu:80/in-notes/rfc/files/rfc1938.txt`

## 05

Crack

What you don't know *can* hurt you if there are accounts on your systems with weak passwords. This chapter shows you how to use Alex Moffett's Crack program to test the "guessability" of the passwords on your systems.

Introduction

Security through obscurity, or by relying on secrets, is a tricky business (see "Rule 1: Security Through Obscurity Doesn't Work" on page 21). While it's risky to rely on a secret to provide security, it's even riskier to rely on a secret that can be guessed by an opponent.

The UNIX password scheme relies on secrets—alphanumeric strings—that exist in a finite space. Passwords, however, are vulnerable to the frailties of human psychology, and even a complex "random" password guessing scheme can be reduced to an ultimately revealing algorithm.

Crack takes an *letc/passwd* file as input, scans the file's contents looking for weak passwords, and then reports its findings. It should not be confused with dozens of other programs—some of which may use the word "crack" or "rip" in their names—that are designed to break either system or application security.

It should also not be confused with the general practice of system "cracking." Crack 5.0a was written by British programmer Alex Muffett with the assistance of several well-known members of the UNIX community.[1] While it finds weak passwords and reports on them—thus potentially aiding system "crackers"—it does not create any security problems that didn't already exist due to either weak passwords or the lack of shadow passwords.[2] Crack is not particularly useful for defeating any particular user's password—it's designed to run against weak passwords in general rather than a given hashed password choice. Despite the misgivings that some may have, Crack is a completely legitimate tool that is widely deployed and run as part of standard system administration practice.

While Crack is a legitimate tool for system security, you should only install and run it with explicit authorization. Obviously, if

---

1. Muffett admits in the appendix that comes with the program that "Passwdcheck" might be a better name for the program. This would free it from the negative connotations of the word "crack," which extend beyond the field of computer security.

2. If there were a single argument for shadow passwords, which can only be viewed by root, Crack would be it. If an attacker already has root privilege, he or she won't benefit from running Crack.

you own the machine, you're free to run Crack. On the other hand, be careful about running it on someone else's systems (owned by your employer, university, ISP, client, etc.) without written permission.

> **Password cracking without explicit authorization may be considered a hostile activity. It may even be illegal in some jurisdictions.** **Caution**

One prominent consultant ran Crack on a client's system in order to assess system security. He was caught, tried, convicted, and sentenced to five years of probation, 480 hours of community service, 90 days of deferred jail time, and a $68,000 fine for his efforts.[3]

Crack doesn't actually "crack"—as in "decrypt"—the hashed UNIX passwords in the *passwd* file. When Crack is invoked, it first creates a set of dictionaries from simple word lists that contain one word per line. One dictionary is compiled directly from words contained in the password file (like usernames). Another is compiled from permutations of usernames contained in the password file— "Joe User" becomes "JUser, JoeU, resueoj, etc." Other dictionaries are compiled from the word lists that either come with the distribution or can be added by the user. A stream of permutated guesses are generated by applying mangling rules to the dictionaries—these rules might force words to all uppercase or lowercase, make them plural, reverse the order of characters, substitute the number "3" for the letter "E," etc. Crack then encrypts the permutated guesses—using the system's password hashing algorithm—and compares them against the hashed passwords in */etc/passwd*. A separate script produces a readable report in either plain or HTML format.

Crack can be computationally expensive. The program includes several provisions for making the computation requirements easier to manage. It can be set to run only during off-hours, for example. It can be "niced" so it runs as a background process. It can also be

---

3. See http://www.lightlink.com/spacenka/fors/

run over the network so that more than one machine can partici-
pate in the cracking.

The maturity of the program shows: Crack provides API's for
integration with arbitrary *crypt()* functions (for password systems
that are hardened with algorithm changes) and for handling arbitrary password formats (for oddball systems that don't conform to
the traditional UNIX format).

Like most good UNIX security tools, Crack runs on a variety of
UNIX implementations, including Solaris, Linux, FreeBSD, Net-
BSD, OSF, and Ultrix.

The Crack Report

The result of a Crack run is a simple report that contains entries for
the user passwords it was able to guess as well as warnings about
errors in the password file. For each guessed password, it lists the
username, the password, the source file, and the user's shell.

As you can see below, Crack can't handle */etc/passwd* entries for
system accounts like "nobody"—it reports an error instead. A
sample run against a generic Linux box might generate output like
Listing 5.1.

Listing 5.1 *Sample Crack Output*

```
---- passwords cracked as of Wed Jan 20 06:47:17 PST 1999 -
---

Guessed alice [90410]   [/etc/passwd /bin/bash]
Guessed bob [chicago]   [/etc/passwd /bin/bash]
Guessed carol [lorac]   [/etc/passwd /bin/bash]
Guessed dave [asdfg]   [/etc/passwd /bin/bash]
Guessed mallory [password]   [/etc/passwd /bin/bash]
Guessed trent [trent]   [/etc/passwd /bin/bash]

---- errors and warnings ----

ignoring locked entry: adm:*:3:4:adm:/var/adm:
ignoring locked entry: bin:*:1:1:bin:/bin:
ignoring locked entry: daemon:*:2:2:daemon:/sbin:
ignoring locked entry: ftp:*:14:50:FTP User:/home/ftp:
ignoring locked entry: games:*:12:100:games:/usr/games:
ignoring locked entry: halt:*:7:0:halt:/sbin:/sbin/halt
ignoring locked entry: lp:*:4:7:lp:/var/spool/lpd:
ignoring locked entry: mail:*:8:12:mail:/var/spool/mail:
```

```
ignoring locked entry: news:*:9:13:news:/var/spool/news:
ignoring locked entry: nobody:*:99:99:Nobody:/:
ignoring locked entry: sync:*:5:0:sync:/sbin:/bin/sync

---- done ----
```

In this sample output, six users have guessable passwords. In fact, each selected a password that contains a fundamental weakness. Alice chose a ZIP code (a famous one at that). Bob chose a place name. Carol picked her username spelled backwards (one of the first things Crack checks for). Dave went wrong with a common QWERTY keyboard string. Mallory used the old standby "password." Trent was trusting enough to use his unadorned username—the first guess even a casual attacker will make.

Crack Dictionaries
The Crack 5 distribution includes a generous collection of word lists. They include approximately 1.5 millions words drawn from:

- place names, male names, female names and family names

- operating systems like DOS and UNIX

- reference works like the Current Index to Statistics, a ZIP code directory, the CIA World Fact Book, dictionaries, and Roget's Thesaurus

- various languages, including Chinese, Danish, Dutch, Finnish, French, German, Japanese, Norwegian, Spanish, Swedish, and Yiddish (*oy gevalt*)

- the works of various classic authors including Shakespeare, Milton, and Lewis Carroll

- religious texts including the King James Bible, the Koran, and various myths and legends

- topics like biology and sports

- pop culture, including Monty Python, Star Trek, cartoon characters, and movies

Tip

> Many of Crack's dictionaries are drawn from Paul Leyland's excellent word list site—hosted by Oxford University, the eminent bastion of lexical knowledge where you can find additional dictionaries covering everything from Afrikaans to Turkish. See
> `ftp://ftp.ox.ac.uk/pub/wordlists/`

Installing Crack

Download Crack 5 from Alex Muffett's home page at `http://www.users.dircon.co.uk/~crypto/` or from one of several mirror sites:

`ftp://ftp.cert.org/pub/tools/crack/`

`ftp://ftp.cert.dfn.de/pub/tools/password/Crack/`

`ftp://ftp.win.tue.nl/pub/security/`

`http://www.thehub.com.au/~bc/crack/`

Alternatively, you can copy it from the *crack* directory on the CD-ROM that accompanies this book.

Unpack the archive in an appropriate directory (maybe */usr/local/sbin*, if you're running Linux) with commands like

```
# gunzip crack5.0.tar.gz
# tar xvof crack5.0.tar
```

This will create the Crack directory (*c50a*).

Caution

> Give careful consideration to where you install Crack. You probably don't want to make it available to your users to run against each other. Consider recursively setting the Crack directory permissions so that only root can read it and execute its contents. Don't save the results of your Crack runs—instead, take immediate action to mitigate the discovered problems (see the Caution on page 107).

Next you have to edit the main "Crack" script, configuring appropriate values for CRACK_PATH, C5FLAGS, CC, CFLAGS and LIBS. This shouldn't be too difficult—if you get stuck, the manual has several tips and potential workarounds. On a Red Hat Linux system, the default settings "just work."

If you're running Red Hat Linux, you may need to double-back to **Tip** Alex's site and download a replacement for the file *src/util/Makefile*. The replacement file is *c50-linux-util-makefile.txt*. If you're running Netscape Navigator, don't just cut and paste (this can affect the file's formatting)—use the "Save As" command.

If you're running Red Hat Linux, you're ready to compile the source code. If you're not, you may have some tweaking to do, depending on the platform you're running and the password algorithm your system uses. The manual contains many pointers on how to get things ready.

From the Crack directory, issue the command

```
# ./Crack -makeonly
```

This will build the binaries and store them in the *run/bin* directory.

Configuring Crack

If you're going to run Crack over a network, you will need to build Crack from source on each machine.

If your system uses shadow passwords, you will need to merge your hashed passwords and your */etc/password* file back into an equivalent of the old style */etc/passwd* file. This can be done manually or via a script provided in the *scripts* directory. The script *shadmgr.sv* is designed for System V systems, but works fine on shadowed Red Hat Linux boxen. To create a merged file called *shadow4crack* in the Crack directory, run a command like this:

```
# bsh shadmgr.sv > ../shadow4crack
```

For many situations, the default word lists shipped with Crack will be sufficient. You can provide additional word lists (say, from the Oxford site cited above, or your own) by adding them to the *dict* directory. This may be appropriate for systems used by speakers of a language not included by default (Swahili, for example).

Once your word lists are in place, you need to transform them into the compressed format Crack prefers with the command:

```
# ./Crack -makedict
```

Running Crack

Once you've run the "-makeonly" and a "-makedict," you should be ready to start cracking. Issue the command:

```
# ./Crack -debug /etc/passwd
```

and Crack will go to work. The "-debug" flag will display Crack's verbose inner workings.

The general form for invoking Crack is

```
Crack [options] [-fmt format] [file ...]
```

where "file" is usually *letc/passwd* (though it may be your merged shadow file, *shadow4crack*, or a manually created file) and the "-fmt" flag specifies BSD 4.4 or other variants.

You don't want to run Crack for the first time during a busy time for the system. If you must run Crack during normal business hours, you can diminish it's impact on system resources by "nic-ing" it:

```
# ./Crack -debug -nice 10 /etc/passwd
```

Caution
You should be prepared for the possibility that you may need to terminate Crack due to system limitations or time constraints. The correct way to do this is with the "plaster" script in the *scripts* directory.

Once Crack has completed its analysis, you can view the results by running the "Reporter" command, which takes the general form:

```
# ./Reporter [-quiet] [-html]
```

The "-quiet" flag suppresses reporting of errors in the password file. After you've seen them once, that may be enough. The "-html" flag spits out an HTML file instead of plain text.

Guesses are reported chronologically. So, if Alice's password is guessed on your first run, it will be listed on subsequent runs (until she gets it together). This can become very annoying, but it also serves as a reminder that you still need to deal with the problem.

Caution

The handling of guessed passwords should be specified in your security policy. The safest way to handle a guessed password is to disable the account immediately (by changing the user's password entry for shell to */bin/false* and the hashed password to "*") and then contact the user offline.

Table 5.1 depicts some of the options you can use to control how Crack runs.

Table 5.1 *Some Crack Options*

Flag	What It Does
-debug	Reveals the inner workings of the Crack script. I prefer this option, just in case something goes wrong.
-recover	Restarts a terminated Crack run (see below). You can save time with this option after a crash.
-fgnd	Runs Crack in the foreground (with a high priority). Contrast this with "-nice."
-fmt format	Specifies non-traditional password file formats (BSD 4.4, for example, which is specified as "BSD").
-mail	Sends mail to users with guessed passwords (see below for a discussion of the risks of this option).
-network	Runs Crack over a network (assuming you've installed Crack on the networked hosts).
-nice N	Runs Crack at a lower priority: the higher N is, the lower the priority. Contrast with "-fgnd."
-makedict	Builds Crack dictionaries at install time.

Crack Tips and Tricks

- Crack can be set to run during off-peak hours, when it's less likely to interfere with real work that the system is trying accomplish. You can tweak the file *scripts/pauser* in order to put Crack to sleep at arbitrary times of day or when they are more than x users on the system.

- You can have Crack send mail to each user with a cracked password with the "-mail" flag, which invokes the "nastygram" script with the username as input. Be sure to customize the script before invoking this option—the default isn't all that nasty, but it's not all that polite either. Try to observe proper Netiquette.[4]

Caution Use of the mail option is deprecated. As Muffett points out, if your system's mail logs are world-readable, other users and potential attackers will be able to see that the password cracker sent a warning to so-and-so, an easy tip-off that there may be a hole to exploit. Plus, if the account is no longer active, sending mail to it will accomplish nothing. A stronger response is to disable the account and ask questions later.

- If a Crack run is terminated accidentally, you can restart by using the "-recover" flag. Issue the following commands, replacing "Dhostname.N" with the appropriate filename:

```
# mv run/Dhostname.N run/tempfilename
# ./Crack -recover -fmt spf run/tempfilename
```

- You can distribute the job of password cracking across various hosts on a network by editing the file *conf/network.conf* and using the "-network" flag. This is done from a "master cracking" host, which needs to have Perl installed. Optimally, the network should be running NFS. The manual contains network configuration details.

---

4. See http://www.albion.com/netiquette/

- The Crack 5 distribution includes some nice extras like "Crack6," which is a single line of Perl code that runs a primitive password cracker, and "Crack7," a brute-force cracker.

- If you have problems with Crack, read the fine manual. If you're still stuck, the author suggests you post to the newsgroup `comp.security.unix` with the subject line "Crack5."

- Don't assume that Crack is foolproof. Just because your Crack runs don't discover weak passwords, it doesn't mean they don't exist. Remember that there's always someone out there smarter or better equipped than you. Perhaps an attacker can run Crack against your system with bigger and better word lists—or with word lists drawn from obscure lexicons. Perhaps your copy of Crack has been subverted. Use Crack *in addition to*, rather than *instead of*, sound password policy and user education.

## 06

Filesystem Security

Filesystem security lies at the core of UNIX system security. The UNIX filesystem controls who can access information and what they can do with it. Even if the outer wall of account security is breached, attackers must still defeat filesystem defenses predicated on an elaborate system of file ownership and permissions. This chapters covers the basics of filesystem controls. It also covers the innermost layer of protection—when all else fails, cryptography can keep data private. Verifying software is covered as well as integrity checking and backups. The chapter also includes a discussion of cryptographic filesystems.

111

The Unix Filesystem

Filesystem Basics

One of the reasons filesystem security is so important is this: on UNIX systems, *everything* is a file. A collection of user data is a file. A directory is a file. A process is a file. A command is a file. A network connection? Yes, even it is a file.

Consider this partial listing of UNIX file types:

- Regular files—ASCII text files, binary data files, binary executable files, etc.

- Directories—Binary files containing a list of other files

- Special files—Including device files commonly found in the */dev* directory that encode information about items like hard drives

- Links—Including hard links, which associate two or more filenames with the same storage location, and soft (symbolic) links, which point to other files

- Sockets—Special files used for communications between processes

Files of these various types are organized in a hierarchical tree structure that starts with a single directory called "root" (denoted with a forward slash "/"). All the items in the tree are collectively known as the "filesystem." Though any particular UNIX system may, in fact, be comprised of a number of disk-based and network-based filesystems, it provides a single tree structure to its users. Each of the items in this tree is more fully described by a number of attributes, including one or more names, an owner, a group, a set of permissions, a length, and other items. Most of these attributes are stored on disk in data structures called "inodes." Each inode within a particular filesystem has a unique number; each file has a distinct inode.

The inode is the focus of all file activity in the UNIX filesystem. UNIX filesystem security is based on three critical pieces of information stored in inodes:

- UID—the file's owner

- GID—the file's group

- mode—the file's permission settings

The "File Permissions" section below describes why these are so important. Additional information contained in inodes includes:

- file size—in bytes

- file type—file, directory, link, etc.

- ctime—when the inode was last modified

- mtime—when the file was last modified

- atime—when the file was last accessed

- nlink—the number of hard links

As you'll read in the next chapter, some of these attributes can be also be relevant to security. When attackers tamper with your files, they often leave a footprint in the form of altered inode settings. This footprint can sometimes be useful as evidence in your search for the attackers, even if they try to cover their tracks. See "Maintaining Filesystem Integrity" on page 139 and "Tripwire" on page 151.

Tip

Filesystem Structure

In order to manage UNIX filesystem security, it's useful to understand the lay of the land. While this overview may be of nominal value to a UNIX guru, it's easy for mere mortals or those just starting out with UNIX to get confused (especially if they come from the Windows or Macintosh worlds, where user confusion about directory structures is endemic). Even experienced system administrators get can tripped up, especially as they move from one UNIX-like system to another. No two UNIX implementations have the same exact directory structure.

Table 6.1 presents an idealized overview of the main directories within the root directory. All files and directories live within the directory structure that begins at this point, even if they are actually stored on separate disks or separate computers.

Table 6.1 *The UNIX Directory Structure*

Directory	Contents
/bin	executable files for user commands (binaries)
/dev	special device files
/etc	system executables, configuration files, administrative files; reserved for configuration files in Red Hat Linux (no binaries)
/home	user home directories (*/u*, */users*, */Users* are alternatives)
/lib	contains shared libraries needed to boot the system and run the commands in the root filesystem
/lost+found	lost files disconnected from the particular filesystem
/mnt	temporarily mounted filesystems (e.g., floppies, CD-ROMs, etc.)
/proc	a pseudo-filesystem which is used as an interface to kernel data structures and running processes (useful for debugging)
/sbin	reserved for executables used only by root, and only those needed to boot and mount */usr*
/tmp	temporary scratch files
/usr	executables for user and system commands, header files, shared libraries, man pages, local programs (in */usr/local*)
/var	spool files for mail, printing, cron, etc.; accounting files, logging files

The layout of the Linux filesystem is specified by a standards document: the *Filesystem Hierarchy Standard (FHS)*. The current version is 2.0. It is meant for Unix distribution developers, package developers, and system implementors. You can find out more at `http://www.pathname.com/fhs/`

Tip

Filesystem Types

Modern UNIX implementations usually support different kinds of filesystems in addition their native filesystem. Linux is particularly strong in this regard. Among the filesystems that are supported by the Linux kernel:

- ext2—a high-performance filesystem used for both fixed and removable disks (the second version of the ext filesystem, which was derived from the Minix filesystem)

- msdos—used by MS-DOS and Windows; filenames can be no longer than an 8 character name followed by an optional period and 3 character extension

- umsdos—an extended DOS filesystem used by Linux; supports long filenames, UID/GID, permissions, and special files under the DOS filesystem

- iso9660—a CD-ROM filesystem conforming to the ISO 9660 standard

- hpfs—the High Performance Filesystem, used in OS/2

- minix—used in the Minux OS; the first Linux filesystem

- nfs—the network filesystem used to access disks located on remote computers

- swap—a disk partition to be used for swapping

File Permissions

File permissions are the linchpin of UNIX filesystem security. UNIX is designed to be a multi-user system and it behaves that way even if there's only one user that ever logs in. Access to files is

controlled in a compartmentalized way: each file is owned by a
particular user and group.

As discussed in the "Account Security Basics" chapter, each
UNIX user is associated with a unique username and user ID number (UID). Additionally, every user is associated with one or more
groups. Primary group membership is defined in the */etc/passwd*
file. Additional group memberships are defined in the */etc/group*
file. For example, the user johndoe is associated with UID 123 and
group 12 (staff). He is also a member of group 230 (pppusers).

Every file in the UNIX filesystem is owned by one user and one
group. Typically, a file is owned by the user that created it and that
user's primary group (though BSD systems sometimes assign group
ownership to the group that owns the directory the file lives in).

Each file and directory has three sets of permissions associated
with it: one set for the owner of the file, one set for members of the
group the file is associated with, and one set for all other users
(commonly referred to as "the world" or "others").

Each set of permissions contains three identical permission bits
that control the following:

- read (r)—If set, the file or directory may be read.

- write (w)—If set, the file or directory may be written or
  modified.

- execute (x)—If set, the file or directory may be executed and
  searched.

Together, these nine bits are commonly known as the "mode
bits."

The mode bits are commonly expressed as a sequence of ten
characters, with a character for each of the mode settings along
with one character indicating the file type. The output of the `ls -l`
command reflects this method of display.

```
$ ls -l
-rw-------  1 jrandom  hackers  2967 Aug 30 1994 private
drwxr-x---  2 jrandom  hackers    96 Mar  2 09:47 backups
-rw-rw-rw-  1 jrandom  albion     15 Apr 14 1998 mbox
```

The `-rw-rw-rw-` in the last entry, for example, starts with "-,"
indicating that *mbox* is a regular file. The owner, group, and world
all have the same level of access(`rw-`), meaning that anyone can

read or write to this file. The second entry—backups—is a directory (indicated by the "d") that the owner can read, write, or execute/search (rwx), the group can read or execute/search but not write (r-x), and the world can't do anything (---). This symbolic depiction of permissions mode bits is summarized in Figure 6.1.

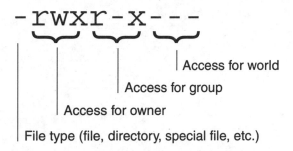

Figure 6.1 *Interpreting Permissions*

The permission bits can also be represented as a single octal number. To do this, take the nine mode bits and break them into three chunks of three bits each: one for owner, one for group, one for world (others). Then add the values shown in Figure 6.2.

Table 6.2 *Permission Bits to Octal Number*

Permission	Owner	Group	World
read	400	40	4
write	200	20	2
execute	100	10	1
none	0	0	0

For example, say you've granted owner read and write permission for a file and given the group and others just read permission: rw-r--r--. This can be written as an octal number—the "absolute mode." Add the following numbers from the table:

```
mode = owner (read) + owner (write) + group (read) + world (read)
mode = 400 + 200 + 40 + 4
mode = 644
```

This method of deducing the absolute mode is used by the chmod command. Some absolute modes are compared with the "symbolic" equivalents in Table 6.3 below.

Table 6.3 *Absolute vs. Symbolic Mode*

Absolute	Symbolic
777	rwxrwxrwx
755	rwxr-xr-x
750	rwxr-x---
700	rwx------
666	rw-rw-rw-
644	rw-r--r--
640	rw-r-----
600	rw-------
444	r--r--r--
400	r--------

If a file is executable, a fourth set of three bits can be significant. One is the "sticky bit," which tells UNIX to leave the executable in memory (to stick around) even after the program is finished. The sticky bit is a hold-over from the olden days and is no longer widely used.

More important are the "set user ID" (SUID) and "set group ID" (SGID) bits. When you execute a SUID file, your user ID is set to the user ID of the owner of that file for as long as the program runs. If the file is owned by root, you are the superuser. In the same way, when you execute a SGID file, your group ID is set to the file's group. So, for example, the ps (process status) command runs SUID root—it reads from system memory, which normal users can't do.

SUID programs are intended to enhance security. The SUID bit pro-   **Tip**
vides a way for users to do a variety of useful things, from tape
backups to printing, without needing access to the root account.
That said, these programs can represent major security holes, especially if they are set to SUID root (i.e., the SUID bit is set and the
owner is root). These files should be monitored (see "SUID/SGID" on
page 121).

The chmod Command

You use the `chmod` command to change the permission settings of
files. This command takes two arguments: *perm*, the permissions
to set on the files; and *files*, the names of the files. The `-R` flag
applies the permission settings recursively throughout the named
file hierarchy starting at the current location. The `chmod` command
can only be run by the owner or by root.

The permissions argument can be specified in either absolute or
symbolic mode. Using absolute mode, the form `chmod 666 myfiles`
sets the permissions of *myfiles* to `rw-rw-rw-`.

Symbolic mode is a bit more complex to explain but may be easier to use. The argument is composed of three parts: *who op permission,* where

- *who* is one of user (u), group (g), others (o), or all (a or ugo)

- *op* is one of +, - or = ... "+" causes the permissions selected to
  be added to the existing permissions of each file; "-" causes
  them to be removed; and "=" causes them to be the only permissions that the file has

- and *permission* is any combinations of read (r), write (w), and
  execute (x), set-user-id or set-group-id (s), or the sticky bit (t).

If *who* is omitted, "a" is assumed.

So, if I need to give the group read access to the file *foo*, the following would work:

```
$ chmod g+r foo
```

Related to `chmod` are the `chown` (change ownership) and `chgrp`
(change group commands). These commands take the form `chown`

user `myfile`. The `chown` command can change owner and group in one stroke: `chown user.group myfile` (some systems use a ":" as a delimiter).

The umask value

When a new file or directory is created, it receives a default set of permissions based on the user's permission mask, or "umask." While the `chmod` command is used to specify the permissions that should be turned on, the `umask` command specifies the permissions that should be turned off. It uses a simple three-digit argument format that specifies the types of access that should be prohibited—or masked out—when a file or directory is created.

Bits set by the umask clear the corresponding permissions bits in the file mode. To determine the three-digit argument for the `umask` command, subtract the numeric equivalent of the file mode you want from 777 (`rwxrwxrwx`). If you want directories to be created with mode 755 and files with 644, then you want a umask of 022 (777-755).

The umask is typically set up in the system-wide login file and in the individual login files *.login* or *.profile* using a command in the form of

`umask value`

Common values are summarized in Table 6.4. Notice that files are not given execute permission regardless of the umask setting.

Table 6.4 *Umask Permission Values for Directories/Files*

Umask	Permissions	User	Group	Others
000	777/666	`rwx/rw-`	`rwx/rw-`	`rwx/rw-`
022	755/644	`rwx/rw-`	`r-x/r--`	`r-x/r--`
077	700/600	`rwx/rw-`	`---/---`	`---/---`
133	644/644	`rw-/rw-`	`r--/r--`	`r--/r--`
333	444/444	`r--/r--`	`r--/r--`	`r--/r--`
377	400/400	`r--/r--`	`---/---`	`---/---`

On most systems, the default umask value is 022.

SUID/SGID

The set user-id (SUID) and set group-id (SGID) properties allow users to run programs with special privileges. UNIX actually has two types of user IDs. The "real user ID" is the user ID established during the login process. The second type of ID is known as the "effective user ID"—this can be changed during the course of a login session by the SUID and SGID bits.

Ordinarily, when a user runs a command, the process inherits the privileges of the user's login shell and the effective user ID is the same as the real user ID. When the SUID bit is set, however, the process inherits the privileges of the command's owner. This has many practical applications. When a user runs the passwd command, for example, he or she can make limited changes to the */etc/passwd* file, even though the file is owned by root. This is possible only because the passwd command runs with the SUID permission of root.

You can identify a SUID program by inspecting its permission mode. If the "x" is changed to a "s," the program is SUID. For example, both the passwd and ps commands are SUID:

```
% ls -l /bin/su /bin/login
-rws- x -x   1 root    root       15572 Dec 29  1997
/bin/login
-rwsr-xr-x   1 root    root       12672 Oct 27  1997 /bin/su
```

This capability, while very useful, can be dangerous. A classic attack on UNIX system security is to create a copy of the shell that is SUID root and then hide it. By invoking this back door, the attacker gains root privileges. While only root can create a SUID version of the shell owned by root, imagine that you're logged in as root and leave your terminal unattended. Someone walks by and types the following:

```
# cp /bin/bash /home/mallory/.bash
# chmod 4777 /home/mallory/.bash
```

Mallory now has an SUID root copy of bash at his disposal. He can run now commands with full root privilege.

Most SUID programs are SUID root, though there's no reason why they can't be owned by regular users. In most cases, SUID root programs don't pose a problem—assuming they're well-coded, and the use of root privilege is tightly controlled. But it's a good idea to know which programs on your system are SUID root.

You can use the `find` command to discover SUID and SGID files. The following syntax works using the GNU version of `find` (included with Red Hat and other Linux distributions) and perhaps with others as well:

```
# find / -type f \( -perm -4000 -o -perm -2000 \) -ls
```

This tells `find` to list all regular files ("f") with the SUID ("4000") or SGID ("2000") bits set. You should run this for each local filesystem (excluding NFS-mounted filesystems). On many UNIX systems, you can use the "-local" flag to exclude NFS filesystems:

```
# find / -local -type f \( -perm -4000 -o -perm -2000 \) -
exec ls -ld '{}' \;
```

Caution

> Be aware that an attacker installing back door SUID root programs can elude detection by modifying the `find` command. For more thorough-going protection, use a filesystem integrity checking program like Tripwire.

Caution

> Mounted filesystems—including NFS partitions, floppy disks, and CD-ROMs—may contain hostile SUID/SGID programs. Whenever practical, mount filesystems using the mount program's "nosuid" option: e.g., `/etc/mount -o nosuid /dev/fd0a/ mnt/floppy`

Cryptography

We've already seen how cryptography is used to protect user passwords and enforce account security (see "The Password Mechanism" on page 53). It is also widely used to protect messages while they're being transmitted (see "IP Security" on page 270 and "Protecting Against Transmission Risks" on page 317). It can also be used to check filesystem security. This section covers how to use cryptographic checksums to determine if unauthorized changes have been made to files—an art that's elevated by the Tripwire tool (see page 151). Most importantly, cryptographic techniques can be used to secure sensitive files or even entire filesystems.

If one imagines UNIX system security as a series of concentric defenses, encryption lies at the core. When all other safeguards fail to protect the confidentiality and integrity of your data, strong encryption can. Network-based attackers might exploit some obscure network service to gain access to a system you use. Passwords can be cracked; permissions can be hacked; one by one the rings of defense fail. Your directory of sensitive files are under their fingertips when, at last they're in. But wait! These files are protected by strong crypto—the cracker loses!

Net hackers aside, every UNIX system contains a huge file security loophole: the root user. Passwords and permissions mean nought to root, who can snoop user data at will. Even the most trusted sysadmin can make a mistake that compromises the root account. Root access can also be stolen by a wide variety of means, from buffer overflow attacks to coercion. If the confidentiality of user data is critical, that data must be encrypted.

Cryptography (crypto) is the art and science of keeping files and messages secure. It works by mathematically transforming a "plaintext" (or "cleartext") message into a disguised "ciphertext"—a process known as "encryption." "Decryption" involves turning the ciphertext back into plaintext. The mathematical function used for encryption and decryption is called a cryptographic algorithm or "cipher."

Most cryptosystems rely on a key, which can be one of a large number of values (the "keyspace"). The key is used to determine *how* data is encrypted or decrypted. In general, the security of the algorithm lies in the key; security should not depend on the secrecy of the algorithm.

"Symmetric" ciphers use the same key for encryption and decryption. "Public-key" (or "asymmetric") ciphers use different but related keys for encryption and decryption: a stranger can use your public key to encrypt a message that only you, holder of your private key, can decrypt.

Symmetric ciphers fall into two broad classes: stream ciphers, which work on plaintext one bit at a time, and block ciphers, which work on groups of bits (blocks).

Tip

> These pages provide only summary information about crypto. For a detailed overview of the field, I recommend Bruce Schneier's *Applied Cryptography*. For a citation, see page 433.

US Export Restrictions

The politics of cryptography are beyond the scope of this book. According to the US government, strong cryptography is a munition; export is regulated by the International Traffic in Arms Regulation (ITAR). The ITAR category for "Auxiliary Military Equipment" includes "Cryptographic (including key management) systems, equipment, modules, integrated circuits, components or software with the capability of maintaining secrecy or confidentiality of information or information systems."[1]

From the point of view of practical system security, this sucks. Many implementations of UNIX are crippled by their creators in order to avoid creating a US-only product. In many cases, even weak DES crypto is set aside as a separate product. This disease has struck both commercial vendors and freeware distributions. One remedy is to deploy a UNIX not created in the US—like Open-BSD, which is distributed by a group based in Canada.

Practical Crypto Algorithms

There are several crypto algorithms which are widely implemented in the UNIX universe.

- **crypt**—The original UNIX encryption program based on the WWII-era Enigma machine. It can be easily broken—unlike the *crypt (3)* library (see the "Crypt Breakers Workbench (CBW)" on page 148). Nonetheless, it can be fun to play with. Try improving security by encrypting a compressed file several times, using a different key with each round. For real encryption, use DES or PGP.

---

1. See http://www.epic.org/crypto/export_controls/ITAR.html

- **DES**—The Data Encryption Standard was developed by NIST (National Institute of Standards and Technology) in the 1970s. It remains a worldwide standard.[2] This symmetric cipher uses a 56-bit key. A modified form is used in the UNIX password encoding system. Some UNIX systems include a general purpose implementation; it's not as ubiquitous as it could be due to US crypto export regulations. The security of DES is suspect; DES-cracking times continue to plunge—see
  `http://www.eff.org/descracker/`

NIST no longer supports the use of the DES for many applications. **Tip** Triple DES is a method for using the DES algorithm in three operations—NIST advises that it should be used instead of DES (see the draft FIPS at `http://csrc.nist.gov/fips/dfips46-3.pdf`). Eventually, NIST will promulgate a more advanced standard (AES). In the meantime, you can find Eric A. Young's encryption library, *libdes*, at `ftp://ftp.psy.uq.oz.au/pub/Crypto/DES/`

- **IDEA**—The International Data Encryption Algorithm (IDEA) was first developed by Xuejia Lai and James Massey in 1990. IDEA is a block cipher that operates on 64-bit plaintext blocks; the key is 128 bits long. IDEA is implemented in Pretty Good Privacy (PGP), a widely-used crypto program.

- **RC4**—This stream cipher was developed by Ron Rivest for RSA Data Security, Inc. in 1987. It uses keys of variable length. It is sometimes used for communications security (see "Setting Up a TLS/SSL Server" on page 320).

- **Blowfish**—This block cipher was developed by Bruce Schneier in 1993 as a general replacement for DES. It can be deployed for communications security. It is also used by at least one UNIX variant to encode passwords (see "Alternative Algorithms" on page 79).

---

2. See Federal Information Processing Standards (FIPS) Publication 46-2 (1993), *Announcing the Standard for DATA ENCRYPTION STANDARD (DES)*, at
`http://www.itl.nist.gov/div897/pubs/fip46-2.htm`

- **RSA**—This leading public-key cipher was developed by Ron
  Rivest, Adi Shamir, and Leonard Adleman. It is widely used to
  protect Internet communications. RSA Data Security's patent is
  due to expire in September 2000 (see the footnote on
  page 320).

One-Way Hash Functions

One-way hash functions process a message of arbitrary length and
return a fixed-length hash value (say, 128 bits). In particular, they
are difficult to reverse—given a hash value, it should be hard to
compute the message it was generated from. In addition, it should
be extremely hard to find two random messages that hash to the
same value.

We've already seen how a one-way hash function is used to
store user passwords. This kind of function has other security uses
as well. Like virtual fingerprints, they can be used to validate the
integrity of messages and files. So-called "message digest" algorithms can be used to verify the integrity of documents that are distributed over insecure networks. Take an arbitrary document and
calculate its, say, MD5 hash value. Send the document along with
its MD5 hash value to someone else. The receiving party can then
take the document, run MD5, and check the result against the hash
value you derived. If the two hash values match, your recipient can
be confident that the document was not accidentally damaged or
altered in transit.

The same process can be used with system and user files—a hash
value or message digest match can ensure that your files haven't
been deliberately tampered with. If information about a critical
system file is hashed today, tomorrow's hash should match. Given
crackers' propensity for "rootkitting" systems—installing altered
system binaries to facilitate future access—systematic integrity
checks using message digest algorithms or one-way hash functions
can be an important detection safeguard. While it's preferable to
deter an attack, if your effort fails, you want to know about it as
soon as possible.

> Hashing functions like MD5 that perform data integrity checks are **Tip**
> not subject to US export controls under ITAR—cryptographic soft-
> ware that is solely limited to a data authentication function is
> excluded from the US Munitions List.

There are several tools that help automate the process of filesystem integrity checking. Tripwire is the most advanced of these programs—the next chapter covers Tripwire in depth (see page 151). Tripwire uses several one-way hash functions—all of these can be used on their own as well:

- **MD5**—This successor to MD4 and MD2 is the most widely implemented message digest algorithm. It was developed by Ronald L. Rivest, released into the public domain by RSA Data Security, Inc., and described by RFC 1321.[3] MD5 processes text in 512-bit blocks and returns a 128-bit hash value. According to the RFC: "It is conjectured that the difficulty of coming up with two messages having the same message digest is on the order of 2^{64} operations, and that the difficulty of coming up with any message having a given message digest is on the order of 2^{128} operations."

> You can find source code for MD5—courtesy of Jim Ellis at CERT— **Tip**
> at http://www.cert.org/ftp/tools/md5/ or on the accompanying
> CD-ROM.

- **SHA**—The Secure Hash Algorithm was designed at NIST with the help of the National Security Agency. It lies at the core of the Secure Hash Standard which, in turn, is designed to ensure the security of the Digital Signature Algorithm (DSA). SHA is closely modeled after Ron Rivest's MD4. It produces a 160-bit message digest. The Digital Signature Algorithm relies on SHA to generate a compressed message digest, which is then signed instead of the entire message.[4]

---

3. See http://www.faqs.org/rfcs/rfc1321.html
4. For more on SHA, see Federal Information Processing Standards (FIPS) Publication 180-1, 1995 April 17, *Announcing the Standard for SECURE HASH STANDARD*, at
http://www.itl.nist.gov/div897/pubs/fip180-1.htm

- **HAVAL**—Based on MD5, Haval was developed by Yuliang Zheng, Josef Pieprzyk, and Jennifer Seberry. It can output hash values of variable length, from 128 bits to 256 bits. It can be configured to run a variable number of rounds.

- **Snefru**—A one-way hash function with a colorful name (after a pharaoh), Snefru outputs 128-bit or 256-bit values. Like HAVAL, it can be configured to run a variable number of rounds. Its creator, Ralph Merkle, suggests a minimum of 8 rounds to ensure security. Given multiple rounds, Snefru is slow—one way to speed Tripwire up is to eliminate file checking with Snefru.

Tip

> You can find source code for Snefru at
> `ftp://coast.cs.purdue.edu/pub/tools/unix/snefru/` or on the accompanying CD-ROM.

Digital Signatures

One-way hash functions are often used with public-key algorithms to create digital signatures. Like a handwritten signature, a digital signature provides proof-of-authorship (authentication). Unlike a conventional signature, a digital signature can also indicate whether the signed document has been modified. In its simplest form, a digital signature is a message that is encrypted with the author's private key. This is like public-key crypto run backwards. Public-key crypto provides for two keys: a public key used to encrypt a message and a private key that decrypts messages once they are received. Using digital signatures, the message is encrypted with the private key so that anyone with the public key can decrypt it.

In reality, public-key algorithms run too slowly to sign long documents. Most digital signature protocols use one-way hash functions to create message digests: why sign the whole document when signing the message digest works just as well? This is faster and requires less storage space.

PGP

Originally created by Philip R. Zimmermann in 1991, PGP has had a colorful history.[5] It was the subject of a series of disputes due to its use of the patented RSA public-key cipher. It also got tangled in US crypto export controls—Zimmermann was the target of a three-year criminal investigation. The government held that US export restrictions for cryptographic software were violated when the freeware program managed to cross the US border. Despite the notoriety, PGP became the leading program for email encryption; version 2.6 was widely distributed and implemented on UNIX and other systems. The program is now owned by Network Associates (an entity formed by the mergers of McAfee, Network General, Helix, and Zimmerman's company, Pretty Good Privacy, Inc.). A "free for non-commercial use" version is available from MIT.

PGP is primarily designed to protect messages, especially electronic mail. It uses the IDEA cipher for data encryption, RSA for key management and digital signatures, and MD5 as a one-way hash function. PGP messages feature layered security: not only are the contents disguised, but so is the sender's signature. An eavesdropper only knows the recipient for certain.

PGP can also be used to encrypt locally-stored files. In Listing 6.1, I encrypt the file *foo* using the "-c" flag. I enter a passphrase which is not echoed by the program.

Listing 6.1 *Encrypting a File with PGP*

```
$ ls -al | grep foo
-rw-r--r--  1 jrandom       21906 Mar 15 11:04 foo
$ pgp -c foo
Pretty Good Privacy(tm) 2.6.1 - Public-key encryption for
the masses.
(c) 1990-1994 Philip Zimmermann, Phil's Pretty Good
Software. 29 Aug 94
Distributed by the Massachusetts Institute of Technology.
Uses RSAREF.
Export of this software may be restricted by the U.S.
government.
Current time: 1999/03/15 19:05 GMT
You need a pass phrase to encrypt the file.
```

5. "PGP," "Pretty Good," and "Pretty Good Privacy" are trademarks of Network Associates, Inc.

```
Enter pass phrase: This is the end of the world
Enter same pass phrase again: Just a moment....
Ciphertext file: foo.pgp
$ ls -al | grep foo
-rw-r--r--   1 jrandom        21906 Mar 15 11:04 foo
-rw-------   1 jrandom        21862 Mar 15 11:05 foo.pgp
```

After encrypting *foo*, I have two files: the original plaintext and *foo.pgp*. If I need to decrypt, a simple `pgp foo` suffices, as shown in Listing 6.2.

Listing 6.2 *Decrypting a File with PGP*

```
$ pgp foo
Pretty Good Privacy(tm) 2.6.1 - Public-key encryption for
the masses.
(c) 1990-1994 Philip Zimmermann, Phil's Pretty Good
Software. 29 Aug 94
Distributed by the Massachusetts Institute of Technology.
Uses RSAREF.
Export of this software may be restricted by the U.S.
government.
Current time: 1999/03/15 19:05 GMT
File is conventionally encrypted.
You need a pass phrase to decrypt this file.
Enter pass phrase: Just a moment....Pass phrase appears
good. .
Plaintext filename: foo
?Output file 'foo' already exists.  Overwrite (y/N)? y
$ ls -al | grep foo
-rw-------   1 jrandom        21906 Mar 15 11:05 foo
-rw-------   1 jrandom        21862 Mar 15 11:05 foo.pgp
```

Caution   Note that PGP (and many other encryption programs don't automatically delete the plaintext file after encrypting it. PGP can be used to "wipe" the files from the filesystem (instead of merely deleting inodes).

The examples above are from a UNIX system running PGP version 2.6.1. Version 6.5.1 is the latest for Linux and Solaris. Starting with version 5, the program offered a slightly different command syntax:

- `pgpe`—for encrypting

- `pgps`—for signing

- pgpv—for verifying/decrypting

- pgpk—for key management

The command, pgpe -c foo, would be used to encrypt the file *foo*.

Listing 6.3 illustrates how to create a public/private key pair using version 5.

Listing 6.3 *Creating PGP Keys*

```
$ pgpk -g
Choose the type of your public key:
    1)  DSS/Diffie-Hellman - New algorithm for 5.0 (default)
    2)  RSA
Choose 1 or 2: 2
Pick your public/private keypair key size:
    1)   768 bits- Commercial grade, probably not currently
breakable
    2)  1024 bits- High commercial grade, secure for many
years
    3)  2048 bits- "Military" grade, secure for the
forseeable future
Choose 1, 2 or 3, or enter desired number of bits
(768 - 2048): 3
You need a user ID for your public key.  The desired form
for this user ID is your FULL name, followed by your E-mail
address enclosed in <angle brackets>, if you have an E-mail
address.  For example:
    Joe Smith <user@domain.com>
If you violate this standard, you will lose much of the
benefits of PGP 5.0's keyserver and email integration.
Enter a user ID for your public key: J. Random
<jrandom@example.com>
Enter the validity period of your key in days from 0 - 999
0 is forever (and the default): 0
You need a pass phrase to protect your private key(s).
Your pass phrase can be any sentence or phrase and may have
many words, spaces, punctuation, or any other printable
characters.
Enter pass phrase: This is the end of the world
Enter again, for confirmation:
Enter pass phrase: This is the end of the world
Collecting randomness for key...
We need to generate 810 random bits.  This is done by
reading /dev/random.  Depending on your system, you may be
able to speed this process by typing on your keyboard
```

```
and/or moving your mouse.
-Enough, thank you.
.......................................
Keypair created successfully.
If you wish to send this new key to a server, enter the URL
of the server, below.  If not, enter nothing.
```

As of this writing, the release of freeware PGP source code is lagging behind the development of the commercial version. Version 2.6.2 is the last for which source code is available. This is problematic for UNIX sites that wish to install and compile PGP freeware from source. You can download the freeware version at MIT, but you're stuck with an old version that—while functional—doesn't include new features like corporate key management.

Tip

> Network Associates has built PGP into a suite of tools called the PGP Data Security Suite. It offers a PGP SDK (Software Development) Kit as well as versions of Windows and Macintosh platforms.

An effort is underway to create an open PGP standard. The OpenPGP working group seeks "to provide IETF standards for the algorithms and formats of PGP processed objects as well as providing the MIME framework for exchanging them via e-mail or other transport protocols."[6] Work to date is summarized in RFC 2440.[7]

You can download the freeware version of PGP at the URL
`http://web.mit.edu/network/pgp.html`

Be prepared, however, to answer some questions, like:

- Are you a citizen or national of the United States or a person who has been lawfully admitted for permanent residence in the United States under the Immigration and Naturalization Act?

- Do you agree not to export PGP, or RSAREF to the extent incorporated therein, in violation of the export control laws of the United States of America as implemented by the United States Department of State Office of Defense Trade Controls?

---

6. See `http://www.ietf.org/html.charters/`
`openpgp-charter.html`
7. See `http://www.faqs.org/rfcs/rfc2440.html`

- Do you agree to the terms and conditions of the RSAREF license (in rsalicen.txt)?

- Will you use PGP Freeware solely for non-commercial purposes?

Alternately, you can go the Network Associates' site and answer several *other* questions—from what's your phone number to how many copies of PGP do you plan purchase (the default is greater than zero).[8]

Finally, you may wish to check on the progress of the GNU Privacy Guard (GnuPG), a free implementation of the OpenPGP standard. As of this writing, it hasn't reached version 1.0, but the work to date is promising. See `http://www.d.shuttle.de/isil/gnupg/`

Verifying Software

One of the paradoxes of this book is that it advocates both strong UNIX system security and the use of freely-available security tools. As I point out in the Introduction, trust is a relative concept (page 28). Any tool or program or library you download from the Internet or receive from some other untrusted source could harm or subvert the security of your system.

There are really two problems here: Can you trust the author and source of the program? Assuming the answer is yes, here's a second question: can you trust that the program you're downloading is actually the one the author wrote?

While ultimately you can't trust anything you didn't code yourself (and you might not even trust your own secure programming skills), there are reputable programs, programmers, security firms, and security sites (and reputable books, too). While it's possible for a security expert who's been years or decades building a solid reputation to go bad, it's an unlikely scenario. Furthermore, the open-source approach acts as a safety net—word that a program contains hostile code or features will most likely get out sooner or

---

8. While this book was in production, the download page for UNIX version of PGP either disappeared or moved. You can find a link to the freeware download site at
`http://www.nai.com/asp_set/products/tns/pgp_freeware.asp`

later. I recommend that security practitioners carefully evaluate security tools before downloading them (see "Evaluating Security Tools" on page 15). In most situations, reasonable due diligence should be sufficient.

The question of verifying authorship is more pressing in some ways. That's where the one-way hash functions and digital signatures described above come in handy.

Trojan Horses

A Trojan Horse is an "apparently useful program containing hidden functions that can exploit the privileges of the user, with a resulting security threat. A Trojan horse does things that the program user did not intend."[9] It usually performs a useful function while it also subverts security—a security-checking program, for example, that mails the /etc/passwd file to an intruder. This method of attack was first described by Homer almost 3,000 years ago. After a nine-year siege of the city-state of Troy, the Greeks apparently gave up, leaving behind a huge wooden horse as a gift, a propitiatory offering to the goddess Minerva. After much debate, the Trojans were deceived into bringing the horse through the gates. At night, armed Greek soldiers enclosed in the body of the horse burst out, burned the city, and beheaded its inhabitants.[10]

Since the development of computing technology recapitulates the development of civilization, it's not surprising that this mytho-poetic form of deception has become a standard way to breach the fortress of computer security. Trojan Horse attacks have taken many forms over the years—they can be launched via email, FTP or web sites, or from disk. In early 1999, a rash of trojans were let loose on the Internet. One trojaned version of Microsoft's Internet Explorer web browser was delivered via email: "As a user of the Microsoft Internet Explorer, Microsoft Corporation provides you with this upgrade for your web browser [sic]. It will fix some bugs found in your Internet Explorer. To install the upgrade, please save the attached file (*ie0199.exe*) in some folder and run it." The

---

9.   Rita C. Summers, *Secure Computing Threats and Safeguards* (McGraw-Hill, 1997).
10. Thomas Bulfinch, *Mythology* (New York: Random House), p. 186.

upgrade was *not* from Microsoft[11]—whether it could be trusted even if it was is another question. A more insidious breach was the Trojan Horse version of the TCP/Wrappers tool that was left in the download directory of a reputable and popular security site. It provided root access to intruders, and sent them an email on successful compilation. This was a case in which both the author (Wietse Venema) and site were trustworthy, but they were burned by a third party interloper.

> **Once a system has accepted a Trojan Horse, it can no longer be trusted. It should be rebuilt from scratch, preferably from original distribution media.** **Caution**

It's best to avoid Trojan Horses. Here are some steps to you can take to lessen the risk:

- Restrict downloads—Only download reputable programs from reputable sites. Avoid downloading anything from "hacker" or cracker sites; university sources are usually more trustworthy.

- Trust, but verify—Many program distributions include a digital signature or message digest; these should be verified along with the public key. See "Verifying with MD5" on page 136 and "Verifying with PGP" on page 137.

- Avoid running pre-compiled binaries. Build from source code.

- Review source code, if possible.

- When installing untrusted programs, use a test system.

- Never execute anything sent to you via unsolicited mail.

- Never execute content such as Java applets or JavaScript from an untrusted web site.

---

11. This should be obvious from the reference to the phrase "web browser." In its anti-trust defense, Microsoft claimed that there was no such thing, only bits of "browsing technology" integrated into the Windows operating system.

Caution   Do not rely on timestamps, file sizes, or other file attributes when trying to determine if a file is a Trojan Horse. This information can be easily forged by the creator of the Trojan Horse.

Verifying with MD5

MD5 checksums sometimes accompany software. You can use these to verify a package. For example, if you go to download the COPS system checker from the CERT FTP site, you'll find a checksums file with the following entries:

```
MD5 (cops.1.04.README) = 3e9af35c6dd4ed014b784efed61a04e6
MD5 (cops.1.04.tar.gz) = dc28e7985fc28fb61138470c11eecbe5
```

You can run the GNU-based md5sum utility (part of the textutils package) which is included with Red Hat Linux, or the md5 command included with BSD systems to verify the downloaded files as shown here:[12]

```
# md5sum cops.1.04.tar.gz
1fa416872934e5bee99068f9989cb8b0  cops.1.04.tar.gz
```

In this case, there isn't a match. Perhaps the package was damaged in transit. In any case, it can't be verified. In general, the checksumming approach is not a strong method of verification. If an attacker can replace the legitimate package with a Trojan Horse version, he or she can replace the checksums file at the same time. If he does so, every well-meaning sysadmin who downloads the Trojan will get a perfect MD5 match.

Note that MD5 can be used to verify system files as well. Say you run the following check on the important lilo (Linux Loader) system binary when you first install your system:

```
# md5sum lilo
a0d91b8d96f9ea6ab5d2e5ec5a73d5ab  lilo
```

The hash value should remain the same (until you upgrade). This verification capability is built into the RPM mechanism (see "RPM Verification and Signature Checking" on page 140). It is also used by Tripwire and other integrity-checking tools.

---

12. See ftp://ftp.gnu.org/gnu/textutils/

Verifying with PGP

PGP is very handy for verifying software and other files that have been downloaded from the net. The author of a security tool, for example, can create a detached signature for the archived tool, using his or her public key. The author then makes the package available along with the detached signature and his or her public key. You download all three files, add the author's public key to your keyring, and then verify the package. PGP will sign the package with the author's key, and check the resulting signature against the one included with the package. If there's a match, you can assume that the package has not been tampered with (as long as you can trust the author's key).

This is simpler than it sounds. I'll use the Abacus Logcheck by Craig H. Rowland to illustrate.[13] The distribution consists of three files:

- *logcheck-1.1.tar.gz*—the compressed logcheck package

- *logcheck-1.1.tar.gz.asc*—a detached PGP signature for the package

- *crowland.asc*—Rowland's public key

The detached signature looks like this:

```
-----BEGIN PGP MESSAGE-----
Version: 2.6.2i

iQCVAwUANIfQAa5kS8WYq/59AQGczwP/QRaYCCMsWcOmy68+DK14VspM1HPIoi5g
3iw1R91iPqgJhEOx+1ZKHY4qHsoOWvvnxGkAL2GbDXelDktcJsA5oNrxMQptzIL8
zFrOxqqNAPHamIsCuri9KzfzbttFR1Xi318GWookhw6qD8sQ7qvs5WxghvnGibFT
zu7vxTxhNLA=
=mX31
-----END PGP MESSAGE-----
```

13. See http://www.psionic.com/abacus/abacus_logcheck.html

Here's what the key looks like:

```
-----BEGIN PGP PUBLIC KEY BLOCK-----
Version: 2.6.2i
mQCNAzIgq+YAAAEEAKzSfNtR71e9ZtXvyOq27WO2kOwUl1YywBqeoOcEtbiHMnUB
19V5iDQbl8Sp/ZssrlR7QzYeFxf6ZRLDegr44ou5EKYhmSlrA+4JkGXyLU2XU7pc
QN2QuYnkI7RN2MFFbOXU6TvmXwdb551x9alwe8y2B1CTswANza5kS8WYq/59AAUR
tCdDcmFpZyBILiBSb3dsYW5kIDxjcm93bGFuZEBwc21vbmljLmNvbT6JAJUDBRAz
g6iormRLxZir/nOBAbHqA/94+33YozmL9kvEnCld4YMrV4zX96aF9xvXAK4YV37b
laPYzr5+AKRUGR8QcLmQ6c3jtO8pQSP95oFQg+tzfEC8FxHQIWkMxb8ty/iEEjEe
9INwKrNC39f2l03707ebuTdWK9cVO7vJxVqCL9H1+KHMkAiZ8tIpTh5jshYVDMai
bg==
=QXe7
-----END PGP PUBLIC KEY BLOCK-----
```

The first step is to add the key to your keyring, using pgpk.

```
$ pgpk -a crowland.asc
Adding keys:
Key ring: 'crowland.asc'
Type Bits KeyID       Created      Expires      Algorithm
Use
pub   1024 0x98ABFE7D 1996-08-25 ----------- RSA
Sign & Encrypt
uid  Craig H. Rowland <crowland@psionic.com>
1 matching key found
Add these keys to your keyring? [Y/n] y? y
Keys added successfully.
```

Then you verify the package using pgpv. PGP is smart enough to know that the detached signature is associated with a package with a similar filename. It confirms the signature and reports on the key that made it.

```
# pgpv logcheck-1.1.tar.gz.asc
This signature applies to another message
File to check signature against [logcheck-1.1.tar.gz]:
Good signature made 1997-12-05 09:57 GMI by key:
  1024 bits, Key ID 98ABFE7D, Created 1996-08-25
    "Craig H. Rowland <crowland@psionic.com>"
WARNING: The signing key is not trusted to belong to:
Craig H. Rowland <crowland@psionic.com>
```

Caution   Without confirmation of the signing key, there's no way to know that a man-in-the-middle didn't place a fake package along with a fake signature and key.

Maintaining Filesystem Integrity

The main purpose behind the UNIX permissions scheme—and all filesystem safeguards—is to maintain the integrity of the system and user files. Integrity is a core attribute of a secure system. You need to rest assured that the file you wrote yesterday is the same file you'll open today. Attackers and malicious users may attempt to subvert filesystems in dozens of ways, from taking advantage of misconfigured permissions to planting Trojan Horses and viruses.

The previous section covered verifying software. The same techniques—and cryptographic checksums in particular—can be used to verify the integrity of filesystems.

The outstanding implementation of a filesystem checking tool is Tripwire (covered starting on page 151). There are other tools that perform the same function—Hobgoblin is an example (see page 148). The find command can also be helpful (see "SUID/SGID" on page 121) as can the commands covered in the next two sections.

The sum and cksum Commands

Historically, UNIX systems have included the sum command, which performs a 16-bit checksum calculation on a specified file. In most modern UNIX implementations, the sum command is considered obsolete and has been replaced by the cksum command, which performs a 32-bit Cyclic Redundancy Check (CRC).

The syntax of cksum is simple: cksum file. The command will return the 32-bit CRC value, the number of octets, and the filename:

```
$ ls -l | grep bar
-rw-------   1 jrandom     losers       30237 Mar 13 18:42 bar
$ cksum bar
164310067 30237 bar
```

Caution

> The sum and cksum commands should not be considered reliable enough to verify the integrity of system files. Attackers can modifyfiles so that they have the same checksum as the original file. This is possible because these commands were designed to detect accidental modifications. They are not strong enough to prevent deliberate attempts to yield a specific checksum. It's better to use MD5 for this purpose. See
> ```
> http://www.cert.org/advisories/
> CA-94.05.MD5.checksums.html
> ```

RPM Verification and Signature Checking

RPM (Red Hat Package Manager) is a versatile software installation manager developed by Red Hat Software and included with their Linux distributions. It can be used to build, install, query, verify, update, and uninstall individual software packages. An RPM "package" includes an archive of files as well as package information.

The RPM package eliminates some of the headaches associated with maintaining current software. The RPM man page contains an exhaustive accounting of its many options. What interests us here is RPM's verification features. When you use RPM to install a package, RPM adds information about each installed file to a database, including

- an MD5 checksum

- file size

- file type

- owner

- group

- permissions mode

When RPM is run with the "--verify" flag, it compares the values from the original files with the currently installed files and reports on discrepancies. For example, the following verifies the current timed binary:

```
# rpm --verify timed-0.10-2
```

In this case, no news is good news.

```
# rpm --verify Tripwire-1.30-1
S.5....T   /usr/local/bin/tw/siggen
S.5....T   /usr/local/bin/tw/tripwire
S.5....T c /usr/local/bin/tw/tw.config
.......T   /var/tripwire/tw.db_TEST
```

Here, several Tripwire files have been altered. But this is due to the normal activity of installing and running the program.

The general form of the RPM signature check command is

```
rpm --checksig <package_file>+
```

This checks the PGP signature built into a package to ensure the integrity and the origin of the package.

Cryptographic Filesystems

The "cryptographic filesystem" is one of the more compelling approaches to filesystem security. It follows a relatively simple dictum: if a system stores secret data, it should routinely store it in encrypted form. While there's nothing stopping a user from using a tool like PGP to encrypt sensitive data for storage, the process can be cumbersome, time-consuming, and prone to error. Each time one needs to work on the files, they must be decrypted "by hand"; each time work is completed, the files must be encrypted again. This method of operation violates the rule that security safeguards should be easy to use. It also creates a window of vulnerability during the time the working files are stored in the clear. Why shouldn't the encryption and decryption be handled by the filesystem in a transparent way, with minimal user intervention, so that secret information is never stored in the clear?

CFS

The reasoning just introduced is the core idea behind the Cryptographic Filesystem (CFS) proposed and implemented by Matt Blaze.[14] CFS provides a transparent interface to directories and files

---

14. Matt Blaze, "A Cryptographic Filesystem for Unix." Proceedings of First ACM Conference on Computer and Communications Security, Fairfax, VA, November 1993. See ftp://coast.cs.purdue.edu/pub/doc/cryptography/Crypto-File-System.ps.Z

that are automatically encrypted with user-supplied keys. A single command associates a key with a directory; from then on, the directory's contents are automatically encrypted when they are written and decrypted when they're opened.

Typically, CFS-enabled directories are mounted as part of a virtual filesystem at the mount-point */crypt*.

CFS uses DES to encrypt files. CFS clients run a server daemon (*cfsd*) based on the Network Filesystem (NFS) protocol (see "NFS" on page 297)—CFS can use either local or network filesystems for underlying storage.

One potential drawback of CFS is speed. CFS requires additional data copies with each file request. Under normal UNIX operation, when a user application needs to access a file, the request goes to the kernel, which then retrieves it from the filesystem. With CFS in place, the application goes to the kernel, which invokes *cfsd*, which calls to the kernel, which retrieves it from the filesystem. Then, the file has to be decrypted and passed back to the application.

Tests run by Blaze indicate that file operations under CFS can be several times slower than normal UNIX file operations. Real world tests indicate that CFS operations are about 1.3 times slower. This difference may be acceptable when you factor in the slowness of the alternative—manually encrypting each and every secret file every time it's worked on.

Caution   Another potential downside of CFS is its experimental nature. As with any experimental filesystem, there's an opportunity for severe data loss or corruption.

Conceptually, both CFS and cryptographic filesystems in general are elegant. Many security safeguards are designed to protect servers by authenticating users who are intrinsically mistrusted. CFS works in reverse—by enforcing security for sensitive user data that must live on servers that are intrinsically mistrusted.

A Red Hat Linux version of CFS—packaged as an RPM by Georg P. Israel—can be downloaded from

`http://www.replay.com/redhat/cfs.html`

Tip

TCFS

A research group in Italy has been working on the Transparent Cryptographic Filesystem (TCFS), a Linux package inspired by CFS. TCFS is designed with even greater transparency—users don't even have to know their files are encrypted. Whereas CFS sits on top of the native filesystem, TCFS integrates with the Linux kernel, resulting in better performance. TCFS operates like NFS: a TCFS filesystem can be accessed by applications using the same system calls as NFS (*open*, *read*, *write*,...). Blocks of data are correctly decrypted only if the right key is available to the kernel.

You can find out more about TCFS at `http://tcfs.dia.unisa.it/`

Tip

While CFS or TCFS can slow down an attacker, they can't protect user files from a compromised root account. The superuser can modify the kernel, the crypto software, or keep a log of every keystroke.

Caution

Backups

It's difficult to overstate the importance of regular data backups. Nothing compares to the experience of losing data, especially huge chunks of data. Every user and every system administrator loses data from time to time. The wise and the strong can recover because of sound backup strategies and execution.

The Varieties of Computer Failure

There are so many ways that data can be lost or compromised. Shall we count the ways?

- Hardware failure—hard drives crash (even new hard drives sometimes)

- Software failure—operating systems and applications sometimes have bugs that can destroy data

- User error—it's very easy to delete critical files by mistake

- Sysadmin error—it can be very destructive when it happens

- Electronic break-ins—the system crackers are out there probing systems

- Theft—what if someone comes in and lifts your ecommerce server?

- Natural disaster—lightning, hurricanes, tornados, and earthquakes all happen

Backup Strategies

There are four types of backups:

- A day-zero backup—A copy of every file as it exists when you first build or install a system. A "virgin" backup can be invaluable if someone breaks into your system and changes system files.

- A full backup—A copy of every file on your system made on a regular basis.

- An incremental backup—A copy of those item in the filesystem that have changed since the most recent full backup or incremental backup.

- An ad hoc backup—A copy of working files made during the course of a project. In addition to system-wide backups, users should make ad hoc backups of their work each day.

Backup Commands

Most Unix systems include a number of commands that can facilitate system backups.

- cp—While usually used to copy single files, the `cp` (copy) command supports a recursive option (-R) that copies a directory and all its files and subdirectories. To copy all the contents of *mydir* to *mydir2*: `cp -R mydir mydir2`. Use of the vestigial alternative "-r" is deprecated since it doesn't copy through symbolic links on some platforms.

- `tar`—This utility is an old standby, first introduced with the Sixth Edition of AT&T UNIX. John Gilmore wrote the first public domain version. The `tar` (TApe aRchiver) command can create, add files to, or extract files from a tar archive (or "tarfile"). An archive is a file that contains other files plus information about them, such as file name, owner, timestamps, and access permissions. The `tar` utility was originally designed to work with tape archives but it can be used with other media. It's commonly used to package files for network delivery. Historically, `tar` has had limitations that make it unsuitable for some backup applications—it couldn't handle pathnames with more than a hundred characters, for example. While the latest `tar` supports new archive formats, `dump` and `restore` may be a better overall backup solution. See `man tar` on any UNIX system.

> To unpack files from a tarfile, run tar with the extract and verbose **Tip**
> flags: `tar xv yourtarfile.Z`
> If the archive is compressed (*.tar.Z), run: `tar xvZ yourtar-`
> `file.tar.Z`
> If the archive is gzipped, run: `tar xvz yourtarfile.tar.gz`

- `cpio`—This SVR4 and GNU utility copies files into or out of a cpio or tar archive. It is comparable to `tar`.

Running Dump and Restore

While `cp` and `tar` are useful for ad hoc backups, the `dump` command is more thorough—it takes an entire filesystem and copies ("dumps") it to backup media. It's particularly useful for doing incremental backups. A canonical way to ensure complete backups is to run a "level 0" or full backup followed by regular, incremental backups—`dump` supports ten levels and will backup all files that have changed since the last dump of a lower level. `Dump` stores information about the backups that have already been run in the file */etc/dumpdates*.

By default, `dump` will backup to tape media. Listing 6.4 shows a level 0 dump of a SCSI disk drive (*/dev/rsd0a*) to tape (*/dev/rst0*).

Listing 6.4 *A Full filesystem Backup Using Dump*

```
# dump 0f0 /dev/rst0 1500 /dev/sd0a
  DUMP: Date of this level 0 dump: Fri May  8 00:10:25 1999
  DUMP: Date of last level 0 dump: the epoch
  DUMP: Dumping /dev/rsd0a (/) to /dev/rst0
  DUMP: mapping (Pass I) [regular files]
  DUMP: mapping (Pass II) [directories]
  DUMP: estimated 298223 removable disk blocks on 0.19 removable disk(s).
  DUMP: dumping (Pass III) [directories]
  DUMP: dumping (Pass IV) [regular files]
  DUMP: 7.28% done, finished in 1:03
  DUMP: 21.63% done, finished in 0:36
  DUMP: 36.56% done, finished in 0:26
  DUMP: 50.95% done, finished in 0:19
  DUMP: 66.54% done, finished in 0:12
  DUMP: 81.37% done, finished in 0:06
  DUMP: 95.63% done, finished in 0:01
  DUMP: DUMP: 298482 removable disk blocks on 1 removable disk(s)
  DUMP: DUMP IS DONE
  DUMP: Disk ejecting
```

Many system administrators use the *cron* mechanism to back up filesystems with dump overnight or during quiet times. While this can ensure that backups are regular, it's includes an element of risk. It's safest to run dump in single-user mode to avoid the possibility of corruption that might occur when a filesystem is changing at the same time it is being backed up.

The restore command can be used to restore an entire filesystem or to retrieve individual files. It can read in the directory contents of a dumped filesystem and supports an interactive mode that allows the operator to move around in the backup filesystem and choose specific files to restore.

> The dump and restore combo have a shaky security history. The   **Caution**
> restore command is particularly risky since it runs SUID root.
> Like any SUID root program, you run restore at your own risk.

Backup Blunders

The following pointers will help you avoid getting burned by backup problems.

- Verify backups—Any number of things can go wrong with even the best backup system and strategies. Check the integrity of your backup media on a regular basis by running test restores.

- Protect backup media—Backup media need to be protected, since they contain copies of every file on your computer. Lock them up! If security is important at your site, don't leave backups running overnight unattended: somebody could swipe your tape and, with it, all of your users' files.

- Write-protect your backup tapes—Moveable tabs on both DAT and 8-mm. tapes allow you to take prophylactic measures against accidental erasure.

- Regularly send a set of backups to an off-site location—You're not prepared for disaster if you back up your system and leave the backup tapes sitting next to your computer. Fire, flood, or theft could eliminate your backups along with your system. For ultimate protection, you might contract with one of the firms that send encrypted data via modem from servers to archives hidden in reinforced concrete bunkers—a legacy of years when corporations feared thermonuclear war.

- Be mindful of media limits—Some kinds of tape cannot be used over and over again without degrading. Know and respect the vendor-recommended limits.

- Print paper records—Hard copies of important configuration and system files are very difficult for an attacker to alter.

- Train the personnel responsible for backups—The function is critical enough to warrant special training in operating backup software and hardware.

Filesystem Security Tools Survey

CFS

CFS by Matt Blaze pushes encryption services into the UNIX filesystem. It supports secure storage at the system level through a standard Unix filesystem interface to encrypted files (see "CFS" on page 141).

For more information:
`ftp://ftp.research.att.com/dist/mab/`

To download:
`http://www.replay.com/redhat/cfs.html`

Crypt Breakers Workbench (CBW)

An integrated workbench of tools that help a cryptanalyst read files encrypted with the BSD4.2 crypt command. Originally written by Robert W. Baldwin. The README file presents a step-by-step sequence of commands to test the program and demonstrate how easily crypt files can be broken. There are 31 steps in all. CBW is available on the accompanying CD-ROM.

To download:
`ftp://coast.cs.purdue.edu/pub/tools/unix/cbw/`

Filereaper

The traditional way of cleaning up temporary files using the find program is vulnerable to certain race condition attacks. This program by Zygo Blaxell takes a number of measures to avoid those problems.

To download:
`ftp://coast.cs.purdue.edu/pub/tools/unix/filereaper/`

Hobgoblin

Hobgoblin uses a template description that specified which files and directories are expected to match. It then scans those files, checks whether they match the descriptions, and reports on any changes.

To download:
`ftp://coast.cs.purdue.edu/pub/tools/unix/hobgoblin/`

libdes

This free kit by Eric A. Young builds a DES encryption library and a DES encryption program. It includes a fast implementation of *crypt(3)*.

To download:
```
ftp://ftp.psy.uq.oz.au/pub/Crypto/DES/

ftp://coast.cs.purdue.edu/pub/tools/unix/libdes/
```

MD5

A message digest algorithm that "fingerprints" message and files (see page 127). Source code is available on the accompanying CD-ROM.

For more information:
```
http://www.faqs.org/rfcs/rfc1321.html
```

To download:
```
http://www.cert.org/ftp/tools/md5/
```

md5sum

Computes and checks MD5 message digests (see page 127). Source code is available on the accompanying CD-ROM.

To download:
```
ftp://ftp.gnu.org/gnu/textutils/
```

Pretty Good Privacy (PGP)

Philip Zimmerman's popular mail and file encryption program (see "PGP" on page 129).

To download a version for non-commercial use:
```
http://web.mit.edu/network/pgp.html
```

To download the non-commercial version for Linux:
```
http://rufus.w3.org/linux/RPM/pgp.html
```

For information about PGP Data Security Suite:
```
http://www.nai.com/asp_set/products/tns/pgp_encryption.asp
```

Trojan

This Perl script by Bruce Barnett can be run by any user to check for Trojan Horses.

To download:
```
ftp://coast.cs.purdue.edu/pub/tools/unix/trojan/trojan.pl
```

Snefru

Source code for the one-way hash function. Available on the accompanying CD-ROM.

To download:

`ftp://coast.cs.purdue.edu/pub/tools/unix/snefru/`

TCFS

Like CFS, the Transparent Cryptographic File System (TCFS) offers on-the-fly encryption and decryption services (see "TCFS" on page 143).

For more information:

`http://tcfs.dia.unisa.it/`

Tripwire

Tripwire is a filesystem integrity checker. It is available on the accompanying CD-ROM.

For more information see "Tripwire" on page 151.

## 07

Tripwire

This chapter shows you how to maintain filesystem integrity using the Tripwire tool. It provides a conceptual overview of the program's design as well as detailed instructions for installation and configuration.

Introduction

Tripwire is an integrity checking tool designed to monitor filesystems for unauthorized modification. It's particularly useful for detecting intruders who might change files in order to facilitate future access; remove or alter system log; leave viruses, worms and logic bombs; or otherwise wreak havoc.

Most UNIX distributions are huge and include tens of thousands of files. There is no practical way for an individual to manually monitor system files for unauthorized changes. Tripwire works by taking mathematical "snapshots" or fingerprints of files and storing them in a database. Later, it compares the files' current snapshots against the original snapshots. Files that have been added, deleted, or changed are flagged by Tripwire, enabling sysadmins to take appropriate measures. Given proper installation, configuration, and monitoring, sysadmins can be quite sure that their "tripwired" systems have not been hacked.

Not only is Tripwire invaluable for detecting intrusions, it can be a major time-saver when recovering from a break-in. Say you suspect that an unauthorized user has gained root access. The perpetrator could easily leave a Trojan Horse or virus behind. This would be very difficult to detect by manual inspection of the 40,000+ files in a bare bones UNIX system. If you've installed Tripwire, however, you can easily check that your critical files have not been tampered with. If you don't have an integrity checker like Tripwire, you're really left with no choice but to re-install your system from scratch—a time-consuming and possibly unnecessary task.

Tripwire Overview

Benefits of Tripwire

Tripwire is one of the most useful and elegant tools in the UNIX security canon. Developed by Eugene Spafford and Gene Kim at Purdue University in 1992, the package was commercialized in 1998 and is now maintained by Tripwire Security Inc. (http://www.tripwiresecurity.com). The company supports both commercial and free versions of the package that will run on most UNIX systems.

Tripwire embodies the best attributes of a good security tool. It's tamper-proof, portable between platforms, configurable, scalable, and self-contained.

- Tamper-proof—In order to detect changes, Tripwire can utilize an arsenal of up to ten signature algorithms or one-way hash functions. The program includes: RSA Data Security Inc.'s MD5, MD4, and MD2 message digest algorithms, Snefru (the Xerox Secure Hash Function), SHA (the Secure Hash Algorithm), and Haval code. It also includes two conventional CRC routines. With the default setup of recording two signatures for each database entry, it becomes extremely difficult for an attacker to cover his or her tracks by, say, padding extra characters. A skilled attacker might be able to make an alteration that doesn't change the size of a file and that matches a single checksum. But two checksums? Practically impossible.[1]

- Portable—The authors recognized that the UNIX world is diverse and thus designed the program for maximum portability across various UNIX platforms. The program supports dozens of UNIX variants. The databases Tripwire produces are encoded as ASCII text that can be manipulated with text processing tools or printed.

- Configurable—Tripwire can monitor changes to file permissions, modification times, and other file parameters on a per file or per directory basis. It can be configured to ignore specified files and directories, or check a directory but not recurse into it.

- Scalable—Tripwire can be set up to cover thousands of machines from a single installation. The package includes a preprocessing language that helps sysadmins re-use configuration files—identically-configured machines can share a configuration file while a unique database file is generated for each unique machine.

---

1. The authors of Tripwire tested over 250,000 files on five computers for duplicate signatures. While the 16-bit CRC produced approximately 25,000 collisions, 128-bit MD4, MD5, and Snefru produced none. See the design document, "The Design and Implementation of Tripwire" by Gene H. Kim and Eugene H. Spafford.

- Self-contained—Tripwire's operations don't rely on external programs. Not only would additional programs be time-consuming to install, but they could present additional security risks.

Summary of Operation

Figure 7.1 sketches out how Tripwire uses two input files—a configuration file (tw.config) describing which directories and files to monitor and a baseline database of signatures—to generate a detailed report on alterations.

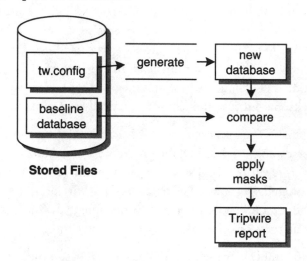

Figure 7.1 *Tripwire's Basic Operations*[2]

When you first run Tripwire, the program creates the baseline database of signatures. The next time you run it, it uses the *tw.config* file to generate a new database of signatures. It then compares the two databases, applies any selection masks that you specified (so that constantly changing files are excluded), and spits out a report that you can read on a terminal, send by email, or print.

Tripwire has four modes of operation: Database Generation, Integrity Checking, Database Update, and Interactive Update.

---

2. This diagram is roughly based on one that appears in the design document, "The Design and Implementation of Tripwire" by Gene H. Kim and Eugene H. Spafford.

Database Generation mode produces the baseline database—
the basis for future comparisons.

Integrity Checking is Tripwire's main mode in which current file
signatures are checked against the baseline.

The two update modes allow you to adjust the Tripwire database in order to eliminate uninteresting results and account for
normal system changes. You don't really need Tripwire to repeatedly report that *letc/passwd* has changed, for example, if user
accounts are being added and deleted on a regular basis.

Listing 7.1 and Listing 7.2 are samples of the output produced
by Tripwire in Integrity Checking mode. Tripwire first reports that
files have changed, without citing the specific differences. In this
case, several users have been added to the system since the last
Tripwire run and thus the *letc/group* and *letc/passwd* files are no
longer the same.

Listing 7.1 *Tripwire Reports on Changes*

```
changed: -rw------- root        419 Nov 11 03:00:12 1998 /etc/group
changed: -rw------- root        708 Nov 11 03:00:37 1998 /etc/passwd
```

Tripwire then supplies the specifics on which attributes have
changed for each file, citing what has been observed and what was
expected, as shown below.

Listing 7.2 *Tripwire Compares What Is and What Should Be*

```
/HH/ Attr         Observed (what it is)        Expected (what it should be)
/HH/ ==========================================================
etc/group
        st_size:  419                          406
       st_mtime:  Wed Nov 11 03:00:12 1998     Tue Nov 10 21:47:18 1998
       st_ctime:  Wed Nov 11 03:00:54 1998     Tue Nov 10 21:47:25 1998
     md5 (sig1):  1v7107JjILdzcmk2KvOss2       2w.G9WImF4YG1dW:v2MNaO
  snefru (sig2):  1kUqQEbLQh1M5MmLTfjZ88       1INUGiJBANqUMc2JZNWPMW

/etc/passwd
        st_size:  708                          704
       st_mtime:  Wed Nov 11 03:00:37 1998     Tue Nov 10 21:53:18 1998
       st_ctime:  Wed Nov 11 03:00:54 1998     Tue Nov 10 21:53:22 1998
     md5 (sig1):  3xyLWCfTxHONvj:VnMD9Vv       3mOa7m2qJ1Bhqq:PUvhkVh
  snefru (sig2):  OLs:Xxeo76EMVIF3tbfEOj       2iwHs11eYHIm6YcqwF4AA4
```

This run compares the current MD5 and Snefru signatures
against the originals and reports different fingerprints. It also
reports on file size and timestamp differences. Since I recently
added users, I'm not concerned about these changes. But if attackers had added bogus accounts in the middle of the night, I'd know.

Planning Considerations

The best time to install Tripwire is immediately after you've built a
"virgin" system, one that's either new or recently upgraded. A system that's been up and running for a while may already be compromised: running Tripwire after this point may be of little or no
value. If it's not possible to install Tripwire when the system is new,
give serious consideration to re-installing system binaries while in
single-user mode. While this isn't trivial, it's the only way to insure
that your system is clean and stays clean.

Tripwire requires some advance storage planning. You need to
store the baseline database as well as the program binary in a
secure place lest an attacker alter these files in a way that defeats
the purpose of the program. The optimal arrangement is to store
these files on a removable read-only medium—like a write-pro-
tected floppy disk, optical disk, or CD-ROM that's inaccessible to
potential attackers. Alternatively, you can place the files on a partition of a secure remote machine and export it read-only. Keep in
mind that mounting a hard drive read-only using the mount command is insufficient since an attacker with root access could easily
remount the drive so that it can be written to.

It's important to consider the trade-offs between security and
performance that Tripwire offers. You can choose to run any of the
program's six signature algorithms and two checksums against any
of your files. It's important to keep in mind, however, that some of
these algorithms are computationally expensive. Snefru, in particular, runs slowly. Only those with an extreme threat model will
want to run all algorithms against every directory and file. By
default, Tripwire uses MD5 and Snefru. These two alone provide
great protection and consume plenty of CPU cycles. I've configured
one of my Tripwire installations to run MD5 against all files and
both MD5 and Snefru against critical system files. Even so, it takes
a half-hour to produce a report on a Pentium Pro system running
Red Hat Linux 5.0. You need to balance your security needs
against available time and CPU cycles.

Anatomy of tw.config

Tripwire's configuration file gives you precise control over the files
and directories that the program monitors. The file *tw.config*

contains a list of these files and directories. Each entry is associated with a selection mask that tells the program what file attribute changes can be safely ignored.

The selection mask is composed of select-flags. Each select-flag covers a different attribute. The "s" select-flag, for example, is for file size, while the "a" is for the access timestamp. Each flag is either added ("+") or deleted ("-") from an item to be monitored. A *tw.config* entry like

```
/home/xyz +s-a
```

tells Tripwire to track file size changes in */home/xyz* while ignoring changes in the access file stamp.

Table 7.1 summarizes Tripwire's select-flags.

Table 7.1 *Tripwire's Attribute Select-flags*

Select-flag	Attribute Covered
-	ignore the following attribute
+	monitor the following attribute
p	permission bits
i	inode number
n	number of links
u	user ID of owner
g	group ID of owner
s	size of file
a	access timestamp
m	modification timestamp
c	inode creation/modification timestamp

Each of Tripwire's signature routines is assigned a number. You can specify which of these are applied to a file/directory entry

(Tripwire applies 1 and 2 by default). Table 7.2 specifies each signature and corresponding number.

Table 7.2 *Tripwire's Signature Numbers*

Signature #	Signature
0	null signature
1	MD5, from RSA Data Security, Inc.
2	Snefru, the Xerox Secure Hash Function
3	CRC-32, 32-bit Cyclic Redundancy Check
4	CRC-16, 16-bit Cyclic Redundancy Check
5	MD4, from RSA Data Security, Inc.
6	MD2, from RSA Data Security, Inc.
7	SHA, the NIST Secure Hash Algorithm
8	Haval, a 128-bit signature algorithm
9	null, reserved for future use

Given Tripwire's flexibility, the selection-masks can get quite complex. The designers compensated for this complexity by creating templates that contain common combinations of selection flags. In most cases, you'll want to use these templates in your *tw.config*. Table 7.3 summarizes the five major templates.

Table 7.3 *Selection-mask Templates*

Template Letter	Template Purpose	Template Select-flags
R	Read-only files	+pinugsm12-ac3456789
L	Log files	+pinug-sacm123456789
N	Ignore nothing	+pinugsamc123456789

Table 7.3 *Selection-mask Templates (Cont'd)*

Template Letter	Template Purpose	Template Select-flags
E	Ignore everything	-pinugsamc123456789
>	Growing log files	+pinug>samc123456789

The R template is the default. So if the entry for */usr/local/bin* looks like this

```
/usr/local/bin      R
```

the effective selection-mask is

```
/usr/local/bin +pinugsm12-ac
```

and Tripwire will report any changes in mode bits, inode number, reference count, uid, gid, file size, modification timestamp, and the MD5 and Snefru signatures. It will ignore changes to the access and inode timestamps.

There are two final operators to consider. A "!" before an entry indicates an inclusive prune. If the entry is a file, it is ignored. If the entry is a directory, it is ignored along with all the files within it. A "=" indicates an exclusive prune. If the entry is a file, it does nothing. If the entry is a directory, the directory will be monitored but not its contents.

The following is a very simple *tw.config* file:

```
#file/dir       selection-mask
/root           R    #check root's home directory
!/root/mbox     R    #but ignore root's mailbox
/usr/local      R-2  #check but save time by skipping
Snefru
=/home          R    #only the directory, not its contents
```

Note that templates can be mixed with select-flags. "R-2" is a simple way of indicating a default check without using Snefru.

Installing Tripwire

To download Tripwire, surf to Tripwire Security Systems, Inc.'s web site at the URL `http://www.tripwiresecurity.com/tripwire`. You can download either the UNIX or the Linux version. For Linux, there are RPM packages for either binaries or source code available. For maximum flexibility, download the source code RPM, which should be called *tripwire-1.3-1.src.rpm* or something similar. While you're there, also download the manual, which is in PDF format.

Log in as root. Use RPM (the RedHat Package Manager) to install the Tripwire source code with a command in the form of

```
$ rpm -ivh tripwire-1.3-1.src.rpm
```

The Tripwire source code will be copied to */usr/src/redhat/BUILD/tripwire-1.3-1*.

Review the README files included in the distribution as well as the FAQ file. You may also wish to review the manual.

Caution

> If you're extremely meticulous, you'll re-install your system binaries before installing Tripwire. This is the only way to ensure that you're starting with a clean system. If you suspect that you've been hacked, definitely re-build your system from the original installation media.

If you're installing on a UNIX box (other than Linux), you may need to check the Makefile, edit the *./include/config.h* file, and make other customizations. Consult the manual for detailed instructions.

From the top-level Tripwire source directory, type the command `make`. This will build the program binaries. The Tripwire binary (*"tripwire"*) and configuration file (*"tw.config"*) will be placed in the directory */usr/local/bin/tw*. If you have problems compiling, consult the manual for trouble-shooting tips.

Tripwire includes a script that tests if your installation was successful. Type the command `make test` at the top-level to invoke the script.

Configuring Tripwire

Edit the *tw.config* file so that it will monitor the right files and directories. You don't want Tripwire to miss checking important files, nor do you want it to report on files that constantly change in the course of normal system operation. The default *tw.config* is quite generous—it's set to monitor most of the files on a stock Linux box. You may want to go ahead and run your first Tripwire report and then adjust *tw.config* based on the output you get.

Run Tripwire in Database Generation mode by running the command `tripwire -initialize`. This creates your baseline database—a file called *tw.db_hostname* where "hostname" is replaced with your machine's hostname.

> By default, the database is placed in a directory *"./databases"*. Note **Tip**
> that in order to change where the database is placed, you'll need to
> recompile Tripwire.

Running Tripwire

Run Tripwire in Integrity Checking mode by running the command `tripwire`. Tripwire will run its comparisons and report on any discrepancies. The report you receive should produce a preamble that looks like Listing 7.3.

Listing 7.3 *Preamble of a Tripwire Report*

```
Tripwire(tm) Intrusion Detection Software v1.3

This release is for single CPU, single-site, end-use
purposes.  For commercial applications or product
information, please visit the Visual Computing Corporation
web site at http://www.visualcomputing.com/tripwire, or
call us at (503) 223-0280.

Tripwire(tm) Copyright 1992-98 by the Purdue Research
Foundation of Purdue University, and distributed by Visual
Computing Corporation under exclusive license arrangements.
```

```
### Phase 1:    Reading configuration file
### Phase 2:    Generating file list
### Phase 3:    Creating file information database
### Phase 4:    Searching for inconsistencies
###
### Total files scanned: 40084
###      Files added: 11
###      Files deleted: 9
###      Files changed: 15
###
### Total file violations: 35
```

You will find that Tripwire flags uninteresting file changes—those that have occurred as a part of normal system operation or those that you already know about. You can update these entries in the database by running Tripwire in either Interactive mode or Database Update mode.

Interactive Mode prompts you to update the database each time it finds a file or directory that has been added, deleted, or changed. To run Tripwire in Interactive mode, type the command `tripwire -interactive` You'll see a notice that a file has been added or deleted and you'll be asked, "Update entry?" as shown in Listing 7.4.

Listing 7.4 *Updating Added or Deleted Entries*

```
added:   -rw-r--r-- root        564 Nov 18 01:41:40 1998
/root/blah.text
---> File: '/root/blah.text'
---> Update entry?  [YN(y)nh?] y

added:   -rw-r--r-- root      99514 Sep 15 00:40:00 1997
/usr/doc/HOWTO/Database-HOWTO
---> File: '/usr/doc/HOWTO/Database-HOWTO'
---> Update entry?  [YN(y)nh?] Y

deleted: -rw-r--r-- root      36304 Sep 15 00:40:00 1997
/usr/doc/HOWTO/Database-HOWTO.gz
---> Updating '/usr/doc/HOWTO/Database-HOWTO.gz'
```

Two files have been added (*"blah.txt"* and a HOWTO) and one has been deleted (the compressed version of the HOWTO). By typing "y" or hitting the return key, you indicate that the additions and deletions should be accounted for in the new Tripwire database. As shown in Listing 7.5, you can update all the files in the same *tw.config* entry by typing "Y."

If a file has changed (as opposed to being added or deleted), Tripwire will note this and then report on the specific attributes that have changed.

Listing 7.5 *Updating Changed Entries*

```
changed: -rw-r--r-- root          495 Nov 18 18:50:25 1998 /etc/group

changed: -rw-r--r-- root          953 Nov 18 23:15:28 1998 /etc/passwd
### Phase 5:   Generating observed/expected pairs for changed files
###
### Attr        Observed (what it is)        Expected (what it should be)
### ========    =====================        ===========================

/etc/group
        st_ino: 6126                         6131
      st_mtime: Wed Nov 18 18:50:25 1998     Sat Nov 14 01:25:50 1998
      st_ctime: Wed Nov 18 18:50:25 1998     Sat Nov 14 01:25:50 1998
---> File: '/etc/group'
---> Update entry?  [YN(y)nh?] y

/etc/passwd
        st_ino: 6135                         6136
---> File: '/etc/passwd'
---> Update entry?  [YN(y)nh?] y
```

Finally, Tripwire confirms that the entries have been updated.

```
Updating entry: /usr/doc/HOWTO/Database-HOWTO
Updating entry: /etc/group
Updating entry: /etc/passwd

### Updating database...
```

Database Update mode provides a method for quickly updating database entries on the command-line. Say you've just installed */usr/local/bin/great.new.file*. You could update the database with the command

```
# tripwire -update /usr/local/bin/great.new.file
```

Note that this command can also be used to update all the files in a directory.

Tripwire Tips and Tricks

- Use *cron* to run Tripwire at regular times. If your system is connected to the Internet, set it to run on at least a daily basis. It's not a bad idea to have Tripwire mail the results to root using a crontab command like `tripwire | /bin/mail root`

- If you use *cron* to do scheduled Tripwire runs, then be sure to run Tripwire at random intervals as well. A potential attacker might view the interval between cron-initiated Tripwire runs as a window of opportunity.

- Tripwire allows you to do checks that run quickly because they exclude certain signatures. This option is helpful if you run Tripwire very frequently from *cron* or if you want to run an Interactive mode check without waiting at your terminal for an extended period. The "-i" select-flag forces Tripwire to ignore specific signatures. For example, if you used MD5 (signature 1) and Snefru (signature 2) to generate your baseline database and now want to do a quick check without Snefru, run the command `tripwire -i 2`

- Tripwire won't traverse mounted file systems. So, if you have the root directory in your *tw.config* ("/"), it won't traverse the separate partitions */usr* and */home*. You need to specify each and every mounted partition that you want Tripwire to check in your *tw.config* file.

- Tripwire databases can be big. If the only read-only medium available for securely storing the Tripwire database is a floppy disk, you'll need to limit the size of the database by setting *tw.config* to ignore less important files, by limiting the number of file attributes monitored, and/or by using only one signature. While these measures may decrease the program's effectiveness to some extent, a circumscribed Tripwire check is preferable to one that can be subverted by an attacker.

- To watch Tripwire in action, run `tripwire -v`. Tripwire will display filenames as they're being checked.

- The man pages for *tw.config* and tripwire contain a wealth of information.

## 08

Logging

Logging significant system events is a critical element of system security. Most UNIX systems are able to run three different logging subsystems: connect-time logging via the *wtmp/utmp* files; process accounting via the *acct* or *pacct* file; and error logging via the *syslog* facility. This chapter covers these logging subsystems and the many commands and programs that allow a sysadmin or security administrator to monitor, audit, and maintain logs. It also covers several add-on tools, from Zap, which helps you stalk an intruder, to syslog-ng, a security-enhanced version of the standard UNIX *syslog* facility.

UNIX maintains several basic log files that track and record what's happening on the system, including who's logging in, who's logging out, and what they're doing. Newer versions of UNIX track additional information such as attempts to log in as superuser, files transferred over the network, email exchanges, and more.

Log files are critical to maintaining system security. They provide data for two critical functions: auditing and monitoring. By providing a recorded history—an audit trail of activities on your system—they allow you or a third party to go back and systematically evaluate the effectiveness of your security program and determine the causes of security breaches and system malfunctions. If push comes to shove, they can be used as evidence that you can present to the authorities.

They can also be used in "real time" to monitor system status, to detect and track intruders, to discover bugs, and to generally head off trouble. You can bird-dog your system by viewing log entries as they're created or you can use a tool like Swatch (see page 197) to watch for you.

Caution

Logging makes users accountable for their actions, particularly in environments with strong user authentication policies and systems. Nonetheless, it's always possible for one user to masquerade as another. Never assume that information contained in a log is sacrosanct—always try to confirm log reports through independent means before taking action.

While the mere existence of a log doesn't provide perfect accountability, logging enables system administrators and security officers to

- discover repeated attempts to defeat system security (say, an attacker trying a brute-force root login)

- track users who assume a high level of privilege (say, those who use the sudo command to execute commands as root)

- track anomalous usage patterns (Carol from accounting works from 9 to 5 but the logs show her logged in at 3 AM; Mallory is hogging CPU time)

- track intruders in real-time

Logging aids detection. It's vital that you know when your systems are being attacked or an intruder has broken in. While logging won't prevent a break-in, it represents a fallback for basic account security. Even if account security fails, and an attacker is able to exploit user privileges, you want this fact to be duly recorded. Once you know what's happening, you can take appropriate actions: cutting a user off, strengthening the network perimeter, monitoring and stalking an intruder to gather forensic evidence, etc. Policies for logging, maintaining logs, log monitoring, and auditing are all important pieces of a complete security policy.

Perhaps the most important security function of logging is deterrence. Elementary human psychology dictates that people will behave differently when they know their actions are being watched. It's not enough to simply set up logging—you should publicize that you've done so in order to instill fear. You want to develop communication strategies designed to impress potential attackers of the likelihood of getting caught (see "Rule 5: The Fear of Getting Caught is the Beginning of Wisdom" on page 23). The goal is to prevent an attacker's or wayward user's intent from reaching the critical point of action.

You should get the word out that your systems are set up for logging. One effective way to do this is with a login banner warning: "WARNING! Use of this system constitutes consent to security monitoring and testing. All activity is logged with your username, host name and IP address."

Unfortunately, log files are themselves vulnerable to attack. Any reasonably competent system cracker attempts to cover his or her tracks by modifying either the log files or, worse, the logging mechanism itself. There are countermeasures which you can take to help preserve the integrity and usefulness of logging subsystems. These are covered later in this chapter.

For a valuable overview of how a cracker covers his or her tracks **Tip** after breaking into a UNIX system, see the Phrack magazine article, "Playing Hide and Seek, Unix style," available at
`http://www.fish.com/security/hide-n-seek.html`.

Logging Subsystems

In most UNIX systems, there are three main logging subsystems:

- Connect-time logging—performed by various programs that write records into */var/log/wtmp* (or */var/adm/wtmp*), and */var/run/utmp* (can be */etc/utmp* or */var/adm/utmp*). Programs such as login update the *wtmp* and *utmp* files so that sysadmins can keep track of who was logged into the system and when that user was logged in.

- Process accounting—performed by the system kernel. Upon termination of a process, one record per process is written to the process accouting file (either *pacct* or *acct*). Process accounting's main purpose is to provide command usage statistics on which to base service charges for use of the system.

- Error logging—performed by the *syslogd(8)* daemon. Various system daemons, user programs, and the kernel report noteworthy conditions via the *syslog(3)* function to the files, */var/adm/messages* and */var/log/syslog*.[1]

In addition, many UNIX programs create log files. Servers that provide network services like HTTP or FTP typically keep detailed logs.

Depending on the UNIX version, log files are typically written to either the */var/log, /var/adm, /usr/adm,* or occasionally the */etc* directories. Most Linux systems keep major logs in */var/log*—I'll use this convention in most of my examples. Common log files are summarized in Table 8.1.

Table 8.1 *Common UNIX Log Files*

Log File	Purpose
access_log	Records HTTP/web traffic
acct/pacct	Records user commands

---

1. This categorization of log files can be found in
http://csrc.nist.gov/nissc/1998/proceedings/paperD1.pdf

Table 8.1 *Common UNIX Log Files (Cont'd)*

Log File	Purpose
aculog	Records modem activity
btmp	Records bad logins
lastlog	Records the most recent successful login time and the last unsuccessful login as well
messages	Records messages from the *syslog* facility (often linked to or from the *syslog* file)
sudolog	Records commands issued using the `sudo` command
sulog	Records use of the `su` command
syslog	Records messages from the *syslog* facility (often linked to or from the *messages* file)
utmp	Records each user currently logged in
wtmp	A permanent record of each time a user logs in and out
xferlog	Logs FTP sessions

The Login Records

The *utmp, wtmp,* and *lastlog* log files are the linchpins of the most important UNIX logging subsystem—the one that keeps track of user logins and logouts. Information about currently logged in users is recorded in the file *utmp*; logins and logouts are recorded in the file *wtmp*; and last logins in the file *lastlog*. Date changes, shutdowns, and reboots are also logged in the *wtmp* file. All records include time stamps.

These files (all but *lastlog*) grow rapidly on busy systems with many users. The *wtmp* file, for example, will increase without bound unless it is periodically truncated. Many systems come configured to rotate *wtmp* on a daily or weekly basis. It is usually pruned daily by scripts run by *cron*. These scripts rename and rotate the *wtmp* files, keeping a week's worth of data on hand.

Typically, *wtmp* is renamed to *wtmp.1* at the end of day one; on day two, *wtmp.1* becomes *wtmp.2*, etc. up to *wtmp.7*.

Caution   No login or connect time accounting is performed if */var/log/wtmp* does not exist. It must be created manually (`touch /var/log/wtmp`).

The Basic Mechanism

Each time a user logs in, the login program looks up the user's UID in the file *lastlog*. If it is found, the timestamp of the last time the user logged in, the terminal line, and the hostname are written to the standard output. The login program then records the new login time in *lastlog*.

After the new lastlog record is written, the file *utmp* is opened and the utmp record for the user inserted. This record remains there until the user logs out at which time it is deleted. The *utmp* file is used by a variety of commands, including `who`, `w`, `users`, and `finger` (see below for more on these commands).

Next, the login program opens the file *wtmp*, and appends the user's utmp record. The same utmp record, with an updated time stamp is later appended to the file when the user logs out. The *wtmp* file is used by the programs `last` and `ac` (see below).

Caution   In older versions of UNIX, the */etc/utmp* file was world-writable (`-rw-rw-rw-`). It shouldn't be, since this allows any user to edit the file (potentially to obscure their presence). Newer UNIX systems ship */etc/utmp* with a more restrictive setting (`-rw-r--r--`).

Monitoring with utmp/wtmp-based Commands

Both the *wtmp* and *utmp* files are in binary format—they can't be tailed (with the `tail` command) or concatenated (with the `cat` command). You need to run one of several commands—including `who`, `w`, `users`, `last`, and `ac`—in order to take advantage of the information they contain.

A system administrator should monitor system security by periodically checking who is logged into the system and what they're doing. This is particularly true for a security-sensitive system, or one with many users. Is the guy on vacation logged on? Is a

business manager compiling programs? Is that one of your programmers in at nine in the morning?

Be attentive. Be curious. Think like a shopkeeper who keeps
close eye on who is coming into and leaving the store. Run w when
you first log in and before you log out at the end of the day (or
night). Observe bad logins—they could presage someone breaking
in. Run ac to see who's hogging system resources—is an email-only
user submitting huge jobs? Eternal vigilance is the price of security.

> **One hole in the logging net is the** su **command, which does not**   **Caution**
> **update** *utmp* **and** *wtmp* **files when a user substitutes one effec-**
> **tive UID for another. This can lead to some strange consequences**
> **such as when a** su'ed **user runs mail or another program that**
> **consults the** *utmp* **file. Fortunately,** su **maintains its own log (see**
> **"sulog" on page 189).**

The who Command

The who command consults the *utmp* file and reports on each user
currently logged in. By default, the output of who includes username, terminal type, the login date and time, and remote host (if
there is one).

```
$ who
root      tty1      May 15 16:09
bob       console   May 15 14:49
alice     ttyp2     May 16 00:13
carol     ttyp3     May 11 13:20
```

The who command will consult the *wtmp* file for previous logins
if that file is named. A command like who /var/log/wtmp will
report on every login since the *wtmp* file was truncated or created.

For those in the midst of an existential crisis, the idiosyncratic
form whoami provides some relief:

```
$ whoami
alice
```

Some vendors include an extended who command with their
UNIX systems. HP-UX, for example, supports 16 different flags
and options. The "-a" flag produces a report "with everything on
it," including username, terminal type, time, idle time, process ID,

and comments. It also indicates the last system boot time and
more, as shown below.

```
$ who -a
      .          system boot  Apr 12 13:15
      .          run-level 3  Apr 12 13:15    3    0   S
NAME     LINE        TIME           IDLE    PID  COMMENTS
LOGIN    console     Apr 12 13:18   old     1699 system console
carol    pts/t0      Apr 26 10:03   3:15   28283 foo.example.com
alice    pts/t1      Apr 26 13:49   .      29009
dave     pts/t2      Apr 23 19:03   old     1923 id= t2 term=0   exit=0
eve      pts/t3      Apr 19 13:07   3:19   26195 foo.bar.com
carol    pts/t4      Apr 23 19:03   old     5570 id= t4 term=0   exit=0
carol    pts/t5      Apr 23 18:05   old     2395 id= t5 term=0   exit=0
mallory  pts/t6      Apr 23 19:03   old     6357 id= t6 term=0   exit=0
alice    pts/t7      Apr 23 02:46   old    16515 id= t7 term=0   exit=0
carol    pts/t8      Apr 23 00:52   old    16824 id= t8 term=0   exit=0
trent    pts/t9      Apr 23 02:52   old    17082 id= t9 term=0   exit=0
LOGIN    dtremote    Apr 25 09:20   old    24861 id=87:0 term=0  exit=4
```

The w Command

The w command consults the *utmp* file and displays information
about each of the users currently on the system as well as the processes they're running. The header shows the current time, how
long the system has been running, how many users are currently
logged on, and the system load averages for the past 1, 5, and 15
minutes.

```
$ w
3:55pm  up 8 days,  2:40,  5 users,  load average: 0.04, 0.06, 0.09
User      tty          login@   idle   JCPU   PCPU  what
carol    pts/t1       2:16pm   18:09                -sh
dave     pts/t2       2:20pm   88:42     1      1   -sh
trent    pts/t3       1:07pm    8:18                nslookup
mallory  pts/t4      10:07pm  133:55                -sh
alice    pts/t5       1:50pm              1      1   w
```

The uptime command is closely related to w. It outputs the
header information cited above.

The users Command

The users command prints a single line listing the users currently
logged in. Each displayed user name corresponds to a login session. So, if a user has more than one login session, that user's name
will appear the same number of times in the output.

```
$ users
alice carol dave bob
```

The last Command

The last command searches back through *wtmp* to show a list of the users who have logged in since the file was first created. It reports both the tty and the date. The output can be verbose; the example output below is trimmed.

```
$ last
alice      ttyp4           Thu May  7 19:50    still logged in
ftp        ftp             Thu May  7 18:42 - 18:42  (00:00)
carol      ttyp5           Thu May  7 18:37    still logged in
alice      ftp             Thu May  7 15:50 - 16:06  (00:15)
bob        ttyp4           Thu May  7 15:46 - 15:50  (00:03)
dave       ftp             Thu May  7 15:00 - 15:01  (00:01)

wtmp begins Sun Mar 14 01:10:36 1999
```

With the "-R" flag ("-h" on BSDish systems), the last command displays the user's hostname as it is stored in *wtmp*. The "-number" flag limits the report to the specified number of lines. To see the last three logins, including remote hosts:

```
$ last -R -3
alice   pts/t7     foo1.example.com Wed Apr 21 23:52    still logged
in
carol   pts/t6     foo2.example.com Tue Apr 20 21:57    still logged
in
eve     pts/t5     foo3.example.com Tue Apr 20 09:45 - 09:48  (00:03)
```

If you specify a user, last will report only on that user's recent activities.

```
$ last carol
carol   pts/t6     Tue Apr 20 21:57    still logged in
carol   pts/t4     Tue Apr 20 21:16    still logged in
carol   pts/t5     Tue Apr 20 18:03    still logged in
carol   pts/t0     Mon Apr 19 15:17 - 15:26 (1+00:09)
carol   pts/t0     Fri Apr 16 16:44 - 18:25  (01:41)
carol   pts/t0     Fri Apr 16 14:12 - 16:12  (02:00)
carol   pts/t0     Thu Apr 15 11:05 - 18:33  (07:28)
carol   pts/t0     Wed Apr 14 22:16 - 01:52  (03:35)
carol   pts/t4     Tue Apr 13 22:07 - 21:15 (6+23:08)
carol   pts/t3     Tue Apr 13 13:03 - 17:30 (1+04:26)
```

The lastb Command

Some UNIX systems also support the `lastb` command, which searches back through the database file */var/adm/btmp* to display information about bad logins (i.e., those that failed due to a bad password). To see the last five bad logins, login as root and issue the following:

```
# lastb -5
Password:
carol     pts/t5          Tue Apr 20 18:03
mallory   pts/t0          Tue Apr 20 16:05
root      pts/t0          Tue Apr 20 16:04
alice     pts/t0          Tue Apr 20 12:05
root      pts/t0          Tue Apr 20 11:56
```

Caution   Access to the *btmp* file should be restricted to users with appropriate privileges—that is, the file should be owned by and readable only by root—because it may contain password information (users commonly enter their password as their username by mistake).

The ac Command

The `ac` command reports on users' connect time (in hours) based on the logins and logouts in the current */var/log/wtmp* file. If used without flags, it reports a total.

```
$ ac
total      136.25
```

The "-d" flag produces total connect hours by date.

```
$ ac -d
Mar 15      total      19.89
Mar 16      total       4.52
Mar 17      total      17.35
Mar 18      total      29.26
Mar 19      total      36.28
Mar 20      total      11.42
Mar 21      total      17.53
```

The "-p" flag reports on connect hours by individual users as well as a total.

```
$ ac -p
mallory                        .        31.02
carol                                   41.08
root                                    10.30
eve                                     29.11
alice                                   14.73
bob                                     10.01
total                                  136.26
```

The lastlog File

As noted above, the *lastlog* file is consulted each time a user logs in. On login, most UNIX systems report on the last successful login, displaying the date and tty. Some System V systems also report on the last unsuccessful login. This looks something like the example below (taken from an HP-UX login session):

```
login: alice
Password: hVse.L2q
Last    successful login for alice: Tue Apr 20 16:05:33 PDT
1999 on pts/t0
Last unsuccessful login for alice: Tue Apr 20 16:05:04 PDT
1999 on pts/t0
```

Check what's reported about successful and unsuccessful logins **Tip**
each time you log in, and teach your users to do the same. Needless
to say, you want to make sure that no one has logged in with your
username or repeatedly racked up unsuccessful login attempts.

If you're running Linux, you can check the last time a given user was on your system by running the `lastlog` command, which formats and prints the contents of the last login log, */var/log/lastlog* (perhaps */var/adm/lastlog* on other systems). The login-name, port (tty), and last login time for each user is displayed, sorted by UID. If a user has never logged in, `lastlog` displays "**Never logged in**"—this is what you should see for most of your system users. Note that you need to run this command as root.

```
# lastlog
Username      Port      From      Latest
root          tty1                Tue Apr 20 22:32:32 1999
bin                               **Never logged in**
daemon                            **Never logged in**
adm                               **Never logged in**
```

```
lp                              **Never logged in**
sync                            **Never logged in**
shutdown                        **Never logged in**
halt                            **Never logged in**
mail                            **Never logged in**
news                            **Never logged in**
uucp                            **Never logged in**
operator                        **Never logged in**
games                           **Never logged in**
gopher                          **Never logged in**
ftp                             **Never logged in**
nobody                          **Never logged in**
postgres                        **Never logged in**
alice          tty3             Tue Apr 20 22:32:32 1999
bob            tty2             Tue Apr 20 09:34:32 1999
carol          tty3             Thu Apr 15 19:50:05 1999
eve            tty3             Thu Apr 07 19:54:45 1999
mallory        tty3             Fri Mar 26 18:39:26 1999
trent          tty1             Tue Apr 20 08:15:49 1999
```

In the above example, lastlog reports on all users since the *last-log* file was created. The report can be restricted to a particular user with the "-u" flag—lastlog -u 102 will report on the user with UID 102. To restrict lastlog reporting to the past week, use the "-t" flag—lastlog -t 7

Logging Shutdowns

Some UNIX systems record system shutdowns and reboots in the *wtmp*. Others maintain a separate shutdown log that records use of the shutdown command. It's advisable to keep an eye out for suspicious shutdowns—an intruder who's editing system files can use a shutdown to initialize changes. The following example is taken from a HP-UX 11 system.

```
# cat /etc/shutdownlog
11:16  Sun Jan 10, 1999.  Halt: (by foo1.example.com!carol)
22:24  Sun Jan 10, 1999.  Reboot:
11:15  Mon Jan 11 1999.   Reboot after panic: Data page fault
11:53  Mon Jan 11 1999.   Reboot after panic: Data page fault
13:30  Mon Jan 11 1999.   Reboot after panic: Data page fault
14:37  Mon Jan 11 1999.   Reboot after panic: Data page fault
19:44  Tue Jan 12, 1999.  Reboot: (by foo1.example.com!carol)
19:40  Mon Jan 18, 1999.  Reboot: (by foo1.example.com!carol)
10:05  Fri Jan 22, 1999.  Reboot: (by foo1.example.com!carol)
14:07  Fri Jan 22, 1999.  Reboot: (by loopback!carol)
13:33  Sun Jan 31, 1999.  Reboot:
```

```
07:53  Tue Feb 02 1999.   Reboot after panic: Data page fault
21:48  Sun Mar 14, 1999.  Reboot: (by foo1.example.com!carol)
09:02  Thu Apr  8, 1999.  Reboot: (by foo1.example.com!carol)
13:16  Mon Apr 12 1999.   Reboot after panic: Data page fault
```

Process Accounting

UNIX can track each and every command run by each and every user. While this facility—known as process accounting—was originally intended to facilitate charging users for CPU time, it can be very useful for tracking down system problems. If you need to know who messed up those vital project files last night, the process accounting subsystem can tell you. It can also help track the activities of an intruder (or a malicious user), subject to two big caveats:

- A sophisticated attacker will attempt to delete or subvert the accounting file

- Process accounting tells what commands a user executed, but not the full command argument

The name and location of the processing accounting file varies in different versions of UNIX. It may be named *pacct* or *acct*. It may live in */var/log* (on Linux systems), */var/account*, */var/adm*, or */usr/adm*.

Turning Accounting On

Unlike connect-time logging, process accounting is not active by default—it must be started up. To turn on process accounting on a Linux or BSD-based box, run the accton command. You must do this as root. The accton command must be in the form: accton file. The file must already exist. First use the touch command to create the *pacct* file:

```
# touch /var/log/pacct
```

Then run accton:

```
# accton /var/log/pacct
```

Once accton is active, you can monitor the commands being executed on your system at any time with the lastcomm command.

To turn accounting off, run the `accton` command without any arguments.

The lastcomm Command

The `lastcomm` command reports on previously executed commands. With no arguments, `lastcomm` displays information about all the commands recorded during the current accounting file's lifetime, including the command name, the user, the tty, how much CPU time the command took to execute, and a timestamp. If a system has many users, the output can be quite long. The example below has been trimmed.

```
# lastcomm
w        S    dave     ttyp2      0.00 secs Tue Apr 20 19:22
ls            dave     ttyp2      0.00 secs Tue Apr 20 19:22
ls            dave     ttyp2      0.00 secs Tue Apr 20 19:22
csh      F    dave     ttyp2      0.00 secs Tue Apr 20 19:21
last          dave     ttyp2      0.00 secs Tue Apr 20 19:21
comsat        root     __         0.00 secs Tue Apr 20 19:14
ac            root     ttyp1      0.00 secs Tue Apr 20 19:17
sa            root     ttyp1      0.00 secs Tue Apr 20 19:17
man           root     ttyp1      0.00 secs Tue Apr 20 19:16
sh            root     ttyp1      0.00 secs Tue Apr 20 19:16
more          root     ttyp1      0.00 secs Tue Apr 20 19:16
uuxqt         uucp     ??         0.00 secs Tue Apr 20 19:17
uucico        uucp     ??         0.00 secs Tue Apr 20 19:15
sa            root     ttyp1      0.00 secs Tue Apr 20 19:16
users         dave     ttyp2      0.00 secs Tue Apr 20 19:16
w        S    dave     ttyp2      0.00 secs Tue Apr 20 19:15
who           dave     ttyp2      0.00 secs Tue Apr 20 19:15
sendmail F    list     __         0.00 secs Tue Apr 20 19:15
procmail S    dave     __         0.00 secs Tue Apr 20 19:15
uux      S    list     __         0.00 secs Tue Apr 20 19:15
procmail F    list     __         0.00 secs Tue Apr 20 19:15
sendmail F    list     __         0.00 secs Tue Apr 20 19:15
sh            list     __         0.00 secs Tue Apr 20 19:15
sendmail S    list     __         0.00 secs Tue Apr 20 19:15
sh            list     __         0.00 secs Tue Apr 20 19:15
sed           list     __         0.00 secs Tue Apr 20 19:15
cat           list     __         0.00 secs Tue Apr 20 19:15
```

> If you don't like `lastcomm`—or if it runs really slowly on your sys-   **Tip**
> tem—try the `spar` tool. See "spar" on page 194.

The sa Command

One problem with process accounting is that the *pacct* file can grow very quickly. Before long, it will consume hundreds of mega-bytes on a busy system. You need to run the `sa` command either interactively or via the *cron* mechanism to keep logging data from overwhelming your system.

The `sa` command reports on, cleans up, and generally maintains the process accounting file. It is able to condense the information in */var/log/pacct* into the summary files */var/log/savacct* and */var/log/usracct* (your path may vary). These summaries contain system statistics according to command name and username—by default, `sa` reads them before and in addition to the *pacct* file so that its reports include all available information.

The output of `sa` is a bit difficult to decipher. The following items are labelled:

- avio—Average number of I/O operations per execution

- cp—Sum of user and system time, in minutes

- cpu—Same as cp

- k—CPU-time averaged core usage, in 1k units

- k*sec—CPU storage integral, in 1k-core seconds

- re—Real time, in minutes

- s—System time, in minutes

- tio—Total number of I/O operations

- u—User time, in minutes

The example `sa` output below was taken from a busy BSD-based mail server.

```
# sa
> sa
9853   196076.40re    0.01cp    15avio    0k
```

```
    6    14354.58re    0.01cp      27avio    0k    csh
    6        0.01re    0.00cp       1avio    0k    hostname
   14        0.24re    0.00cp      14avio    0k    sa
   15        0.28re    0.00cp       2avio    0k    ac
    3        0.02re    0.00cp       4avio    0k    mailDBupda
  505      525.55re    0.00cp      48avio    0k    uucico
  793        0.79re    0.00cp       0avio    0k    uuname
 2205       65.87re    0.00cp       1avio    0k    sh
  795       26.06re    0.00cp      15avio    0k    sendmail
  661       22.45re    0.00cp       1avio    0k    rmail
 1953     4480.67re    0.00cp       6avio    0k    sendmail*
  534       33.71re    0.00cp      17avio    0k    uuxqt
   48        1.19re    0.00cp      41avio    0k    MailFetch
  395       15.68re    0.00cp       7avio    0k    procmail
   89        0.21re    0.00cp       1avio    0k    formail
   13        0.10re    0.00cp       1avio    0k    cat
   20        1.29re    0.00cp       2avio    0k    multigram
   66        0.47re    0.00cp       1avio    0k    sh*
   13        0.05re    0.00cp       1avio    0k    sed
   21        0.03re    0.00cp       3avio    0k    rm
    4     4441.60re    0.00cp      43avio    0k    cron*
    3        0.00re    0.00cp       2avio    0k    expr
    7        0.01re    0.00cp       1avio    0k    date
   40        2.57re    0.00cp       7avio    0k    procmail*
  236        6.51re    0.00cp      19avio    0k    uux
    2        0.00re    0.00cp       1avio    0k    who
    8        0.05re    0.00cp       6avio    0k    w
    6       16.27re    0.00cp    5155avio    0k    find
    6        0.04re    0.00cp       2avio    0k    grep
    2        0.97re    0.00cp      29avio    0k    man
   98      271.19re    0.00cp       1avio    0k    comsat
    2        0.01re    0.00cp       4avio    0k    tset
    2        0.00re    0.00cp       2avio    0k    csh*
    9        0.13re    0.00cp      18avio    0k    ls
    4        0.00re    0.00cp       1avio    0k    stty
    2        0.05re    0.00cp       5avio    0k    su.nowheel
  267        0.89re    0.00cp       8avio    0k    uupoll
  189        1.95re    0.00cp      12avio    0k    mail*
    2        0.00re    0.00cp       2avio    0k    whoami
  189        5.64re    0.00cp       7avio    0k    mail
  258        0.62re    0.00cp       5avio    0k    atrun
   32        0.01re    0.00cp       0avio    0k    uucico*
    2        0.00re    0.00cp       3avio    0k    chmod
    2        0.00re    0.00cp       2avio    0k    touch
  259     7596.80re    0.00cp      23avio    0k    appnmail
    3        0.02re    0.00cp       2avio    0k    mkdirs
    3     3590.81re    0.00cp    1652avio    0k    Mail
    3        0.04re    0.00cp      13avio    0k    nidump
```

```
  6    26649.60re    0.00cp      5avio    0k    nfsd*
 31    98434.84re    0.00cp    870avio    0k    ***other
  6        0.07re    0.00cp     30avio    0k    cp
  7     4435.22re    0.00cp      5avio    0k    tail
  2     4441.62re    0.00cp     83avio    0k    autonfsmo*
  2     8883.20re    0.00cp     16avio    0k    lpd*
  4    17766.40re    0.00cp      0avio    0k    biod*
```

The sa facility can also provide summary reports organized by user, rather than command. Use the "-m" flag as shown in the example below.

```
# sa -m
root       1403     0.00cpu     65374tio     0k*sec
agent       151     0.00cpu      2611tio     0k*sec
uucp       7068     0.00cpu     57712tio     0k*sec
list        370     0.00cpu      1289tio     0k*sec
bob          40     0.01cpu       926tio     0k*sec
dave        821     0.00cpu     17699tio     0k*sec
```

> System V systems have a slightly different process accounting sys- **Tip**
> tem. Accounting is turned on with the startup command (in
> */usr/lib/acct/startup*). The accounting file is usually
> */var/adm/pacct*—it is accessed using the acctcom command (rather
> than the lastcomm command described above).

The syslog Facility

In many respects, the development of UNIX and UNIX clone systems has been somewhat haphazard. At no point did a dedicated software engineer sit down, plan, and implement an overall logging scheme. To this we owe the ascendancy of the *syslog* facility——a general purpose logging facility that was originally developed at the University of California Berkeley as part of the sendmail program. Over the years, *syslog* has been adapted for many logging functions and ported to many UNIX systems including those based on System V and Linux. Even more than the extensive connect-time and process accounting systems described earlier in this chapter, it casts a wide net of protection—any program can log events via syslog. In turn, *syslog* can log to the system console, can write to a file or a device, or can send a message to a user. It can log events locally or on another host over a network.

The *syslog* facility is based on two key elements: */etc/syslogd* (the daemon) and the */etc/syslog.conf* configuration file. By convention, most syslog messages are written to the messages file, which lives in either the */var/adm* or */var/log* directories, though they can be written anywhere.

A typical *syslog* record cites the name of the generating program and a text message. It also includes a Facility (a categorization of the source of the message) and a Priority ranging from "info" (informational) to "emerg" (an emergency)—these are critical to *syslog* behavior but typically don't appear in the logs.

Facilities

Each syslog message is assigned to one of the following major facilities:

- LOG_AUTH—The authorization system: *login*, su, *getty*, etc.

- LOG_AUTHPRIV—The same as LOG_AUTH, but logged to a file readable only by selected individuals

- LOG_CRON—The *cron* daemon

- LOG_DAEMON—Other system daemons, such as *routed*

- LOG_FTP—The file transfer protocol daemons: *ftpd*, *tftpd*

- LOG_KERN—Messages generated by the kernel (as opposed to user processes)

- LOG_LPR—The line printer spooling system: *lpr*, *lpd*

- LOG_MAIL—The mail system

- LOG_NEWS—The network news system

- LOG_SYSLOG—Messages generated internally by *syslogd(8)*

- LOG_USER—Messages generated by random user processes; the default facility if none is specified

- LOG_UUCP—The UUCP system

- LOG_LOCAL0...LOG_LOCAL7—Reserved for local use

Syslog Priorities

The *syslog* daemon assigns one of several different priority levels to
each event:

- LOG_EMERG—A panic condition (normally broadcast to all
  users)

- LOG_ALERT—A condition that should be corrected immediately, such as a corrupted system database

- LOG_CRIT—Critical conditions, e.g., hard drive errors

- LOG_ERR—Errors

- LOG_WARNING—Warning messages

- LOG_NOTICE—Conditions that are not error conditions, but
  might require special handling

- LOG_INFO—Informational messages

- LOG_DEBUG—Messages that contain information normally
  of use only when debugging a program

syslog.conf

The *syslog.conf* file specifies the logging behavior of the *syslogd*
program, which consults the configuration file when it starts up.
Most UNIX systems ship with a reasonable baseline of *syslog.conf*
settings. Nonetheless, it's a system administrator's duty to review
these settings to ensure that the level of logging is appropriate and
consistent with security policy.

The file consists of individual entries for different programs or
message categories, each on its own line. For each message category, a selector field and an action field are presented. These fields
are separated by a tab:

- the selector field specifies the types of messages (facilities) and
  priorities

- the action field specifies the action to be taken if a message syslogd receives matches the selection criteria

Tip

> Old versions of *syslog.conf* require that tabs separate the fields, not spaces. Newer versions will accept either tabs or spaces. Use tabs if you wish to maintain backward compatibility.

Each selector is composed of a paired facility and priority. As noted in the bulleted list above, the facility can one of the following: auth, authpriv, cron, daemon, ftp, kern, lpr, mail, news, syslog, user, uucp, and local0 through local7. The priority can be one of emerg, alert, crit, err, warning, notice, info, and debug.

When you specify a priority, *syslogd* will log a message whenever that priority or a higher one is generated. So if you specify level "crit," all messages marked crit, alert, or emerg will be logged. Note that the list in the previous section is in priority order.

The action field of each line specifies where a message should be sent when the selector field selects a given message. It takes one of five forms:

- a pathname (preceded by "/")—selected messages are appended to the specified file or device

- a hostname (preceded by "@")—selected messages are forwarded to the *syslog* daemon on the named host

- a list of users (comma delimited)—selected messages are written to those users (if they are logged in)

- an asterisk—selected messages are written to all logged-in users

- a command (preceded by a vertical bar ("|")—selected messages are piped

If, for example, you want to log all mail messages into a single file, the following line would be appropriate (the "#" indicates a comment):

```
# Log all the mail messages in one place.
mail.*      /var/log/maillog
```

The syntax is fairly straightforward—for all mail messages (mail.*), write to the file */var/log/maillog*.

Other facilities (programs) also get their own logs. The UUCP and news facilities can generate a lot of extraneous messages. It makes sense to store them in their own log (say, */var/log/spooler*) and restrict logging to level "err" or higher.

```
# Save mail and news errors of level err and higher in a
# special file.
uucp,news.err     /var/log/spooler
```

When an emergency message comes down the pike (*.emerg), you want all your users to get it. Plus, you want your dedicated loghost (foo7.example.com) to receive and store it.

```
# Everybody gets emergency messages, plus log them on
# another machine.
*.emerg      *
*.emerg      @foo7.example.com
```

Alert messages should be written both to root and to Alice's personal account.

```
# Root and Alice get alert and higher messages.
*.alert     root,alice
```

Sometimes *syslogd* will produce too much information. The kernel (the "kern" facility), for example, can be verbose. You might want to log kernel messages to */dev/console,* or you might want to suppress reporting them altogether. In the example below, the line specifying kernel logging is commented out.

```
# Log all kernel messages to the console.
# Logging much else clutters up the screen.
#kern.*     /dev/console
```

You can specify all facilities in one line. The example below sends everything of level info or higher to */var/log/messages,* except for mail (mail.none). The level "none" disables a facility.

```
# Log anything (except mail) of level info or higher.
# Don't log private authentication messages!
*.info;mail.none;authpriv.none     /var/log/messages
```

Logging Everywhere

Setting up logging is not trivial. Logging policy needs to be an integral part of an overall security plan, so that an adequate audit trail is maintained. You need to preserve the integrity and availability of logs, and decide where they will be kept. Given the relatively low-cost of hard disks and the ubiquity of LANs, it makes sense for substantial installations to be generous in both what is captured and where it is kept. One way to improve availability is to send log messages to multiple devices and hosts.

With a network of any size, it makes sense to send significant messages to one or more dedicated loghosts—security-enhanced machines that do nothing but accept incoming *syslog* messages. Even if a given system is compromised, you may still be able to trust the dedicated loghosts it's been reporting to. Ideally, a dedicated loghost doesn't have any user accounts, and all unnecessary services should be turned off.

In some situations, it makes senses to log to a printer. A network intruder who's compromised a system may be able to cover his or her tracks by altering log files. But it's tough to hack old-fashioned hard copy. This trick was used by Cliff Stoll to track down intruders who were able to alter online log files. Some nights he'd sleep right next to the log printer just in case it ran out of paper. This points to a vulnerability of printer logging—printers have a tendency to run out of supplies or jam. Don't depend on a printer as a sole logging target.

In general, be generous with logging. The more places you send messages to be logged, the more difficult it becomes for an attacker or intruder to erase evidence. The following *syslog.conf* entries will log all messages to a loghost (foo7) and all authentication messages to a printer attached to the local host at */dev/ttya:*

```
auth.*     /dev/ttya
*.*        @foo7.example.com
```

Protecting Syslog

The *syslog* facility is an obvious target for an attacker or intruder. A system that maintains logs for other hosts is particularly vulnerable to denial of service attacks—an attacker could subvert *syslogd* by sending it more messages than it can handle, or by sending gigabytes of *syslog* messages, thus filling the target's disk.

Some versions of UNIX include *syslog* daemons that have been extended with security safeguards. FreeBSD, for example, allows you to launch syslogd in "secure mode"—the "-s" flag tells *syslogd* not to accept any log messages from remote hosts. FreeBSD also allows you to precisely control incoming messages by using the "allowed peer" argument (the "-a" flag)—this allows you to specify the IP addresses and ports that can log to your system.

The logger Command

UNIX is full of small single-purpose programs. The `logger` utility, for example, is very handy. It does one thing and one thing only: it provides a shell command interface to the *syslog(3)* system log module so that you can make entries in the system log.

The syntax is simple: `logger <message>`

If Alice issues a command like

```
$ logger This is the end of the world
```

it will produce a syslog record that looks like this:

```
Apr 23 15:36:49 foo alice: This is the end of the world
```

> **Never fully trust log entries. As the logger example above shows, it's all too easy for fun-loving users or attackers to spoof critical logs.**   **Caution**

Program Logs

A variety of programs maintain logs that reflect the security status of your system. All, some, or none of the following may be active in all, some, or none of your systems, depending on the versions of UNIX you're running.

sulog

Since the substitute user (`su`) command allows one user to obtain the privileges of another, it's security-sensitive. Some UNIX systems keep a log of `su` attempts: */var/adm/sulog;* others make an entry in the *syslog*.

It's a good idea to monitor failed su attempts, particularly those aimed at the root account. The *sulog* contains the date and time of su attempts, the terminal used, and both the su'ing user and the target user. In the example below, alice has su'ed to various users, including root.

```
# cat sulog | more
SU 03/18 21:49 + t3 alice-root
SU 03/26 10:48 + 1 alice-carol
SU 03/26 10:48 + 1 alice-dave
SU 04/16 12:38 + t2 alice-mallory
SU 04/16 12:38 + t2 alice-trent
```

sudolog

The sudo command allows a regular user to issue commands as root. It's considered excellent system administration practice to use the sudo command for routine tasks instead of constantly logging in as root. This command is particularly handy for systems that have more than one user with administrative responsibility—if several people have the root password, there's no easy way to track operator errors.

Each command issued via sudo is logged along with a timestamp, the username of the user that executed sudo, and the working directory the command was issued from. As you can see from the *sudolog* example below, Carol has been doing some serious sysadmin work on host foo1 using her carol account rather than root.

```
Apr  8 09:00:48 foo1 sudo:    carol : PWD=/home/carol ; COM-
MAND=/usr/bin/vi /etc/resolv.conf
Apr  8 09:01:05 foo1 sudo:    carol : PWD=/ ;
COMMAND=/sbin/shutdown -r now
Apr 10 20:36:16 foo1 sudo:    carol : PWD=/etc ;
COMMAND=/usr/bin/vi hosts
Apr 11 11:25:00 foo1 sudo:    carol : PWD=/home/carol/bin ;
COMMAND=/usr/bin/vi stress-dns.pl
Apr 12 15:51:03 foo1 sudo:    carol : PWD=/home/carol ; COM-
MAND=/usr/sbin/useradd
```

uucp logs

The UUCP facility may be obsolete in an age where IP packets are everywhere, but there are still many systems running Unix-to-Unix

Copy Programs (see "UUCP" on page 300). These programs generate several specialized log files. Some of them are quite prosaic, like this excerpt from a */usr/spool/uucp/SYSLOG*:

```
daemon uufoo (4/22-19:28) (924834526.26) received data 4271 bytes 6.08 secs
daemon uufoo (4/22-19:28) (924834527.31) received data 230 bytes 0.50 secs
daemon uufoo (4/22-19:29) (924834543.08) received data 10154 bytes  15.10 secs
agent uufoo (4/22-19:30) (924834608.09) sent data 4816 bytes 6.32 secs
agent uufoo (4/22-19:30) (924834609.13) sent data 91 bytes 0.00 secs
uucp uufoo (4/22-19:30) (924834612.54) sent data 335 bytes 0.01 secs
uucp uufoo (4/22-19:30) (924834613.70) sent data 83 bytes 0.00 secs
```

httpd logs

Web server software like Apache maintains detailed logs about web traffic. These may contain important marketing information (who's viewing your pages) and technical information (there's a broken link that's producing a "404" error).

Apache produces two logs: an *access_log* and an *error_log*. You can specify where these logs are kept; by default, they live in the directory */usr/local/etc/httpd/logs*.

The *access_log* contains the following for each HTTP request:

- Name or IP address of the remote host that made the request

- Remote login name, if any, or "-" if none

- Remote username, if any or "-" if none

- Time that the request was received

- HTTP command that was executed (usually GET)

- Status code (200 is "OK"; 304 is "Not Modified"; 404 is "Not Found"; etc.)

- Number of bytes transferred

Some servers use an extended record format that also includes the "referrer"—an indication of where the page view came from (usually a link at another web site.)

In the sample *access_log* below, you can see that several "GET" requests are answered from various hosts. Note that the last line contains a 404 error due to a spelling mistake.

```
flx1-ppp41.lvdi.net - - [21/Apr/1999:17:39:26 -0700] "GET
/millennium/prologue.html HTTP/1.1" 200 40115
cache-rc01.proxy.aol.com - - [21/Apr/1999:17:40:28 -0700]
"GET /netiquette/ HTTP/1.0" 200 9000
204.84.224.60 - - [21/Apr/1999:17:40:29 -0700] "GET
/netiquette/ HTTP/1.0" 200 9000
cache-rb01.proxy.aol.com - - [21/Apr/1999:17:40:29 -0700]
"GET /netiquette/nqback.gif HTTP/1.0" 200 1055
grape.cslab.vt.edu - - [21/Apr/1999:17:41:15 -0700] "GET
/netiquette/book/TOC0963702513.html HTTP/1.0" 304 -
scooby.northernlight.com - - [21/Apr/1999:17:41:24 -0700]
"GET /blake/indx.html HTTP/1.1" 404 -
```

Unless you're running a web site with restricted access, the *access_log* is not security-sensitive (though sometimes you may find that the competition or some other opponent is checking your stuff out). There are numerous tools for analyzing log data ways to glean important statistical information from these records.

Logging Tools Survey

chklastlog

This tool checks the file */var/adm/lastlog* file for deleted information by cross-checking it against */var/adm/wtmp* for inconsistencies. The program will complain about user IDs with logins recorded in *wtmp* but not in *lastlog*.

To download:

```
ftp://coast.cs.purdue.edu/pub/tools/unix/chklastlog/
```

chkwtmp

This small tool checks the file */var/adm/wtmp* for overwritten information. If an entry overwritten with zero's is found, the timestamps for the entries before and after the deleted entry are printed, indicating the window of time when the deletion was made:

```
5 deletion(s) between Sat Apr 24 18:36:29 1999 and Sat Apr
24 21:51:02 1999
```

This can come in handy if you suspect that one of your users is using a tool like Zap to defeat the logging mechanism (see "Zap" on page 195). Note that you may need adjust the path to the *wtmp* file. This tool is available on the accompanying CD-ROM.

To download:

`ftp://coast.cs.purdue.edu/pub/tools/unix/chkwtmp/`

dump_lastlog

This Perl program dumps the lastlog file for SunOS/Solaris systems (it works on both).

To download:

`ftp://coast.cs.purdue.edu/pub/tools/unix/dump_lastlog.Z`

HostSentry

HostSentry is part of the Abacus suite. It monitors the connect-time accounting records (*wtmp/utmp*) for user login activity. It requires that the Python programming language be installed. This is alpha software at the time of this writing (version 0.02).

For more information:

`http://www.psionic.com/abacus/hostsentry/`

Logcheck

The Logcheck tool by Craig Rowland is designed to look for security violations and unusual activity in log files and send email alert messages. It can be set to either 1) report everything you tell it to specifically look for via keywords, or 2) report everything you didn't tell it to ignore via keywords. Thus, you can look for specific "attack signatures" (BAD SU root) or for any unusual messages (those you haven't filtered). Logcheck utilizes a nifty little program called logtail that remembers the last position it read from in a log file and uses this position on subsequent runs to process new information. In fact, it may be worth installing this package for logtail alone. It's a clone of the *frequentcheck.sh* script from the Trusted Information Systems Gauntlet firewall package. Like HostSentry, Logcheck is part of the Abacus suite of security tools.

For more information:

`http://www.psionic.com/abacus/logcheck/`

loginlog

This is a small program that tails the *wtmp* file and reports all logins to the *syslogd*.

To download:

`ftp://coast.cs.purdue.edu/pub/tools/unix/loginlog.c`

spar

The spar (Show Process Accounting Records) tool is used to select records from a UNIX process accounting file. It is usually faster than `lastcomm` and significantly more flexible and powerful.

For more information:

`ftp://coast.cs.purdue.edu/pub/tools/unix/TAMU/spar.README`

To download:

`ftp://coast.cs.purdue.edu/pub/tools/unix/TAMU/`
`spar-1.2.tar.gz`

surrogate-syslog

This tool by Wietse Venema is a *syslog* facility for systems that have no *syslog* library. It logs directly to a file (default */usr/spool/mqueue/syslog*).

To download:

`ftp://coast.cs.purdue.edu/pub/tools/unix/surrogate/`

Swatch

This "simple watcher" monitors log files. It's available on the accompanying CD-ROM.

For more information see "Swatch" on page 197.

syslog-ng

This "next generation" *syslogd* is designed to replace the *syslogd* that ships with Solaris, BSDi, and Linux (as well as other UNIX systems). It features a digital "fingerprinting" of log information. It generates and stores SHA-1 hash values alongside the actual log file. These hash values protect the integrity of logged information in transit (for more on SHA, see page 127). This kind of protection could be vital if log files are placed in evidence during legal proceedings. At the time of this writing, syslog-ng is still fairly experimental. It will be interesting to see if it's further developed and incorporated as the default syslog in various UNIX distributions.

For more information:

`http://www.balabit.hu/products/syslog-ng.html`

tklogger

The tklogger tool by Doug Hughes monitors logs created by *syslog* (or other logging mechanisms). No special files or interface to *sys-*

log are needed because it works on plain text files and watches for updates to the file specified. The monitored events are user configurable and based either upon file type, pattern matching, or a mixture of the two. The events are color coded.

For more information:

```
ftp://coast.cs.purdue.edu/pub/tools/unix/tklogger/
```

```
ftp://ftp.eng.auburn.edu/pub/doug/tklogger
```

Trimlog

Trimlog by David A. Curry is used to trim system log files to keep them from growing without bound. When invoked, it reads commands from the file %CONFIG% which tell it which files to trim, how to trim them, and by how much they should be trimmed.

To download:

```
ftp://coast.cs.purdue.edu/pub/tools/unix/trimlog/
```

Watcher

Watcher by Kenneth Ingham is a configurable and extensible system monitoring tool that issues a number of user-specified commands, parses the output, checks for items of significance, and reports them to the system administrator.

To download:

```
ftp://coast.cs.purdue.edu/pub/tools/unix/Watcher.tar.Z
```

Zap

The handy Zap tool does one thing well: it wipes out connect-time login data for a specified user. To zero out *wtmp*, *utmp*, and *lastlog* entries for mallory, the command Zap mallory will work—the finger command will subsequently report that Mallory "Never logged in" as shown in this example (which has trimmed finger output):

```
# finger mallory
... On since Sun Apr 25 20:50 (PDT) on tty5  29 seconds
idle
# ./Zap mallory
Zap!
# finger mallory
... Never logged in.
```

If you're tracking an intruder, you can mask yourself from *lastlog* and *wtmp* so that the intruder doesn't know he or she is being watched. You need to be root to run Zap—unprivileged users should not have access. To compile, `cc -O Zap.c -o zap`. Note that you may need to edit the pathnames to the *wtmp*, *utmp*, and *lastlog* files (*/var/log/wtmp*, */var/run/utmp*, and */var/log/lastlog* in Red Hat Linux). This tool is available on the accompanying CD-ROM.

   To download:

```
ftp://coast.cs.purdue.edu/pub/tools/unix/zap.tar.gz
```

## 09

Swatch

UNIX log files provide an avalanche of information. The Swatch tool can be used to reduce the plethora of log records to actionable items. It monitors *syslog* messages as they're written to log files and takes pre-configured actions (e.g., call my pager number) in response to patterns (e.g., evidence that someone is repeatedly trying to login as root). This chapter covers how to install, configure, and run Swatch both for real-time log monitoring and log file auditing.

Introduction

Monitoring is an onerous task for UNIX system administrators, particularly for those who are responsible for the security status of large numbers of hosts. Even a modestly busy server will produce thousands of lines of logging information each day, testing the ability of any one person to sift through it all. It's not surprising that logs are often ignored or used only for auditing purposes after a break-in or security compromise has occurred.

Swatch (the Simple WATCHer) is designed to ease the burden of monitoring and auditing log files. The authors of the program describe managing a facility with a dozen servers and 50 client machines, all of which reported to a single logmaster host—important log messages were getting lost in the chaff. They developed Swatch to sift through the logs and take simple actions in response to reported events (i.e., detected patterns). They had four goals in mind for the program:

- It should be easy to use

- It should support a simple set of actions that could be taken in response to certain messages

- It should support customization by users so they can define their own actions

- It should be reconfigurable on demand without manual intervention[1]

Swatch, the resulting Perl-based program they created, has been widely deployed over the years and further developed by author Todd Atkins. It has become a standard fixture at many UNIX sites, including some large installations. As one sysadmin at Lockheed Martin Astronautics points out: "Swatch is something we REALLY use in a REAL world environment ..."[2] It's become so

---

1. Stephen E. Hansen and E. Todd Atkins, Stanford University. "Automated System Monitoring and Notification with Swatch," 1993 LISA Conference. A Postscript version of this paper is included with the Swatch distribution. Or see
http://www.stanford.edu/~atkins/swatch/lisa93.html
2. Alek Komarnitsky, Swatch: Automated UNIX System Monitoring & Notification. See
http://www.komar.org/komar/alek/pres/swatch/cover.html

"mainstream" that it's bundled with some systems—Red Hat Linux, for example, includes an easy-to-install RPM package for Swatch.

> The log file monitoring and auditing capabilities of a tool like Swatch should be included in every UNIX and Linux distribution—if they're not, ask your vendor why. **Tip**

Overview of Swatch

Swatch can be used in one of three ways. It was originally written to actively monitor messages as they are written to a log file via the UNIX *syslog* utility. It can also be used for auditing—that is, reviewing and checking a log file in a single pass. Finally, it can accept input from a program—this is handy for checking process accounting logs that aren't kept as plain text. These three ways to run Swatch—along with relevant options—are more fully described in "Running Swatch" on page 209.

> While designed for *syslog*, Swatch can monitor any log file, including connect-time records, sulog, web access logs, etc. **Tip**

Regardless of how Swatch is run, the tool is dependent on two critical items: event patterns and corresponding actions, both of which are specified in a *.swatchrc* configuration file.

Patterns
Swatch can act on a wide variety of recorded log events because it matches regular expressions or keywords as they appear in log entries; "reboot," "Filesystem Full," "BAD SU," and "yourcompetitor.com" are all patterns that may require action. Swatch will accept any regular expression that's compatible with Perl, which behaves like the egrep program, which, in turn, was built on the grep program.

> For more on regular expressions as they're used in Swatch, consult the man pages for egrep (or grep) and perl. **Tip**

Actions

In accordance with specifications in the *.swatchrc* configuration file, Swatch watches for particular patterns of events, from bad logins to system halts, and takes one of the following actions:

- echo—displays the message, with either inverted or bold text

- bell—displays the message and sounds the system bell

- mail—mails the message to the user running Swatch

- exec—executes a command or script

- pipe—pipes a message to a program

- write—uses the write command to notify users

- ignore—does nothing

The Swatch Configuration File

The operation of Swatch is set by a relatively simple configuration file that contains four Tab-separated fields:

```
/pattern/[,/pattern/,...]      action[,action,...]
[[HH:]MM:]SS    start:length
```

The first two fields—pattern and action—are the most critical. The pattern is a regular expression to be matched. It's enclosed by forward-slashes ("/"). If you want to track the activities of the user Mallory, the pattern "/mallory/" will catch all log entries that mention him. If you want to see all *inetd* messages, "/inetd/" picks them up. A "*" indicates that the preceding item will be matched zero or more times. Two regular expressions may be joined by a pipe "|"—the resulting regular expression matches any string containing either subexpression. The pattern "/(panic|halt)/" will match either panic or halt.

The action consists of one of the bulleted items above: echo, bell, mail, exec, pipe, write, or ignore. The most common action is to echo the message. The appearance of the echoed text can be further specified by any of the keywords: normal, bold, underscore, blink, or inverse—although some terminals don't support bold, underscore, or blink.

> If you're running Red Hat Linux and bash, the bold, underscore and blink modes won't work. You're stuck with normal (the default) or inverse, which gives the message emphasis.

Caution

The bell action (bell=*n*) rings the system bell for *n* number of times. Urgent messages can set the bell to ring several times. The bell is handy for those moments when you're in the office but away from the terminal running Swatch—set it to ring three times, for example, whenever there are three failed logins to the root account.

The echo and bell actions are well-represented in the "Personal Swatch configuration file" included in the Swatch 2.2 distribution. It's set to echo bad logins and logging errors in inverse mode and ring the bell three times on important events. Other items—like sendmail, news, network time—are ignored. For the most part, kernel problems ("file system full") also ring bells.

Listing 9.1 *A Personal Swatch Configuration File*

```
#
# Personal Swatch configuration file
#

# Alert me of bad login attempts and find out who is
# on that system
/INVALID|REPEATED|INCOMPLETE/       echo=inverse,bell=3

# Important program errors
/LOGIN/                             echo=inverse,bell=3
/passwd/                            echo=bold,bell=3
/ruserok/                           echo=bold,bell=3

# Ignore this stuff
/sendmail/,/nntp/,/xntp|ntpd/,/faxspooler/      ignore

# Report unusual tftp info
/tftpd.*(ncd|kfps|normal exit)/     ignore
/tftpd/                             echo,bell=3
```

```
# Kernel problems
/(panic|halt|SunOS Release)/          echo=bold,bell
/file system full/                    echo=bold,bell=3
/vmunix.*(at|on)/                     ignore
/vmunix/                              echo,bell

/fingerd.*(root|[Tt]ip|guest)/        echo,bell=3
/atkins/                              echo=inverse,bell=3

/su:/                                 echo=bold
/.*/                                  echo
```

Note how the author matches his username. It's not a bad idea to track activity on your own account. The last line uses a wild card to echo everything not specified above.

The "personal" *.swatchrc* won't be sufficient if you're responsible for a critical server or a cluster of servers. Important servers need to be monitored around the clock, and immediate action needs to be taken if they're in danger of going down. The Swatch distribution includes a more aggressive sample *.swatchrc* for constant monitoring (*swatchrc.monitor*). Here, stronger actions are taken. In some cases, mail is sent. With repeated bad login attempts, a script is executed that fingers the user attempting the logins. A system crash executes a script that pages the sysadmin.

In Listing 9.2, I've forced action items to a second line where both pattern and action wouldn't fit on a single line.

Listing 9.2 *A Swatch Configuration File for Servers*

```
#
# Swatch configuration file for constant monitoring
#

# Bad login attempts
/INVALID|REPEATED|INCOMPLETE/
     echo,bell=3,exec="/eecf/adm/bin/badloginfinger $0"

# Machine room temperature
/WizMON/
     echo=inverse,bell

# System crashes and halts
/(Gordon-Biersch|Anchor)/&&/(panic|halt)/
     echo,bell,mail,exec="call_pager 3667615 0911"
/(isl|coffee)/&&/(panic|halt)/
     echo,bell,mail,exec="call_pager 3667615 1911"
```

```
/Sierra/&&/(panic|halt)/
     echo,bell,mail,exec="call_pager 3667615 2911"
/(gloworm|stjames)/&&/(panic|halt)/
     echo,bell,mail,exec="call_pager 3667615 3911"
/(osiris|shemesh)/&&/(panic|halt)/
     echo,bell,mail,exec="call_pager 3667615 4911"
/(panic|halt)/                echo,bell,mail

# System reboots
/(gloworm|stjames)/&&/SunOS Release/
     echo,bell,mail,exec="call_pager 3667615 3411"
/(osiris|shemesh)/&&/SunOS Release/
     echo,bell,mail,exec="call_pager 3667615 4411"
/(Gordon-Biersch|Anchor)/&&/SunOS Release/
     echo,bell,mail,exec="call_pager 3667615 0411"
/Sierra/&&/SunOS Release/
     echo,bell,mail,exec="call_pager 3667615 2411"
/(isl|coffee)/&&/SunOS Release/
     echo,bell,mail,exec="call_pager 3667615 1411"
/SunOS Release/               echo,bell,mail
```

> **The sample configuration files included with Swatch 2.2 are writ-** **Caution**
> **ten for a machine running SunOS. You will need to customize**
> **these files for your particular system and system configuration.**

The third and fourth fields in a *.swatchrc* entry help minimize and control redundant messages. The optional third field can contain a time interval, which should be specified in one of three formats:

- SS—Just seconds

- MM:SS—Minutes and seconds

- HH:MM:SS—Hours, minutes and seconds

When an interval is included, Swatch will wait before it takes action on identical patterns for the specified amount of time. It then reports on multiple instances of the pattern, citing the number of occurences since last notification (in the form "40 seen in 01:00:00"). This important setting can be used to restrict a flood of distracting items that otherwise might drown out critical patterns.

The fourth field is also optional and must only exist if the time interval is specified. It specifies the location of the timestamp in the log message as well as the length of the timestamp. It's specified in the form "start:length."

Major 3.0 Changes

As of this writing, Atkins has released a beta version of Swatch version 3. While this new version is not finished, it appears to be a significant upgrade. The configuration file has a completely different format, although you can still use your old configuration files if you use the "--old-style-config" switch.

The good news is that the author re-wrote a lot of the code to take advantage of features and modules available with Perl 5. Version 3 requires Perl 5 and the following modules:

- Time::HiRes

- Date::Calc

- File::Tail

Of these, the File::Tail module fulfills a critical role—it replaces the UNIX `tail` command for monitoring files.

Tip

> You can download the latest Swatch 3 at the URL
> `ftp://ftp.stanford.edu/general/security-tools/swatch/`
> If your Perl installation doesn't include the needed modules, you
> can download them at `http://www.cpan.org`

Version 3 also adds the seven colors that color terminals recognize, each of which can be used to mark a particular type of event.

Installing Swatch

Swatch 2.2 is available from numerous sources. If you're running Red Hat Linux, a Swatch RPM package is included in the main distribution. For other UNIX and Linux systems, I suggest that you download Swatch from the main Swatch archive at:

`ftp://ftp.stanford.edu/general/security-tools/swatch/`

As of this writing, a beta version of Swatch 3 is available at the above URL.

You can also find Swatch on the accompanying CD-ROM.

To install the RPM package, issue a command like:

```
# rpm -i swatch-2.2-7.noarch.rpm
```

It will copy and install the following files:

```
/usr/bin/swatch
/usr/doc/swatch-2.2
/usr/doc/swatch-2.2/Changes
/usr/doc/swatch-2.2/README
/usr/doc/swatch-2.2/config_files
/usr/doc/swatch-2.2/config_files/swatchrc.monitor
/usr/doc/swatch-2.2/config_files/swatchrc.personal
/usr/doc/swatch-2.2/config_files/syslog.conf-client
/usr/doc/swatch-2.2/config_files/syslog.conf-master
/usr/doc/swatch-2.2/config_files/syslog.conf-server
/usr/doc/swatch-2.2/lisa93_paper.ps
/usr/lib/sw_actions.pl
/usr/lib/sw_history.pl
/usr/man/man5/swatch.5
/usr/man/man8/swatch.8
```

Once this is done, you're ready to run. Type the default command: `swatch`

To install the tarball version, decompress like this:

```
# gunzip swatch-2.2.tar.gz
```

then, extract the archive.

```
# tar xvof swatch-2.2.tar
```

This will create a swatch-2.2 subdirectory with the following contents:

```
swatch-2.2/
swatch-2.2/Changes
swatch-2.2/Contents
swatch-2.2/README
swatch-2.2/config_files/
swatch-2.2/config_files/syslog.conf-master
swatch-2.2/config_files/syslog.conf-server
swatch-2.2/config_files/swatchrc.personal
swatch-2.2/config_files/swatchrc.monitor
swatch-2.2/config_files/syslog.conf-client
swatch-2.2/install.pl
swatch-2.2/install.sh
swatch-2.2/lisa93_paper.ps
swatch-2.2/sw_actions.pl
```

```
swatch-2.2/sw_history.pl
swatch-2.2/swatch.pl
swatch-2.2/swatch.conf.man
swatch-2.2/swatch.prog.man
swatch-2.2/utils/
swatch-2.2/utils/call_pager.pl
swatch-2.2/utils/badloginfinger.pl
```

Change directory to it (cd swatch-2.2) and run the script
sh.install.sh. The install script will prompt you to answer nine
questions about your system's configuration and how you want to
install Swatch:

```
# sh install.sh
Enter the directory where swatch
is to be installed (default '/usr/local/etc')
What user should own the installed swatch files?
 (default 'root')
What group should own the installed swatch files?
 (default 'wheel')
What should the permissions be for the installed swatch
script?
 (default '755')
What should the permissions be for the installed swatch
libraries and man pages?
 (default '444')
Enter the name of the directory where the
perl library files are located (default
'/usr/local/lib/perl') /usr/lib/perl5
Enter the name of the directory where you wish to
install the swatch library files (default '/usr/lib/perl5')
What directory should the swatch man pages be installed
(default '/usr/local/man')
What should the extension be for the swatch program manual
page? (default '8')
What should the extension be for the swatch configuration
file manual page? (default '5')
Here is what I have...
     Perl library: /usr/lib/perl5
     Swatch binary location: /usr/local/etc
     Swatch manual page location: /usr/local/man
     Swatch program manual page extention: 8
     Swatch configuration file manual page extention: 5
     Swatch data file permissions: 0444
     Swatch program permissions: 0755
     Swatch owner: root
     Swatch group: wheel
```

```
Are these values okay (y or n)? y
Are you ready for me to start the installation (y or n)? y
Installing swatch...done.
Installing sw_actions.pl...done.
Installing sw_history.pl...done.
Installing swatch.prog.man...done.
Installing swatch.conf.man...done.
```

In this example, I was able to accept all the default values offered by Swatch except for the location of the main Perl directory. Had you run these commands, you would now be ready to run Swatch (though you may want to do some configuration work first).

Configuring Swatch

Swatch allows for two opposing approaches to setting up pattern/action rules: default accept and default deny. You can set Swatch to report on all messages and then suppress those that aren't interesting. Or you can set Swatch to report on nothing and then add the items that you wish to see.

Swatch 2.2 includes five sample configuration files:

- *swatchrc.monitor*—appropriate for a server

- *swatchrc.personal*—appropriate for a personal workstation

- *syslog.conf-client*—a replacement *syslog.conf* for a client systems

- *syslog.conf-master*—a replacement *syslog.conf* for a logging "master" system

- *syslog.conf-server*—a replacement *syslog.conf* for a server

Check your system's *syslog* configuration file */etc/syslog.conf*. If the configuration seems appropriate, leave it alone. Take a look at the sample *syslog.conf* files, however—they may include entries that you can add.

Alternatively, you can set up *syslog.conf* to write everything to single file and set Swatch to report on everything it finds. This can be useful to testing purposes. You can then add reject entries to

your *.swatchrc* file until all the messages that remain are
interesting.

For example, I set my */etc/syslog.conf* to record all events to the
messages file as well as to a terminal (tty8 in this case):

```
# Sample syslog.conf -- let's see it all
*.*     /var/log/messages
*.*     /dev/tty8
```

Tip

> In order for changes to the *syslog.conf* file to take effect, you need
> to restart *syslogd* or send a HUP signal to the daemon by running
> the `kill` command in the form `kill -HUP process-id` You can
> find the process ID by running the `ps` command. If you're running
> Linux, you can find the process ID by issuing a command like `cat`
> `/var/run/syslogd.pid`

With the *syslog* volume turned all the way up, I then set up a
generous *.swatchrc* file, designed to highlight failed logins and the
activities of both root and alice, ignore the flood of sendmail messages, and simply echo everything else.

```
# A Generous swatchrc
/FAILED LOGIN/                  echo=inverse
/TOO MANY LOGIN TRIES/          echo=inverse,bell=3,mail=root
# Ignoring this stuff
/sendmail/                      ignore
# Special stuff
/root/                          echo=inverse,bell=4
/alice/                         echo,bell
/.*/                            echo
```

This produces verbose Swatch sessions. I then go back, edit the
.swatchrc so Swatch ignores additional superfluous messages, and
so on until the proper balance is struck between echoing everything
and ignoring too much.

Undoubtedly, while monitoring security-sensitive messages,
you're sure to notice an unusual pattern of events that you wish to
be alert for. Someone on a host in Germany would occasionally
launch a series of telnet attempts against a client's system—a pattern I discovered while auditing recent log files. Using a *.swatchrc*

with one entry—"/telnet/ echo"—I noticed dozens of entries like the following, during a five-minute period.

```
May 3 02:59:14 foo inetd[18545]: telnet/tcp: Connection from
bar.blarstadt.de (130.83.44.150) at Mon May 3 02:59:14 1999
May 3 02:59:14 foo telnetd[18537]: getpid: peer died: Error 0
```

In response, I added the following to foo's *.swatchrc:*

```
/bar.blarstadt.de/    mail=security@example.com    5:00
```

Next time a user on the host bar.blarstadt.de tries to telnet in, the security administrator will be notified and can take appropriate action—the offending host could be blocked at either the firewall or with TCP/Wrappers. Perhaps this is just an anomaly: no action is required for now. Sometimes security is a game of waiting and watching. At other times, it is a game of striking back. The Swatch distribution includes two scripts that take strong action:

- Backfinger (*badloginfinger.pl*)— fingers a host that failed to log in and writes the result to a logfile

- CallPager (*call_pager.pl*)—uses the `tip` command to place a call to a pager via a modem (usage: call_pager phone_number_of_pager number_to_send_to_pager)

The CallPager script is invoked generously in the sample server *.swatchrc* on page 202. This is very handy for sysadmins who need to maintain 7x24 uptime. The Backfinger may or may not work, depending on if and how finger is configured on the other end.

Running Swatch

Running Swatch is easy. There are three basic ways to run it: as an active monitor; as an auditing tool that takes a single pass through a log file; and as the recipient of piped input from another program.

Active Monitoring

Calling Swatch with no options:

```
# swatch
```

is the same as typing the following on the command line:

```
# swatch -c ~/.swatchrc -t /var/log/syslog
```

This opens an active monitoring session on */var/log/syslog*, using the *.swatchrc* in the user's home directory. After Swatch starts up, it prints a small banner with the process ID and a date/time stamp, followed by matched messages:

```
*** swatch-2.2 (pid:396) started at Sat May  1 23:59:55 PDT
1999
May  1 23:49:04 localhost named[217]: starting.  named
4.9.6-REL Thu Nov  6 23:29:57 EST 1997
/usr/src/bs/BUILD/bind-4.9.6/named
May  1 23:49:04 localhost named[218]: Ready to answer
queries.
May  1 23:50:18 localhost PAM_pwdb[341]: (login) session
opened for user root by (uid=0)
May  1 23:50:18 localhost PAM_pwdb[341]: ROOT LOGIN ON tty1
```

Table 9.1 summarizes the options that can be used when running Swatch.

Table 9.1 *Swatch Options*

Option	Description
-t *filename*	Actively monitor messages as they are written to *filename*
-f *filename*	Make a single pass through the named *file*
-p *program_name*	Examine input piped in from the named *program*
-c *filename*	Use *filename* as the configuration file
-r *restart_time*	Automatically restart at *restart_time*, which can be represented as either "+hh:mm" (to restart after hh hours and mm minutes) or "hh:mm[am|pm]" (restart at the specified time)

Table 9.1 *Swatch Options (Cont'd)*

Option	Description
-P *pattern_separator*	Use the specified *pattern_separator* when parsing the patterns in the configuration file—a comma is the default
-A *action_separator*	Use the specified *action_separator* when parsing the actions in the configuration file—a comma is the default
-I *input_record_ separator*	Use the specified *input_record_separator* as the character(s) which mark the boundary of each input record—a carriage return is the default

Auditing Arbitrary Logfiles

Swatch can examine any of the many text logfiles kept on UNIX and Linux systems. If I wanted to look at visits from Example.com employees to one of my client's web sites (let's call her Alice), I would set up a *.swatchrc-ex* file with one pattern ("/example.com/"), tell Swatch to use it with the "-c" flag, and use the "-f" flag to point Swatch at the site's *access_log*:

```
# swatch -c .swatchrc-ex -f /var/opt/www/alice_access_log
```

Swatch takes a single pass on the 100 MB logfile and finds thousands of messages that look like:

```
foobar.example.com - - [02/May/1999:23:37:17 -0700] "GET
/futureplans/index.html HTTP/1.1" 200 17684
```

Perhaps someone is interested in purchasing Alice's secret cookie recipe. Log file auditing with the "-f" flag can yield all kinds of information. It can be particularly helpful when a system administrator has been away from the terminal for the long-delayed vacation and wants to catch up.

> When examining an arbitrary logfile that doesn't separate records with a carriage return, you may need to use the "-I" flag to specify an input_record_separator.   **Tip**

Receiving Input from Another Program

Swatch can examine process accounting files, which are stored in binary format, with the help of the "-p" flag, which tells Swatch to take input from the named program. If I want to know about Alice's recent logins, I set up a configuration file with one line:

```
/alice/    echo
```

Then I pipe the output of the last command through Swatch:

```
# swatch -c .swatchrcalice -p last
*** swatch-2.2 (pid:389) started at Mon May 3 01:25:07 PDT
1999
alice     tty4         Thu Apr 29 19:39 - crash  (03:18)
alice     tty4         Thu Apr 29 16:13 - 17:38  (01:25)
alice     tty4         Thu Apr 29 16:00 - 16:05  (00:05)
alice     tty2         Wed Apr 28 23:37 - 15:33  (15:56)
alice     tty2         Wed Apr 28 15:57 - down   (06:48)
alice     tty3         Wed Apr 28 10:40 - down   (00:21)
alice     tty2         Wed Apr 28 08:23 - 10:40  (02:16)
alice     tty3         Tue Apr 27 23:32 - down   (00:12)
alice     tty2         Sun Apr 25 20:31 - down   (03:02)
alice     tty2         Sun Apr 25 20:29 - 20:31  (00:02)
alice     tty2         Sun Apr 25 20:27 - 20:29  (00:01)
```

No matter how you run it, Swatch is a fast, flexible, and easy-to-use tool that you can use on the frontlines of system security. In a networked environment where anything and everything can happen, regular and active logfile monitoring with a tool like Swatch is the sysadmin's best defense.

## 10

Vulnerability Testing

This chapter describes vulnerability testing—the process of systematically checking hosts for known configuration errors, bugs, and other security problems. This can be accomplished manually, with the assistance of security checklists and vulnerability databases, or programmatically, with a variety of system-checking tools. The chapter covers host-based tools that check the security posture of a single system, tools that check and then actively fix specific problems, and network-based tools that can detect vulnerabilities from the outside.

The Art of Security Checking

Let's consider a very likely scenario. You've been tasked with connecting a system to the Internet. A strong security policy is in place. You've examined the security of your accounts, and double-checked by running Crack. You've reviewed filesystem security and hardened it by deploying cryptography. As a precaution, you've installed Tripwire to monitor critical system binaries. Your logging system is up and running, including process accounting. You're running Swatch to monitor system events in real-time. You still need to check the system's network security standing but, from the point-of-view of system security, you should be ready to go.

Or maybe not. With a new system, or one that's being placed in a more hostile environment (like the Internet), it's wise to check and double-check your work with a host-based security audit or review. This kind of examination is distinct from the logging and auditing described in the Logging chapter (see page 167). Instead of looking back at a record of what's happened, a vulnerability test or host-based audit examines what might happen in the future. Instead of detecting abuse, a host-based audit is intended to prevent it. A good host-based audit or security review touches on almost every aspect of system security—users, passwords, home directories, system files, world-writable and SUID/SGID files, and services offered—with the goal of finding and then fixing system security vulnerabilities and configuration errors. It acts as a failsafe that can potentially catch errors, omissions, and oversights.

Checklists

One way to review system security is to run through a checklist. Security checklists are a long-standing tradition in computer security (and in computer security books). They usually contain items that pertain to known vulnerabilities and configuration errors. The system administrator examines each item on the list and cross-checks it against the system being reviewed. If the system is compliant, the item gets checked off. Potential vulnerabilities are fixed on the spot thus preventing their exploitation. Once all items are checked off and accounted for, the sysadmin proclaims the system "secure," and the system is deployed.

Or maybe not. A good checklist can encourage a sysadmin to discover a number of security weaknesses he may not have considered. At the same time, the checklist approach to security has intrinsic problems. No single checklist can ever be complete. Even an exhaustive checklist may be out of date—new vulnerabilities are found every day. Even an exhaustive and up-to-date checklist is only as good as the person using it. Humans have a tendency to develop blind spots to things they see every day or don't want to notice. Sysadmins, in spite of their heightened discipline, are no exception. A sysadmin might think to himself: "I've seen that checklist item about updating my sendmail installation, but that's a big bother—I'll think about it some other time." Even worse, the checklist approach may induce a false sense of security—we've checked all the items on all the lists, therefore we're ready to connect our systems to the Internet.

You need to think like the enemy (Rule 9 on page 27). Assume that a skilled attacker or intruder has seen all the checklists and will work around them with new exploits and variations on old favorites.

As long as you keep the limitations of the checklist review in mind, it can be useful and instructive; there are good security checklists out there. Some general computer security lists may be applicable to some extent—others are system-specific. Probably the most exhaustive checklists available for UNIX systems are contained in Appendix A of *Practical Unix and Internet Security*—they encapsulate much of the helpful information in this venerable tome (see the Bibliography). Another good UNIX security checklist was put out by the Australian Computer Emergency Response Team (AUSCERT). Here's an excerpt with exemplary checklist items (including one not mentioned elsewhere in this work):[1]

---

1. AUSCERT, "UNIX Computer Security Checklist (Version 1.1)" at
`ftp://ftp.auscert.org.au/pub/`
`auscert/papers/unix_security_checklist` or
`http://www.cert.org/ftp/tech_tips/AUSCERT_checklist1.1`

4.7 Root account
*   DO restrict the number of people who know the root
password. These should be the same users registered with
groupid 0(e.g., wheel group on SunOS). Typically this is
limited to at most 3 or 4 people.
*   DO NOT log in as root over the network, in accordance
with site security policy.
*   DO su from user accounts rather than logging in as
root. This provides greater accountability.
*   ENSURE root does not have a ~/.rhosts file.
*   ENSURE "." is not in root's search path.
*   ENSURE root's login files do not source any other
files not owned by root or which are group or world
writable.
*   ENSURE root cron job files do not source any other
files not owned by root or which are group or world
writable.
*   DO use absolute path names when root. e.g., /bin/su,
/bin/find, /bin/passwd. This is to stop the possibility of
root accidentally executing a trojan horse. To execute
commands in the current directory, root should prefix the
command with "./", e.g., ./command.

Vulnerability Databases

Another way to "sanity check" your security posture is to consult
security vulnerability databases. These allow you to search for
publicly-known vulnerabilities that could affect your specific system. Several of these are available on the World Wide Web, but
beware of snake oil. Some are put out by reputable vendors; others
by hackers. Some are spotty; others are exhaustive.[2]

You can create your own checklist from items found in these
databases and then meticulously make sure each problem is dealt
with appropriately. It's also wise to regularly check vendor sites for
security patches. Some distributions, like Red Hat Linux, are constantly patched (especially right after a major upgrade).[3]

Tip   One the strongest vulnerability databases is maintained by Internet
Security Systems Inc. You can search ISS's X-force database at
http://www.iss.net/cgi-bin/xforce/xforce_index.pl

---

2. Some are simple pages, like the "Incomplete List of UNIX Security
Vulnerabilities" at http://www.cs.iastate.edu/~ghelmer/
unixsecurity/unix_vuln.htm, or Fyodor's Exploit World at
http://www.insecure.org/sploits.html
3. See http://www.redhat.com/support/docs/errata.html

Host-based Tools

Manually reviewing checklists and other sources of security information can take a long time. The process is also prone to error and human foibles. To compensate, there are several tools that automate the process. Built on a foundation of known vulnerabilities, vulnerability-testing programs like COPS and Tiger work against a checklist on the sysadmin's behalf, checking items like:

- system configuration errors

- unsafe permissions settings

- world-writable files

- SUID/SGID files

- *crontab* entries

- sendmail and FTP setups

- weak or null passwords

- changes to system files

Running a system-checker like COPS or Tiger for the first time can be an eye-opener. Both programs produce voluminous reports on their findings, exposing all sorts of vulnerabilities. Neither program, however, extends beyond the border of the system it's running on. System-checkers check systems, not other hosts or networks.

> Both COPS and Tiger can check system binaries for alterations, but **Tip**
> you're much better off relying on Tripwire for this critical security
> check (see "Tripwire" on page 151).

COPS and Tiger are covered in their own chapters (see page 227 and page 235). Both passively check system security; that is, they find problems but don't fix them. Corrections are left to the sysadmin. These programs suffer from what is potentially a more serious problem—they haven't been updated in a while. As a result, they may lag behind other tools in detection of recently discovered security holes.

Caution   COPS (1990) and Tiger (1993) are "oldies gut goodies." While still
               fundamentally sound, they haven't been updated to reflect new
               vulnerabilities or vulnerabilities specific to Linux. They still do a
               good job checking "old" or legacy systems, but use them with
               caution on newer systems.

Whatever tool you use, you should run vulnerability tests at regular intervals (daily on critical hosts), and whenever

- a new system is installed (to get a baseline)

- a compromise is suspected

- a compromise is confirmed

In addition, you should run random tests at unusual times—to
guard against the attacker who, having determined your schedule,
might be ducking out of site during regularly scheduled checks.

Tools That Fix Problems

Another class of tools can find security problems and fix them. The
Titan tool, for example, will check systems running Solaris, report
on discovered problems, request permission to make repairs, and
then correct the problems (the team working on Titan includes
COPS and SATAN protagonist Dan Farmer). A somewhat obscure
tool called S4 checks and corrects systems running Digital UNIX.
For summaries of these tools, see the "Vulnerability Testing Tools
Survey" on page 220.

Theoretically, it makes sense for a checking tool to make needed
changes. This further reduces the chance of operator error. At the
same time, it increases the chance of program error. For this reason, you want to be sure any program you use comes from a reputable source (like the Titan team) before trusting it to do the right
thing for your system's security and usability.

The disclaimer in the README file for the S4 tool is quite clear
about the risks of automatic fixes:

```
S4 IS DESTRUCTIVE! ITS NATURAL TENDENCY IS TO SHUT DOWN OR
ELIMINATE ALL NETWORK SERVICES CONSIDERED INSECURE BY THE
AUTHOR! YOU CANNOT INSTALL S4 SAFELY ON A LIVE SYSTEM!
THINGS WHICH ARE OFFICIALLY SUPPORTED ON DIGITAL UNIX MAY NO
LONGER WORK AFTER S4 IS INSTALLED! YOU MUST INSTALL THIS ON
A SCRATCH MACHINE AT LEAST ONCE BEFORE TRYING IT ANYWHERE
ELSE! THIS TOOL IS FREE BUT UNSUPPORTED, USE AT YOUR OWN
RISK! AM I BEING CLEAR ENOUGH???????
```

The above disclaimer is crystal clear. Nonetheless, it bears restatement—don't run security-fixing tools on production systems, even if you know what you're doing.   **Caution**

Not every testing program that makes changes is destructive, however. The chkacct tool runs a fairly benign set of home directory checks and fixes and it can be run by "users." For a brief description, see page 220.

Network Security Scanners

All the tools mentioned above restrict their activity to the system they're running on. There is a substantial class of tools that use network communication channels to probe other hosts for vulnerabilities. Although mentioned here, these tools are beyond the scope of this book, which is focused on system security and network security as it pertains to system security, rather than network security per se. As the 1995 release of SATAN (another Dan Farmer production) proved, these tools can be controversial.[4] While SATAN and similar tools won't hasten the collapse of Western Civilization (or even USENET), they do provide script kiddies and other malfeasants an easy way to make a pest of themselves.

SATAN has the catchy moniker, but there are dozens of network scanning and probing tools available on the Internet. SAINT is an

---

4. The name "SATAN" (System Administrator's Tool for Analyzing Networks) fueled the publicity fire. Farmer credits Muffy Barkocy for coming up with the acronym.

updated program based on SATAN. The nmap tool can probe for
open ports and even does operating system detection—there are
many more like it.[5] All of these tools can be used to check hosts for
defensive purposes or as part of an attack or intrusion, illustrating
the general security rule "Good and Evil Blend into Gray" (see
page 25). Vigilant sysadmins will obtain these tools and run them
against the networked systems they're responsible for. If anyone
can find a vulnerability using SATAN, you need to know about it
now.

SATAN is listed on page 224, SAINT on page 224, and nmap
on page 223. Courtney (page 221) is a counter-measure to
SATAN-like probes.

Caution   **Never run a network scanner against remote systems or those
outside your area without express authorization. It may look like
an intrusion or attempted intrusion to the sysadmin on the other
end. Unauthorized network and port scans can cost you your job,
your gig, and/or your professional reputation. Always get written
authorization for systematic probes.**

Vulnerability Testing Tools Survey

chkacct

Chkacct is a tool that checks the security of user accounts. It
checks file permissions and can correct them. It looks for world-
writable files and inspects dot files. It can be made available to
users or reserved for system or security administrators.

On the down side, this GNU-licensed tool requires some configuration (see *chkacct.src*). To it's credit, however, its output is "user
friendly." Here's a sample report in interactive mode ("-i")—in
which no problems were detected:

```
# ./chkacct -i
Press RETURN/NEWLINE to begin>
Step one (three total) - Evaluating your account's dot
files.
```

---

5. You can find over a dozen more at the AntiCode web site,
`http://www.AntiCode.com/cgi-bin/`
`showdsc.anticode?cat=network-scanners.html`

```
...Step one complete.
Step two (three total) - Evaluating the file permissions in
your account.
(If you're a disk hog, this may take a while)
......Step two complete.
Step three (three total) - Checking the contents of your
rhosts file.
Congratulations!  You don't have a .rhosts file!
(If I had a cookie, I would give you one.)
Step 3 complete.
Chkacct is complete.  If you still have questions about
this program, please see a System Administrator.
If you are interested in reading an article on Unix
security, type "yes" and hit RETURN/NEWLINE now.
If not, simply hit RETURN/NEWLINE and chkacct will exit.>
yes
There were no obvious problems with your Unix account.
(I owe you a cookie.)
```

This tool is available on the accompanying CD-ROM.

For more information:

```
http://www.cs.purdue.edu/coast/projects/
recommendations/tools/chkacct.html
```

To download:

```
ftp://coast.cs.purdue.edu/pub/tools/unix/chkacct/
```

COPS

COPS is a system-checking tool by Dan Farmer and Gene Spafford that reports on system configuration errors and more. It's available on the accompanying CD-ROM

For more information see "COPS" on page 227.

To download:

```
ftp://coast.cs.purdue.edu/pub/tools/unix/cops/1.04/
```

Courtney

Courtney monitors a network, detects the signature of SATAN probes, and attempts to identify their source. It takes input from tcpdump and counts the number of new service requests a machine generates within a certain time window. If one machine connects to numerous services within that time window, Courtney identifies that machine as a potential SATAN host.

To download:

```
ftp://coast.cs.purdue.edu/pub/tools/unix/courtney/
```

Internet Security Scanner (ISS)

The ISS tool by Christopher Klaus is a "multi-level" security scanner. It will interrogate all computers within a specified IP address range, and determine the security posture of each with respect to several common system vulnerabilities. It relies on published CERT and CIAC advisories as well as other sources of information about known security holes. Ironically, this tool became the subject of a CERT advisory.[6]

The original ISS was written for SunOS 5.5.1. While that's not a problem in and of itself, it may not be ready to compile on machines besides SunOS. ISS has evolved into a far more capable commercial product available from Internet Security Systems, Inc.[7]

To download the non-commercial version of ISS:

ftp://coast.cs.purdue.edu/pub/tools/unix/iss/

Merlin

Merlin is a Perl-based utility that helps you use other tools. It provides a web browser interface to COPS 1.04, Tiger 2.2.3, Crack 4.1, and Tripwire 1.2. Merlin utilizes an HTTP server that only accepts requests from the localhost, that utilizes an arbitrary free socket port, and that generates a "magic cookie" value for each session.

For more information:

http://ciac.llnl.gov/ciac/ToolsMerlin.html

To download:

ftp://ciac.llnl.gov/pub/ciac/sectools/unix/merlin/

Nessus

Nessus is a network security scanner. It's built on a client-server architecture that allows for numerous "plug-ins." This open source project is headed by Renaud Deraison. It runs under many flavors of UNIX and Linux, as well as Windows NT. There is also a Java client (NessusJ). Nessus has received mixed reviews on USENET. As with any new security tool, and especially any new network-scanning program, proceed with caution.

---

6. See http://www.cert.org/advisories/CA-93.14.Internet.Security.Scanner.html
7. For more information on the commercial version of ISS, see http://www.iss.net/prod/isb.php3

For more information:
`http://www.nessus.org/`

nmap

The nmap tool is a port scanner (a network mapper). It can scan for open ports across an entire network or on a single host. I like this quote from InfoWorld included on the nmap web site: "If your goal is to understand your network from a 40,000-foot view, then Windows port scanning tools will suffice. But if you're serious about your security and looking for the holes that crackers will find, then take the time to install a Linux box and use nmap." The author, Fyodor, has incorporated a wide variety of scanning techniques into nmap. According to the author, nmap supports:

- Vanilla TCP connect() scanning

- TCP SYN (half open) scanning

- TCP FIN, Xmas, or NULL (stealth) scanning

- TCP ftp proxy (bounce attack) scanning

- SYN/FIN scanning using IP fragments (bypasses packet filters)

- UDP raw ICMP port unreachable scanning

- ICMP scanning (ping-sweep)

- TCP Ping scanning

The nmap tool can also use TCP/IP fingerprinting to identify what operating system a remote host is running. This tool falls into the gray area between a legitimate sysadmin tool and a cracker tool. If you're responsible for a network, you need to run it—because, if you don't, script kiddies will do it for you.

For more information:
`http://www.insecure.org/nmap/index.html`

Titan

Titan is a collection of programs for SunOS 4.1.X and Solaris 2.X—each of which either fixes (or "tightens") one or more potential security vulnerabilities. It can be used to actively fix problems, as a security learning tool, or to conduct security audits. It includes

default configurations for servers, firewalls, and desktops
(*Server.config*, *Firewall.config*, and *Desktop.config*).

Conceived and created by Brad Powell, this Bourne shell-based
package has been developed by a team including Dan Farmer and
Matthew Archibald. One of the goals of its simple modular design
is to make it easy for anyone who can write a shell script or program to add to it. It does not replace COPS, Tiger, and other security-checking tools. Titan might stand for "Toolkit for Interactively
Toughening Advanced Networks and Systems," or it might be
named for its ability to "tighten" system security. As of this writing, Titan only runs on Sun systems. Eventually it is likely be
ported to other UNIX systems.

For more information:
```
http://www.trouble.org/titan/index.html
```

```
http://www.fish.com/titan/
```

SAINT

SAINT (Security Administrator's Integrated Network Tool) ain't
SATAN but it's based on it. World Wide Digital Security, Inc. has
been maintaining this SATAN update/clone for some time now.

For more information:
```
http://www.wwdsi.com/saint/index.html
```

SATAN

SATAN (System Administrator's Tool for Analyzing Networks) is
designed to help systems administrators check security. It can also
be used by network-based intruders to search for vulnerabilities
and vulnerable systems. Like ISS, it was the subject of a CERT
Advisory. According to CERT: "SATAN was designed as a security
tool for system and network administrators. However, given its
wide distribution, ease of use, and ability to scan remote networks,
SATAN is also likely to be used to locate vulnerable hosts for malicious reasons."[8]

SATAN incorporates a checklist of networking-related security
problems, probes specified systems or subnets via the network, and
reports on its findings. It probes for vulnerabilities in

---

8. See `http://www.cert.org/advisories/CA-95.06.satan.html`

- NFS—exports via unprivileged programs or portmapper

- NIS—password file access

- rexd—whether it is properly blocked at the firewall

- sendmail—various vulnerabilities

- FTP—problems with FTP , wu-ftpd, or TFTP configuration

- remote shell access—if it is properly disabled or "wrapped"

- X windows—if hosts provide unrestricted access

- modems—those with unrestricted dial access via TCP

The reports include suggestions for changing configurations, installing bug fixes, restricting services, and/or disabling services, along with mini-tutorials about each of the problems. The program also has an "exploratory mode" that can probe unspecified hosts.

There was a mini-furor when SATAN—written by Dan Farmer and Wietse Venema—was first released in 1995. The program is able to change the acronym from "SATAN" to "SANTA"—some folks feel better about running a program called "SANTA" than running one called "SATAN." A countermeasure tool called Courtney that can detect SATAN probes is available. SATAN has not been updated in a long while. Another network-checking program—SAINT—is based on SATAN.

For more information:
`http://www.fish.com/~zen/satan/satan.html`

To download:
`http://www.fish.com/~zen/satan/satan-1.1.1.tar.gz`

`ftp://ftp.porcupine.org/pub/security/satan-1.1.1.tar.Z`

S4

The goal of S4 (Secure System Setup Script) is to lock down a base UNIX installation in advance of providing network services. It checks for problems and fixes them. S4 runs on Digital UNIX systems. It prompts the user for confirmation, logs what it does, and provides a script to undo some of the changes it makes—proceed with caution.

For more information:

`ftp://coast.cs.purdue.edu/pub/tools/unix/s4/`

Tiger

A system-checking tool from Texas A&M University. It's available on the accompanying CD-ROM.

For more information see "Tiger" on page 235.

## 11

COPS

This chapter illustrates how a model system-checking or vulnerability testing program works. COPS (Computer Oracle and Password System) is designed to find and reports on common security problems, from world-writable directories to weak passwords. First, it needs to be installed and configured for a specific system. Once it's up and running, you'll need to fix the problems it finds, and then run it on a regular basis to monitor system security.

Introduction

The COPS (Computer Oracle and Password System) package
checks a Unix system for common procedural errors. COPS was
presented at the summer 1990 USENIX Conference by authors
Dan Farmer and Eugene H. Spafford, in the wake of the Internet
worm.[1] While the program was a milestone at the time of its
release—showing how vulnerability testing could be rationalized—
this combination of C code and shell scripts has not been updated
in some time. Nonetheless, it remains a valuable tool for double-
checking the security status of UNIX systems.

The Scope of COPS

COPS sets out a wide net. It looks for administrative errors,
account problems, and unauthorized permissions or privileges.
Specifically, it checks:

- for dangerous permissions on important system files and
  directories

- for world-readable/writable file systems

- all files for SUID status

- the *letc/passwd* file for null passwords

- the *letc/group* file

- user passwords for guessability

- the commands in *letc/rc** to make sure none of the files or paths
  are world-writable

- the *crontab* file to make sure none of the files or paths are
  world-writable

- user home directories to make sure none are world-writable

- certain user files to make sure none are world-writable

---

1.   The COPS distribution includes Farmer's and Spafford's paper,
"COPS and Robbers, UN*X System Security." See
/docs/COPS.report.ms

- the FTP setup

- for illegitimate filesystem changes

COPS can be run at regular intervals by the cron mechanism with reports mailed to the system administrator. This can provide ongoing feedback on common problem areas. It can be particularly helpful for raising the security awareness of beginning system administrators.

COPS Downsides

Farmer and Spafford point out some disadvantages of COPS in their paper, some of which are generic to all system-checking tools. Running COPS and getting a relatively clean report can create a false sense of security on the part of the system administrator. This is especially dangerous given that this tool is several years old and therefore will not catch recently-discovered security holes. Sysadmins should run COPS pro forma, fully aware that they are getting only a partial snapshot of system security.

Another drawback of COPS is that it reports problems but doesn't present solutions. The issues it flags are complex enough to require the intervention of a skilled and experienced system administrator. This is a kind of Catch-22. If an experienced sysadmin is on board, the need for COPS is diminished. If you need to run COPS, then you may need to rely on an experienced sysadmin to fix the problems it finds. Still, anyone who works with COPS enough can learn a trick or two.

Finally, like many security tools, COPS can be run by a system cracker to find vulnerabilities in the target system. Thus, it has become the system administrator's responsibility to run COPS at least once to make sure any gaping security holes are closed.

> **Some might argue that an old security tool that hasn't been kept**   **Caution**
> **up-to-date is worse than none at all. I believe COPS still has**
> **value, as a model and as a checker for older UNIX installations.**
> **But you should never lose sight of its limitations, especially for**
> **systems connected to the Internet.**

A Sample COPS Report

COPS' reports are fairly straightforward and verbose. I ran COPS on an older system—a PC running Nextstep 3.3[2]—and was surprised at the number of vulnerabilities the program found. The report output below illustrates COPS' major checks.

Permissions Checking

COPS will look for permission problems, one of the banes of UNIX system security. Directories that are world-writable can be particularly hazardous, especially if they're in root's path (the root user could easily execute a malicious program planted in such a directory).

COPS found serious problems:

```
Warning!  Directory /LocalApps is _World_ writable and in
roots path!
Warning!  Directory /NextDeveloper/Demos is _World_
writable and in roots path!
Warning!  / is _World_ writable!
Warning!  /usr/spool/mail is _World_ writable!
Warning!  /usr/lib/crontab is _World_ readable!
```

The program flagged the fact that the sysadmin made the */LocalApps* directory world-writable. While this allows any user to install programs there, this configuration is unnecessary in this case and should be fixed (users should install programs in their home directories; programs that need to be shared should be installed by the sysadmin).

Next, COPS found additional potential permissions problems.

```
Warning!  User root's home directory / is mode 01777!
Warning!  User uucp's home directory /usr/spool/uucppublic
is mode 0777!
Warning!  User me's home directory /me is mode 0777!
```

These are all default conditions for this version of UNIX. The liberal permissions setting on root's home directory is troubling.

---

2. Nextstep has been updated over the years and renamed Openstep, Rhapsody, and now Mac OS X Server—see
http://www.apple.com/macosx/server/

The default account "me" has other problems (see the following "Caution").

Checking /etc/passwd

COPS contains a program that checks for weak passwords. It works like Crack (see page 99), but Crack is better (it's more focused and it's been updated). While it won't hurt to have COPS check your passwords, give serious consideration to running the more-specific tool.

COPS also checks the structure of the */etc/passwd* file, looking for incorrect numbers of fields, duplicate UIDs, non-alphanumeric usernames, non-numeric UIDs, non-root users with UID 0, blank lines, password-less accounts, and invalid login directories.

In the sample run, COPS flagged two accounts without passwords and one with a negative UID.

```
Warning!  Password file, line 6, no password:
       root::0:1:Operator:/:/bin/csh
Warning!  Password file, line 7, negative user id:
       nobody:*:-2:-2::/private:
Warning!  Password file, line 13, no password:
       me::20:20:My Account:/me:/bin/csh
```

Since Nextstep uses a utility called NetInfo to store and retrieve passwords, these accounts are not problematic. The passwords are there—they're just not stored in a place where COPS knows to look.

> Under Nextstep, the /me account is a default account intended for guests, testing purposes, and demos. It's a bad idea, as evidenced by the CERT Advisory—see http://www.cert.org/advisories/CA-91.06.NeXIstep.vulnerability.html

Caution

CRC Checks

COPS includes a checksumming program, like Tripwire, that can test for filesystem corruption or security breaches. It parses a list of system files to check and creates CRC checksums (signatures). On a subsequent run, it compares the baseline checksums to the current checksums and reports on changes.

The CRC check is simple but effective. In the sample run, it detected a legitimate update to *crontab*.

```
ATTENTION:

CRC Security Report for Mon May 3 20:30:25 PDT 1999
from host foo
replaced -rw-r--r-- root        wheel   Oct  6 15:38:55
1998 /etc/crontab
```

Tip

> COPS can check filesystem integrity but, for better protection, install and run Tripwire (see page 151).

Installing COPS

1. Download COPS from the Coast Archive:

```
ftp://coast.cs.purdue.edu/pub/tools/unix/cops/
```

Or copy from the accompanying CD-ROM.

2. Unpack it with commands like:

```
# gunzip cops.1.04.tar.Z
```

```
# tar xvof cops.1.04.tar
```

3. Review the "README" files, starting with *README.1* or *README.FIRST* then *README.1*.

4. Decide whether to install the shell version or the Perl version. The shell version is more portable across systems: review *README.2.sh*. If you want to try the Perl version, review *README.2.pl*.

5. Assuming you'll try the shell version first, run the script *reconfig*. This script looks for the locations of needed commands and utilities and changes the paths in the COPS distribution files accordingly.

```
# ./reconfig
```

6. Edit line 7 in the *makefile* to specify where COPS should be installed. If you're installing on Red Hat Linux, uncomment the "BRAINDEADFLAGS" line (by removing the '#') in the *makefile* (otherwise COPs will not compile).

7. Compile COPS:

```
# make
```

Configuring COPS

COPS is a great general purpose tool with many, many options.

Edit the files *is_able.lst* and *crc_list* to reflect your system.

COPS will check *is_able.lst* for the permissions of sensitive files. Depending on the layout of the system's filesystem, the defaults may or may not be appropriate.

COPS can be set to run at regular intervals via the *cron* mechanism and can deliver regular reports via email.

> **Caution**
>
> The COPS directory should be readable, writable, and executable only by the owner of the directory—you don't want others to be able to run COPS, change the scripts, or otherwise find or hide vulnerabilities. You should check the permissions of this directory, and fix them with a `chmod 700` command if necessary.

In some cases, COPS runs checks that other (newer) programs do better. While COPS can check passwords, I recommend that you install and run Crack instead. While COPS can run CRC checks on system files, I recommend Tripwire instead.

Running COPS

1. To run COPS, `cd` to the directory where you installed COPS and enter the command:

```
# ./cops -v -s . -b cops_errs
```

2. Evaluate the COPS report. The header of a COPS session looks something like this:

```
ATTENTION:
Security Report for Mon May 3 20:30:32 PDT 1999
from host foo
```

3. Evaluate the results. Review the *docs/warnings* file for an explanation of COPS warnings.

4. Fix flagged problems.

Tip   There's much more to COPS than presented in this brief chapter.
COPS is a great learning tool that's extensively documented. But
Tiger (see page 235) is a bit more up-to-date and thus more valu-
able for the purposes of thorough system checking.

## 12

Tiger

Tiger is a flexible tool that checks for known security problems. It's more up-to-date than COPS and more thorough. It also is one of the few security tools that includes detailed explanations of its output. This chapter provides an overview of what Tiger does and how to install, configure, and run it.

Introduction

Tiger is a UNIX security checker that scans system configuration files, file systems, and user configuration files for possible security problems. Tiger is meant to be run as a general sanity check before a system is connected to the Internet. Its main goal is to seek out circumstances that could lead to compromise of the root account. Once installed, it can methodically check for common problems, including altered system files, "strange" files, weak passwords, and unnecessary or new SUID/SGID executables.

Tiger was written at Texas A&M University as part of the TAMU suite of security tools—the suite was developed in response to a series of coordinated Internet intrusions that occurred at the university in the summer of 1992.[1] The authors made extra efforts to ensure that the tool is easy-to-use so that users (as opposed to system administrators) can routinely monitor and learn about UNIX system security. It produces detailed reports that optionally include clear explanations of the meaning of each item found.

Tiger is composed of a portable collection of Bourne shell scripts, C code, and data files. It can be run on almost any UNIX system; it contains specific support for

- AIX

- HPUX

- IRIX

- Linux

- Nextstep

- SunOS

- UNICOS

---

1. The incidents leading up to Tiger's creation are documented in "Texas A&M Network Security Package Overview" by Dave Safford, Doug Schales, and Dave Hess. See `ftp://coast.cs.purdue.edu/ pub/tools/unix/tiger/TAMU/OVERVIEW`

For most of these platforms, version 2.2.3 of Tiger is appropriate. Version 2.2.4 was released in 1998—it contains modifications specific to Red Hat Linux 5.2.

> While Tiger is portable, it relies to some extent on fixed operating system "signatures" that contain items like a list of all SUID/SGID files. To make it work optimally on a system not listed above, you'll need to make extensive customizations.

Caution

Tiger is similar in design to COPS. It is, however, a newer tool that's been more extensively developed. Like Tripwire, it can check the signature of important system files (though you're better off using Tripwire for this purpose—see page 151). It can also be configured to run Crack as part of its checks and report on weak passwords.

Tiger Checks

Tiger is designed to check a broad assortment of files and directories. Specifically, it looks at

- file and directory access permissions
- SUID/SGID executables
- *crontab* entries
- mail aliases
- NFS exports
- *inetd* entries
- PATH variables
- *.rhosts* and *.netrc* files
- unusual files
- alterations to key binaries (via signatures generated from CD-ROM)
- binaries for which security patches exist
- embedded pathnames

As one might expect, these checks can be time and resource-consuming. Tiger can be run on an ad-hoc basis or at regular intervals through the *cron* mechanism. Tiger also includes its own special cron-like mechanism that allows you to run certain scripts at specified intervals (*tigercron*). This helps conserve computing resources on production machines.

Tiger Reporting

The authors put quite a bit of work into making the Tiger's report format useful. Tiger labels all report items with an error classification:

```
--FAIL--  The problem that was found was extremely serious.
--WARN--  The problem that was found may be serious, but
will require human inspection.
--INFO--  A possible problem was found, or a change in
configuration is being suggested.
--ERROR-- A test was not able to be performed for some rea-
son.
```

This allows the user to quickly find and act on priority items.

Tiger can also provide explanations of the problems it finds. Explanations can be inserted directly into the report (using the "-e" flag)—this produces verbose output. A separate list of explanations can be also generated from a report (using the tigexp command—./tigexp -f report-file). Finally, you can look up the explanation of a single specific report item (using a command like ./tigexp msgid where *msgid* is the message ID number).

Caution

In some instances, Tiger will report on vulnerabilities—like those contained in old CERT advisories—that no longer exist (much of Tiger was written in 1993 and hasn't been updated since). Carefully evaluate the timeliness of Tiger warnings before taking action.

Installing Tiger

Once nice feature of Tiger is that it's not necessary to install and configure it in order to run it. You can do a "test run" in three easy steps:

1. Download Tiger from the COAST Archive:

```
ftp://coast.cs.purdue.edu/pub/tools/unix/tiger/TAMU/
```

Or copy it from the accompanying CD-ROM.

2. Unpack it with these commands:

```
# gunzip tiger-2.2.4.tar.gz

# tar xvof tiger-2.2.4.tar
```

3. Change to the unpacked Tiger directory (cd tiger-2.2.4) and run the command:

```
# ./tiger
```

If you plan to run Tiger on a regular basis as part of a security checking routine, it's advisable to fully install Tiger and tightly configure it to your system's or site's security needs and policy. This involves a few more steps:

4. Edit the *Makefile* for your system configuration. The *Makefile* specifies the four distinct directories that Tiger uses. Edit these for your system:

- TIGERHOME—contains the *tiger, tigercron*, and *tigexp* scripts, as well as the *scripts* subdirectory (where the checking scripts live) and *systems* subdirectory (where binaries live); the default is */usr/local/tiger*

- TIGERWORK—used for scratch files; the default is */usr/spool/tiger/work* or */var/spool/tiger/work*

- TIGERLOG—this is where security reports will go; the default is */usr/spool/tiger/logs* or */var/spool/tiger/logs*

- TIGERBIN—where binaries live (if they're not in TIGER-HOME/systems); the default is */usr/spool/tiger/bin* or */var/spool/tiger/bin*

> **The TIGERHOME directory must not be the same directory that you unpacked Tiger into. Your Tiger installation will become unusable if you don't keep the two separate. For example, I unpacked into */usr/local/toolz/tiger-2.2.4* but installed into */usr/local/tiger***Caution**

5. Invoke a full install with the command

```
# ./make install
```

This will build the directories specified in the *Makefile*.

Configuring Tiger

Once you've installed Tiger, there are a couple of configuration files you'll want to look at: *tigerrc* and *site*.

Tiger is controlled by the *tigerrc* configuration file. The Tiger package includes several example *tigerrc* files, including one that runs all of Tiger's checks (*tigerrc-all*).

Caution   The default *tigerrc* file included with the Tiger distribution is customized for Texas A&M systems—some Tiger checks are disabled. You should consider copying *tigerrc-all* or *tigerrc-dist* to *tigerrc* and then editing it for your systems.

While running all the checks may seem like a good idea, this produces very long reports. In fact, the more verbose the reports are, the harder it is to identify security-critical items. Once you have Tiger up and running, you'll want to restrict the checks to those that are important for your system.

You may also need to edit the *site* file, which is used to set Tiger up for a specific host. Of particular interest is the entry for Crack. If you want Tiger to initiate Crack runs for weak passwords, you'll need to specify the path to the Crack script (*/usr/local/etc/crack/Crack* or */usr/local/sbin/c50a* or whatever). The Tiger distribution includes a file *site-sample*, which you can edit and rename to *site*.

Running Tiger

To run a complete tiger report with explanations for each item found (the -e flag), run the command:

```
# ./tiger -c tigerrc-all -e
```

Note that the "-c" flag specifies use of the *tigerrc-all* file and the "-e" flag adds the explanations.

While running a check, Tiger is verbose—it echoes each system check. A typical Tiger session looks like this:

```
# ./tiger
Configuring...
 Will try to check using config for 'i686' running Linux
2.0.32...
--CONFIG-- [con005c] Using configuration files for Linux
2.0.32.
21:10> Beginning security report for host foo.
21:10> Starting file systems scans in background...
21:10> Running Crack (password cracker) in background...
21:10> Checking password files...
21:10> Checking group files...
21:10> Checking user accounts...
21:10> Checking .rhosts files...
21:10> Checking .netrc files...
21:10> Checking PATH settings...
21:10> Checking anonymous ftp setup...
21:10> Checking mail aliases...
21:10> Checking cron entries...
21:11> Checking 'inetd' configuration...
21:11> Checking NFS export entries...
21:11> Checking permissions and ownership of system files...
+ kill -TERM 1047
+ rm -f run/Kfoo.683
+ exit 0
21:11> Checking for altered or out of date binaries...
21:12> Checking for indications of breakin...
21:12> Performing system specific checks...
21:12> Waiting for filesystems scans to complete...
21:23> Filesystems scans completed...
21:23> Performing check of embedded pathnames...
21:26> Security report completed for foo.
Security report is in `/var/spool/tiger/logs/
security.report.foo.990512-21:10'.
```

As noted above, Tiger can be run at regular intervals from *cron*, but this can be problematic and resource-consuming for large systems. It also provides an attacker or intruder with a window of opportunity for committing and then covering up malicious acts.

Tiger provides a way to set the timing of individual script runs. While this still leaves open a window of vulnerability, it keeps the *crontab* file from getting cluttered up. This capability is controlled by the *cronrc* file; the tigercron script does the work. The *cronrc* file is fairly self-explanatory:

```
#
# Sample 'tigercron' cronrc file...
#
# By running 'tigercron' from 'cron' say, once an hour:
#
# 0 * * * * .../tigercron >/dev/null 2>&1
#
# You can run the different checks in stages, without
# having to clutter up the crontab for root.
#
#----------------------------------------------------------------
#
# Field 1:  Comma separated list of hours (0-23) or '*'
# when this should be run.
#
# Field 2:  Comma separated list of days of month or '*'
# when this should be run.
#
# Field 3:  Comma separated list of days of week or '*'
# when this should be run.  Days of week must be
# exactly as 'date' prints.
#
# Remaining fields:  Scripts to execute
#
0,8,16 * * check_known
2 * * check_accounts check_rhosts check_netrc check_anonftp
1 * * check_perms check_signatures check_group check_passwd
3 * Mon check_inetd check_exports check_aliases check_path
check_cron
2 * Sun find_files
2 1 * crack_run
```

A Sample Tiger Report

With the "-e" flag enabled, Tiger reporting is self-explanatory.
Below are excerpts from a report run on a Pentium Pro machine
("i686") running Red Hat Linux 5.0 (Linux 2.0.32). This should
give you an idea of what Tiger does.

```
Wed May 12 21:50:28 PDT 1999
21:50> Beginning security report for xerxes (i686 Linux
2.0.32).

# Performing check of passwd files...

# Performing check of group files...
```

```
# Performing check of user accounts...
# Checking accounts from /etc/passwd.
--WARN-- [acc001w] Login ID adm is disabled, but still has
a valid shell (/bin/sh).
```

The listed login ID is disabled in some manner ('*' in
passwd field, etc),but the login shell for the login ID is
a valid shell (from /etc/shells or the system equivalent). A valid shell can potentially enable the login ID
to continue to be used. The login shell should be changed
to something that doesn't exist, or to something like
/bin/false.

Tiger reports on several system accounts that are included with Red Hat Linux. While this may be a weakness, it's probably an acceptable risk in most situations.

The next series of items are more serious—Red Hat Linux has a much more permissive view of appropriate system file permissions than Tiger. While none of the listed permissions settings is likely to lead to an imminent system breach, Tiger's suggestions for tightening them make sense. In general, the less a potential attacker or intruder can read, the better. In particular, the *rc.d* directory should be protected—it controls the start-up process, the perfect time for an attacker to set a rogue program to launch.

```
# Performing check of system file permissions...
--WARN-- [perm006w] /root/.bashrc should not have world
read.
```

The configuration files (.login, .profile, etc) should be
not be writable by non-root users. In addition, the
.rhosts file should not be readable or writable by non-root
users.

```
--WARN-- [perm006w] /root/.cshrc should not have world
read.
```

The configuration files (.login, .profile, etc) should be
not be writable by non-root users. In addition, the
.rhosts file should not be readable or writable by non-root
users.

```
--FAIL-- [perm007f] /etc/aliases should not have world
read.
```

The /etc/aliases, /etc/aliases.dir and /etc/aliases.pag

files should not be writable by non-root users. On SunOS 4
systems, these files are shipped world writable. The
permissions should be 644 on all three files. If left
writable, program aliases can be added which can allow
unauthorized access.

--FAIL-- [perm007f] /etc/aliases.db should not have world
read.

The /etc/aliases, /etc/aliases.dir and /etc/aliases.pag
files should not be writable by non-root users. On SunOS 4
systems, these files are shipped world writable. The
permissions should be 644 on all three files. If left
writable, program aliases can be added which can allow
unauthorized access.

--WARN-- [perm008w] /etc/exports should not have world
read.

The /etc/exports (or equivalent) file should not be
writable by anyone other than root. If a non-root user can
modify the file, unauthorized privileges can be obtained.
There is also no reason for this file to be readable by
anyone other than root. Making it unreadable, reduces the
information available to an intruder attempting to gain
privileged access.

--WARN-- [perm003w] /etc/fstab should not have world read.

The access permissions of the indicated file are not what
is considered best for security. Unless you have a reason
for not doing so, the permissions should be corrected.

--WARN-- [perm012w] /etc/inetd.conf should not have world
read.

The /etc/inetd.conf file defines the network daemons
controlled by `inetd'. If this file is writable by non-
root users, then unauthorized access can be obtained. In
addition, it is not necessary that this file be readable by
non-root users. Making the file unreadable reduces the
information available to an intruder attempting to gain
privileges.

---FAIL-- [perm015f] /etc/rc.d should not have world read.

The 'rc.*' scripts are executed during system startup. If
they are writable by non-root users, then unauthorized

access or privileges can be obtained. In addition, there
is no need for these files to be world readable. Making
them unreadable reduces the information available to
an intruder attempting to gain privileges.

--FAIL-- [perm015f] /etc/rc.d should not have world search.

The 'rc.*' scripts are executed during system startup. If
they are writable by non-root users, then unauthorized
access or privileges can be obtained. In addition, there
is no need for these files to be world readable. Making
them unreadable reduces the information available to
an intruder attempting to gain privileges.

Next, Tiger checks the signatures of system files. If an intruder
or attacker has installed a Trojan Horse in place of a system file,
Tiger should catch it. In this instance, Tiger discovers that I
installed an updated version of the bash shell.

```
# Performing signature check of system binaries...
--WARN-- [sig004w] None of the following versions of
/bin/bash (-rwxr-xr x) matched the /bin/bash on this
machine.
>>>>>> Linux 2.0.32
```

No match was found for the signature of the indicated file.
This indicates either a local modification has been performed, replacing the binary, or that the file has been
altered by an intruder. If you are not aware of any local
modifications, you should check this carefully.

Tiger checks the mail spool directory for misuse. It finds a
"bogus" file, which was created in error (rather than by an
intruder).

```
# Checking for known intrusion signs...

# Performing check of files in system mail spool...
--WARN-- [kis008w] File "BOGUS.P01" in the mail spool,
owned by `519'.
```

The indicated file in the system mail spool does not have a
name which matches the owner. This indicates either an
attempt to create a mailbox for another user (allowing
someone else to read that persons mail), or that the mail
spool is being used to store files. These files should be
checked, and if unusual, the system should be examined for
other signs of intrusion.

Tiger then checks SUID binaries for potential problems. I've cut several messages similar to the two listed below. Tiger knows about a CERT-documented vulnerability and is smart enough to report on a file that might be affected. In this case, the potential hole was closed several years ago.

The warning about relative pathnames in the uucp program is not all that serious. On the other hand, it raises the question: why is the UUCP facility installed on this machine in the first place?

```
# Checking setuid executables...

--WARN-- [misc013w] /usr/X11R6/bin/xterm: see CERT Advisory
CA-93:17 about a security hole in xterm.

CERT Advisory CA-93:17

The xterm utility contains a vulnerability which allows any
file to be overwritten, or the ownership of the file
changed.  Consult vendors for patches for supported
versions of xterm.  MIT Patch 26 for X11R5 contains a patch
for the MIT distribution.

--WARN-- [fsys002w] setuid program /usr/bin/uucp has
relative pathnames.

The listed program is a setuid executable, and it appears
to contain relative pathnames (do not start with a '/').
This often represents a security hole in the program.
These relative pathnames can be caused by system()* or
popen()* calls which do not use full pathnames to the
executable, or, on systems which support dynamic linking,
relative pathnames indicating the directories containing
the libraries.  In any case, these need to be checked.

*Note:  system() and popen() should *never* be used from a
program which is executing with privileges.
```

Before I ran Tiger, I deliberately inserted a SUID root Trojan Horse. As root, I created a copy of the bash shell, copied it to Mallory's home directory, and turned the SUID bit on (chmod u+s)—this provides Mallory with a root shell. I wanted to see if Tiger would detect this bit of hackery. It did.

```
-rwS--x--- root    mallory  /home/mallory/bash
-rws--x--x root    root     /usr/X11R6/bin/kterm
```

```
-rws--x--x root       root    /usr/bin/sperl5.00401
-rwsr-sr-x root       mail    /usr/bin/mh/inc
-rwsr-xr-x root       root    /usr/X11R6/bin/xserver-wrapper
-rwsr-xr-x root       root    /usr/bin/mh/msgchk
```

Tiger checks for unusual file names. Here it found odd temporary files left behind by Swatch. As suggested by the explanation, this can be suppressed by the *tigerrc* configuration file.

```
# Checking unusual file names...
--ALERT-- [fsys005a] Unusual filename `..swatch..1071' found:
-rw-r--r--  1 root     root          550 May 19  1998
/tmp/..swatch..1071

The listed file has an unusual filenames.  These include
files with multiple leading '.', filenames with spaces,
etc.  The variable FS_FILES can be set in the 'tigerrc'
file to specify the filename patterns which are reported.
```

Tiger checks for world-writable directories that might aid an attacker or intruder in hiding files. I've redacted the output below—there's nothing here of particular concern.

```
# Checking for writable directories...
--INFO-- [fsys008i] The following directories are world writable:
/var/lib/texmf/fonts/
/var/lib/texmf/texfonts/
/var/spool/fax/outgoing/
/var/spool/fax/outgoing/locks/
/var/spool/samba/

The listed directories are world writable.  These provide a
location for intruders to store files.  They should be
checked for unusual files.
```

Finally, Tiger runs Crack against the shadow password file and finds a handful of accounts with weak passwords. You should carefully evaluate whether or not you want to set Tiger up to run Crack. If you install Tiger so that it can be run by unprivileged accounts, this may not be a good idea. I find it convenient to consolidate as much security reporting as possible under the Tiger umbrella.

```
# Running Crack on password files...
Crack 5.0a: The Password Cracker.
(c) Alec Muffett, 1991, 1992, 1993, 1994, 1995, 1996
```

```
System: Linux foo 2.0.32 #1 Wed Nov 19 00:46:45 EST 1997 i686 unknown
Home: /usr/local/sbin/c50a
Invoked: /usr/local/sbin/c50a/Crack /usr/local/sbin/c50a/run/tmppass
Stamp: linux-2-unknown


Crack: making utilities in run/bin/linux-2-unknown
find . -name "*~" -print | xargs -n50 rm -f
( cd src; for dir in * ; do ( cd $dir ; make clean ) ; done )
make[1]: Entering directory `/usr/local/sbin/c50a/src/lib'
rm -f dawglib.o debug.o rules.o stringlib.o *~
make[1]: Leaving directory `/usr/local/sbin/c50a/src/lib'
make[1]: Entering directory `/usr/local/sbin/c50a/src/libdes'
/bin/rm -f *.o tags core rpw destest des speed libdes.a
.nfs* *.old *.bak destest rpw des speed
make[1]: Leaving directory `/usr/local/sbin/c50a/src/libdes'
make[1]: Entering directory `/usr/local/sbin/c50a/src/util'
rm -f *.o *~
make[1]: Leaving directory `/usr/local/sbin/c50a/src/util'
make[1]: Entering directory `/usr/local/sbin/c50a/src/lib'
make[1]: `../../run/bin/linux-2-unknown/libc5.a' is up to date.
make[1]: Leaving directory `/usr/local/sbin/c50a/src/lib'
make[1]: Entering directory `/usr/local/sbin/c50a/src/util'
all made in util
make[1]: Leaving directory `/usr/local/sbin/c50a/src/util'
Crack: The dictionaries seem up to date...
Crack: Sorting out and merging feedback, please be patient...
Crack: Merging password files...
Crack: Creating gecos-derived dictionaries
mkgecosd: making non-permuted words dictionary
mkgecosd: making permuted words dictionary
Crack: launching: cracker -kill run/Kxerxes.2259
Done
---- passwords cracked as of Wed May 12 21:51:41 PDT 1999 ----

Guessed alice [password]
[/usr/local/sbin/c50a/run/tmppass /bin/bash]
Guessed mallory [myword]
[/usr/local/sbin/c50a/run/tmppass /bin/bash]
Guessed bob [heaven]    [/usr/local/sbin/c50a/run/tmppass
/bin/bash]
Guessed trent [trustme]    [/usr/local/sbin/c50a/run/tmppass
/bin/bash]

---- done ----
find . -name "*~" -print | xargs -n50 rm -f
( cd src; for dir in * ; do ( cd $dir ; make clean ) ; done )
make[1]: Entering directory `/usr/local/sbin/c50a/src/lib'
rm -f dawglib.o debug.o rules.o stringlib.o *~
make[1]: Leaving directory `/usr/local/sbin/c50a/src/lib'
```

```
make[1]: Entering directory `/usr/local/sbin/c50a/src/libdes'
/bin/rm -f *.o tags core rpw destest des speed libdes.a
.nfs* *.old *.bak destest rpw des speed
make[1]: Leaving directory `/usr/local/sbin/c50a/src/libdes'
make[1]: Entering directory `/usr/local/sbin/c50a/src/util'
rm -f *.o *~
make[1]: Leaving directory `/usr/local/sbin/c50a/src/util'
scripts/plaster
scripts/fbmerge
rm -f run/[DIEGTKM]*
rm -f run/dict/gecos.*
rm -f run/dict/gcperm.*
```

As you can see, a Tiger report can expose an eclectic mix of security holes, quirks, and false alarms. The more you refine and customize Tiger, the more valuable it will be.

13

Network Security Basics

No UNIX box is an island. UNIX has been a major force behind the development of the Internet since the first Internet Protocol implementation was added to Berkeley UNIX in 1982. Connectivity with the Internet is a given for most UNIX systems, along with the need to consider network security in close conjunction with system security. This chapter introduces TCP/IP networking and covers some of the security concerns raised by TCP/IP services commonly offered by UNIX systems. It touches on the concept of protocol layers and how transmissions can be protected at each layer. It concludes by covering the `netstat` command.

251

TCP/IP Networking

Defense by Dispersion

The risky nature of connecting computers to networks is so widely known that it has become a "meme"—a unit of thought that spreads like a mental virus from person to person. Even Hollywood has embraced the notion of the dangerous network with crackers at every port.

Ironically, the technology behind today's networks was developed by the United States Department of Defense with security in mind. At the heart of most current networking is a classic "defense by dispersion" strategy first suggested by Rand researcher Paul Baran under a defense contract in 1962. It called for a network topology that distributed authority among a large number of geographically dispersed computers. The idea is stunning in its simplicity—in the case of nuclear attack, military command-and-control communications could be maintained even if many or even most of the networked systems were totally destroyed. This topology was first implemented in the Advanced Research Projects Agency Network (ARPANET), a forerunner of the Internet built in the early 1970s.

In order for dispersed and diverse computers to communicate, it was first necessary to develop a series of protocols—communications standards that specify the formulas for sending and receiving messages, message formats, and error handling. During the late 1970s, defense researchers developed a scalable, platform-independent set of protocols officially known as the TCP/IP Internet Protocol Suite that was widely deployed on the ARPANET starting in 1980. Enter UNIX. TCP/IP was integrated with the University of California's Berkeley UNIX in the early 1980s. This implementation quickly spread to other UNIX implementations and other operating systems along with a set of standard application-level utilities like Telnet and FTP. The combination of open standards like TCP/IP and an open system like UNIX created fertile ground for the explosive growth of the Internet which continues to the present time.

Packet Switching

The concept of packet switching is key to understanding how TCP/IP works. A packet (also known as a "datagram") is a unit of transmission. The easiest way to understand packet switching is to contrast it with another common approach to network communications: circuit switching. Circuit-switched networks are created by forging a dedicated connection (or circuit) between two points. The telephone system is the canonical example of a circuit-switched network. When you make a call, a circuit is established from your phone through the local central office across trunk lines to a remote central office and then on to the phone of the party you're calling. You have a guaranteed dedicated connection to the other end that you pay for regardless of whether you're talking or not.

In packet-switched networks, traffic is broken into packets that contain identifying information such as its destination. A file that's being transmitted from one system to another is divided into packets, sent one at a time over the network, and reassembled at the other end. Multiple streams of packets are combined, or multiplexed, in an efficient manner so that many machines can share the network medium simultaneously. Unlike the circuit-switched phone network, there's no guaranteed connection between machines. If the network is congested, computers may have to wait before sending additional packets. Still, packet-switching confers a major advantage: multiple communications between computers can proceed concurrently, without the expense of having to maintain a dedicated circuit.

The Internet Protocol

The part of the TCP/IP suite that defines packets as the basic unit of information on an internetwork is the Internet Protocol (IP). IP lies at the core of the Internet and many of its component networks. It defines the header of each packet—a structured collection of bytes that identifies the sender as well as the destination along with a number of other fields. The header is followed by the packet's data contents, a larger block of arbitrary data that will generally be recombined with related data at the receiving end.

IP can be used to connect two computers in a number of ways. One common way is by creating a Local Area Network (LAN). In a LAN, each computer contains a network interface device that connects it to a passive network medium such as copper wire or coaxial cable. Ethernet is a very common scheme for building a LAN that was developed at Xerox PARC in the early 1970s.

IP can also connect two computers via a serial line, typically with two modems and a telephone line acting as a bridge. The Point-to-Point Protocol (PPP) supports the use of IP over phone lines and is very widely deployed by Internet Service Providers. Finally, IP can also be encapsulated within packets defined by other protocols, such as ATM (Asynchronous Transfer Mode) or X.25.

Viewed from another perspective, IP can be used to join two separate networks into an internetwork. This is archetypically accomplished by inserting a computer called a router (or "gateway") between the two networks. A router is a computer that connects two networks and passes packets between them according to predetermined rules. Take a simple example of two networks. All packets on network 1 that are bound for network 2 are captured by the router and sent to network 2. All packets on network 2 that are bound for network 1 are captured and send to network 1.

The concept of the router connecting two networks is deceptively simple. A router doesn't just connect two computers (or "hosts"): it connects two networks. Consider the case of three networks, connected by two routers, or x networks, connected by x-1 routers. All of a sudden, each router's task in determining where to send packets becomes far more complex and the amount of information it must store greatly increases. One of the beauties of IP, fortunately, is its scalability. An IP router doesn't need to know about the topology of every host on every network it connects— routing decisions are made on the basis of the destination network, not the destination host. Since routing is based on networks, the amount of information that a router must hold is proportional to the number of networks on the Internet, not the number of hosts.

IP Addresses

One of the beauties of the Internet is how transparent the complexity of routing packets is to its users. It doesn't matter whether you're sending a packet down the hall or across the world, pulling in a web page or sending mail to Timbuktu. This is in stark contrast to earlier network schemes such as UUCP that required users to specify each hop needed to get from system A to system Z. Part of this "magic" is due to the elegant design of the IP addressing scheme.

Each computer—or more exactly, each interface—on an IP network has a unique 32-bit IP address, a set of four 8-bit numbers or octets. Since humans don't typically think in terms of 8-bit numbers, IP addresses are commonly written as four decimal integers separated by decimal points. Each integer represents the value of one octet of the Internet address. The 32-bit IP address

```
10000000 00001010 00011110 00000010
```

is written as

```
128.10.30.2
```

Each address actually contains a pair of identifiers: one for the network the host is on (the netid), and one for the host on that network (the hostid). This has a number of important implications. The prominence of the netid makes routing much more efficient: a router only needs to know a path to a specific network rather than a specific host. An IP address really specifies a network connection, rather than an individual machine. In the case of the host with two network connections (say, for packet filtering between a trusted network and the Internet), the host needs two IP addresses. This binding of netid and hostid also means that when a machine changes networks, it needs to change its IP address as well.

Every IP address belongs to one of three classic forms: Class A, Class B, and Class C. These correspond to three network classes. Given an IP address, its class can be determined from the first few bits (the high-order bits) in the address. Each class devotes a varying number of the remaining bits to the netid and the hostid. Naturally, as more bits are devoted to the netid, there are fewer individual hosts that can be specified by the hostid. Table 13.1 summarizes the three major classes.

Table 13.1 *IP Addresses*

Class	High-order Bits (value)	netid (size)	hostid (size)	Maximum Number of Hosts
Class A	0	7 bits	24 bits	16,777,216
Class B	10	14 bits	16 bits	65,546
Class C	110	21 bits	8 bits	256

Actually, each of the maximum number of hosts depicted in the table should be decremented by two. Hostid zero is never assigned to a specific host. It is reserved for identifying networks. Similarly, the highest possible host value in a network serves as the broadcast address—an address which reaches all of that network's hosts.

To help you understand the table above, the IP address mentioned earlier, 128.10.30.2, belongs to a class B network; the first two bits in the IP address are "10." Further, the network address is 128.10.0.0 and the broadcast address is 128.10.255.255.

There are also Class D addresses (reserved for multicasting) and Class E addresses (reserved for experimental use). Neither concerns us here.

Protocol Layering

TCP/IP is a protocol suite rather than a monolithic entity. It consists of a variety of standards that work cooperatively to establish and maintain communication. The reason TCP/IP's designers created an interlocking set of protocols becomes clear when you consider

- the survivability design goal

- all the difficulties that can come up in data communication.

Networks are prone to hardware failure: a robust communication protocol needs to be able to detect when a host has crashed and route around it. Anyone who's ever surfed the World Wide Web knows that network congestion is an ongoing feature of the Internet: the protocol needs to be able to relieve hosts that are bogged down by too much packet traffic. Sometimes packets are sucked into virtual black holes and the network suffers packet loss: the protocols have to know when this has happened and compensate. At other times, data is corrupted in transit by anything from electromagnetic interference to sequence errors: the protocol must detect and compensate for data corruption as well.

To make these problems more manageable, the TCP/IP designers created a vertical stack of protocols that run on top of each other on each connected host. The morass of potential problems is thus neatly divided layer by layer, with a protocol (or protocols) at each layer that's specializing in handling a particular problem.

There are four conceptual layers—Application, Transport, Internet, Network Interface—that sit on a fifth layer of network hardware. Each of the four conceptual layers is explained in Table 13.2.

Table 13.2 *TCP/IP Protocol Layers*

Layer	Layer Name	Description
4	Application	This highest level provides support for applications that allow users to access TCP/IP services. An application sends data to and receives data from the protocol running at the Transport Layer (layer 3).
3	Transport	This layer provides for end-to-end communications from one application to another. It divides the stream of data into packets and passes each packet along with a destination address to the Internet Layer (layer 2). It also receives data from layer 2 and passes it to layer 4. Some layer 3 protocols ensure the data arrives without error and in sequence (i.e., TCP).

Table 13.2 *TCP/IP Protocol Layers (Cont'd)*

Layer	Layer Name	Description
2	Internet	This layer of the IP protocol handles communication between one machine and another. It accepts a packet from the Transport Layer along with the destination address. It encapsulates the packet and uses the routing algorithm to determine whether to deliver directly or send to a router. It then delivers the packet directly to the appropriate network interface for delivery. It also accepts packets from layer 1 and uses the routing algorithm to determine whether they should be processed locally (to layer 3) or forwarded (back to layer 1).
1	Network Interface	This lowest level is responsible for establishing, maintaining, and releasing data connections between network hardware.

Note this layering model is similar to but distinct from the seven-layer model promulgated by the International Standards Organization, formally known as the ISO Reference Model for Open System Interconnection. Like the ISO model, the TCP/IP model operates according to set rules:

- Beneath the conceptual layers is a layer of network hardware that forms the physical link between two systems.

- Each successive higher layer is progressively less concerned with the details of network traffic and more concerned with the details of user applications.

- Each layer can only communicate with the layers directly above and below it in the stack.

- Messages get passed down through the lower layers at the transmitting end and back up through the layers at the receiving end.

- The layering is organized so that layer *n* at the receiving end receives exactly the same object sent by layer *n* at the transmitting end.

This last item is conceptually important.

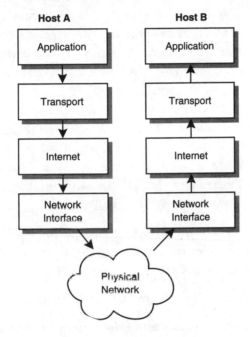

Figure 13.1 *A Message Passing Through the Layers*

While the concept of layered protocols is interesting, it is an abstraction as far as system security is concerned. The nitty-gritty lies in what each layer actually does. The next chapter, "UNIX Network Services" (see page 275), reviews the major services that are offered at the Application Layer. The Firewall chapter (see page 323) covers some of the important issues surrounding routing and what happens at the Internet Layer. The next section looks at the Transport Layer and its two major protocols: UDP and TCP.

Transport Protocols

The TCP/IP protocol suite includes two major transport layer protocols: the Transmission Control Protocol (TCP) and the User Datagram Protocol (UDP).

Protocol Ports

Both TCP and UDP utilize an abstraction known as "ports." Ports solve a vexing problem. The ultimate destination for a message is a process running on a host. UNIX hosts, however, run many processes at once and dynamically create and destroy them on the fly. How can a sender find the right process to send a message to?

Protocol ports serve as abstract destination points for messages. Each port is identified by a positive integer. Each message carries both a destination port number for the receiving end and a source port number that replies should go to.

Port numbers are a vital part of the Internet standards landscape—communication would be hindered in the absence of agreed-upon conventions for mapping port numbers to services. The Internet Assigned Numbers Authority (IANA) divides port numbers into three ranges: the Well Known Ports, the Registered Ports, and the Dynamic and/or Private Ports.

- Well Known Ports—those from 0 through 1023. On most systems, these are reserved for root processes or programs executed by privileged users.

- Registered Ports—those from 1024 through 49151

- Dynamic and/or Private Ports—those from 49152 through 65535

For overviews of the port numbering scheme, see the tables "Common TCP Ports and Services" on page 262 and "Common UDP Ports and Services" on page 264.

For a complete list of the Well Known Ports, see Appendix C on page 363.

Tip   For a complete and current list of IANA port assignments, see
`ftp://ftp.isi.edu/in-notes/iana/assignments/port-numbers`

TCP

TCP provides for reliable, end-to-end connection between processes running on either networked computers or the same computer. TCP connections act as "virtual circuits" that are somewhat analogous to circuit-switched telephone calls. Protocol software on one machine "calls" the corresponding software on the remote machine. Once a connection is up, the software on both machines communicate continuously to ensure that the data is sent correctly. If communication fails, both machines detect the failure and report to the appropriate applications.

TCP is predicated on a technique known as "positive acknowledgment with retransmission." The recipient must communicate back to the sender by sending an acknowledgement message when it receives data. The sender keeps a record of each packet sent and waits for an acknowledgement before sending the next packet.

A TCP connection is established by a three-way handshake that guarantees that two hosts are ready to communicate as peers. The protocol inserts two special bits into each packet header in order to negotiate a new connection: SYN and ACK. To start a connection, the requesting host sends a packet that has the SYN bit set and the ACK bit unset. The receiving host responds by sending back a packet with both the SYN and ACK bits set. Finally, the requesting host sends a third packet with the SYN bit unset and the ACK bit set.

TCP is based on work done by Vinton G. Cerf (the "father" of the **Tip** Internet) and Robert E. Kahn in the early 1970s. In 1981, Jon Postel formalized it in RFC 793. For more information, see
`http://www.faqs.org/rfcs/rfc793.html`

TCP is designed to support services that require a reliable bidirectional stream of data. FTP and Telnet applications, for example, are built on TCP.

Table 13.3 summarizes some common TCP services and their corresponding ports.

Table 13.3 *Common TCP Ports and Services*

Port #	Service	Function
7	echo	Echoes characters and packets (for testing purposes)
9	discard	Accepts connections but discards the data (for testing purposes)
13	daytime	Time of day in human-readable form
19	chargen	A character generator
20	ftp-data	File Transfer Protocol—default data
21	ftp	File Transfer Protocol—control
22	ssh	Secure Shell
23	telnet	Provides a network virtual terminal
25	smtp	Simple Mail Transfer Protocol for exchanging email
37	time	Time of day in machine-readable form
42	nameserver	TCP host nameservice (obsolete)
43	whois	whois lookup service provided by Network Information Centers (NICs)
53	domain	Domain Name Service (DNS)
79	finger	Returns public information about a user or machine
80	http	Hypertext Transfer Protocol for the World Wide Web
110	pop3	Post Office Protocol (POP), version 3
111	sunrpc	Sun Microsystems' Remote Procedure Call (RPC)

Table 13.3 *Common TCP Ports and Services (Cont'd)*

Port #	Service	Function
113	auth	Authentication service that identifies the username associated with a TCP connection
119	nntp	Network News Transfer Protocol (NNTP) for USENET
512	exec	Executes commands on a remote host
513	login	Logs in to a remote host
514	shell	Retrieves a shell from a remote host
515	printer	For remote printing
2049	NFS	Network File System (NFS) over TCP
6000-6063	X	X Windows

UDP

The User Datagram Protocol is an unreliable connectionless delivery service that relies on IP to transport messages between machines. The protocol provides a procedure for application programs to send messages to other programs with a minimum of protocol mechanism. In contrast to TCP, the protocol is transaction-oriented—delivery and duplicate protection are not guaranteed. An application that uses UDP is fully responsible for handling problems like message loss, duplication, delay, and out-of-order delivery.

Like IP, UDP makes a "best effort" to deliver packets. UDP runs quite reliably on a LAN and less reliably over the public Internet. The advantages of UDP are its simplicity and economy—less overhead results in greater throughput.

UDP is used for resolving hostnames, transmitting routing information, Sun Microsystem's Network Filesystem (NFS), and several obscure services that can miss a packet here and there without catastrophic results.

Tip   UDP was formalized by Jon Postel in RFC 768. For more information,
                 see `http://www.faqs.org/rfcs/rfc768.html`

Table 13.4 summarizes some common UDP services and their
corresponding ports. Note that the UDP port numbers follow their
TCP counterparts as closely as possible.

Table 13.4 *Common UDP Ports and Services*

Port #	Service	Function
7	echo	Echoes characters and packets (for testing purposes)
9	discard	Does nothing
13	daytime	Time of day in human-readable form
37	time	Time of day in machine-readable form
53	domain	Domain Name Service (DNS)
69	tftp	Trivial File Transfer Protocol
79	finger	Returns public information about a user or machine
110	pop3	Post Office Protocol (POP), version 3
111	sunrpc	Sun Microsystems' Remote Procedure Call (RPC)
123	ntp	Network Time Protocol (NTP)
161	snmp	Simple Network Management Protocol (SNMP)
512	biff	Incoming mail alerts
513	who	Provides information who is logged in
514	syslog	System logging facility
517	talk	Requests a talk (chat) session
518	ntalk	The new talk

Table 13.4 *Common UDP Ports and Services (Cont'd)*

Port #	Service	Function
520	route	Routing Information Protocol (RIP)
2049	NFS	Network Filesystem (NFS)

ICMP

One final TCP/IP protocol deserves mention: the Internet Control Message Protocol (ICMP). ICMP is a special messaging mechanism that allows routers to report errors or unexpected circumstances. ICMP is an integral part of the Internet Protocol. An ICMP message is sent from the IP software on one machine to the IP software on another.

One of the most significant uses of ICMP is to test reachability. The ICMP echo request and echo reply message types are used by the `ping` command via a simple mechanism: A host sends an echo request to a second host; the receiving host receives the request and sends back an echo reply. Ping is invaluable when building a network. A successful result means that the machine is routing packets, that intermediate machines are routing correctly, and that IP and ICMP are working on both ends.

ICMP is described in detail in RFC 792 by Jon Postel. For more information, see `http://www.faqs.org/rfcs/rfc792.html`   **Tip**

UNIX Network Server Basics

UNIX TCP/IP services are provided by a variety of servers or daemons, some of which are invoked automatically at startup time (usually through the */etc/rc** files) and are always running, and others which are invoked only when needed.

Among the daemons invoked at startup is the sendmail daemon (see "SMTP/sendmail" on page 284) and the NFS daemon, *nfsd* (see "NFS" on page 297).

/etc/inetd.conf

Most of the network services invoked on demand are controlled by *inetd*—a sort of "superserver" that listens on many network ports at once and starts various daemons as they're needed. When it's launched at boot time, *inetd* reads the contents of the */etc/inetd.conf* file and stands ready to initiate processes in response to requests for services like Telnet, FTP, and finger.

Caution | Basic network security hinges on the services enabled in the *inetd.conf* file. This file should be closely scrutinized: any and all unnecessary services should be commented out. If your system doesn't need to accept incoming Telnet sessions, for example, the Telnet server should be disabled in *inetd.conf*. If you're not sure whether a server is needed, try turning it off. You can always restore it if something breaks.

The *inetd.conf* file consists of many service entries, each of which has six or seven fields separated by tabs or spaces:

- Service name—from the */etc/services* file (see below)

- Socket type—either stream or datagram (a "socket" is an abstraction provided by UNIX that allows an application to access TCP/IP)

- Protocol type—either TCP or UDP

- Wait/nowait—With a "wait" entry, the server processes all subsequent connections on the port; with a "nowait" entry, *inetd* forks a new server process for each new connection

- User—The UID that the server process should run under

- Server-program—Contains the pathname of the program to be executed by *inetd* when a request is found on a socket

A well-organized *inetd.conf* file might look something like Listing 13.1.[1] Note that the authors have added generous comments about various services.

---

1. This example is based on the file that ships with Red Hat Linux 5.0.

Listing 13.1 *A Sample inetd.conf File*

```
# inetd.conf
# This file describes the services that will be available
# through the INETD TCP/IP super server.  To re-configure
# the running INETD process, edit this file, then send the
# INETD process a SIGHUP signal.
#
# Version: @(#)/etc/inetd.conf 3.10 05/27/93
#
# <service_name> <sock_type> <proto> <flags> <user>
#    <server_path> <args>
#
# Echo, discard, daytime, and chargen are used primarily
# for tesing.
#
# To re-read this file after changes, just do a
# 'killall -HUP inetd'
#
#echo stream tcp nowait root internal
#echo dgram udp wait root internal
#discard stream tcp nowait root internal
#discard dgram udp wait root internal
#daytime stream tcp nowait root internal
#daytime dgram udp wait root internal
#chargen stream tcp nowait root internal
#chargen dgram udp wait root internal
#
# These are standard services.
#
ftp stream tcp nowait root /usr/sbin/tcpd in.ftpd -l -a
telnet stream tcp nowait root    /usr/sbin/tcpd
     in.telnetd
gopher stream tcp nowait root    /usr/sbin/tcpd gn

# do not uncomment smtp unless you *really* know what you
# are doing.
# smtp is handled by the sendmail daemon now, not smtpd.
# It does NOT run from here, it is started at boot time
# from /etc/rc.d/rc#.d.
#smtp stream tcp nowait root    /usr/bin/smtpd smtpd
#nntp stream tcp nowait root /usr/sbin/tcpd in.nntpd
#
# Shell, login, exec and talk are BSD protocols.
#
shell stream tcp nowait root /usr/sbin/tcpd in.rshd
login stream tcp nowait root /usr/sbin/tcpd in.rlogind
#exec stream tcp nowait root /usr/sbin/tcpd in.rexecd
talk dgram udp wait root /usr/sbin/tcpd in.talkd
```

```
ntalk dgram udp wait root /usr/sbin/tcpd in.ntalkd
#dtalk stream tcp waut nobody /usr/sbin/tcpd in.dtalkd
#
# Pop and imap mail services et al
#
pop-2 stream tcp nowait root /usr/sbin/tcpd
     ipop2d
pop-3 stream tcp nowait root /usr/sbin/tcpd
     ipop3d
imap stream tcp nowait root /usr/sbin/tcpd
     imapd
#
# The Internet UUCP service.
#
#uucp stream tcp nowait uucp /usr/sbin/tcpd
/usr/lib/uucp/uucico -l
#
# Tftp service is provided primarily for booting.  Most
# sites run this only on machines acting as "boot servers."
# Do not uncomment this unless you *need* it.
#
#tftp dgram udp wait root /usr/sbin/tcpd in.tftpd
#bootps dgram udp wait root /usr/sbin/tcpd bootpd
#
# Finger, systat and netstat give out user information
# which may be valuable to potential "system crackers."
# Many sites choose to disable some or all of these
# services to improve security.
#
finger stream tcp nowait root /usr/sbin/tcpd in.fingerd
#cfinger stream tcp nowait root /usr/sbin/tcpd in.cfingerd
#systat stream tcp nowait guest /usr/sbin/tcpd /bin/ps
     -auwwx
#netstat stream tcp nowait guest /usr/sbin/tcpd
     /bin/netstat -f inet
#
# Time service is used for clock syncronization.
#
time stream tcp nowait nobody /usr/sbin/tcpd in.timed
time dgram udp wait nobody /usr/sbin/tcpd in.timed
#
# Authentication
#
auth   stream  tcp     nowait    nobody
/usr/sbin/in.identd in.identd -l -e -o
#
# End of inetd.conf
```

There's a school of security thinking which would like to see all services turned off in the *inetd.conf* files that ship with new systems. This would force sysadmins and users to deliberately turn on a service that is needed while denying crackers unnecessary open ports. While the above example file is generally conservative, it turns on *imapd*, a mail daemon that's been exploited many times on systems that don't even use it (see "IMAP" on page 296) as well as POP, a mail service with intrinsic weaknesses (see "POP" on page 295).

Always run the command `kill -HUP inetd` after editing the **Tip** *inetd.conf* file in order to force your changes to take effect.

/etc/services

A service is a combination of port and protocol. Both client and server programs consult the */etc/services* file, which lists service names, port numbers, and aliases. Many of these are defined by RFCs (several important RFCs are cited in the next chapter; all of them can be found at `http://www.faqs.org`). Well Known Ports and associated service names are listed in Appendix C on page 363.

TCP Wrappers

In response a series of attacks on systems at Eindhoven University of Technology in the Netherlands, Wietse Venema developed a simple but elegant tool to control and monitor incoming network traffic called TCP Wrappers. TCP Wrappers amends the *inetd* method of invoking network services. It works by "wrapping" around default network server programs like FTP and Telnet. When a connection is made, TCP Wrappers is initially invoked instead of the default service. It subjects the incoming connection to simple access controls (via two files—*/etc/hosts.allow* and */etc/host.deny*), logs the name of the remote host, and then runs the original network server program.

Tip

> You can find out more about (or download) TCP Wrappers at
> `ftp://ftp.porcupine.org/pub/security/`
> You may also wish to review an account of how it works at
> `http://www.ja.net/CERT/Hinxman/TCP_wrapper.html`
> Note that TCP Wrappers is included with Red Hat and other Linux
> distributions.

IP Security

The Internet Protocol was not designed for security. Its overriding purpose is to move packets from one machine to another. Its designers made no intrinsic provisions for authenticating hosts or protecting the privacy of communications in transit. Thus, it's not surprising that attacks on IP-based communications have increased with the spread of IP networking.

Given IP's lack of authentication controls, many attacks are based on spoofing and trickery. Say Host A is set to accept connections from Host B. Host M can spoof Host A into thinking it's Host B (IP spoofing). Given IP's lack of encryption, Host M can sit in between A and B, intercepting and then forwarding their communications (data spoofing or a man-in-the-middle attack).

Some attackers will use any one of dozens of packet sniffers—programs that can listen to the transmissions between two machines and find interesting patterns (like username/password combinations). Other attackers may try connection hijacking to take over a telnet or other interactive session.

The weakness of IP is compounded by weakness in many of the services that run over it (see the next chapter, "UNIX Network Services" on page 275).

The current version of the Internet Protocol is version 4 (IPv4). Given its vulnerabilities, security has been a major design consideration of the next generation IP—IP version 6 (IPv6). Additionally, protocol designers have promulgated a "secure" IP called IPSec that works with either IPv4 or IPv6.

In general, encryption features like confidentiality can be added to any of the layers of the TCP/IP stack (depicted in Figure 13.1 on page 259): Application, Transport, Internet, or Network Interface.

A good example of application-level encryption is the Secure Shell (SSH) tool.[2] SSH allows users to log into another computer over a network, to execute commands on a remote machine, and to move files from one machine to another while providing strong authentication and secure communications. It is intended as a replacement for `rlogin`, `rsh`, and `rcp` (for SSH URLs, see the Tip on page 284).

Transport-layer security can be provided by Secure Sockets Layer (SSL) technology (also known as Transport Layer Security or TLS). This method of protecting transmissions is widely used in "secure web servers"—an SSL-enabled web server can communicate confidentially with an SSL-enabled web browser. I cover this in "Protecting Against Transmission Risks" on page 317.

IP-level encryption can be provided by IPSec (see below). Finally, network interface (or link-level) encryption can be provided by dedicated encryption hardware.

IPSec

IPSec provides an architecture for a variety of security services for either IPv4 or IPv6. It works at the Internet Layer, providing confidentiality, integrity, and authentication for that layer and those above. Eventually, all Internet communications should be protected this way—it's more efficient to systematically encrypt and decrypt incoming and outgoing packets than to deploy dozens of encryption-aware applications. While various add-on technology is being widely deployed on corporate Internet sites to form "virtual private networks" (VPNs), IPSec is the preferred long-term solution, forming a real private network.

> You can find out more about IPSec in RFC 2041, "Security Architecture for the Internet Protocol" by Stephen Kent and Randall Atkinson—see http://www.faqs.org/rfcs/rfc2401.html   **Tip**

---

2. Not to be confused with the Site Security Handbook (SSH), http://www.faqs.org/rfcs/rfc2504.html

Monitoring with Netstat

A live Internet connection requires constant monitoring. You need
to be able to find out which machines your host is connected to and
what they are doing. The netstat command is designed for this
purpose. It lists all current TCP/IP connections along with the host
and port number of each end of the connection.

Monitoring with netstat on a regular basis—looking for
unusual or unauthorized connections—is a good sysadmin practice. The netstat command is quite flexible. It will list all UNIX
domain sockets that are active as well as IP sockets. You can
restrict its output to IP sockets by using the "-f inet" option, as
shown in the abbreviated example below. Note that the following
examples are taken from a machine running HP-UX and should
work on BSD-derived systems—the syntax is slightly different on
Linux and Solaris systems.

```
$ netstat -f inet
Active Internet connections
Proto Recv-Q Send-Q  Local Address   Foreign Address      (state)
tcp  0   0  foo1.example.com.smtp  gate.ey.com.60072      TIME_WAIT
tcp  0   0  foo1.example.com.1023  foo2.example.com.login ESTABLISHED
tcp  0 140  www.albion.com.http    202.102.187.56.1206    FIN_WAIT_1
tcp  0   0  foo1.example.com.telnet host.blar.com.2913    ESTABLISHED
```

The first line of this sample output indicates that port 60072 on
"foreign" host named gate.ey.com is connecting to the local SMTP
port on foo1.example.com (presumably to send mail). The second
shows a login across the LAN, from a user on host foo2 to host
foo2. The third shows an incoming web/http connection from the
machine with the IP address 202.102.187.56. The last line shows
an incoming telnet session from host.blar.com.

You can broaden the scope of netstat reporting to include all
sockets, including those that are just listening, by using the "-a"
flag. In the sample below, you'll see what appears in the previous
example as well as various ports in the "listening" state.

```
$ netstat -a -f inet
Active Internet connections (including servers)
Proto Recv-Q Send-Q  Local Address       Foreign Address    (state)
...
tcp      0      0  *.printer             *.*                LISTEN
tcp      0      0  *.portmap             *.*                LISTEN
tcp      0      0  *.pop3                *.*                LISTEN
tcp      0      0  *.pop                 *.*                LISTEN
```

```
tcp       0      0   *.http            *.*                    LISTEN
tcp       0      0   *.2121            *.*                    LISTEN
tcp       0      0   *.domain          *.*                    LISTEN
tcp       0      0   *.time            *.*                    LISTEN
tcp       0      0   *.smtp            *.*                    LISTEN
tcp       0      0   *.telnet          *.*                    LISTEN
tcp       0      0   *.ftp             *.*                    LISTEN
tcp       0      0   *.49173           *.*                    LISTEN
tcp       0      0   *.49172           *.*                    LISTEN
tcp       0      0   *.chargen         *.*                    LISTEN
tcp       0      0   *.daytime         *.*                    LISTEN
tcp       0      0   *.discard         *.*                    LISTEN
tcp       0      0   *.echo            *.*                    LISTEN
tcp       0      0   *.49153           *.*                    LISTEN
udp       0      0   *.177             *.*
udp       0      0   *.syslog          *.*
udp       0      0   localhost.domain  *.*
udp       0      0   fool.domain       *.*
udp       0      0   www.domain        *.*
udp       0      0   mail.domain       *.*
udp       0      0   pop.domain        *.*
udp       0      0   ftp.domain        *.*
udp       0      0   www.domain        *.*
```

One handy way to run netstat is to have it print cumulative packet reports to the screen. In the form below, netstat reports at an interval of five seconds. Sit back and watch the packets flow.

```
$ netstat -a -f inet 5
(lo0)-> input     output        (Total)-> input     output
       packets    packets                 packets    packets
       131713     131713                  1017397    1106592
       131715     131715                  1017413    1106611
       131723     131723                  1017445    1106639
       131725     131725                  1017458    1106652
       131729     131729                  1017459    1106653
```

There are many other tools for watching what's happening on a network-connected UNIX machine. As a built-in UNIX utility, net-stat is both ubiquitous and useful.

## 14

UNIX Network Services

The conceptual barrier between the strictly local and the wider network has dissolved as every major UNIX implementation now includes a dizzying array of network-capable applications and services, from the hoary (circa 1971 FTP) to the hot (HTTP). At the same time, the scope of UNIX system software has expanded to include more and more network utilities. This chapter covers the security risks of several major network services and attempts to describe how these risks can be managed with sound techniques and tools. The risks associated with running HTTP/WWW services are covered in the next chapter.

275

FTP

The File Transfer Protocol (FTP) allows files to be transferred from one system to another across a network. FTP is implemented in UNIX in two pieces: the *ftp* client and the *ftpd* server. During an FTP session, a bi-directional data channel is constructed in order to transfer a part of a file, an entire file, or a number of files. FTP (i.e., *ftpd*, the daemon) typically uses TCP port 21 for sending commands and sometimes TCP port 20 for data. Often the client and server will negotiate to use a set of port numbers greater than 1024.

Tip

> When measured in Internet time, FTP is ancient—over 200 years old![1] It was first specified by Abhay Bhushan at MIT in 1971. The current specification was drafted by Jon Postel and Joyce Reynolds as RFC 959. To find out more about the colorful history of FTP, see http://www.faqs.org/rfcs/rfc959.html

Using FTP is a snap. You provide a hostname, username/password, and a path to the file, and the program will fetch it. Modern FTP clients offer a plethora of features, like the ability to retrieve files using either the FTP or HTTP protocols (`man ftp` tells you more).

Many organizations offer anonymous FTP, which allows network users without an account to fetch and deposit files using a special directory. These users simply enter "ftp" (preferred) or "anonymous" (for older systems) as the username and their email address as the password. The start of a typical anonymous ftp session might look like this:

```
$ ftp gnudist.gnu.org

Connected to gnudist.gnu.org.
220 ProFTPD 1.2.0pre1 Server (ProFTPD) [gnudist.gnu.org]
Name (gnudist.gnu.org:alice): ftp
331 Anonymous login ok, send your complete e-mail address
as password.
Password: *******
230-Welcome, archive user! ...
230 Anonymous access granted, restrictions apply.
```

---

1. One calendar year equals seven Internet years ;-)

```
Remote system type is UNIX.
Using binary mode to transfer files.
ftp>
```

From this point, entering a "?" will list available FTP commands, including dir (to list directory contents), cd (to change directory), or get (to retrieve a file).

Active vs. Passive

There are two FTP modes: active and passive. In active mode, the ftp client initiates a session by using a random port to contact server port 21, and the server responds by opening a data channel back to the client (an "active open"). The data channel goes from server port 20 to the same random port number that initiated the session. In passive mode, the client initiates a session, is allocated a random port on the server, and then opens the data channel, which the server uses to send data back to the client.

In older FTP implementations, active mode is the default. This complicates the construction of firewalls. Since the server opens the data channel, the firewall has to anticipate opening a random port on the client—most firewalls are constructed to allow incoming "calls" only to specified safe ports, such as SMTP (see "Firewalls" on page 323).

Newer FTP clients—like those implemented in web browsers—support passive mode. This is a good thing from the perspective of a firewall, which can honor outgoing client requests without having to allow incoming connections from untrusted FTP servers.

> **Caution**
>
> In some ways, using passive mode merely transfers the risks of accepting calls on random ports from the client to the server. Since there are many more clients than servers, and it's easier to secure a single server than numerous clients, this arrangement improves overall security. RFC 1579 by firewall guru Steven M. Bellovin explores the merits of active vs. passive mode. See
> `http://www.faqs.org/rfcs/rfc1579.html`

FTP Server Setup

Most UNIX implementations include an FTP daemon (*ftpd*), which can be started by *inetd* or as a standalone daemon (by using the "-D" flag). Alternatively, it can be invoked through a wrapper tool like TCP Wrappers (see page 269 for a brief description of this tool).

Commonly, the */etc/ftpusers* file specifies accounts that are not allowed to transfer files with FTP—this file should list system accounts (and others who are not welcome).

Ordinarily, when a user starts an FTP session using a valid username and password, that user is not restricted to his or her home directory. You can use the */etc/ftpchroot* file to specify users who will get a restricted FTP environment—the root directory of the FTP session for these users will be changed to the user's home directory by the *chroot()* system call.

In the case of anonymous FTP, *ftpd* makes additional provisions to restrict access privileges. The server performs a *chroot()* to the home (or "root") directory of the ftp user (*~ftp*) which is set up with a mini-filesystem of its own. This directory—along with sub-directories for bin, etc, and pub—must be constructed with care. The *~ftp* directory, *~ftp/bin,* and *~ftp/etc* should all be owned by root. The *~ftp/pub* directory is traditionally where publicly accessible files are stored for download. It should also be owned by root. See man ftpd for more information on the specific *ftpd* you're running. There's also a Perl script by C. Paul Ferroni that checks the ftp root directory. See ftp://ftp.cle.ab.com/pub/ftpcheck.v2.3

The Risks of FTP

Most UNIX implementations are configured to run an FTP server "out of the box." This is probably a mistake. The hoary UNIX *ftpd* is one of the most hacked pieces of software on the planet. Major UNIX vendors seem historically incapable of producing a secure *ftpd*—the open exchange of information embodied in the FTP standard conflicts with traditional security concerns. The sad history of FTP security holes is documented by the CERT organization:

- December 1997—After several years of discussion, CERT issues an advisory documenting "FTP Bounce," an exploit that allows an attacker to establish a connection between an FTP server and an arbitrary port on another system that can be used to bypass access controls.[2]

- May 1997—CERT releases advisory on the "ftpd Signal Handling Vulnerability" that allows regular and anonymous users to access arbitrary files with root privileges.[3]

- November 1995—CERT releases advisory on the Washington University *ftpd* (wu-ftpd), a popular replacement for the standard UNIX *ftpd*. A misconfiguration/path problem allows users to gain root access.[4]

- April 1994—CERT announces that wu-ftpd source code has been subverted by a Trojan Horse that provides a back-door password for any username other than "anonymous."[5]

One potential source of security problems is cited by the man page as a "bug": an FTP server must run as root in order to create sockets with privileged port numbers. It maintains the effective user ID of the logged-in user, reverting to root only when binding addresses to sockets. Quoting the man page: "The possible security holes have been extensively scrutinized, but are possibly incomplete." The Troll Ftpd (see "Tip" on page 280) is an *ftpd* replacement that doesn't switch UID.

Certain FTP configurations are inherently insecure. Arguably, any anonymous FTP site exposes the owner to risk. Even worse, some sites leave open directories on their servers so that network users can leave files for local users. These "drop-off" directories can be extremely risky since software pirates and other malfeasants can use such directories to deposit illegally copied software applications, pornography, cracked password files and such. There's little stopping an attacker from launching a denial-of-service attack

---

2. See http://www.cert.org/advisories/
CA-97.27.FTP_bounce.html
3. See http://www.cert.org/advisories/CA-97.16.ftpd.html
4. See http://www.cert.org/advisories/CA-95.16.
wu-ftpd.vul.html
5. See http://www.cert.org/advisories/CA-94.07.
wuarchive.ftpd.trojan.horse.html

by transferring massive files to such a directory and filling up the hard drive.

Even without a drop-off configuration, FTP is vulnerable to an attacker who starts multiple anonymous FTP sessions in order to consume all available bandwidth to the server. Finally, like other Internet services, FTP sends username/password combinations in the clear. These unencrypted transmissions can be intercepted by a packet sniffer.

Protecting Against FTP Risks

Given the established pattern of FTP vulnerabilities, consider one of the following steps:

- Disable the FTP server—FTP services are often installed by default on machines that don't need to run them. You can check to see if your system is allowing FTP by checking */etc/inetd.conf* with a command like

  ```
  grep -i '^ftp' /etc/inetd.conf
  ```

  You can disable FTP services by commenting out the appropriate line in */etc/inetd.conf*. Be sure to remove the user ftp from the password file and delete its home directory. Alternatively, the file */etc/nologin* can be used to disable FTP access. If the file exists, *ftpd* displays it and then exits.

- Install wu-ftpd (see "wu-ftpd" on page 282).

- Install ProFTPD (see "ProFTPd" on page 282).

Tip

If you're running Linux, consider installing the Troll Ftpd, a lightweight implementation that dispenses with "bloated legacy code" and doesn't require ~*ftp* support files for anonymous FTP configuration. It contains a significant security feature: it doesn't change the effective user ID. Two caveats: it relies on Linux-specific system calls, and the author describes it as a "random hack" rather than a product (not that this would deter anyone running Linux in the first place). For more information, see

`http://www.troll.no/freebies/ftpd.html`

If you need to run FTP, consider the following steps:

- As with any security-sensitive software, make sure you've installed the latest version of your UNIX vendor's *ftpd*.

- Newer versions of *ftpd* support extensive logging. The "-l" flag logs successful and failed ftp sessions to *syslog*. Additional flags support further logging for anonymous FTP transfers (-S) and current ftp users (-U). Set your *ftpd* to log extensively and monitor the output on a regular basis (daily on a busy site).

- Provide a restricted FTP environment by setting up the file */etc/ftpchroot*.

- If you need anonymous FTP, review the anonymous FTP configuration guidelines posted by CERT at
  `http://www.cert.org/advisories/CA-93.10.`
  `anonymous.FTP.activity.html`
  This document was released in 1993 in response to a rash of FTP problems.

- If you need anonymous FTP, make sure that the anonymous FTP home directory (*~ftp*) is not owned by the user ftp. This might allow attackers to add or modify files. The FTP root directory and all its children should be owned by root. Note this contradicts the advice provided by some dated man pages.

- If you need anonymous FTP, host it on a machine that's outside your trusted internal network or intranet. Depending on your firewall configuration, you may be able to situate the host in the Demilitarized Zone (DMZ) (see "Screened Subnet" on page 331).

- If you need to provide "drop-off" service, institute a policy that requires the sysadmin to check incoming files before they're made publicly available.

- Contain the risk of a denial-of-service attack by locating the anonymous FTP directory on an isolated partition or disk or by placing a disk quota on the ftp user.

- If your FTP configuration supports it, contain the risk of a denial-of-service attack by limiting the maximum number of concurrent sessions that the server will support. Consider setting a tight session time-out value (the default can be as long as 15 minutes).

- Deliver a warning message ("Unauthorized access prohibited") to potential FTP abusers via the files */etc/ftpwelcome* and *~ftp/etc/motd* (for anonymous users).

wu-ftpd

Wuarchive-ftpd (wu-ftpd) is a popular replacement FTP daemon developed at Washington University (wustl.edu) by Bryan D. O'Connor. It's currently supported by Academ Consulting Services. The wu-ftpd is deployed on many high-volume anonymous FTP sites.

For more information, see the FAQ at

`http://www.cetis.hvu.nl/~koos/wu-ftpd-faq.html`

To download wu-ftpd, see `http://www.academ.com/academ/wu-ftpd/`

ProFTPd

ProFTPd (the Professional FTP Daemon) is a newer *ftpd* modelled after the Apache web server. While the author admits it's not a lightweight bit of code, he believes that it's more secure than wu-ftpd. For more information , see

`http://www.proftpd.org/index.html`

Future Directions for FTP

Even the best FTP implementations suffer from a flaw in the underlying protocol. In both active mode and passive mode, the protocol assumes, in the absence of any authentication method, that the client or server that opens the data channel is the same client or server attached to the associated control channel. Taking the case of a server listening for a client on a given TCP port after the control connection has been set up: an attacker could guess the port the server is using and bombard it with connection attempts. In this interception scenario, any data being sent to the client would go to the attacker's system instead. Alternately, the attacker could send data to the server, replacing data the client meant to send.

This potential vulnerability is described by David Sacerdote in a 1996 paper entitled "Some problems with the File Transfer Protocol, a failure of common implementations, and suggestions for repair."[6] He suggests a couple of potential solutions, including amending the FTP protocol so that clients and servers confirm IP addresses and port numbers over the control channel before sending any data. While it doesn't appear that this problem area has been exploited, it illustrates how gnarly it can be to implement secure versions of protocols established in a more trusting era.

Telnet

Telnet is a standard for logging into a remote host over the Internet. It provides a general purpose, bi-directional communications facility that allows a local terminal program to interact and synchronize with a remote terminal "server" process. Telnet is built around the concept of a "Network Virtual Terminal"—an imaginary device which provides a network-wide, intermediate representation of a canonical terminal, thus freeing users and server processes from having to worry about the characteristics of each other's terminals and terminal handling conventions.

The UNIX implementation of the Telnet protocol is divided into the telnet client and the *telnetd* server. By convention, *telnetd* listens on TCP port 23.

> **Tip** Like FTP, Telnet has been around for a long time. There are dozens of RFC documents primarily concerned with Telnet. The first was drafted by Jon Postel and Joyce Reynolds as RFC 854. See `http://www.faqs.org/rfcs/rfc854.html`

Telnet presents some glaring security problems. Since it sends information in the clear, it's vulnerable to packet sniffing. An attacker can capture the username/password combinations used to start telnet sessions. Telnet can also be hijacked—once a user is logged in, an attacker can take control of the session.

---

6. See `http://www.rootshell.com/docs/ftp-paper.txt`

The best protection against these vulnerabilities is to implement encryption, either at the IP or Transport Layers (with IPSec or SSL), or with a tool like Secure Shell. Alternatively, authentication security can be beefed up with one-time passwords.

Tip

> The most recent version of SSH has been commercialized. You can find out more about Secure Shell by consulting the FAQ at `http://www.uni-karlsruhe.de/~ig25/ssh-faq/` or by surfing to the home page for SSH Communications Security Ltd. at `http://www.ssh.fi/`

SMTP/sendmail

The Simple Mail Transfer Program (SMTP) is the TCP/IP standard for exchanging email between computers. It specifies how the underlying mail delivery system passes formatted messages from end point to end point. It does not concern itself with the user interface to mail, how the mail system accepts mail, or how mail is stored. Nor does it require a specific transmission subsystem, though by convention SMTP communication occurs on TCP port 25.

Tip

> Email has been a core network service since the first computer networks were built. See Jon Postel's RFC 821 for a circa 1982 explanation of SMTP—See `http://www.faqs.org/rfcs/rfc821.html` Also of interest: David H. Crocker's seminal RFC 822, the guide to email syntax—See `http://www.faqs.org/rfcs/rfc822.html`

Sendmail Basics

On most UNIX systems, the sendmail program implements both the client and the server side of SMTP. The sendmail facility is known as a Mail Transport Agent (MTA), as opposed to a Mail User Agent (MUA). It processes mail for delivery to individuals and mailing lists, relays mail from one machine to another, appends mail to files, and provides mail as standard input to programs. Newer versions contain extensive options for defeating spam or Unsolicited Commercial Email (UCE), the bane of every Internet mail user.

As a Mail Transport Agent, sendmail acts like the Postal Service, minus the actual letter carriers. Like post offices and mail sorting facilities, it serves as a relay, receiving, parsing, sorting, and directing email to delivery agents ("letter carriers") that in turn make final delivery. The delivery agents are typically servers running protocols like the Post Office Protocol (POP) or Internet Message Application Protocol (IMAP), which provide for local storage and the delivery of mail to end user programs like */bin/mail* or Netscape Messenger.

Sendmail has two main components: a binary program (usually */usr/lib/sendmail*) and a configuration file (*sendmail.cf*). The *sendmail.cf* file is organized into complex sets of rules that rewrite mail headers, check for errors, and select mail delivery agents. Since sendmail consults each rule each time it parses the configuration file, the rule syntax is optimized for program speed rather than human comprehensibility. The rules have been variously described as "modem noise, Mr. Dithers swearing in the comic strip 'Blondie', and an explosion in a punctuation factory."[7]

Additional components include the system-wide aliases file, which maps usernames to aliases, and optional *.forward* files maintained in the home directories of individual users. The *.forward* mechanism allows users to set up their own forwarding aliases.

Sendmail has a long and colorful history in the UNIX and Internet communities, dating back to 1979 when the program's author Eric Allman wrote a predecessor called delivermail while at University of California at Berkeley. The program has been iterated on many times over the years: version 5 (also known as IDA) was superseded by version 8 in 1993 (the latest version as of this writing is 8.9.3).

In many respects, sendmail is a proven solution: it's installed on over 75% of Internet mail servers and tens of millions of mail clients. In 1998, Allman formed a company, Sendmail, Inc., with a dual business model: to provide corporations and ISPs with commercial-grade product and services, and to share its commercial

---

7. "Explosion in a Punctuation Factory," Bryan Costales. See
http://www.networkcomputing.com/unixworld/
tutorial/01/01.txt.html

success by continuing to develop the "free" open source software version of sendmail. The Sendmail Pro commercial version features a Graphical User Interface for configuration, an installation "wizard," printed documentation, and technical support. The company has also rolled out a Windows NT version (Sendmail for NT) that's integrated with NT's administration and management tools.

Tip

> You can find out more about Sendmail, Inc. at `http://www.sendmail.com` and the open source version at `http://www.sendmail.org` There's an extensive FAQ document that can be found at `http://www.sendmail.org/faq/`

Sendmail Risks

Since its inception, the sendmail facility has faced adverse security risks—it's complex; it runs as root; it accepts connections from any computer on the Internet; and it supports a rich command language. It's been the subject of numerous hacks and exploits, dating back to the Internet Worm and even earlier.

- January 1997—According to CERT, a serious security hole known as the "MIME Conversion Buffer Overflow" was introduced in sendmail version 8.8.3 that allows remote users to execute arbitrary commands with root privileges. Attackers could exploit this hole by sending a carefully crafted email message to a system running a vulnerable version of sendmail.[8]

- November 1996—CERT describes a long-standing coding error that allows any local user to gain root access. Usually, only root can start sendmail in daemon mode so that it can "listen" for incoming mail connections on port 25. As of version 8.7, this restriction could be bypassed by restarting sendmail with the SIGHUP signal.[9]

- August 1995—CERT reports on a vulnerability in sendmail version 5 (IDA) that enables intruders to gain unauthorized

---

8. See `http://www.cert.org/advisories/CA-97.05.sendmail.html`
9. See `http://www.cert.org/advisories/CA-96.24.sendmail.daemon.mode.html`

privileges, including root. The solution is to upgrade to version 8.[10]

Protecting Against Sendmail Risks

The overall security picture for sendmail is not as bleak as these reports might indicate. For every exploit, there is a fix, and newer versions have been methodically hardened.

UNIX vendors have been notorious, however, about shipping old versions of sendmail in current releases. If possible, you want to run the latest version—the developers are producing security fixes and other enhancements on a regular basis. You can find out what version of sendmail your system is running by running the command

```
$ /usr/lib/sendmail -d0 -bt < /dev/null | grep -i Version
Version 8.8.6 (PHNE_15509)
```

or by telnetting to port 25:

```
$ telnet localhost 25
Trying...
Connected to localhost.example.com.
Escape character is '^]'.
220 localhost.example.com ESMTP Sendmail 8.8.6
(PHNE_15509)/8.8.6; Thu, 14 Jan 1999 18:35:12 -0800 (PST)
Quit
221 localhost.example.com closing connection
Connection closed by foreign host.
$
```

Caution

Unfortunately, some UNIX vendors make proprietary changes to the sendmail program—including hooks to non-standard name services like NIS+ or NetInfo—so it may not be possible to replace your sendmail with the latest canonical release from sendmail.org.

Here are some additional security tips for sendmail installations.

---

10. See http://www.cert.org/advisories/CA-95.08. sendmail.v.5.vulnerability.html

- Use the sendmail restricted shell program (smrsh) instead of /bin/sh in the "programmailer" definition in sendmail. It gives you improved administrative control over the programs sendmail executes on behalf of users. The *smrsh* program is included in the sendmail Version 8 distribution, in the subdirectory *smrsh*.

- Use mail.local—If you run /bin/mail based on BSD 4.3 UNIX, replace /bin/mail with mail.local, which is included in the sendmail distribution. As of Solaris 2.5 and beyond, mail.local is included with the standard distribution. It is also included with some other operating systems distributions, such as FreeBSD. Although the current version of mail.local is not a perfect solution, it addresses certain active vulnerabilities.

- Delete SUID executable copies of old versions of mail programs. If you leave SUID executable copies of older versions of sendmail installed in */usr/lib* (on some systems it may be installed elsewhere), the vulnerabilities in those versions could be exploited by an intruder.

Sendmail vs. Spam

Spam is the bane of Internet email. These unwanted solicitations are often relayed through the mail servers of innocent sites (which then face the wrath of recipients). Sendmail offers relay control options to specify what hosts or domains are allowed to relay through sendmail. A database file specifies domains, users, or IP ranges that are allowed or denied entry into sendmail.

In addition, sendmail can hook into the Mail Abuse Prevention System's Realtime Blackhole List (MAPS RBL). The RBL is a third-party database of known domains and IP addresses where spam has originated. For more information on the Realtime Blackhole List, see http://maps.vix.com/rbl/

> S/MIME (Secure/ Multipurpose Internet Mail Extensions) is a proto-col that adds authentication and message integrity (using digital signatures) and privacy (using encryption) to Internet MIME (Multi-purpose Internet Mail Extensions) messages (described in RFC 1521). For more information on S/MIME, see RFC 2311 at `http://www.faqs.org/rfcs/rfc2311.html` or S/MIME Central at `http://www.rsa.com/smime/`
>
> **Tip**

DNS

The Domain Name System provides a cooperative, distributed sys-tem for mapping names to addresses. This critical piece of protocol infrastructure allows client computers to determine IP addresses from hostnames and vice versa. This process is called resolving. DNS also plays a critical role in determining where mail should be sent.

The machines on the original Internet had short simple names consisting of a string of characters. The Network Information Cen-ter (NIC) gave out names and managed this flat namespace. As the net grew, this simple system broke down—there were only so many unique names that could be assigned, and the NIC faced an admin-istrative burden of having to administer names for thousands of sites, each with hundreds of hosts. DNS was designed to provide a decentralized system that delegated authority for part of the namespace and distributed responsibility for resolving names and addresses.

DNS establishes a hierarchy of name servers, each of which has a zone of authority that it is responsible for. When a client needs a name resolved, it forms a domain name query and sends it to the appropriate name server, which then checks to see if the domain name lies within its zone of authority. If it does, the name server sends a response based on its database. If not, the name server either seeks out the name server that has the answer or provides the client with a reference to the right name server.

DNS stores several different types of records about each host. This provides for a great deal of flexibility and means that DNS will be able to add additional protocol suites (or new versions) in

the future. When a client makes a request, it specifies what type of
record or records it needs.

Table 14.1 *Some DNS Record Types*

Type	Meaning	Contents
A	Host address	IP address
CNAME	Canonical Name	An alias or nickname for the official, or canonical, name.
MX	Mail Exchanger	Name of the host that acts as a mail exchanger for the domain
PTR	Pointer	Maps IP addresses to a hostname
AAAA	Host address	IP version 6 address

Let's take a look at an example to see how this works. Say a
user wants to send mail to null@example.com. The mail system
performs a DNS query for example.com's MX record, which can
specify multiple machines each of which is capable of handling
example.com's mail. DNS will reply with a set of MX records that
are ranked from the highest preference to the lowest, and the mail
system can try each one in turn (after resolving the IP addresses). In
this case, mail.example.com is the mail exchanger. Once the mail
resolves mail.example.com's IP address, it sends the mail on.

DNS runs on TCP port 53 and/or UDP port 53. It uses UDP for
quick and dirty name resolution and TCP for zone transfers—
wholesale DNS database copies between a primary name server
and a secondary one. The most popular software for managing
DNS is BIND (Berkeley Internet Name Domain), which was first
introduced with BSD 4.3. BIND includes reference implementations of

• a DNS server (*named*)

• a DNS resolver library, and

• tools for verifying the proper operation of the DNS server

The current version of BIND is Version 8. Use of Version 4 is discouraged, particularly since it's no longer being patched. To find out more about BIND, see the Internet Software Consortium's site at `http://www.isc.org/bind.html` **Tip**

DNS service is security critical, especially since access to many services are allowed or denied on the basis of hostnames. If you run BIND, run Version 8. It's important to restrict zone transfers so that attackers can't get detailed information about your internal network configuration. This can be done with a firewall by blocking incoming TCP connections on port 53. DNS servers should be run on machines without user accounts. Make sure all the files associated with name service are owned by root.

DNS is also vulnerable to spoofing attacks—a name server can be loaded with spurious information. One way to strengthen security is to set up two name servers, one on each side of the firewall.

finger

The finger utility provides a simple system for sharing semi-personal and professional information like phone numbers and work schedules. If a user on host X wants to find out about a user on host Y, finger makes a network connection to host Y. If host Y is running a *fingerd*, the daemon relays information about the user in question through the connection back to host X, where finger displays it. This venerable network service runs on TCP (port 79). It can reveal some or all of the following:

- username

- real name

- terminal name and write status (with a "*" before the terminal name if write permission is denied)

- idle time

- login time

- office location

- office phone number

- the remote host

- user's home directory

- home phone number

- login shell

- mail status

- contents of the *.plan* file in the user's home directory

- contents of the *.project* file in the user's home directory

Finger can also be used to get summary information about all the users logged in to a system. In short, finger is a major security risk.

Tip

Finger was first described (along with name) as an RFC in 1977. It is currently formalized by David Paul Zimmerman in RFC 1288 (see `http://www.faqs.org/rfcs/rfc1288.html`).

Weak finger implementations have been implicated in numerous security breaches, including the infamous Internet worm. But even sound implementations beg the question: why would any sane system administrator want to give random crackers access to sensitive and perhaps confidential information? If there's any service that's a throwback to the early days when the Internet was run on a trusted and collegial basis, this is it.

Here's what the output of a finger session might look like when probing for a single user:[11]

```
$ finger dnull
Login name: dnull                In real life: David Null
Office: 013 Foo Hall, x1234      Home phone: 555-7890
Directory: /home/dnull           Shell: /bin/csh
Last login Sat Jun 23 10:47 on ttyp0 from hackme.opensite
No unread mail
Project:
Plan:
```
_____

11. This is derived from a sample in RFC 1288.

```
                    Work Schedule, Summer 2001
                  Opensite Operations, 999-555-1234
                    Monday        5pm - 12am
                    Tuesday       5pm - 12am
                    Wednesday     9am -  5pm
                    Thursday      9am -  5pm
                    Saturday      9am -  5pm
                      larf larf hoo hoo
```

Imagine that this type of information is publicly available for every system user. Now, adopt the point-of-view of an attacker. You know who the users are, the hosts they use, where they work, and when they work—more than enough for a social engineering attack.

Protecting Against Finger Risks

Many sites disable finger so that incoming finger requests are answered with "Connection refused." Others replace it with something else, preferably a facility that gives the legitimate requester a clue about how to contact someone.

You can disable finger by commenting out the appropriate line in */etc/inetd.conf*.

If you want some sort of message to go out in reply to finger requests, you can write a shell script, store it as an executable in say, */usr/local/etc/alt_finger*, and then edit the finger entry in */etc/inetd.conf* to point to it. The script might look like:

```
#!/bin/sh
#
# This sample script replaces regular finger output
#
/bin/echo Welcome to Anon Corporation, Inc. "  " 'date'
/bin/cat << ETX
Thanks for trying to contact us. To contact a specific
employee, please utilize the services of our company
operator at 1-999-555-5678.
ETX
exit 0
```

The Ph Name Server

As an alternative to finger, you can install the Ph Name Server from the Computing and Communications Services Office (CCSO), University of Illinois at Urbana-Champaign (the program is also known as "CCSO"). Ph provides an Internet-based virtual phone book. It allows an organization to load arbitrary contact information into a database and provide that information to both local users and over the Internet. The database is optimized to keep a relatively small amount of information about a relatively large number of people.

Ph is implemented as a client-server protocol. The Ph server listens on TCP port 105. A requesting client connects to the server and issues commands which the server then answers until the connection is either closed by the client or aborted by server.

Ph provides for granular control over the information available to random Internet requesters. The administrator of a Ph system is called a "hero." The hero user can mark Ph database fields so that they can only be viewed by local users—a sharp contrast to the promiscuous approach implemented in finger.

True to its academic roots, Ph is implemented at hundreds of universities. It is specified in RFC 2378 (for more information, see `http://www.faqs.org/rfcs/rfc2378.html`). You can download Ph (look for the "qi" distribution) from `ftp://uiarchive.uiuc.edu/pub/packages/ph/`

The way Ph is deployed has a significant limitation: you can't use it to find any one person without already knowing that person's organizational affiliation ("If I only knew where you were, I could find you."). Each organization's server is independent of all the others that run on the Internet. They contain divergent schema and don't communicate.

RFC 2258 by Joann J. Ordille suggests a grand project: to integrate hundreds of publicly available Ph servers from around the world so that users can perform fast cross-server searches. While I don't know whether Ordille's plan will ever get off the ground, I love its name: the Internet Nomenclator Project. For more information, see `http://www.faqs.org/rfcs/rfc2258.html`

GNU Finger

Perhaps the users at your site want, need, and/or expect finger service. Perhaps your site runs as an MIT-style "open lab" where information is routinely and generously shared. On the other hand, maybe you're taken with the friendly and fun aspects of finger. You may want to consider replacing the default finger that comes with your version of UNIX with GNU Finger. GNU Finger is a finger on steroids. It allows a site to set up a central finger server that polls hosts and keeps track of who is logged in where. The finger server can then honor site-wide finger requests. GNU Finger provides generous options for the information that is delivered—it can even include pictures of users (though the documentation states that this option is unsupported).

GNU Finger contains an interesting security enhancement: the ability of users to control finger output via *.fingerrc* files in their home directory. When the GNU Finger server receives a request for information about a user, it checks to see if there's a *.fingerrc* script in the user's home directory. If an executable script exists, it is executed with the normal finger output as input. The output of the script is then passed back to the finger daemon for display on the requesting end. This facility can be used

- to disable finger entirely for a particular user by linking *.fingerrc* to */bin/true*

- to replace finger output with the output of a shell script that might look like the one above (see "Protecting Against Finger Risks" on page 293)

- to filter finger output

> You can download and find out more about GNU Finger at **Tip**
> `http://www.gnu.org` It comes with a lively and well-written manual
> by Jan Brittenson and Brian Fox that can be found at
> `http://www.gnu.org/manual/finger/index.html`

POP

As the Internet developed, it became clear that while every system needed email access, not every system could support or needed to support a complex Mail Transfer Agent (MTA) like sendmail (see "SMTP/sendmail" on page 284). The Post Office Protocol (POP) was developed in order to enable a client to retrieve mail by accessing a maildrop on a mail server. This is somewhat analogous to getting mail from a PO box at the Post Office rather than from a mailbox outside your home.

The current version of POP (Version 3) is widely deployed on UNIX servers in general and on the mail servers maintained by Internet Service Providers in particular. POP operates in a fairly basic manner. A POP server listens on TCP port 110. When a client wishes to connect, it establishes a TCP connection with the server, which sends a greeting. The client sends commands that the server responds to until the connection is closed or aborted.

Tip

The POP3 protocol is described in RFC 1939. For more information, see `http://www.faqs.org/rfcs/rfc1939.html`

POP is vulnerable to eavesdropping. In a default configuration, a POP client authenticates itself with a simple password. Often this is the same password that is used for general login purposes. An attacker armed with a packet sniffer has a good shot at intercepting passwords, especially since they're sent again and again as clients retrieve mail during the course of the day.

POP3 supports an alternative authentication mechanism via the APOP command. APOP relies on a shared secret between the client and server, which alleviates the need to send a password in the clear. If possible, configure POP servers and clients to utilize APOP.

Tip

The Eudora division of Qualcomm offers a free POP server for UNIX called Qpopper, which was originally developed at UC Berkeley. It provides a major security feature: APOP authentication can be added at compile time. It also supports Kerberos. You can find more information at `http://www.eudora.com/freeware/qpop.html`

Caution

Qpopper 2.41 and prior versions are vulnerable to buffer overflows which allow remote users to obtain root access. Upgrade your server if you are running any qpopper older than 2.5.

IMAP

The Internet Message Access Protocol (IMAP) is similar to the Post Office Protocol. It allows a client to access mail messages on a server. IMAP is newer than POP, and it's considerably more powerful and complex. While POP sends email to the client, where it is read and managed locally, IMAP enables a client to manipulate email messages on the server as if they were stored locally.

> The current version of IMAP (IMAP4) is documented by RFC 2060. **Tip**
> For more information, see
> `http://www.faqs.org/rfcs/rfc2060.html`

IMAP has been subject to security problems in the past, including a nasty implementation bug discovered in 1997 that allowed attackers to gain privileged access (see `http://www.cert.org/advisories/CA-97.09.imap_pop.html` for details).

> The IMAP included with Red Hat Linux 4.1 contained a buffer **Caution**
> overrun which allowed remote users to gain root access. Be sure
> to patch a Red Hat 4.1 system, or upgrade to a newer
> distribution.

NFS

The Network File System (NFS) allows users to transparently access files and programs across a network (usually a LAN). On an NFS-enabled client, a user can work with files that reside on a variety of servers, server architectures, and across a variety of operating systems—the remote files appear to be part of the local filesystem. NFS is ubiquitous—it has been implemented on almost all versions of UNIX in addition to the Apple Macintosh, Windows, MS-DOS, OS/2, and VMS. Client file requests are converted to NFS protocol requests, and are sent to the server system over the network. The server receives the request, performs the actual file system operation, and then sends a response back to the client.

Promulgated by Sun Microsystems,[12] NFS enables file systems to be exported by a server and imported by clients in a "stateless" best effort way. It handles the creation of new files, the actual sharing of files, file locking, and the management of file ownership.

---

12. See Sun's NFS white paper at `http://www.sun.com/software/white-papers/wp-nfs/`

NFS is built on Remote Procedure Call (RPC) primitives and uses RPC's authentication methods to ensure security. It originally ran over UDP for performance reasons. It can now run over the more reliable TCP. Clients and server negotiate which protocol to use.

A server grants access to a given filesystem by adding an entry for that filesystem to the server's */etc/exports* file. A client gains access to that filesystem with the *mount* system call, which requests a file handle for the filesystem. Once the filesystem is mounted by the client, the server issues a file handle to the client for each file (or directory) the client accesses. If the file is removed on the server side by another NFS user, the file handle becomes stale and will produce an error.

Tip

The mount call is an implementation of the mount protocol, which is described in RFC 1094. See
`http://www.faqs.org/rfcs/rfc1094.html` Also, RPC is defined in
RFC 1057—see `http://www.faqs.org/rfcs/rfc1057.html`

Unfortunately, NFS has little built-in security. It was developed in olden times (1985), when the slogan "the network is the computer" referred to LANs rather than the global Internet.

Information transmitted by NFS over the network is not encrypted—thus, it's subject to eavesdropping and/or interception.

NFS uses the same authentication scheme as the UNIX filesystem and thus inherits UNIX's file system vulnerabilities.[13] NFS servers accept client requests when the client's IP address appears on a list of trusted hosts. Under this scheme, users can be impersonated, since most of the permission checking is performed on the client. An imposter can trick a server by temporarily assigning the IP address of a victim to his own workstation. From that point on, the imposter can assume a false user ID to make NFS requests and thus access, alter, or even destroy private or confidential data on the server.

---

13. It is possible, however, to configure NFS so that it utilizes one of two authentication services: either one based on the Diffie-Hellman key exchange protocol and one based on Kerberos.

> In 1992, a group of vendors including IBM, Digital, and Sun under-
> took a revision to the NFS protocol resulting in NFS Version 3. While
> it offers substantial performance improvements via local file cach-
> ing, it fails to address the protocol's fundamental security
> weaknesses.

Tip

A handful of general rules will help improve NFS security:

- Dedicate a system to NFS service and don't allow users to log into it.

- Implement authentication services with Kerberos, rather than relying on UNIX-style authentication.

- Limit the number and scope of exports as much as possible. Carefully configure */etc/exports* so that only known and autho-rized local clients can access it. If clients only need access to part of a filesystem, export just that part.

- Limit the number and scope of client mounts. Not every client needs access to every NFS server.

- When feasible, filesystems should be exported read-only.

- Filesystems should never be exported to any hosts outside the LAN. If possible, all external access to NFS service should be blocked by a firewall.

Finally, consider whether your installation really needs to be configured with NFS in the first place. NFS was created in an era when hard disks were expensive. By deploying diskless worksta-tions and sharing a common file space, organizations could save money. Disk space is cheap now. NFS has also been deployed to allow users to access their home directories no matter which machine they log into. While this "open lab" configuration is con-ceptually attractive, we live in the PC era now—most users have their own boxes that they use more or less exclusively. NFS can be an operational nightmare as well—when the server is down, work can grind to a halt. Your organization or site may be able to save time, money, and security woes by tossing NFS and installing lots of disks, a high-speed LAN, a software distribution program like rdist, and intranet web servers.

systat

The systat service provides information to the network about who
is logged into your computer. It uses TCP port 11 to deliver status
information, often the output of the who or w commands. Many
systems have this service turned off by default. This is a good idea,
since this information can be used for social engineering and other
nefarious purposes. If your system is running systat, turn it off in
/etc/inetd.conf. You can test if your system offering systat by telnetting to port 11. It should refuse the connection.

UUCP

The Unix-to-Unix Copy (UUCP) facility is a dial-up networking
and file exchange scheme that was widely deployed on UNIX systems in the 1980s. Created in 1977, UUCP was popular because it
was bundled with almost every UNIX distribution and because it
provided rudimentary networking using relatively inexpensive
dial-up modems and telephone lines. UUCP was used primarily for
the point-to-point exchange of email and USENET news, though it
could also be used as a generic file transfer facility or to execute
commands on a remote system. Mail and news articles would be
temporarily stored (spooled) on one UUCP host and then transmitted when the uucico program was invoked—typically by *cron*, and
often during off-hours to save a phone charges.

I'm using the past tense in describing UUCP because it has been
largely been superseded by the Point-to-Point Protocol (PPP),
which uses the same hardware but offers a full range of Internet
services, by the POP and IMAP protocols for retrieving mail, and
by the Network News Transfer Protocol for exchanging USENET
articles. As one of its primary programmers pointed out over ten
years ago: "UUCP is a dead protocol."[14] Nonetheless, it is still used
by many legacy systems—one of my old NeXT machines has
faithfully polled for mail every hour for the past ten years—and it

---

14. P. Honeymoon, as quoted by Steve Simmons in "Living without
Root." See http://www.raptor.com/lib/noroot.pdf

is still shipped with UNIX and with Linux. A few pointers are in
order.

There are three versions of UUCP: Version 2, the original that
was produced at AT&T in 1977; HoneyDanBer, also known as
BNU (Basic Networking Utilities); and Taylor, written by Ian
Lance Taylor. Most Linux distributions run Taylor UUCP, which is
covered by the GNU Public License; most commercial UNIXes
ship with BNU. From a functional point of view, the different versions are quite similar. They do, however, rely on different sets of
configuration files.

> You can check if your Linux system is running Taylor UUCP by run-   **Tip**
> ning the command: /usr/sbin/uuchk This will report on your UUCP
> set-up. Adding the "-v" flag will report the version number. If you're
> running BNU UUCP, the command /usr/lib/uucp/uucheck -v
> reports on the security of the *Permissions* file.

UUCP can also be run over TCP/IP rather than point-to-point
dial-up connections. This capability was added to UUCP during
the late 1980s as a stop-gap measure during the transition from
dial-up connectivity to TCP/IP. The *uucpd* daemon listens on TCP
port 540 for a connection request from a sending system's uucico
program.

As one of the oldest UNIX utilities, UUCP is fairly secure, at
least in so far as vulnerability after vulnerability has been patched
over the decades. UUCP programs run with the UID of the ficti-
tious uucp user; it can only read and write files that are owned by
that user. UUCP can configured to restrict or eliminate file retriev-
als from remote systems; it's also possible to prevent remote systems from executing commands. Version 2 supports the use of
callback, so that UUCP can make sure an incoming connection is
coming from a specific system rather than an imposter.

> Make sure the account for the uucp user has a password—many   **Caution**
> default UNIX installations create this user but don't assign a
> password (assuming, perhaps, that the sysadmin knows to do it).
> Log in as root and use the command passwd uucp

If you're running UUCP, be sure to run a tight ship. Review the documentation and man pages for security concerns. Eliminate remote file retrieval and remote command execution. Protect the UUCP control and configuration files. Disable the *uucpd* daemon.

Caution   If you're not running UUCP, it might be wise to remove it from your system entirely. As an unused system resource, it adds no value and provides yet another way for attackers to breach your system. An unnoticed and unconfigured UUCP subsystem would make a nice back door for intruders to gain direct dial-up access to your machine.

You can find UUCP files in */etc/uucp* (perhaps in */usr/lib/uucp*), in either */usr/spool/uucp* or */var/spool/uucp*, and in */var/log/uccp*. In a Red Hat Linux system, you'll find UUCP documentation and sample configurations in */usr/doc/uucp-1.06.1*. All this material should be blown away if you're not using UUCP.

## 15

HTTP/WWW Security

There's nothing inherently insecure about the HTTP protocol which underpins the World Wide Web, at least relative to older protocols like FTP and Telnet. The immense ubiquity and popularity of the web, however, makes it a favorite target for system crackers who seem to take great pleasure in defeating the system security of web servers and replacing popular web pages with cryptic and juvenile messages. This chapter explains some of the risks involved on both the server and client side and suggests security tools (starting with a secure server) and methods. It also describes TLS/SSL (Transport Layer Security/Secure Sockets Layer).

HTTP Basics

The Hypertext Transfer Protocol (HTTP) is a fairly simple but very important protocol that allows users ("browsers" or "surfers") to request and receive hypermedia content from the World Wide Web (WWW) and other distributed information systems. By default, the HTTP daemon (*httpd*) runs on top of TCP and listens on TCP port 80. It can, however, use other ports and even other protocols that provide a reliable data stream (at least in theory).

HTTP is a request/response protocol. In order to retrieve information, a web browsing client program like Netscape Navigator (technically known as a "user agent") establishes a TCP connection to a server like Apache and makes a request for a resource (a "GET"). The server examines the request and responds in accordance with the configuration of the server and the content the server contains. A server might send a Hypertext Markup Language (HTML) file, text, graphics, audio, video, or a Java applet, which the browser (hopefully) displays. A server might also run a program in response to a browser request, either through the Common Gateway Interface (CGI) or through the server's Application Programming Interface (API).

HTTP is both flexible and generic. While its original function was to retrieve information from the web, it can also be used as a "meta" protocol for connecting to other Internet systems, including those supported by the SMTP, NNTP, FTP, Gopher, and WAIS protocols. Through the use of proxies and gateways, HTTP allows basic hypermedia access to resources available from diverse applications.

The popularity of the WWW—and the ubiquity of the HTTP protocol—is one of the most amazing developments in the history of the Internet. Despite the hegemony of one particular PC operating system vendor, UNIX and TCP/IP form its foundation. The WWW was invented in 1990 by Tim Berners-Lee while he was at the European Laboratory for Particle Physics (CERN). Berners-Lee was working as part of team that wanted to facilitate the exchange of online research documents among physicists when he wrote the original WWW server and browser software on a NeXT computer. When a team at University of Illinois at Champaign-Urbana released a browser called Mosaic for the Macintosh and Windows operating systems, the web took off like wildfire. Mosaic was commercialized by the company that became Netscape Communications and renamed Netscape Navigator.

> Due to the web's fantastic growth, HTTP is the dominant protocol   **Tip**
> on the Internet. Everything you ever wanted to know about HTTP
> can be found at the World Wide Web Consortium's HTTP overview
> page—See `http://www.w3.org/Protocols/` The latest version of
> HTTP is 1.1, specified in RFC 2068—See
> `http://www.faqs.org/rfcs/rfc2068.html`

One handy way to test HTTP connectivity—and to illustrate potential HTTP security holes—is to telnet into a web server host on port 80. You can type "GET /" to view the site's root HTML document (say, an *index.html*) as illustrated below (minus the HTML content):

```
$ telnet www.example.com 80
Trying...
Connected to www.example.com.
Escape character is '^]'.
GET /
<HTML>
<HEAD>
snip snip
</BODY>
</HTML>
Connection closed by foreign host.
```

Alternatively, you can pipe the GET request to the server by issuing a command like

```
$ echo 'GET /' | telnet www.example.com 80
```

Of course, you achieve the same results—and get a graphical display of the output—by sparking up Netscape Navigator and letting it issue requests transparently on your behalf.

HTTP/WWW Security Risks

Web security risks can be classified into three general categories:

- threats to the web server and the LAN it's connected to

- threats to the web browsing client

- threats to the communication channel between the server and client

Web Server Risks

The widespread deployment of web servers poses a network security paradox. The general goal of network security is to keep strangers off the network. Yet the general goal of a web server is to solicit strangers to visit your site in a controlled manner. There's plenty of room for conflict in the middle ground between these divergent goals.

There are several generic threats that every web server faces. Bugs in the HTTP server software, misconfiguration, insecure CGI programs, and the lack of strong encryption can allow attackers

- to alter or replace content the server provides

- to gain access to confidential documents protected by the server's access controls

- to execute arbitrary commands on the server and thus subvert the server's system security

- to violate user privacy by inspecting log files

- to launch denial-of-service attacks that incapacitate either the server or the network connection

All of these threats have manifested themselves in the short history of the web. On September 13, 1998, The New York Times suffered a humiliating breach of web security.[1] The team of crackers known as HFG (H4CK1NG 4 G1RL13Z) gained control of the paper's web site and replaced the home page with a hairy collection

---

1. For more on this attack, see
    http://www.dailyflame.com/006-nyt.html

of soft porn, cryptic flames, and communiques regarding impris-
oned cracker Kevin Mitnick, Times reporter John Markoff, and
others. Instead of the day's headlines, browsers found rants like:

> F1RST 0FF, WE HAVE T0 SAY.. WE 0WN YER DUMB ASS.
> 4ND R3MEMB3R, DUMB ASS 1S OFT3N CUTE 4SS. AND
> WE L1KE CUTE ASS. S3C0ND, TH3R3 AR3 S0 MANY
> L0S3RS H3R3, 1TZ HARD T0 P1CK WH1CH T0 1NSULT
> THE M0ST.

Needless to say, the attack undermined the national paper of
record's most priceless asset: the trust of its browsers. Similar
"content displacement" attacks have undermined thousands of
government, corporate, and personal sites. In July 1998, an anti-
nuclear group of crackers subverted over 300 sites at once, replacing home pages with a rambling world peace message.[2]

Many of these attacks represent a complete compromise of system security. Web servers face more moderate dangers as well. The
HTTP 1.0 protocol includes a "Basic Authentication" scheme that
involves a simple challenge and response. By providing a username
and password, a user can gain access to protected web resources.
Unfortunately, both username and password are transmitted in the
clear where they can be intercepted by eavesdroppers.

Running CGI programs on a web server presents an array of
risks to system security. CGI programs that accept and process user
input are particularly vulnerable—insecure code can allow an
attacker to execute arbitrary commands on the server with either
the same privileges as *httpd* or the user that owns the script
(depending on whether the server is configured properly). This
canonical security hole is illustrated in the following sample attack
on the *campas* CGI:

```
$ telnet www.example.com 80
Trying 200.xx.xx.xx...
Connected to www.example.com
Escape character is '^]'.
GET /cgi-bin/campas?%0acat%0a/etc/passwd%0a
<PRE>
root:x:0:1:Super-User:/export/home/root:/sbin/sh
```

---

2. See http://www.wired.com/news/news/
technology/story/13446.html

```
daemon:x:1:1::/:
bin:x:2:2::/usr/bin:
sys:x:3:3::/:
adm:x:4:4:Admin:/var/adm:
lp:x:71:8:Line Printer Admin:/usr/spool/lp:
smtp:x:0:0:Mail Daemon User:/:/bin/false
 .... continue :P
```

Here, a random browser, with a few keystrokes, is able to display the contents of */etc/passwd,* which can then be subjected to a password cracking program.

Tip

This risk is briefly described in a CERT advisory—See
`http://www.cert.org/advisories/CA-97.25.CGI_metachar.html`
You can find plenty of sample CGI exploits at
`http://www.rootshell.com`—just feed "CGI" into the search engine.

One area of web server security that rarely gets much attention is maintaining the confidentiality of the web server logs. Web server software commonly maintains detailed information about who has visited the site, what they viewed, etc. When system security is breached, it's possible for this potentially sensitive information to leak, thus compromising the implicit trust your visitors have placed in your site.

Finally, web servers are very much at risk from denial-of-service attacks. This risk arises from the fundamental security paradox presented by web and other information servers—you want to provide a service to a worldwide public, but this leaves you vulnerable to those willing to abuse the privilege. There are ways to mitigate this risk, but it remains intrinsic to making private resources publicly available.

Web Client Risks

Browsing the web is a generically insecure activity. Bugs, inappropriate "active content" and scripts, and sloppy web server administration can leave web surfers vulnerable to:

- application and system crashes

- malicious code including viruses and Trojan Horses

- loss of confidential information, and

- breaches of privacy

Sadly, the systems that are most vulnerable to client-side web risks are those with a minimal or non-existent system security model: Microsoft Windows and the Macintosh. An inventory of bugs and security problems associated with browsers like Microsoft Internet Explorer and Netscape Navigator is beyond the focus of this book. Fortunately, many of these problems have received widespread publicity in the mainstream press ("New hole found in Netscape ... News at 11"). Scripting vulnerabilities illustrate the phenomenon nicely.

Both major web browsers support the ability to download scripts embedded in an HTML page and execute them within the browser. Often, these programs are designed to interact with the user and transmit information between the browser and the server. Several times, significant bugs have been discovered in Netscape's JavaScript and Microsoft's VBscript—for example, see
`http://www.cert.org/advisories/CA-97.20.javascript.html`

Even without bugs, it's trivial for a malicious webmaster to include scripts in HTML pages that can either breach confidentiality or cause serious damage. One common line of attack is to create a JavaScript that spoofs an error message or a prompt for a user's net login ID and password. Dannie J. Gregoire calls these "Spartan Horses"—they're similar to Trojan Horses but simpler. Major sites like HotMail have been victimized by this trivial cracking method, which Gregoire documents and demonstrates at
`http://www.thetopoftheworld.com/spartanhorse/`

Other client risks result from breaches of privacy. Many web sites write an identifying cookie to the client—cookies can track users and leak where they've surfed to. According to the RFC that specifies cookie handling, client software should provide a way to specify domains for which cookies should or should not be saved.[3] Unfortunately, this capability has not been implemented.

---

3. See `http://www.faqs.org/rfcs/rfc2109.html`

Transmission Risks

Information being transmitted between web client and web server can be intercepted by eavesdroppers on either end of the link or anywhere in between, including

- the client's LAN

- the server's LAN

- the client's ISP

- the server's ISP

- any intermediary networks between the two ISPs

The terms "secure web server" and "web browser security" refer to the ability of both sides to exchange encrypted information that should be useless to eavesdroppers. Barring a "secure" encrypted link between client and server, any information transmitted between the two is subject to packet-sniffing and other interception techniques.

Tip

> No review of web security risks would be complete without reference to "The World Wide Web Security FAQ" by Lincoln D. Stein. This can be discovered at `http://www.w3.org/Security/Faq/`

Protecting Against Web Server Risks

Choosing Secure Server Software

There are dozens of *httpd* servers available that run on UNIX, from expensive commercial packages and collaboratively-developed open source packages to obsolete daemons dating back to the birth of the web. If the web server function is mission-critical, you should evaluate them all for functionality and security.

Tip

> The WebServer Compare site at `http://webcompare.internet.com` contains extensive feature-by-feature comparisons of software for UNIX and other platforms.

Here's a partial list of web server software that is known to run on Linux:

- AOLserver 2.3 by America Online Inc.

- Allegro RomPager 2.20 by Allegro Software

- Apache 1.3 by The Apache Group

- EmWeb Embedded Web Server R3_03 by Agranat Systems, Inc.

- Hawkeye 1.3.3 by Hawkeye Project

- Java Server 1.1 by Sun Microsystems

- Roxen 1.3 by Idonex AB

- Spyglass MicroServer 2.0 by Spyglass

- WebControl 2.0 by Rapid Logic, Inc.

- Xitami 2.2b by iMatix

- Zeus Web Application Server 3 by Zeus Technology

- vqServer 1.03 by vqSoft

You could evaluate all these packages, or you could run with the herd and default to the "market leader" — Apache. Apache has been the most popular web server on the Internet since 1996. Netcraft does a monthly survey of the web server installed base; the most recent as of this writing (May 1999)[4] found that over half of the web sites on the Internet are using Apache (and most of these are UNIX boxes since the Windows version of Apache is still experimental). It is more widely deployed than all other web servers combined.

A popular program isn't necessarily a secure program. Apache benefits, however, from the vetting that's integral to the open source software development model. More specifically, the Apache code benefits from ubiquity. Bugs are promptly discovered and squashed.

Among the security features offered by Apache in its latest incarnation (version 1.3) are:

---

4. See http://www.netcraft.com/survey/

- access can be prohibited by domain name, IP address, user, and group

- user groups can be configured (rather than a single user list)

- the user access control list can be modified without restarting the server

- CGI execution can be performed under the UID of the owner

- permissions for directory-based documents are hierarchical

- part of a document can be hidden based on security rules

- SSL versions 2 and 3 are supported

- a password mechanism is available

- security rules can be based on URLs

Tip

You can find out more about Apache and the Apache Group at
`http:///www.apache.org`

Caution

You probably don't want to run NCSA's *httpd,* one of the original web servers, since it's no longer under development or supported. The National Center for Supercomputing Applications recommends running Apache instead. See
`http://hoohoo.ncsa.uiuc.edu/`

Server Configuration Tips

In general, web servers should be hardened with a combination of good system security practice, configuration, and tools. The following guidelines may help:

- Dedicate a host to web serving and disallow gratuitous interactive logins to it. Delete user accounts except for the webmaster account.

- Disable unnecessary services from */etc/inetd.conf*. If your site needs FTP capabilities, dedicate another host as an FTP server. Other services that should be disabled or restricted include Telnet, finger, netstat/systat, and chargen/echo.

- Remove unnecessary shells and interpreters. If you're not running Perl-based CGI scripts, remove Perl.

- Disable support for options like automatic directory listings, symbolic link following, and server side includes.

- Monitor web logs closely.

- Deploy "secure" web server software, i.e., software that supports Secure Sockets Layer (SSL).

- Consider running the server in a *chroot* environment.

- Use a firewall to control access to the server (see "Firewalls" on page 323).

It's important to carefully plan who will have access to the content directories on a secure server. Most web servers support a variety of access control schemes. You usually can limit access to specified IP addresses or DNS hostnames or to specified users who must present a password to access a particular directory. If a web server hosts confidential company information, you will need to take steps to ensure the material stays in the right hands.

> **You must take extra care when hosting Common Gateway Interface (CGI) programs on a web server. A CGI program can do anything to the system hosting it, from providing access to outsiders to erasing critical files. For more information, see the WWW Security FAQ at**
> `http://www.w3.org/Security/Faq/`
> **the Perl-CGI FAQ at**
> `ftp://ftp.plig.org/pub/CPAN/doc/FAQs/cgi/perl-cgi-faq.html`
> **and the book *Web Security and Commerce* by Simson Garfinkel (see the Bibliography).**

Caution

Protecting Against Web Client Risks

For many UNIX installations, "web client" means "Netscape Navigator" or "Netscape Communicator" (a newer product name describing the suite of Netscape client apps).

Good Client Security Practices

Some general rules can help maintain client security. Netscape has done a good job of finding and patching security holes over the years. Be sure to install and run the latest UNIX version for your platform since it may contain security-related fixes. Give serious thought to the security settings the program offers—your browsing will be safer (if a bit crippled) if you disable both JavaScript and Java. Clean out your cache and cookie files on a regular basis. Avoid disreputable sites and use the "save" option in preference the "open" option for untrusted files.

In order to head off "Spartan Horse" attacks (described in "Web Client Risks" on page 308), be sure to educate your users about social engineering and the risk that their passwords could be stolen via deceptive code.

Mozilla

In 1998, Netscape decided to release the source code for Navigator and created a separate organization to oversee its publication and maintenance: Mozilla.org.

This was an unprecedented move for a large commercial software organization and a reflection of the fact that Netscape's management and programmers understood the net's gift economy. It was also a brilliant counterpunch to Microsoft's attempts to destroy the company. Instead of being presented as a fixed target, Netscape's technology as developed by hundreds of programmers within and outside the company has assumed a certain degree of formlessness. The book *The 48 Laws of Power*[5] describes the advantages of formlessness (Law 48):

> By taking a shape, by having a visible plan, you open yourself to attack. Instead of taking a form for your enemy to grasp, keep yourself adaptable and on the move. Accept the fact that nothing is certain, and no law is fixed. The best way to protect your-

---

5.   Greene, Robert. *The 48 Laws of Power.* Viking Penguin, 1998.

self is to be as fluid and formless as water; never bet on stability or lasting order. Everything changes.

> **Tip** You can discover more about Mozilla and download source code for the UNIX versions by surfing to `http://www.mozilla.org`

Navigator's conversion to an open source model should be a boon for those concerned about security, at least in the long-term. The code is being subjected to review by programmers and security experts outside the company for the first time.

While Netscape could not release source for any of the program's cryptographic functions (including the implementation of SSL) due to US export restrictions, the code contains "hooks" so that programmers working outside the US can add these functions on their own. One group released working cryptographic code for Mozilla within 24 hours of the source code's release on April 1, 1998.

> **Tip** You can find out about the good work of the Mozilla Crypto group and download code at
> `http://mozilla-crypto.ssleay.org/index.php`

Lynx

Lynx is a command-line browser that's included with some UNIX implementations. It's been around for a long time. While it doesn't offer "pretty pictures" (or support for security risks like Java), it is both fast and efficient. One historical limitation of Lynx: it doesn't support SSL by default.

> **Tip** If you rely on Lynx, consider installing the Lynx 2.8.1 SSL Patch which can be found at `http://www.moxienet.com/lynx/`

User Privacy

The risk of personal information being leaked during the course of web surfing and commerce is substantial. Some sites require that users register before being able to gain access to content. Most sites maintain server logs that can leak potential sensitive information including IP address, ISP, previous URLs visited, and the kind of computer and browser the user is running. Others push cookies down the pipe that could later be used to correlate the sites a user visits.

There's no sure way to ensure that your users aren't leaking personal or even confidential information during the course of web browsing, and new potential threats to privacy such as Netscape's "What's Related" feature could appear at any time.[6] Barring the development of a privacy infrastructure (covered below), user education is the best prevention.

Looking at the problem from the other side, you should consider these simple steps for protecting the privacy of your web site visitors:

- Don't require users to register in the first place.

- Gather only user email addresses as opposed to complete contact info.

- Don't share email addresses with third parties.

- Don't make your log files accessible on the web.

- Delete your log files when they're no longer needed, or move them to a secure offline medium.

Tip

> In response to widespread concern about user privacy, the Electronic Frontier Foundation (EFF) and several leading web companies formed an organization devoted to increasing users' trust and confidence in the web. TRUSTe maintains resources for both web developers (including a privacy policy wizard) and web users at
> http://www.etrust.org

Eventually, the protection of user privacy will be embodied by a technical standard. The World Wide Web Consortium (W3C) has started work on a specification called The Platform for Privacy Preferences (P3P) that will allow users to control the disclosure of

---

6. See http://www.anonymizer.com/content/whatsrelated.shtml for an explanation of the risks of What's Related.

identity information based on their own preferences. According to the W3C's site:[7]

> The P3P specification will enable Web sites to express their privacy practices and users to exercise preferences over those practices. P3P products will allow users to be informed of site practices, to delegate decisions to their computer when possible, and allow users to tailor their relationship to specific sites. Sites with practices that fall within the range of a user's preference could, at the option of the user, be accessed "seamlessly," otherwise users will be notified of a site's practices and have the opportunity to agree to those terms or other terms and continue browsing if they wish.

Tip

One "brute force" method of protecting privacy is to use an anonymizing proxy server that strips any identifying information from your web requests. Check out http://www.anonymizer.com, the Lucent Personalized Web Assistant at http://lpwa.com:8000/, and AT&T's Crowds protocol at http://www.research.att.com/projects/crowds/.

Protecting Against Transmission Risks

From the point of view of the user, web browsing can breach privacy, allowing TCP/IP excels at providing an anonymous stream of data between two machines, but it does not provide for confidentiality, integrity, and authentication. There are several complementary and competing schemes for adding a security layer to the TCP/IP suite, including Secure Shell (SSH) and Microsoft's PCT. In the rough and tumble marketplace of working code, the Secure Sockets Layer (SSL) prevails.

SSL

SSL was designed by Netscape as a protocol for providing data security layered between application protocols (such as HTTP, Telnet, NNTP, or FTP) and the lower TCP/IP layers. It provides three basic security features:

- Confidentiality—Privacy is implemented through symmetric cryptography. The keys for symmetric encryption are generated

---

7. See http://www.w3.org/P3P/

uniquely for each connection and are based on a negotiated
secret.

- Server authentication—Clients check for a valid server
  X.509v3 certificate, either an RSA public key certificate, a Digital Signature Standard (DSS) certificate, or a Diffie-Hellman
  certificate. Typically, certificates are issued by a trusted Certificate Authority.

- Message integrity—Message integrity is protected by a MAC
  (Message Authentication Code) integrity check, a one-way hash
  computed from a message and some secret data. It is difficult to
  forge without knowing the secret data.

In addition, SSL provides for optional client authentication,
though this feature is not widely used. SSL's other features—and
server authentication in particular—are widely deployed on the
World Wide Web in support of electronic commerce. While different web browsers indicate a secure SSL connection in different
ways, a URL that starts with "https://" indicates that a secure connection between client and server has been built.

Tip

You can find out more about SSL from Netscape—see
`http://home.netscape.com/products/`
`security/ssl/index.html`
In addition, Netscape provides SSLRef, a reference version of the
protocol. See `http://home.netscape.com/products/`
`security/ssl/reference.html`

TLS

SSL is an open, nonproprietary protocol. Although Netscape has
patented the underlying technology, it freely licenses it. The latest
version—SSL 3.0—is in the process of being adopted and adapted
as an Internet standard by the Internet Engineering Task Force.
The new standard is called TLS (Transport Layer Security). It's
being drafted by the Transport Layer Security Working Group,
which should eventually produce an RFC document.

Tip

You can find out more about TLS by reviewing the working group's
site at `http://www.ietf.org/html.charters/tls-charter.html`

While a complete description of TLS/SLL is beyond the scope of this work, I'll present a brief sketch of how TLS should work.

TLS is designed to set-up a secure "session"—an association between a client and a server used to avoid the expensive negotiation of new security parameters for each addition connection.

The proposed protocol is divided into two separate layers: the TLS Handshake Protocol, which sits "on top," and the TLS Record Protocol.

The TLS Handshake Protocol establishes the cryptographic parameters of a secure session. As a TLS-enabled client and a TLS-enabled server establish communication, they agree on a protocol version, select cryptographic algorithms, optionally authenticate each other, and use public-key encryption techniques to generate shared secrets.

According to the preliminary specification,[8] the TLS Handshake Protocol involves the following steps:

- Exchange "hello" messages to agree on algorithms, exchange random values, and check for session resumption.

- Exchange the necessary cryptographic parameters to allow the client and server to agree on a "pre-master secret."

- Exchange certificates and cryptographic information to allow the client and server to authenticate themselves.

- Generate a master secret from the pre-master secret and exchanged random values.

- Provide security parameters to the record layer.

- Allow the client and server to verify that their peer has calculated the same security parameters and that the handshake occurred without tampering by an attacker.

Once the client and server have "shaken hands" and agreed on session parameters, the TLS Record Protocol does the actual work of reading and writing data across the link. It takes a message to be

---

8. See http://www.ietf.org/internet-drafts/draft-ietf-tls-protocol-06.txt

transmitted, fragments the data into manageable blocks, optionally compresses the data, applies a message authentication code
(MAC), encrypts the data, and transmits the result. Received data
is decrypted, verified, decompressed, and reassembled, and is then
delivered to higher level clients.

Setting Up a TLS/SSL Server

Most commercial web server products—including those from
Netscape—implement SSL. While the vagaries of setting up these
secure servers is best left to the accompanying documentation, I'd
be remiss if I didn't point that there's a "free" implementation of
TLS/SSL called SSLeay (each letter is pronounced separately)
which was coded from protocol descriptions by Australian programmer Eric A. Young. I put the "free" in quotation marks since
SSLeay uses several encryption algorithms, some of which may
require commercial licensing. SSLeay implements five different
algorithms: DES, RSA, RC4, IDEA, and Blowfish. The RSA algorithm is patented in the US. You may need to get a license from
RSA Data Security in order to deploy it with SSLeay on US-based
commercial servers.[9]

Tip

> You can find more information about the SSLeay library or down-
> load it by surfing to the official site—http://www.ssleay.org/ You
> can also download several SSLeay-based applications—including
> SSL-hardened versions of FTP and Telnet by Tim J. Hudson.

In December1998, several programmers in the UK launched a
collaborative, open source effort to build a commercial-grade
TLS/SSL toolkit based on SSLeay. The OpenSSL Project's home
page asks a reasonable question: "Why buy an SSL toolkit as a
black-box when you can get an open box for free?"

---

9. See http://www.rsa.com/ Here's an excerpt from the company's
FAQ: "RSA is patented under U.S. Patent 4,405,829, issued September
29, 1983 and held by RSA Data Security, Inc.; the patent expires 17 years
after issue, in the year 2000. RSA Data Security has a standard, royalty-
based licensing policy, which can be modified for special circumstances.
However, RSA Data Security usually allows free non-commercial use of
RSA, with written permission, for academic or university research
purposes."

Find out more about the OpenSSL project and download source   **Tip**
code at http://www.openssl.org/

Both SSLeay and OpenSSL can be integrated with the Apache web server. Programmer Ben Laurie has developed an Apache-SSL package that provides a set of patches for Apache, some extra source files, a few README files, and example configuration files.[10] The patches need to be applied to the Apache source code, and the result compiled and linked with either SSLeay or OpenSSL.

You can download Laurie's Apache-SSL package, along with server   **Tip**
documentation, from http://www.apache-ssl.org/

If you're interested in the Apache/SSL combination, but are daunted by either patent restrictions or the complexity of working with source code, a commercial package called Stronghold from C2Net Software, Inc. integrates Apache with an SSL implementation and provides tech support and documentation.[11]

TCP/IP Ports for TLS/SSL

In theory, TLS/SSL can transparently secure any TCP-based protocol running on any port if both sides know the other side is using TLS/SSL. For practical reasons, separate port numbers have been reserved for each of the protocols that can be secured by TLS/SSL, thus permitting packet filtering firewalls to allow such secure traffic through.

Table 15.1 summarizes the SSL port numbers that have been reserved by the Internet Assigned Numbers Authority (IANA). While many of the secured versions of common net protocols are not in wide use, they are likely to be deployed in the coming years as network security concerns become more prominent.

---

10. Ben, along with Peter Laurie, wrote a good book on Apache. *Apache: The Definitive Guide* (Sebastopol, CA: O'Reilly, 1997).
11. It costs about $1000. See
http://www.c2.org/products/stronghold/

Table 15.1 *TLS/SSL Assigned Port Numbers*

Keyword	Port #	Description
nsiiops	261/tcp	IIOP Name Service over TLS/SSL
https	443/tcp	http protocol over TLS/SSL
ddm-ssl	448/tcp	DDM-SSL
smtps	465/tcp	smtp protocol over TLS/SSL
nntps	563/tcp	nntp protocol over TLS/SSL
sshell	614/tcp	SSLshell
ldaps	636/tcp	ldap protocol over TLS/SSL
ftps-data	989/tcp	ftp protocol, data, over TLS/SSL
ftps	990/tcp	ftp, control, over TLS/SSL
telnets	992/tcp	telnet protocol over TLS/SSL
imaps	993/tcp	imap4 protocol over TLS/SSL
ircs	994/tcp	irc protocol over TLS/SSL
pop3s	995/tcp	pop3 protocol over TLS/SSL

## 16

Firewalls

This chapter explains what firewalls are and why
they're an important part of a defense-in-depth
strategy for a UNIX-based and Internet-connected
network. It presents some of the policy issues
related to firewalls, common firewall designs, and
an overview of firewall tools.

In its simplest incarnation, a firewall is a component or set of
components that restricts access between a protected network (typically a LAN) and the Internet. It can be implemented as hardware
in the form of a router or computer, software running on a gateway
system, or some combination.

The term originally comes from the building industry. Firewalls
are commonly built of fireproof materials and are often built
between adjacent apartments or buildings. With a firewall in place,
a fire that breaks out on one side of the wall can be contained, preventing it from spreading to neighboring units or structures. Steve
Bellovin was the first to use the term in the context of computer
security in an email message to a colleague in 1987.[1] Like many
Internet terms, the metaphor between the physical firewall and the
network firewall is rich—in many ways, there are fires breaking
out all the time on the net. Very few organizations are interested in
feeling the heat.

Why Firewalls?

Marcus J. Ranum and Matt Curtin, authors of the Firewall FAQ,[2]
summarize the justification for firewalls quite nicely:

> The Internet, like any other society, is plagued with the kind of
> jerks who enjoy the electronic equivalent of writing on other
> people's walls with spraypaint, tearing their mailboxes off, or
> just sitting in the street blowing their car horns. Some people try
> to get real work done over the Internet, and others have sensi-
> tive or proprietary data they must protect. Usually, a firewall's
> purpose is to keep the jerks out of your network while still let-
> ting you get your job done.

Firewalls are like traffic cops that do one of two things—let traffic go through, or block traffic. Like real-world cops, firewalls can
be either permissive—in so far as they allow a generous flow of
traffic—or paranoid in so far as they reject all but specific, pre-
authorized blocks of traffic. In this way, they embody the security
policy that the organization wishes to enforce.

---

1. Bellovin, along with Cheswick, wrote the seminal book *Firewalls and
Internet Security: Repelling the Wily Hacker* (Addison-Wesley, 1994).
2. See http://www.clark.net/pub/mjr/pubs/fwfaq/index.htm

Like the ramparts of a medieval castle, well-implemented fire-walls can be a critical part of a defense-in-depth strategy. Without a firewall, a LAN or subnet is extremely vulnerable to external attack on services like NFS of NIS, on weak passwords, and on misconfigured systems. Overall network security completely relies on maintenance of a consistent, high-level of security on each and every host—a difficult state to preserve across a complex network.

Firewalls can:

- control access to internal systems so that only mail or public information servers are reachable from the outside

- block access to particular Internet sites on a per-machine or per-user basis

- improve network security by filtering insecure services like NFS

- reduce cost and increase efficiency by allowing sysadmins to concentrate security efforts on a single system as opposed to each and every host on a LAN

- enhance privacy by blocking external access to services like finger and DNS, which could leak information to attackers

- monitor communications between an internal network and the Internet in order to track down network penetrations or insider malfeasance

- establish an encrypted link between two remote locations (sometimes referred to as a virtual private network)

Policy Considerations

There are two levels of network security policy that need to be established before an effective firewall can be implemented. At the top level is a service access policy which specifically lays out what services will be allowed or restricted across the firewall, how those services may be used, and how exceptions are handled. A realistic balance must be struck between protecting the network from known risks and allowing users access to needed network resources. A service access policy might state, for example, that only restricted access to mail and information servers will be allowed from the Internet, or it may be extended to allow some access from the Internet to certain hosts but only by authenticated users.

At a lower level is the firewall design policy that will dictate what restriction mechanisms are implemented. There are two basic and exclusive strategies that inform firewall policy:

- Default permit—permit any service unless it is expressly denied, allowing all services to pass by default, with the exception of those that the service access policy specifically disallows. This conforms to an "open lab" access model that maximizes functionality.

- Default deny—deny any service unless it is expressly permitted, denying all services by default, with the exception of those that the service access policy specifically allows. This conforms to the classic access model used in many areas of information security.

Neither strategy is full-proof. Default permit is easier to set up in some ways; the main task is to identify and deny risky protocols. While a default deny strategy closely tailored to the organization's service access policy provides a higher level of security, it can be inconvenient for users. One reason for this is that many services— like X Windows, FTP, and RPC—are difficult to filter. Another is that, as newer services—such as RealAudio—become available, users will be blocked from using them until the firewall administrators reconfigure the firewall.

Like many security policy dichotomies, the two approaches need to be balanced and iterated upon. In some cases, requested services need to be denied because the security risk is too high. In others, a risky service may be essential to the mission of the organization and will be accommodated despite the risk.

Firewall Hazards

With the corporate rush to exploit the Internet, there's a tendency to seek out "stock" firewall products for purchase. There's no such thing as a stock firewall—like many methods of improving computer security, a firewall requires tight customization to the unique

needs and circumstances of a given site. If you seek a standard
solution, you're on the wrong path. The thought of corporate customers asking vendors for the capability to misconfigure their firewalls is disheartening.

The Computer Security Institute held a "meet the enemy" tele-
conference with a group of hackers.[3] When asked about commercial firewall packages, the hackers made some interesting
observations:

> First of all, with any big commercial firewall that comes in a
> package, if you don't have the knowledge to configure it, it's
> useless to you anyway. It's like going out and buying a car and
> not knowing how to drive it.

A commercial firewall package creates its own risk. As one
hacker points out:

> Two thousand people install 'Super Firewall X' at their sites,
> then you and I sit down for a week or two and crack 'Super
> Firewall X' —hey, we've just cracked two thousand sites.

Another hacker offered a gem of wisdom concerning how essential trained firewall administrators are:

> You have to have someone dedicated to the security of your net-
> work. You can't have three people doing the job. You have to
> have someone who knows it inside and out—someone who can
> recognize that when the system has problems, it's not just
> because Bob did something weird last shift.

Firewalls can breed a false sense of security. Some sites seem to
feel that having a firewall, any firewall, makes their site secure
against any form of attack. There's a saying amongst firewall
gurus: it's altogether possible to have a vault for a front door and
screen doors in the back. As a perimeter defense, a firewall is only
one piece of the puzzle—one tactic of many needed to provide an
Internet site with defense-in-depth.

A firewall will not protect an organization from attacks by
insiders who operate behind the firewall. Some companies have

---

3. See `http://www.gocsi.com/hacker.htm` Some of these individuals
might be more accurately described as "crackers," but I'm following the
usage of the source document.

responded to this problem by installing internal firewalls within
their organizations. There's a misconception that you can dial your
firewall from a very secure setting to, say, a medium secure setting.
As Bill Cheswick has pointed out: "Hacking is binary by nature
(0/1). You get hacked or you don't. There isn't a half-way secure
firewall."[4]

Internal firewalls can both decrease usability and tempt well-
meaning employees to find ways to defeat them (this applies to
other security measures as well). Brent Chapman tells a chilling
tale of a computer company that had a strict "no modems" policy
that engineers hated. Security managers thought the engineers had
no choice but to go along, but a common hack was "to go to Frye's
get a V.32 modem, plug it into the SPARC, and unplug nearest fax
line and plug into a modem at night. (A) former employee kept getting in this way over and over." The lessons?[5]

> 1) Most companies try to hire people who are problem solvers.
> If the firewall is a problem, they will solve it.
> 2) Management didn't realize difficulties with using the secure
> network. Engineers didn't think about the security implications
> of what they were doing.

Types of Firewalls

Over the past several years, many types of firewalls have evolved.
They can be roughly categorized as either network-level firewalls
or application-level firewalls, though the distinction between the
two gets weaker as firewall technologies are mixed and matched in
the marketplace.

Network-level Firewalls

A basic instance of a network-level firewall is a single router that
sits between the Internet and an internal network and filters individual packets based on their source, destination addresses and
ports. A packet-filtering router (known as a "choke" in firewall
lingo) can be deployed in a variety of ways to block connections
from or to specific hosts or networks, and to block connections to

---

4. From a Birds of a Feather meeting noted at http://www.cs.
purdue.edu/coast/firewalls/firewalls_bof_95.txt
5. Ibid.

specific ports. A site might wish to block connections from hostile or untrustworthy addresses, or it may block connections from all external addresses with an exception for SMTP so that mail can be exchanged with the outside.

Network-level firewalls tend to be fast and transparent to users. They can be relatively easy to set up and cheap, in so far as many organizations already have routers connected to the Internet. They can be programmed with straightforward rules like "block packets for unused services" or "allow incoming TCP connections to information servers but no other internal hosts." They are also flexible. Say someone on subnet 123.4.5.0 is attacking one of your hosts: you can configure a network-level firewall to block all access from that subnet.

Packet-filtering routers have some potential weaknesses, however. Older routers do not support extensive logging—your first sign of misconfiguration could be a break-in. Packet-filtering rules can also be complex to specify—filter rulesets can get so convoluted that holes may be hard to detect.

Application Gateways

A common way to overcome some of the weaknesses of packet filtering is to deploy an application-level firewall, a host that runs proxy services—software applications that forward and filter connections for services such as Telnet and FTP. The host running the proxy service is referred to as an "application gateway" or a "bastion host." It can be combined with a packet-filtering router to provide better security and flexibility than if either were used alone.

Classic Firewall Configurations

Packet-filtering Firewall

This is probably the simplest firewall configuration. You install a packet-filtering router at the Internet gateway and then configure the router's packet-filtering in order to selectively block, or "filter," protocols and addresses. Internal systems may have direct access to the Internet while all or most access to internal systems from the Internet is blocked, depending on the policy.

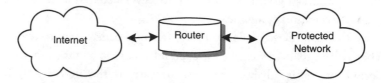

Figure 16.1 *A Packet-filtering Firewall*

Dual-Homed Host

Superior to the packet-filtering firewall in many ways, the dual-homed host (also known as a "dual-homed gateway") is a simple configuration that is relatively easy to implement and offers good security. Many early Internet firewalls were built around a single UNIX host configured as a "bastion host"—a host that acts as an application forwarder, traffic logger, and service provider. Naturally, a bastion host must be as secure as possible since it's the focal point for attack on the network.

A dual-homed host has two network interfaces—one connected to the internal network and one connected to the Internet. The host blocks all traffic passing through it and runs proxy services. In order to work properly, the computer must never forward packets directly from one interface to the other. This can be set up on many UNIX systems by setting the kernel variable *ip_forwarding* to zero (i.e., off).

This kind of firewall offers a greater degree of security than a packet-filtering firewall since it achieves a total block and conforms to the default deny policy. All services are denied unless they are specifically permitted, since no services pass except those for which proxies exist.

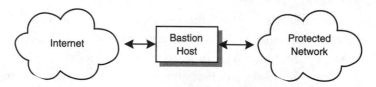

Figure 16.2 *A Dual-homed Host Firewall*

Screened Host

In a screened host firewall, access to and from a single bastion host is controlled by means of a router with some form of packet-screening capability to block off access between the protected network and the Internet. Traffic is permitted only to the bastion host, which runs proxy software similar to what would run on a dual-homed gateway.

Screened host gateways are flexible. They offer the opportunity to selectively permit traffic through the screening router for applications that are considered trustworthy, or between mutually trusted networks. The disadvantage of this configuration is that there are now two security critical systems to be aware of: the bastion host and the router.

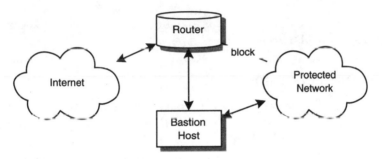

Figure 16.3 *A Screened Host Firewall*

Screened Subnet

In a screened subnet firewall, a small isolated network is placed between the internal network and the Internet. Two routers are used to create an inner, screened subnet—the "DMZ" (Demilitarized Zone). The DMZ houses the bastion host as well as information servers, modem pools, and other systems that require controlled access. Access to the DMZ subnet is protected by screening rules in the routers, which restrict traffic so that hosts on the subnet are the only systems reachable by both the internal network and the Internet.

The screened subnet firewall is a variation of the dual-homed gateway and screened host firewalls. The DMZ makes it very difficult for an outsider to direct traffic at the hidden private network.

If the routing is blocked, then, as with a dual-homed gateway, all traffic must pass through an application on the bastion host.

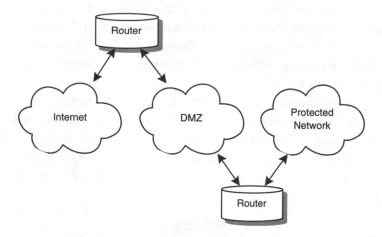

Figure 16.4 *A Screened Subnet Firewall*

Firewall Planning

Traditionally, many organizations have "rolled their own" firewalls, using UNIX hosts and routers. In the past few years, firewall capabilities have been built into many UNIX implementations and a wide variety of both free and commercial firewall toolkits have become available. Additionally, it is possible for an organization to outsource firewall services: a large number of Internet Service Providers and other service organizations provide monitored firewall services.

Risk Assessment

All computer security planning starts with a risk assessment: what am I trying to protect and what are the risks? Unfortunately, the risks are substantial when connecting a private network to the Internet or to any untrusted networks. If you're connecting systems to the Internet, their security will be probed, even if you perceive that "there's nothing of value" for anyone to steal. Many small-time home LAN operators have been surprised to find their Linux boxes on the receiving end of rootkit exploits: you can find their desperate calls for help on the comp.security.unix newsgroup. At the other end of the spectrum, serious ecommerce companies view firewall implementation as a mission-critical part of preserving the trust online customers demonstrate with each order.

Policies
You must adopt high-level policies outlining the services that the firewall will support and specifying the choice for default deny or default permit. You should also integrate firewall policy into the overall site security policy.

Personnel
In all but the smallest installations, firewall administration is a full-time job. There is no replacement for trained, full-time system administrators who are available to monitor performance, upgrade systems, apply bug fixes and patches, and otherwise make sure that systems are secure and protected from intruders. A poorly-maintained firewall may be worse than no firewall at all since it may permit break-ins while providing an illusion that the site is still secure. A site's security policy should clearly reflect the importance of strong firewall administration.

A firewall is not an excuse to pay less attention to site system administration. It is, in fact, the opposite: if a firewall is penetrated, a poorly administered site could be wide-open to intrusions and resultant damage. A firewall in no way reduces the need for highly skilled system administration.

Budget
At the high-end, it can cost hundreds of thousands of dollars to install and configure firewalls across an entire corporation. At the low-end, an old PC running Linux can do it for free. Be sure to factor in maintenance costs: even that freebie firewall will need ongoing monitoring and upgrades.

Minimum Requirements
Once you've established policy, analyzed risk, and accounted for costs, you are ready to develop a set of design requirements for your firewall system. Following is a list of possible requirements extracted from the NIST publication, "Keeping Your Site Comfortably Secure: An Introduction to Internet Firewalls."[6]

---

6. John P. Wack and Lisa J. Carnahan, NIST Special Publication 800-10. See http://csrc.nist.gov/nistpubs/800-10/

- The firewall should be able to support a "deny all services except those specifically permitted" design policy, even if that is not the policy used.

- The firewall should support your security policy, not impose one.

- The firewall should be flexible; it should be able to accommodate new services and needs if the security policy of the organization changes.

- The firewall should contain advanced authentication measures or should contain the hooks for installing advanced authentication measures.

- The firewall should employ filtering techniques to permit or deny services to specified host systems as needed.

- The IP filtering language should be flexible, user-friendly to program, and should filter on as many attributes as possible, including source and destination IP address, protocol type, source and destination TCP/UDP port, and inbound and outbound interface.

- The firewall should use proxy servers for services such as FTP and Telnet, so that advanced authentication measures can be employed and centralized at the firewall. If services such as NNTP, X, http, or gopher are required, the firewall should contain the corresponding proxy services.

- The firewall should contain the ability to centralize SMTP access, to reduce direct SMTP connections between site and remote systems. This results in centralized handling of site e-mail.

- The firewall should accommodate public access to the site, such that public information servers can be protected by the firewall but can be segregated from site systems that do not require public access.

- The firewall should contain the ability to concentrate and filter dial-in access.

- The firewall should contain mechanisms for logging traffic and suspicious activity, as well as mechanisms for log reduction so that logs are readable and understandable.

- A secured version of UNIX should be part of the firewall, with other security tools as necessary to ensure firewall host integrity. The operating system should have all patches installed.

- The firewall should be developed in a manner that its strength and correctness is verifiable. It should be simple in design so that it can be understood and maintained.

- The firewall and any corresponding operating system should be updated with patches and other bug fixes in a timely manner.

Firewall Tools Survey

Packet-filtering and other firewall features are built into many modern UNIX systems, including Linux and the *BSD systems. In addtion, a wide variety of firewall tools are available, from code in the public domain to expansive and expensive commercial products. Many tools are integrated with "toolkits." Others are standalone.

> **Tip**
>
> An extensive list of commercial firewall products maintained by Catherine Fulmer can be found at
> `http://www.waterw.com/~manowar/vendor.html`

The following are free tools that are available on the net. Note that many of these programs come with licensing restrictions.

Freestone

SOS Corp. makes this freeware version of its Brimstone firewall available. Freestone is a portable, fully-functional firewall implementation that supports niceties like FTP and Telnet proxies which can be extended with an access control list mechanism. Installation and configuration is complex and takes many steps. Here's an excerpt from the README: "Freestone should be thought of as providing many of the tools needed to make a secure firewall, rather than being a turnkey solution."

For more information:

http://www.soscorp.com/products/Freestone.html

To download:

ftp://ftp.soscorp.com/pub/sos/freestone/

ftp://ftp.cs.columbia.edu/pub/sos/freestone/

IP Filter

IP Filter is a TCP/IP packet filter designed for use in a firewall environment. It can be configured as a loadable kernel module (preferred) or incorporated into a UNIX kernel. Scripts are provided to
install and patch system files as needed. IP Filter can explicitly
deny/permit any packet from passing through, distinguish between
various interfaces, filter by IP networks or hosts, or selectively filter
any IP protocol. It includes provisions for logging and testing. IP
Filter is included with several free UNIX implementations, including FreeBSD, OpenBSD, and NetBSD.

For more information:

http://cheops.anu.edu.au/~avalon/ip-filter.html

To download:

ftp://coombs.anu.edu.au/pub/net/ip-filter/

Juniper Firewall Toolkit

Juniper is a toolkit for building secure and effective Internet firewalls. It's designed to work on a dual-homed bastion host that
does not forward packets between interfaces. Juniper implements
transparent proxy facilities to allow machines on internal,
unrouted networks to transparently access the Internet as if they
were directly connected. Juniper was turned into an open source
product in 1998. It runs on BSD/OS, FreeBSD, NetBSD, and
Linux.

For more information:

http://www.obtuse.com/juniper/

To download:

ftp://ftp.obtuse.com/pub/juniper/

Mediator One

The Mediator One Firewall is a complete shareware firewall package designed to run on a single system. It provides a collection of
hardened proxies as well as authentication and auditing

capabilities for network connections. A browser-based interface can be used to configure, control, and query the firewall.

For more information:

```
http://www.comnet.com.au/htmls/mediator1.html
```

To download, use this site:

```
http://www.comnet.com.au/htmls/mediator_registration.html
```

SOCKS

SOCKS is a networking proxy protocol that enables hosts on one side of a SOCKS server to gain full access to hosts on the other side of a SOCKS server without requiring direct IP reachability. SOCKS includes two primary components: the SOCKS server and the SOCKS client library. The server authenticates and authorizes connection requests, establishes proxy connections, and relays data. The client library sits between the client's application and transport layers. Because of its simplicity, SOCKS has been widely used as a circuit-level firewall: hosts behind a SOCKS server can gain full access to the Internet while clients remain hidden to the Internet hosts they access. There are two versions of SOCKS available. SOCKS V4 performs three functions: connection requests, proxy circuit setups, and application data relays. SOCKS V5 adds authentication.

For more information:

```
http://www.socks.nec.com/
```

```
http://www.socks.nec.com/rfc/rfc1928.txt
```

To download:

```
http://www.socks.nec.com/cgi-bin/download.pl
```

```
ftp://ftp.nec.com/pub/socks/
```

Tcpr

Tcpr is a set of Perl scripts that forwards FTP and Telnet commands across a firewall. Forwarding takes place at the application level, so it's easy to control. No recompilation of C code is necessary. Tcpr consists of an *inetd*-type server that interprets commands, a relay program, and a client that talks to the server. The client asks the server for a relay connection to some specified remote host at a specified TCP port number; the server invokes the relay program and returns a proxy port number to the client. The client then invokes telnet or ftp, telling them to connect to the relay host at the proxy port number. The relay program then transfers data between the client host and the remote host. Tcpr was written for SunOS and Perl 4.

For more information:
`ftp://coast.cs.purdue.edu/pub/tools/unix/tcpr/`

TIS Firewall Toolkit

The TIS Internet Firewall Toolkit is a freely available set of programs and "configuration practices" for building network firewalls on UNIX systems. Toolkit components can be used in isolation or mixed and matched with other firewall components. The toolkit is designed to support the implementation of firewalls based on the "that which is not expressly permitted is denied" approach. It supports the construction of dual-homed gateways, screened host gateways, and screened subnet gateways. TIS, which merged with Network Associates in 1998, now sells a commercial firewall package: the Gauntlet Internet Firewall.

For more information:
`http://www.tis.com/prodserv/fwtk/index.html`

To download (email confirmation required):
`http://www.tis.com/prodserv/fwtk/readme.html`

`ftp://ftp.tis.com/pub/firewalls/toolkit/`

udprelay

The udprelay package by Tom Fitzgerald implements a daemon process that runs on a firewall host and forwards UDP packets into and out of the firewalled network, as directed by a configuration file.

To download, use this site:
`ftp://coast.cs.purdue.edu/pub/tools/unix/`
`udprelay-0.2.tar.gz`

xforward

The xforward package by Win Treese is used to relay X Window System connections across network firewalls.

To download:
`ftp://crl.dec.com/pub/DEC/xforward.tar.Z`

Xp-BETA

Xp-BETA is an application gateway for the X11 protocol that uses Socks and/or the CERN WWW Proxy.

To download:

`ftp://ftp.mri.co.jp/pub/Xp-BETA`

A Linux Firewall with ipchains

The presence of firewall capabilities at the kernel level is one of the many benefits of Linux. The firewall utility ipfwadm (based on the BSD ipfw) provides sysadmins with many options for integrating firewall capabilities on their Linux boxes. In 1998, various Linux developers undertook a major re-write of the previous Linux IPv4 firewall code dubbed "ipchains."

> The ipchains tool is required to administer the IP packet filters in Linux kernel versions 2.1.102 and above. Systems running the 2.0 kernel series can download a kernel patch. To check if your system has ipchains, look for the file `/proc/net/ip_fwchains`   **Tip**

The ipchains tool is set up with filters that determine how packets are handled. The filters are controlled by three firewall chains—or lists of rules—called input, forward, and output. When a packet arrives, the kernel uses the input chain to determine whether it lives or dies. If it survives, the packet is routed. If the packet is destined for another machine, the kernel consults the forward chain. Finally, the kernel consults the output chain before sending it on its way.

> For more information on ipchains, see the Linux IPCHAINS-HOWTO by Paul Russell, at `http://www.rustcorp.com/linux/ipchains/HOWTO.html` and the Official IPCHAINS Home Page at `http://www.rustcorp.com/linux/ipchains/`.   **Tip**

Innovations like ipchains demonstrate that the art of building firewalls continues to evolve. Eventually, system and application security may improve to the point that perimeter defenses like firewalls are rendered moot. This change, if it comes at all, will be driven by the complex connectivity requirements of extensively internetworked businesses. In the meantime, Internet-connected sites will continue to deploy firewalls; vendors will improve the underlying technology; and sysadmins will struggle with their configuration and maintenance. You can keep current with developments in the field of firewalls by subscribing to the Firewall Wizards List—see `http://www.nfr.net/forum/ firewall-wizards.html` for more information.

The Tools CD-ROM

The CD-ROM that accompanies this work contains source code for several UNIX security tools. This appendix displays the contents of the CD-ROM. It also presents some tips about using the tools.

Mounting the CD-ROM

Before you can access the files, you may need to mount the
CD-ROM using the mount command. This command usually takes
the form:

```
# mount CD-ROM_device mount_point
```

The CD-ROM device varies depending on the system you're
using. In Linux, it may be */dev/cdrom*. The mount point is the par-
ent directory of the CD-ROM once it is mounted. The directories
/cdrom or */mnt/cdrom* would be conventional mount points. An
example command under Linux might look like:

```
# /bin/mount -r /dev/cdrom /cdrom
```

The "-r" flag indicates a read-only filesystem ("-o ro" is synonymous). Check your system's man page for mount for more details
(man mount). It's possible that your system is configured to auto-
mount CD-ROMs. It's also possible that you may need to be root
in order to run the mount command.

Tips on the Tools

Keep a few things in mind while working with the enclosed tools.

- The files for each tool are stored in a top-level directory (i.e.,
  the files for the COPS tool are in the */cops* directory).

- Most tools have a README file—read it first.

- The files for most of the tools are tarred and either compressed
  (*.tar.Z*) or gzipped (*.tgz* or *.tar.gz*) with GNU zip (gzip). Most
  systems support these formats; for those that don't, GNU zip is
  included on the accompanying CD-ROM. When available,
  RPM versions for Linux i386 are included.

- Some of the tar files are signed by the author with a PGP key.
  Others included MD5 checksums. If feasible, verify the packages—See "Verifying Software" on page 133.

- Most of the tools are in source form. That means you need to
  compile and install them. Most of the packages include a

Makefile—the `make` command simplifies the compilation process. One C source file has been provided: *snefru.c*. To compile it, issue the command:

```
cc -o snefru snefru.c
```

- Online sources for the packages are listed in the footnotes.

- Most of the programs are covered by the GNU General Public License—see page 397.

Table A.1 *Tools on CD-ROM*

Tool	Purpose	Page	Files
Crypt Breakers Workbench[a]	Breaks crypt files	148	/cbw/README.local /cbw/cbw.tar.Z
chkacct[b]	Checks the security of user accounts	220	/chkacct/README /chkacct/chkacct-src.tar.sig /chkacct/chkacct.v1.1.tar.Z /chkacct/chkacct.v1.tar.Z
chkwtmp[c]	Checks the *wtmp* file	192	/chkwtmp/ chkwtmp.README/ chkwtmp/ chkwtmp-1.0.tar.Z
Crack 5.0a[d]	Finds and reports on weak passwords	99	/crack/Crack_5.0a.tar.gz /crack/c50a.txt /crack/c50a.tgz.asc
COPS[e]	Reports on vulnerabilities	227	/cops/cops.1.04.README /cops/cops.1.04.tar.gz
gzip[f]	Compresses files	342	/gzip/gzip-1.2.4a.tar.gz
MD5[g]	Calculates MD5 message digests	127, 136	/md5/MD5.README /md5/MD5.tar.Z /md5/MD5.tar.Z.asc /md5/jim_ellis.asc

Table A.1 *Tools on CD-ROM (Cont'd)*

Tool	Purpose	Page	Files
md5sum[h]	Calculates MD5 message digests	127, 136	/md5sum/ textutils-1.22.tar.gz
Snefru[i]	One-way hash function	128	/snefru/README
Swatch[j]	Monitors system logs	197	/swatch/README /swatch/swatch-2.2.tar.gz /swatch/swatch-2.2.tar.asc /swatch /swatch-2.2-7.src.rpm /swatch/swatch-3.0b1.tar.gz
Tiger[k]	Reports on vulnerabilities	235	/tiger/tiger.README /tiger/tiger-2.2.4.tgz /tiger/tiger-2.2.4.lsm /tiger/tiger-2.2.3.tar.gz
Tripwire[l]	Checks filesystem integrity	151	/tripwire/
Zap	Hides user from logs	195	/zap/zap.tar.gz

a. ftp://coast.cs.purdue.edu/pub/tools/unix/cbw/
b. ftp://coast.cs.purdue.edu/pub/tools/unix/chkacct/
c. ftp://coast.cs.purdue.edu/pub/tools/unix/chkwtmp/
d. http://www.users.dircon.co.uk/~crypto/
e. ftp://coast.cs.purdue.edu/pub/tools/unix/cops/
f. ftp://ftp.gnu.org/gnu/gzip/
g. http://www.cert.org/ftp/tools/md5/
h. ftp://ftp.gnu.org/gnu/textutils/
i. ftp://coast.cs.purdue.edu/pub/tools/unix/snefru/
j. ftp://ftp.stanford.edu/general/security-tools/swatch/
k. ftp://coast.cs.purdue.edu/pub/tools/unix/tiger/TAMU/
l. ftp://contrib.redhat.com/libc5/SRPMS/tripwire-1.2-3.src.rpm

Internet Resources

This appendix presents a short selection of security
and UNIX-related resources that can be accessed
via the World Wide Web, including security
"supersites," tool archives, reference sites and
portals, organizations, periodicals, open source/
Linux sites, underground/cracker sites, and
Internet mailing lists.

Security Supersites

These sites are remarkable for their depth of security coverage—
they offer advisories, tools, documents, links, research programs,
and more. They all provide extensive UNIX security resources as
well as resources for other platforms.

CERIAS /COAST

`http://www.cerias.purdue.edu`—As part of its research and educational mission at Purdue University, CERIAS (the Center for
Education and Research in Information Assurance and Security)
hosts the leading security site on the net. Along with COAST
(Computer Operations, Audit, and Security Technology), it offers a
comprehensive collection of security tools, documents, and links.
See the COAST Hotlist of security links at
`http://www.cs.purdue.edu/coast/hotlist/`, the COAST Library
at `http://www.cs.purdue.edu/coast/coast-library.html`, and the
COAST Security FTP Archive at `ftp://coast.cs.purdue.edu/pub/`

CERT® Coordination Center

`http://www.cert.org`—Best known for its security advisories,
CERT maintains an extensive set of Internet and UNIX security-
related documents; it takes the lead in coordinating the efforts of
various response teams when responding to large-scale incidents.
CERT is part of the Survivable Systems Initiative at the Software
Engineering Institute, a federally-funded research and development
center at Carnegie Mellon University.

CIAC (Computer Incident Advisory Capability)

`http://ciac.llnl.gov`—This comprehensive site developed by the
US Department of Energy provides bulletins, resources on hoaxes
and viruses, and a collection of security tools.

Computer Security Resource Clearinghouse

`http://csrc.ncsl.nist.gov`—This National Institute of Standards
and Technology (NIST) site offers a wide variety of computer security resources, including conferences, publications, policies, and
more. Topics include authentication, common criteria, emerging

technologies, encryption and keys, incident handling, security objects, testing, and virus information.

Security Tool Archives

Here are several reputable places to download UNIX security tools.

AusCERT Software Security Tools

`http://www.auscert.org.au/Information/tools.html`—An annotated collection of tools developed at AusCERT and elsewhere; see "Australian Computer Emergency Response Team (Aus-CERT)" on page 353

CERT

`http://www.cert.org/ftp/tools/`—A conservative collection of leading tools

CIAC Security Tools

`http://ciac.llnl.gov/ciac/SecurityTools.html`—Nicely organized, with sections for DOS, Windows, and Macintosh as well as UNIX

COAST Security FTP Archive

`ftp://coast.cs.purdue.edu/pub/tools/unix/`—The definitive collection of UNIX security tools; if it's not here, it may not exist

Defense Information Systems Agency (DISA)

`http://199.211.123.12/netsecurity/tools.htm`—An annotated collection of network security tools.

The Freefire Project

`http://sites.inka.de/sites/lina/freefire-1/tools.html`—With the motto, "Support for Developers of Free Security Solutions," this site offers an extensive collection of links to free security tools.

Operating Systems Lab at North Carolina State University

ftp://ftp.csc.ncsu.edu/pub/security/—A wide-ranging collection of tools and documents

NSA Security and Assessment Tools Inventory

http://www.sans.org/NSA/sectools.htm—An annotated list compiled by Gregory Stocksdale of the National Security Agency

NSA Intrusion Detection Tools Inventory

http://www.sans.org/NSA/idtools.htm—Another site compiled by Gregory Stocksdale

Wietse's tools and papers

ftp://ftp.porcupine.org/pub/security/index.html—The collected works of leading security researcher and toolsmith Wietse Venema

Security Reference Sites

This grab bag includes security portals, libraries, a crypto site, and even an information vault.

advICE

http://www.8lgm.org—A resource center for information about hackers, security, and networking from the NetworkICE Corporation (ICE = Intrusion Countermeasure Enhancements); it can also be found at http://www.netice.com/Advice/default.htm

all.net

http://all.net—Fred Cohen's site; it has several great security articles and offers the Deception Toolkit (DTK) as well as security games

Computer and Network Security Reference Index

http://www.telstra.com.au/info/security.html—An extensive collection of links to computer and network security resources

Counterpane Systems

http://www.counterpane.com—Bruce Schneier's site. It features well-written and authoritative cryptography resources, including the free monthly email newsletter, Crypto-gram.

Cryptography A-2-Z

http://www.ssh.fi/tech/crypto/—Cryptography sources and resources

ZDTV Cybercrime

http://www.zdnet.com/zdtv/cybercrime/—This show/web site provides timely, consumer-oriented coverage of security and privacy issues.

FreeBSD Hypertext Man Pages

http://www.freebsd.org/cgi/man.cgi?—This very handy man page-to-HTML gateways offers complete sets of man pages for FreeBSD, OpenBSD, Red Hat Linux, and other UNIX systems.

Illustrative Risks to the Public in the Use of Computer Systems and Related Technology

http://www.csl.sri.com/~neumann/illustrative.html—See "The RISKS Forum" on page 361

NIH Computer Security Information

http://www.alw.nih.gov/Security/security.html—An extensive collection of resources compiled at the National Institutes of Health (NIH)

NSA Glossary of Terms Used in Security and Intrusion Detection

http://www.sans.org/NSA/glossary.htm—A work-in-progress compiled by Greg Stocksdale

The Orange Book

http://www.radium.ncsc.mil/tpep/library/rainbow/ 5200.28-STD.html—Official title: *Department of Defense Trusted Computer System Evaluation Criteria*

Rainbow Series Library

http://www.radium.ncsc.mil/tpep/library/rainbow/—Home of multi-hued government security standards, including the Orange Book (see above)

Raptor Systems' Security Library

http://www.raptor.com/lib/—A collection of security documents in PDF and Postscript format

securityinfo.com

http://www.securityinfo.com—"The Information Security Blueprint Web site"; sponsored by information security vendors

SecurityPortal

http://securityportal.com—An independent site that features a variety of security resources

Security Search

http://www.securitysearch.net—A Yahoo-like security search engine/portal site

SGI Security Info Vault

http://www.sgi.com/Support/security/vault.html—The Information Vault is a collection of links to documents, books, and reference sources on computer security.

The Single UNIX Specification

http://www.opengroup.org/onlinepubs/7908799/toc.htm—Offers a keyword search on the Single UNIX Specification

X-Force Database

http://www.iss.net/cgi-bin/xforce/xforce_index.pl—A complete and up-to-date security vulnerabilities database sorted by platform

Yahoo

`http://dir.yahoo.com/Computers_and_Internet/`
`Security_and_Encryption/`—An extensive listing of security and encryption sites

FAQs

Here's a partial list of the many Frequently Asked Questions documents on security-related topics.

Internet FAQ Archives

`http://www.faqs.org/faqs/computer-security/`—A well-maintained and comprehensive listing of security FAQs

comp.security.unix and comp.security.misc FAQ

`http://www.faqs.org/faqs/computer-security/most-common-qs/`
—Compiled by Alan J. Rosenthal

computer-security/compromise FAQ

`http://www.faqs.org/faqs/computer-security/`
`compromise-faq/`—Compiled by Christopher Klaus

Cryptography FAQ

`http://www.cis.ohio-state.edu/hypertext/faq/usenet/`
`cryptography-faq/top.html`—A thorough, ten-part document

Firewalls FAQ

`http://www.faqs.org/faqs/firewalls-faq/`—Compiled by Marcus J. Ranum and Matt Curtin

How To Become A Hacker

`http://www.tuxedo.org/~esr/faqs/hacker-howto.html`—A classic by Eric S. Raymond that answers the oft-asked question: "How can I learn to be a wizard hacker?"

Linux IPCHAINS-HOWTO

`http://www.rustcorp.com/linux/ipchains/HOWTO.html`—
Compiled by Paul Russell

Linux LAN & Internet Firewall Security FAQ

`http://rlz.ne.mediaone.net/linux/faq/index3.html`—Compiled by Robert L. Ziegler

Linux Security HOWTO

`http://metalab.unc.edu/LDP/HOWTO/Security-HOWTO.html`— Compiled by Kevin Fenzi and Dave Wreski

NetBSD, FreeBSD, and OpenBSD FAQ

`http://www.faqs.org/faqs/386bsd-faq/part1/`—A very detailed compilation by Dave Burgess

Perl CGI Programming FAQ

`http://ftp.plig.org/pub/CPAN/doc/FAQs/cgi/` `perl-cgi-faq.html`–Compiled by Shishir Gundavaram and Tom Christiansen

Secure UNIX Programming FAQ

`http://www.faqs.org/faqs/unix-faq/programmer/` `secure-programming/`—Compiled by Thamer Al-Herbish

Sendmail Frequently FAQ

`http://www.sendmail.org/faq/`—Very thorough (and necessary)

SGI Security FAQ

`http://www-viz.tamu.edu/~sgi-faq/faq/html-1/security.html`— Covers IRIX

Snake Oil FAQ

`http://www.interhack.net/people/cmcurtin/` `snake-oil-faq.html`—A warning about extremely bad cryptographic products; compiled by Matt Curtin

The Solaris Security FAQ

`http://www.sunworld.com/common/security-faq.html`—Compiled by Peter Baer Galvin

SSH (Secure Shell) FAQ

`http://www.faqs.org/faqs/computer-security/ssh-faq/`—
Compiled by Thomas Koenig

Tru64 UNIX FAQ

`http://www.unix.digital.com/unix/faq/index.html`—Covers the
OS formerly known as DIGITAL UNIX

Trusted Computer System Evaluation Criteria (TCSEC) FAQ

`http://www.radium.ncsc.mil/tpep/process/faq-sect3.html`—
Used to grade or rate the security offered by a computer system
product. Answers the question: "What are the requirements for a
D/C1/C2/B1/B2/B3/A1 System?"

The World Wide Web Security FAQ

`http://www.w3.org/Security/Faq/`—Compiled by Lincoln D. Stein

Organizations

There are many organizations devoted to computer security: some
of them non-profit; others for profit.

Australian Computer Emergency Response Team (AusCERT)

`http://www.auscert.orq.au`—Provides a single, trusted point of
contact in Australia for the Internet community to deal with computer security incidents and their prevention

The Computer Security Institute (CSI)

`http://www.gocsi.com`—A membership organization dedicated to
serving and training the information, computer, and network security professional

DOD-CERT

`http://www.assist.mil`—The Department of Defense Computer
Emergency Response Team (DOD-CERT) offers security documents, guidelines, policies, and tools, in addition to its regular inci-
dence response duties.

Electronic Frontier Foundation (EFF)

http://www.eff.org—A non-profit, non-partisan organization working in the public interest to protect fundamental civil liberties, including privacy and freedom of expression, in the arena of computers and the Internet

Forum of Incident Response and Security Teams (FIRST)

http://www.first.org—A coalition of computer security incident response teams from government, commercial, and academic organizations

International Computer Security Association (ICSA)

http://www.icsa.net—Promoted as "The objective source for security assurance services," this site provides a formidable professional reference library; see "Information Security magazine" on page 355

Information Systems Security Association (ISSA)

http://www.issa-intl.org—A not-for-profit international organization of information security professionals and practitioners

NSA/CSS

http://www.nsa.gov—"The National Security Agency/Central Security Service is responsible for the centralized coordination, direction, and performance of highly specialized technical functions in support of U.S. Government activities to protect U.S. communications and produce foreign intelligence information." For a good example of a security notice: http://www.nsa.gov/notice.html

The Open Group

http://www.opengroup.org—The consortium that owns the UNIX trademark; find out about The Open Group Security Program at http://www.opengroup.org/security/

The President's Commission on Critical Infrastructure Protection

http://www.pccip.gov—This quote says it all: "The PCCIP was formed to advise and assist the President of the United States by recommending a national strategy for protecting and assuring critical infrastructures from physical and cyber threats."

USENIX
http://www.usenix.org—The Advanced Computing Systems Association; includes SAGE, a special technical group for system administrators

The SANS Institute
http://www.sans.org—A cooperative research and education organization through which more than 62,000 system administrators, security professionals, and network administrators share the lessons they are learning and find solutions for challenges they face.

(ISC)², Inc.
http://www.isc2.org—The International Information Systems Security Certification Consortium offers the CISSP (Certified Information Systems Security Professionals) certificate.

Periodicals
A short list of magazines and periodicals that cover topics related to UNIX and security.

2600 Magazine
http://www.2600.com/mindex.html—The Hacker Quarterly

Cipher
http://www.itd.nrl.navy.mil/ITD/5540/ieee/cipher/—Newsletter of the IEEE Computer Society's Technical Committee on Security and Privacy

Information Security magazine
http://www.infosecuritymag.com—The official publication of ICSA (see page 354)

Infoworld

http://www.infoworld.com—See the "Security Watch" column by Stuart McClure and Joel Scambray

Network Magazine

http://www.networkmagazine.com—Strong network security coverage

Phrack

http://www.phrack.com—A humorous hacker's journal with substantial technical content

SunWorld

http://www.sunworld.com—IDG's magazine for the Sun community

Sys Admin

http://www.samag.com—The Journal for UNIX Systems Administrators

Open Source/Linux Sites

Peer-reviewed open source software can be a boon for security (see "The Benefits of Open Source" on page 18). Linux is the leading open source UNIX variant. Here are some sites relevant to one or both of these.

Bastille Linux

http://www.bastille-linux.org—A project to create a secure Linux distribution based on Red Hat Linux

Caldera Security Advisories

http://www.calderasystems.com/news/security/index.html—For Caldera's OpenLinux distribution

FreeBSD

http://www.freebsd.org—A great resource for FreeBSD and more

Freshmeat

http://www.freshmeat.net—An exhaustive collection of open source programs, compiled by a team lead by Patrick Lenz

GNU Project

http://www.gnu.org—GNU's Not Unix! The GNU Project and the Free Software Foundation develop and promote free software including some security tools. See "The GNU General Public License" on page 397.

Linux Security Audit Project

http://www.lsap.org—The goal is to coordinate a security audit of Linux source code.

Linux Security Resources

http://www.linux-security.org—A security portal in progress

Linux.com

http://www.linux.com—A Linux portal produced by Linux systems vendor VA Linux Systems

Linux Online

http://www.linux.org—The original Linux portal

OpenBSD

http://www.openbsd.org—A security-audited BSD variant

The Open Source Initiative

http://www.opensource.org—Manages and promotes the Open Source trademark for the good of the community; includes the Open Source Definition; home of the Halloween Document, a confidential Microsoft memorandum on Redmond's strategy against Linux and Open Source software

Red Hat Errata

http://www.redhat.com/support/docs/errata.html—The place to check for security-related and other updates; if you're running Red Hat Linux, check here often

Slashdot

http://www.slashdot.org—"News for Nerds. Stuff that Matters."
A very lively news and commentary site; a public commons for the
open source movement where anyone (and everyone, it seems) gets
their own soapbox

Trinux

http://www.trinux.org—A handy Linux security toolkit, oriented
toward network security; according to the home page: "a portable
Linux distribution that boots from 2-3 floppies and runs entirely in
RAM. Trinux contains the latest versions of popular network security tools and is useful for mapping and monitoring TCP/IP
networks."

Underground/Cracker Sites

Most "underground" and cracker sites are poorly conceived and
executed, belying a lack of maturity on the part of their creators.
Here are some of the better ones, offered in accordance with the
"Know Thy Enemy" principle.

AntiOnline

http://www.antionline.com—According to the home page: "The
Internet's Information Security Super Center!" Founder John Vra-
nasevich profiles, tracks, and publishes interviews with system
crackers. This site is funded and growing, but some of its tactics
are dubious. See also the AntiCode Exploit Archive at
http://www.anticode.com, the AntiSearch security search engine
at http://www.antisearch.com, etc.

ATTRITION

http://www.attrition.org—"Service without a smile." This voluminous site offers a library of security advisories, hacker documents, a cross-referenced mirror of web site hacks, and Negation,
a section that refutes AntiOnline.

Cult of the Dead Cow

http://www.cultdeadcow.com—Founded in 1984, the Cult of the Dead Cow (cDc) is the oldest group still active in the computer underground. From their site: "You have never seen us, but you may have felt our wrath. We operate in the bitter darkness outside the known channels. We thrive in the ferro-concrete walls of the technological civilization. We are the stainless steel rats, gnawing at the underpinnings of the 'Information Superhighway,' spreading the power and propaganda of the Cow wherever we go."

Cyphernomicon

http://www.oberlin.edu/~brchkind/cyphernomicon/—The "FAQ" for the Cypherpunks group and mailing list—the title is a take-off on H.P. Lovecraft's mythical *Necronomicon*. The list is devoted to crypto-anarchy and related topics, including digital cash, anonymous remailers, libertarianism, and yes, computer security. See Section 11 "Surveillance, Privacy, And Intelligence Agencies" before subscribing

Fyodor's Playhouse

http://www.insecure.org—By Fyodor; home of the nmap tool and Fyodor's Exploit World

L0pht Heavy Industries

http://www.l0pht.com—This industrious group of hardware and software hackers provides a deep site with security advisories, cracking tools, and more.

Packet Storm Security

http://www.genocide2600.com/~tattooman/—This formidable site with an extensive archive of security files (documents and code) was taken down in 1999 due to legal difficulties ("All Rights Reserved. All Wrongs Avenged"). It should be back at a new URL.

rootshell.com

http://www.rootshell.com—As of this writing, in need of an update

Internet Mailing Lists/Newsgroups

There are several Internet mailing lists and newsgroups relevant to UNIX system security. Follow the URLs to find subscription instructions.

Bugtraq

`http://www.geek-girl.com/bugtraq/index.html`—A full-disclosure UNIX security mailing list

comp.security.unix

`news:comp.security.unix`—Lively discussion of UNIX security issues, debates, complaints, announcements, and more. The *comp.security* hierarchy also includes groups devoted to security announcements, PGP, SSH, etc.

Cu Digest

`http://sun.soci.niu.edu/~cudigest/`—Per the home page: "The Cu Digest is a more-or-less weekly digest/newsletter/journal of debates, news, research, and discussion of legal, social, and other issues related to computer culture."

Firewall Wizards

`http://www.nfr.net/forum/firewall-wizards.html`—This moderated firewall and security-related list is more like a journal than a public soapbox.

The PRIVACY Forum

`http://www.vortex.com/privacy.html`—Built around a moderated email digest for the discussion and analysis of issues relating to the general topic of privacy

redhat.security.general

`news:redhat.security.general`—A mailing list/newsgroup devoted to Red Hat Linux security issues

The RISKS Forum

`http://catless.ncl.ac.uk/Risks`—A seminal mailing list/ USENET newsgroup moderated by Peter G. Neumann. The official title is "Forum On Risks To The Public In Computers And Related Systems."

sci.crypt

`news:sci.crypt`—Devoted to the science of cryptography

www-security

`http://www-ns.rutgers.edu/www-security/www-security-list.html`—The official mailing list of the IETF Web Transaction Security Working Group

Well-Known Port Numbers

Protocol ports are abstractions that act as the logical end points of TCP/IP links. The "Well-Known Ports" are assigned by the Internet Assigned Numbers Authority (IANA) and can only be used by system (or root) processes or by programs executed by privileged users. They range from 0 to 1023. When possible, corresponding TCP and UDP services are assigned the same number.

Ports can be security-sensitive because they sometimes provide an avenue of attack. Repeated attempts to connect to various ports via the Internet can be a sign of an attempted intrusion. For more on ports, see "Protocol Ports" on page 260.

Table C.1 does not include the TLS/SSL Assigned Port Numbers summarized on page 322. Complete listings of port assignments can be found at

`ftp://ftp.isi.edu/in-notes/iana/assignments/port-numbers`

or

`http://www.faqs.org/rfcs/rfc1700.html`

Table C.1 *Port Assignments*

Keyword	Decimal	Description
tcpmux	1/tcp	TCP Port Service Multiplexer
tcpmux	1/udp	TCP Port Service Multiplexer
compressnet	2/tcp	Management Utility
compressnet	2/udp	Management Utility
compressnet	3/tcp	Compression Process
compressnet	3/udp	Compression Process
rje	5/tcp	Remote Job Entry
rje	5/udp	Remote Job Entry
echo	7/tcp	Echo
echo	7/udp	Echo
discard	9/tcp	Discard
discard	9/udp	Discard
systat	11/tcp	Active Users
systat	11/udp	Active Users
daytime	13/tcp	Daytime
daytime	13/udp	Daytime

Table C.1 *Port Assignments (Cont'd)*

Keyword	Decimal	Description
qotd	17/tcp	Quote of the Day
qotd	17/udp	Quote of the Day
msp	18/tcp	Message Send Protocol
msp	18/udp	Message Send Protocol
chargen	19/tcp	Character Generator
chargen	19/udp	Character Generator
ftp-data	20/tcp	File Transfer [Default Data]
ftp-data	20/udp	File Transfer [Default Data]
ftp	21/tcp	File Transfer [Control]
ftp	21/udp	File Transfer [Control]
telnet	23/tcp	Telnet
telnet	23/udp	Telnet
mail	24/tcp	any private mail system
mail	24/udp	any private mail system
smtp	25/tcp	Simple Mail Transfer
smtp	25/udp	Simple Mail Transfer
nsw-fe	27/tcp	NSW User System FE
nsw-fe	27/udp	NSW User System FE
msg-icp	29/tcp	MSG ICP
msg-icp	29/udp	MSG ICP
msg-auth	31/tcp	MSG Authentication
msg-auth	31/udp	MSG Authentication
dsp	33/tcp	Display Support Protocol

Table C.1 *Port Assignments (Cont'd)*

Keyword	Decimal	Description
dsp	33/udp	Display Support Protocol
	35/tcp	any private printer server
	35/udp	any private printer server
time	37/tcp	Time
time	37/udp	Time
rap	38/tcp	Route Access Protocol
rap	38/udp	Route Access Protocol
rlp	39/tcp	Resource Location Protocol
rlp	39/udp	Resource Location Protocol
graphics	41/tcp	Graphics
graphics	41/udp	Graphics
nameserver	42/tcp	Host Name Server
nameserver	42/udp	Host Name Server
nicname	43/tcp	Who Is
nicname	43/udp	Who Is
mpm-flags	44/tcp	MPM FLAGS Protocol
mpm-flags	44/udp	MPM FLAGS Protocol
mpm	45/tcp	Message Processing Module [recv]
mpm	45/udp	Message Processing Module [recv]
mpm-snd	46/tcp	MPM [default send]
mpm-snd	46/udp	MPM [default send]
ni-ftp	47/tcp	NI FTP
ni-ftp	47/udp	NI FTP
auditd	48/tcp	Digital Audit Daemon

Table C.1 *Port Assignments (Cont'd)*

Keyword	Decimal	Description
auditd	48/udp	Digital Audit Daemon
login	49/tcp	Login Host Protocol
login	49/udp	Login Host Protocol
re-mail-ck	50/tcp	Remote Mail Checking Protocol
re-mail-ck	50/udp	Remote Mail Checking Protocol
la-maint	51/tcp	IMP Logical Address Maintenance
la-maint	51/udp	IMP Logical Address Maintenance
xns-time	52/tcp	XNS Time Protocol
xns-time	52/udp	XNS Time Protocol
domain	53/tcp	Domain Name Server
domain	53/udp	Domain Name Server
xns-ch	54/tcp	XNS Clearinghouse
xns-ch	54/udp	XNS Clearinghouse
isi-gl	55/tcp	ISI Graphics Language
isi-gl	55/udp	ISI Graphics Language
xns-auth	56/tcp	XNS Authentication
xns-auth	56/udp	XNS Authentication
	57/tcp	any private terminal access
	57/udp	any private terminal access
xns-mail	58/tcp	XNS Mail
xns-mail	58/udp	XNS Mail
	59/tcp	any private file service
	59/udp	any private file service
ni-mail	61/tcp	NI MAIL

Table C.1 *Port Assignments (Cont'd)*

Keyword	Decimal	Description
ni-mail	61/udp	NI MAIL
acas	62/tcp	ACA Services
acas	62/udp	ACA Services
covia	64/tcp	Communications Integrator (CI)
covia	64/udp	Communications Integrator (CI)
tacacs-ds	65/tcp	TACACS-Database Service
tacacs-ds	65/udp	TACACS-Database Service
sql*net	66/tcp	Oracle SQL*NET
sql*net	66/udp	Oracle SQL*NET
bootps	67/tcp	Bootstrap Protocol Server
bootps	67/udp	Bootstrap Protocol Server
bootpc	68/tcp	Bootstrap Protocol Client
bootpc	68/udp	Bootstrap Protocol Client
tftp	69/tcp	Trivial File Transfer
tftp	69/udp	Trivial File Transfer
gopher	70/tcp	Gopher
gopher	70/udp	Gopher
netrjs-1	71/tcp	Remote Job Service
netrjs-1	71/udp	Remote Job Service
netrjs-2	72/tcp	Remote Job Service
netrjs-2	72/udp	Remote Job Service
netrjs-3	73/tcp	Remote Job Service
netrjs-3	73/udp	Remote Job Service

Table C.1 *Port Assignments (Cont'd)*

Keyword	Decimal	Description
netrjs-4	74/tcp	Remote Job Service
netrjs-4	74/udp	Remote Job Service
	75/tcp	any private dial out service
	75/udp	any private dial out service
deos	76/tcp	Distributed External Object Store
deos	76/udp	Distributed External Object Store
	77/tcp	any private RJE service
	77/udp	any private RJE service
vettcp	78/tcp	vettcp
vettcp	78/udp	vettcp
finger	79/tcp	Finger
finger	79/udp	Finger
www-http	80/tcp	World Wide Web HTTP
www-http	80/udp	World Wide Web HTTP
hosts2-ns	81/tcp	HOSTS2 Name Server
hosts2-ns	81/udp	HOSTS2 Name Server
xfer	82/tcp	XFER Utility
xfer	82/udp	XFER Utility
mit-ml-dev	83/tcp	MIT ML Device
mit-ml-dev	83/udp	MIT ML Device
ctf	84/tcp	Common Trace Facility
ctf	84/udp	Common Trace Facility
mit-ml-dev	85/tcp	MIT ML Device
mit-ml-dev	85/udp	MIT ML Device

Table C.1 *Port Assignments (Cont'd)*

Keyword	Decimal	Description
mfcobol	86/tcp	Micro Focus Cobol
mfcobol	86/udp	Micro Focus Cobol
	87/tcp	any private terminal link
	87/udp	any private terminal link
kerberos	88/tcp	Kerberos
kerberos	88/udp	Kerberos
su-mit-tg	89/tcp	SU/MIT Telnet Gateway
su-mit-tg	89/udp	SU/MIT Telnet Gateway
dnsix	90/tcp	DNSIX Securit Attribute Token Map
dnsix	90/udp	DNSIX Securit Attribute Token Map
mit-dov	91/tcp	MIT Dover Spooler
mit-dov	91/udp	MIT Dover Spooler
npp	92/tcp	Network Printing Protocol
npp	92/udp	Network Printing Protocol
dcp	93/tcp	Device Control Protocol
dcp	93/udp	Device Control Protocol
objcall	94/tcp	Tivoli Object Dispatcher
objcall	94/udp	Tivoli Object Dispatcher
supdup	95/tcp	SUPDUP
supdup	95/udp	SUPDUP
dixie	96/tcp	DIXIE Protocol Specification
dixie	96/udp	DIXIE Protocol Specification
swift-rvf	97/tcp	Swift Remote Vitural File Protocol
swift-rvf	97/udp	Swift Remote Vitural File Protocol

Table C.1 *Port Assignments (Cont'd)*

Keyword	Decimal	Description
tacnews	98/tcp	TAC News
tacnews	98/udp	TAC News
metagram	99/tcp	Metagram Relay
metagram	99/udp	Metagram Relay
newacct	100/tcp	[unauthorized use]
hostname	101/tcp	NIC Host Name Server
hostname	101/udp	NIC Host Name Server
iso-tsap	102/tcp	ISO-TSAP
iso-tsap	102/udp	ISO-TSAP
gppitnp	103/tcp	Genesis Point-to-Point Trans Net
gppitnp	103/udp	Genesis Point-to-Point Trans Net
acr-nema	104/tcp	ACR-NEMA Digital Imag. & Comm. 300
acr-nema	104/udp	ACR-NEMA Digital Imag. & Comm. 300
csnet-ns	105/tcp	Mailbox Name Nameserver
csnet-ns	105/udp	Mailbox Name Nameserver
3com-tsmux	106/tcp	3COM-TSMUX
3com-tsmux	106/udp	3COM TSMUX
rtelnet	107/tcp	Remote Telnet Service
rtelnet	107/udp	Remote Telnet Service
snagas	108/tcp	SNA Gateway Access Server
snagas	108/udp	SNA Gateway Access Server
pop2	109/tcp	Post Office Protocol - Version 2
pop2	109/udp	Post Office Protocol - Version 2
pop3	110/tcp	Post Office Protocol - Version 3

Table C.1 *Port Assignments (Cont'd)*

Keyword	Decimal	Description
pop3	110/udp	Post Office Protocol - Version 3
sunrpc	111/tcp	SUN Remote Procedure Call
sunrpc	111/udp	SUN Remote Procedure Call
mcidas	112/tcp	McIDAS Data Transmission Protocol
mcidas	112/udp	McIDAS Data Transmission Protocol
auth	113/tcp	Authentication Service
auth	113/udp	Authentication Service
audionews	114/tcp	Audio News Multicast
audionews	114/udp	Audio News Multicast
sftp	115/tcp	Simple File Transfer Protocol
sftp	115/udp	Simple File Transfer Protocol
ansanotify	116/tcp	ANSA REX Notify
ansanotify	116/udp	ANSA REX Notify
uucp-path	117/tcp	UUCP Path Service
uucp-path	117/udp	UUCP Path Service
sqlserv	118/tcp	SQL Services
sqlserv	118/udp	SQL Services
nntp	119/tcp	Network News Transfer Protocol
nntp	119/udp	Network News Transfer Protocol
cfdptkt	120/tcp	CFDPTKT
cfdptkt	120/udp	CFDPTKT
erpc	121/tcp	Encore Expedited Remote Pro.Call
erpc	121/udp	Encore Expedited Remote Pro.Call
smakynet	122/tcp	SMAKYNET

Table C.1 *Port Assignments (Cont'd)*

Keyword	Decimal	Description
smakynet	122/udp	SMAKYNET
ntp	123/tcp	Network Time Protocol
ntp	123/udp	Network Time Protocol
ansatrader	124/tcp	ANSA REX Trader
ansatrader	124/udp	ANSA REX Trader
locus-map	125/tcp	Locus PC-Interface Net Map Ser
locus-map	125/udp	Locus PC-Interface Net Map Ser
unitary	126/tcp	Unisys Unitary Login
unitary	126/udp	Unisys Unitary Login
locus-con	127/tcp	Locus PC-Interface Conn Server
locus-con	127/udp	Locus PC-Interface Conn Server
gss-xlicen	128/tcp	GSS X License Verification
gss-xlicen	128/udp	GSS X License Verification
pwdgen	129/tcp	Password Generator Protocol
pwdgen	129/udp	Password Generator Protocol
cisco-fna	130/tcp	cisco FNATIVE
cisco-fna	130/udp	cisco FNATIVE
cisco-tna	131/tcp	cisco TNATIVE
cisco-tna	131/udp	cisco TNATIVE
cisco-sys	132/tcp	cisco SYSMAINT
cisco-sys	132/udp	cisco SYSMAINT
statsrv	133/tcp	Statistics Service
statsrv	133/udp	Statistics Service
ingres-net	134/tcp	INGRES-NET Service

Table C.1 *Port Assignments (Cont'd)*

Keyword	Decimal	Description
ingres-net	134/udp	INGRES-NET Service
loc-srv	135/tcp	Location Service
loc-srv	135/udp	Location Service
profile	136/tcp	PROFILE Naming System
profile	136/udp	PROFILE Naming System
netbios-ns	137/tcp	NETBIOS Name Service
netbios-ns	137/udp	NETBIOS Name Service
netbios-dgm	138/tcp	NETBIOS Datagram Service
netbios-dgm	138/udp	NETBIOS Datagram Service
netbios-ssn	139/tcp	NETBIOS Session Service
netbios-ssn	139/udp	NETBIOS Session Service
emfis-data	140/tcp	EMFIS Data Service
emfis-data	140/udp	EMFIS Data Service
emfis-cntl	141/tcp	EMFIS Control Service
emfis-cntl	141/udp	EMFIS Control Service
bl-idm	142/tcp	Britton-Lee IDM
bl-idm	142/udp	Britton-Lee IDM
imap2	143/tcp	Interim Mail Access Protocol v2
imap2	143/udp	Interim Mail Access Protocol v2
news	144/tcp	NewS
news	144/udp	NewS
uaac	145/tcp	UAAC Protocol
uaac	145/udp	UAAC Protocol
iso-tp0	146/tcp	ISO-IP0

Table C.1 *Port Assignments (Cont'd)*

Keyword	Decimal	Description
iso-tp0	146/udp	ISO-IP0
iso-ip	147/tcp	ISO-IP
iso-ip	147/udp	ISO-IP
cronus	148/tcp	CRONUS-SUPPORT
cronus	148/udp	CRONUS-SUPPORT
aed-512	149/tcp	AED 512 Emulation Service
aed-512	149/udp	AED 512 Emulation Service
sql-net	150/tcp	SQL-NET
sql-net	150/udp	SQL-NET
hems	151/tcp	HEMS
hems	151/udp	HEMS
bftp	152/tcp	Background File Transfer Program
bftp	152/udp	Background File Transfer Program
sgmp	153/tcp	SGMP
sgmp	153/udp	SGMP
netsc-prod	154/tcp	NETSC
netsc-prod	154/udp	NETSC
netsc-dev	155/tcp	NETSC
netsc-dev	155/udp	NETSC
sqlsrv	156/tcp	SQL Service
sqlsrv	156/udp	SQL Service
knet-cmp	157/tcp	KNET/VM Command/Message Protocol
knet-cmp	157/udp	KNET/VM Command/Message Protocol
pcmail-srv	158/tcp	PCMail Server

Table C.1 *Port Assignments (Cont'd)*

Keyword	Decimal	Description
pcmail-srv	158/udp	PCMail Server
nss-routing	159/tcp	NSS-Routing
nss-routing	159/udp	NSS-Routing
sgmp-traps	160/tcp	SGMP-TRAPS
sgmp-traps	160/udp	SGMP-TRAPS
snmp	161/tcp	SNMP
snmp	161/udp	SNMP
snmptrap	162/tcp	SNMPTRAP
snmptrap	162/udp	SNMPTRAP
cmip-man	163/tcp	CMIP/TCP Manager
cmip-man	163/udp	CMIP/TCP Manager
cmip-agent	164/tcp	CMIP/TCP Agent
smip-agent	164/udp	CMIP/TCP Agent
xns-courier	165/tcp	Xerox
xns-courier	165/udp	Xerox
s-net	166/tcp	Sirius Systems
s-net	166/udp	Sirius Systems
namp	167/tcp	NAMP
namp	167/udp	NAMP
rsvd	168/tcp	RSVD
rsvd	168/udp	RSVD
send	169/tcp	SEND
send	169/udp	SEND
print-srv	170/tcp	Network PostScript

Table C.1 *Port Assignments (Cont'd)*

Keyword	Decimal	Description
print-srv	170/udp	Network PostScript
multiplex	171/tcp	Network Innovations Multiplex
multiplex	171/udp	Network Innovations Multiplex
cl/1	172/tcp	Network Innovations CL/1
cl/1	172/udp	Network Innovations CL/1
xyplex-mux	173/tcp	Xyplex
xyplex-mux	173/udp	Xyplex
mailq	174/tcp	MAILQ
mailq	174/udp	MAILQ
vmnet	175/tcp	VMNET
vmnet	175/udp	VMNET
genrad-mux	176/tcp	GENRAD-MUX
genrad-mux	176/udp	GENRAD-MUX
xdmcp	177/tcp	X Display Manager Control Protocol
xdmcp	177/udp	X Display Manager Control Protocol
nextstep	178/tcp	NextStep Window Server
NextStep	178/udp	NextStep Window Server
bgp	179/tcp	Border Gateway Protocol
bgp	179/udp	Border Gateway Protocol
ris	180/tcp	Intergraph
ris	180/udp	Intergraph
unify	181/tcp	Unify
unify	181/udp	Unify
audit	182/tcp	Unisys Audit SITP

Table C.1 *Port Assignments (Cont'd)*

Keyword	Decimal	Description
audit	182/udp	Unisys Audit SITP
ocbinder	183/tcp	OCBinder
ocbinder	183/udp	OCBinder
ocserver	184/tcp	OCServer
ocserver	184/udp	OCServer
remote-kis	185/tcp	Remote-KIS
remote-kis	185/udp	Remote-KIS
kis	186/tcp	KIS Protocol
kis	186/udp	KIS Protocol
aci	187/tcp	Application Communication Interface
aci	187/udp	Application Communication Interface
mumps	188/tcp	Plus Five's MUMPS
mumps	188/udp	Plus Five's MUMPS
qft	189/tcp	Queued File Transport
qft	189/udp	Queued File Transport
gacp	190/tcp	Gateway Access Control Protocol
cacp	190/udp	Gateway Access Control Protocol
prospero	191/tcp	Prospero Directory Service
prospero	191/udp	Prospero Directory Service
osu-nms	192/tcp	OSU Network Monitoring System
osu-nms	192/udp	OSU Network Monitoring System
srmp	193/tcp	Spider Remote Monitoring Protocol
srmp	193/udp	Spider Remote Monitoring Protocol
irc	194/tcp	Internet Relay Chat Protocol

Table C.1 *Port Assignments (Cont'd)*

Keyword	Decimal	Description
irc	194/udp	Internet Relay Chat Protocol
dn6-nlm-aud	195/tcp	DNSIX Network Level Module Audit
dn6-nlm-aud	195/udp	DNSIX Network Level Module Audit
dn6-smm-red	196/tcp	DNSIX Session Mgt Module Audit Redir
dn6-smm-red	196/udp	DNSIX Session Mgt Module Audit Redir
dls	197/tcp	Directory Location Service
dls	197/udp	Directory Location Service
dls-mon	198/tcp	Directory Location Service Monitor
dls-mon	198/udp	Directory Location Service Monitor
smux	199/tcp	SMUX
smux	199/udp	SMUX
src	200/tcp	IBM System Resource Controller
src	200/udp	IBM System Resource Controller
at-rtmp	201/tcp	AppleTalk Routing Maintenance
at-rtmp	201/udp	AppleTalk Routing Maintenance
at-nbp	202/tcp	AppleTalk Name Binding
at-nbp	202/udp	AppleTalk Name Binding
at-3	203/tcp	AppleTalk Unused
at-3	203/udp	AppleTalk Unused
at-echo	204/tcp	AppleTalk Echo
at-echo	204/udp	AppleTalk Echo
at-5	205/tcp	AppleTalk Unused
at-5	205/udp	AppleTalk Unused
at-zis	206/tcp	AppleTalk Zone Information

Table C.1 *Port Assignments (Cont'd)*

Keyword	Decimal	Description
at-zis	206/udp	AppleTalk Zone Information
at-7	207/tcp	AppleTalk Unused
at-7	207/udp	AppleTalk Unused
at-8	208/tcp	AppleTalk Unused
at-8	208/udp	AppleTalk Unused
tam	209/tcp	Trivial Authenticated Mail Protocol
tam	209/udp	Trivial Authenticated Mail Protocol
z39.50	210/tcp	ANSI Z39.50
z39.50	210/udp	ANSI Z39.50
914c/g	211/tcp	Texas Instruments 914C/G Terminal
914c/g	211/udp	Texas Instruments 914C/G Terminal
anet	212/tcp	ATEXSSTR
anet	212/udp	ATEXSSTR
ipx	213/tcp	IPX
ipx	213/udp	IPX
vmpwscs	214/tcp	VM PWSCS
vmpwscs	214/udp	VM PWSCS
softpc	215/tcp	Insignia Solutions
softpc	215/udp	Insignia Solutions
atls	216/tcp	Access Technology License Server
atls	216/udp	Access Technology License Server
dbase	217/tcp	dBASE Unix
dbase	217/udp	dBASE Unix
mpp	218/tcp	Netix Message Posting Protocol

Table C.1 *Port Assignments (Cont'd)*

Keyword	Decimal	Description
mpp	218/udp	Netix Message Posting Protocol
uarps	219/tcp	Unisys ARPs
uarps	219/udp	Unisys ARPs
imap3	220/tcp	Interactive Mail Access Protocol v3
imap3	220/udp	Interactive Mail Access Protocol v3
fln-spx	221/tcp	Berkeley rlogind with SPX auth
fln-spx	221/udp	Berkeley rlogind with SPX auth
rsh-spx	222/tcp	Berkeley rshd with SPX auth
rsh-spx	222/udp	Berkeley rshd with SPX auth
cdc	223/tcp	Certificate Distribution Center
cdc	223/udp	Certificate Distribution Center
sur-meas	243/tcp	Survey Measurement
sur-meas	243/udp	Survey Measurement
link	245/tcp	LINK
link	245/udp	LINK
dsp3270	246/tcp	Display Systems Protocol
dsp3270	246/udp	Display Systems Protocol
pdap	344/tcp	Prospero Data Access Protocol
pdap	344/udp	Prospero Data Access Protocol
pawserv	345/tcp	Perf Analysis Workbench
pawserv	345/udp	Perf Analysis Workbench
zserv	346/tcp	Zebra server
zserv	346/udp	Zebra server
fatserv	347/tcp	Fatmen Server

Table C.1 *Port Assignments (Cont'd)*

Keyword	Decimal	Description
fatserv	347/udp	Fatmen Server
csi-sgwp	348/tcp	Cabletron Management Protocol
csi-sgwp	348/udp	Cabletron Management Protocol
clearcase	371/tcp	Clearcase
clearcase	371/udp	Clearcase
ulistserv	372/tcp	Unix Listserv
ulistserv	372/udp	Unix Listserv
legent-1	373/tcp	Legent Corporation
legent-1	373/udp	Legent Corporation
legent-2	374/tcp	Legent Corporation
legent-2	374/udp	Legent Corporation
hassle	375/tcp	Hassle
hassle	375/udp	Hassle
nip	376/tcp	Amiga Envoy Network Inquiry Proto
nip	376/udp	Amiga Envoy Network Inquiry Proto
tnETOS	377/tcp	NEC Corporation
tnETOS	377/udp	NEC Corporation
dsETOS	378/tcp	NEC Corporation
dsETOS	378/udp	NEC Corporation
is99c	379/tcp	TIA/EIA/IS-99 modem client
is99c	379/udp	TIA/EIA/IS-99 modem client
is99s	380/tcp	TIA/EIA/IS-99 modem server
is99s	380/udp	TIA/EIA/IS-99 modem server
hp-collector	381/tcp	hp performance data collector

Table C.1 *Port Assignments (Cont'd)*

Keyword	Decimal	Description
hp-collector	381/udp	hp performance data collector
hp-managed-node	382/tcp	hp performance data managed node
hp-managed-node	382/udp	hp performance data managed node
hp-alarm-mgr	383/tcp	hp performance data alarm manager
hp-alarm-mgr	383/udp	hp performance data alarm manager
arns	384/tcp	A Remote Network Server System
arns	384/udp	A Remote Network Server System
ibm-app	385/tcp	IBM Application
ibm-app	385/tcp	IBM Application
asa	386/tcp	ASA Message Router Object Def.
asa	386/udp	ASA Message Router Object Def.
aurp	387/tcp	Appletalk Update-Based Routing Pro.
aurp	387/udp	Appletalk Update-Based Routing Pro.
unidata-ldm	388/tcp	Unidata LDM Version 4
unidata-ldm	388/udp	Unidata LDM Version 4
ldap	389/tcp	Lightweight Directory Access Protocol
ldap	389/udp	Lightweight Directory Access Protocol
uis	390/tcp	UIS
uis	390/udp	UIS
synotics-relay	391/tcp	SynOptics SNMP Relay Port
synotics-relay	391/udp	SynOptics SNMP Relay Port
synotics-broker	392/tcp	SynOptics Port Broker Port
synotics-broker	392/udp	SynOptics Port Broker Port

Table C.1 *Port Assignments (Cont'd)*

Keyword	Decimal	Description
dis	393/tcp	Data Interpretation System
dis	393/udp	Data Interpretation System
embl-ndt	394/tcp	EMBL Nucleic Data Transfer
embl-ndt	394/udp	EMBL Nucleic Data Transfer
netcp	395/tcp	NETscout Control Protocol
netcp	395/udp	NETscout Control Protocol
netware-ip	396/tcp	Novell Netware over IP
netware-ip	396/udp	Novell Netware over IP
mptn	397/tcp	Multi Protocol Trans. Net.
mptn	397/udp	Multi Protocol Trans. Net.
kryptolan	398/tcp	Kryptolan
kryptolan	398/udp	Kryptolan
work-sol	400/tcp	Workstation Solutions
work-sol	400/udp	Workstation Solutions
ups	401/tcp	Uninterruptible Power Supply
ups	401/udp	Uninterruptible Power Supply
genie	402/tcp	Genie Protocol
genie	402/udp	Genie Protocol
decap	403/tcp	decap
decap	403/udp	decap
nced	404/tcp	nced
nced	404/udp	nced
ncld	405/tcp	ncld
ncld	405/udp	ncld

Table C.1 *Port Assignments (Cont'd)*

Keyword	Decimal	Description
imsp	406/tcp	Interactive Mail Support Protocol
imsp	406/udp	Interactive Mail Support Protocol
timbuktu	407/tcp	Timbuktu
timbuktu	407/udp	Timbuktu
prm-sm	408/tcp	Prospero Resource Manager Sys. Man.
prm-sm	408/udp	Prospero Resource Manager Sys. Man.
prm-nm	409/tcp	Prospero Resource Manager Node Man.
prm-nm	409/udp	Prospero Resource Manager Node Man.
decladebug	410/tcp	DECLadebug Remote Debug Protocol
decladebug	410/udp	DECLadebug Remote Debug Protocol
rmt	411/tcp	Remote MT Protocol
rmt	411/udp	Remote MT Protocol
synoptics-trap	412/tcp	Trap Convention Port
synoptics-trap	412/udp	Trap Convention Port
smsp	413/tcp	SMSP
smsp	413/udp	SMSP
infoseek	414/tcp	InfoSeek
infoseek	414/udp	InfoSeek
bnet	415/tcp	BNet
bnet	415/udp	BNet
silverplatter	416/tcp	Silverplatter
silverplatter	416/udp	Silverplatter
onmux	417/tcp	Onmux
onmux	417/udp	Onmux

Table C.1 *Port Assignments (Cont'd)*

Keyword	Decimal	Description
hyper-g	418/tcp	Hyper-G
hyper-g	418/udp	Hyper-G
ariel1	419/tcp	Ariel
ariel1	419/udp	Ariel
smpte	420/tcp	SMPTE
smpte	420/udp	SMPTE
ariel2	421/tcp	Ariel
ariel2	421/udp	Ariel
ariel3	422/tcp	Ariel
ariel3	422/udp	Ariel
opc-job-start	423/tcp	IBM Operations Planning and Control Start
opc-job-start	423/udp	IBM Operations Planning and Control Start
opc-job-track	424/tcp	IBM Operations Planning and Control Track
opc-job-track	424/udp	IBM Operations Planning and Control Track
icad-el	425/tcp	ICAD
icad-el	425/udp	ICAD
smartsdp	426/tcp	smartsdp
smartsdp	426/udp	smartsdp
svrloc	427/tcp	Server Location
svrloc	427/udp	Server Location
ocs_cmu	428/tcp	OCS_CMU

Table C.1 *Port Assignments (Cont'd)*

Keyword	Decimal	Description
ocs_cmu	428/udp	OCS_CMU
ocs_amu	429/tcp	OCS_AMU
ocs_amu	429/udp	OCS_AMU
utmpsd	430/tcp	UTMPSD
utmpsd	430/udp	UTMPSD
utmpcd	431/tcp	UTMPCD
utmpcd	431/udp	UTMPCD
iasd	432/tcp	IASD
iasd	432/udp	IASD
nnsp	433/tcp	NNSP
nnsp	433/udp	NNSP
mobileip-agent	434/tcp	MobileIP-Agent
mobileip-agent	434/udp	MobileIP-Agent
mobilip-mn	435/tcp	MobilIP-MN
mobilip-mn	435/udp	MobilIP-MN
dna-cml	436/tcp	DNA-CML
dna-cml	436/udp	DNA-CML
comscm	437/tcp	comscm
comscm	437/udp	comscm
dsfgw	438/tcp	dsfgw
dsfgw	438/udp	dsfgw
dasp	439/tcp	dasp
dasp	439/udp	dasp
sgcp	440/tcp	sgcp

Table C.1 *Port Assignments (Cont'd)*

Keyword	Decimal	Description
sgcp	440/udp	sgcp
decvms-sysmgt	441/tcp	decvms-sysmgt
decvms-sysmgt	441/udp	decvms-sysmgt
cvc_hostd	442/tcp	cvc_hostd
cvc_hostd	442/udp	cvc_hostd
https	443/tcp	https
https	443/udp	https
snpp	444/tcp	Simple Network Paging Protocol
snpp	444/udp	Simple Network Paging Protocol
microsoft-ds	445/tcp	Microsoft-DS
microsoft-ds	445/udp	Microsoft-DS
ddm-rdb	446/tcp	DDM-RDB
ddm-rdb	446/udp	DDM-RDB
ddm-dfm	447/tcp	DDM-RFM
ddm-dfm	447/udp	DDM-RFM
ddm-byte	448/tcp	DDM-BYTE
ddm-byte	448/udp	DDM-BYTE
as-servermap	449/tcp	AS Server Mapper
as-servermap	449/udp	AS Server Mapper
tserver	450/tcp	TServer
tserver	450/udp	TServer
exec	512/tcp	remote process execution
biff	512/udp	used by mail system to notify users of new mail

Table C.1 *Port Assignments (Cont'd)*

Keyword	Decimal	Description
login	513/tcp	remote login a la telnet
who	513/udp	maintains data bases showing who's logged in
cmd	514/tcp	like exec, but automatic authentication
syslog	514/udp	
printer	515/tcp	spooler
printer	515/udp	spooler
talk	517/tcp	like tenex link
talk	517/udp	like tenex link
ntalk	518/tcp	
ntalk	518/udp	
utime	519/tcp	unixtime
utime	519/udp	unixtime
efs	520/tcp	extended file name server
router	520/udp	local routing process (on site)
timed	525/tcp	timeserver
timed	525/udp	timeserver
tempo	526/tcp	newdate
tempo	526/udp	newdate
courier	530/tcp	rpc
courier	530/udp	rpc
conference	531/tcp	chat
conference	531/udp	chat
netnews	532/tcp	readnews

Table C.1 *Port Assignments (Cont'd)*

Keyword	Decimal	Description
netnews	532/udp	readnews
netwall	533/tcp	for emergency broadcasts
netwall	533/udp	for emergency broadcasts
apertus-ldp	539/tcp	Apertus Technologies Load Determination
apertus-ldp	539/udp	Apertus Technologies Load Determination
uucp	540/tcp	uucpd
uucp	540/udp	uucpd
uucp-rlogin	541/tcp	uucp-rlogin
uucp-rlogin	541/udp	uucp-rlogin
klogin	543/tcp	
klogin	543/udp	
kshell	544/tcp	krcmd
kshell	544/udp	krcmd
new-rwho	550/tcp	new-who
new-rwho	550/udp	new-who
dsf	555/tcp	
dsf	555/udp	
remotefs	556/tcp	rfs server
remotefs	556/udp	rfs server
rmonitor	560/tcp	rmonitord
rmonitor	560/udp	rmonitord
monitor	561/tcp	
monitor	561/udp	
chshell	562/tcp	chcmd

Table C.1 *Port Assignments (Cont'd)*

Keyword	Decimal	Description
chshell	562/udp	chcmd
9pfs	564/tcp	plan 9 file service
9pfs	564/udp	plan 9 file service
whoami	565/tcp	whoami
whoami	565/udp	whoami
meter	570/tcp	demon
meter	570/udp	demon
meter	571/tcp	udemon
meter	571/udp	udemon
ipcserver	600/tcp	Sun IPC server
ipcserver	600/udp	Sun IPC server
urm	606/tcp	Cray Unified Resource Manager
urm	606/udp	Cray Unified Resource Manager
nqs	607/tcp	nqs
nqs	607/udp	nqs
sift-uft	608/tcp	Sender-Initiated/Unsolicited File Transfer
sift-uft	608/udp	Sender-Initiated/Unsolicited File Transfer
npmp-trap	609/tcp	npmp-trap
npmp-trap	609/udp	npmp-trap
npmp-local	610/tcp	npmp-local
npmp-local	610/udp	npmp-local
npmp-gui	611/tcp	npmp-gui
npmp-gui	611/udp	npmp-gui
ginad	634/tcp	ginad

Table C.1 *Port Assignments (Cont'd)*

Keyword	Decimal	Description
ginad	634/udp	ginad
mdqs	666/tcp	
mdqs	666/udp	
doom	666/tcp	doom Id Software
doom	666/tcp	doom Id Software
elcsd	704/tcp	errlog copy/server daemon
elcsd	704/udp	errlog copy/server daemon
entrustmanager	709/tcp	EntrustManager
entrustmanager	709/udp	EntrustManager
netviewdm1	729/tcp	IBM NetView DM/6000 Server/Client
netviewdm1	729/udp	IBM NetView DM/6000 Server/Client
netviewdm2	730/tcp	IBM NetView DM/6000 send/tcp
netviewdm2	730/udp	IBM NetView DM/6000 send/tcp
netviewdm3	731/tcp	IBM NetView DM/6000 receive/tcp
netviewdm3	731/udp	IBM NetView DM/6000 receive/tcp
netgw	741/tcp	netGW
netgw	741/udp	netGW
netrcs	742/tcp	Network based Rev. Cont. Sys.
netrcs	742/udp	Network based Rev. Cont. Sys.
flexlm	744/tcp	Flexible License Manager
flexlm	744/udp	Flexible License Manager
fujitsu-dev	747/tcp	Fujitsu Device Control
fujitsu-dev	747/udp	Fujitsu Device Control
ris-cm	748/tcp	Russell Info Sci Calendar Manager

Table C.1 *Port Assignments (Cont'd)*

Keyword	Decimal	Description
ris-cm	748/udp	Russell Info Sci Calendar Manager
kerberos-adm	749/tcp	kerberos administration
kerberos-adm	749/udp	kerberos administration
rfile	750/tcp	
loadav	750/udp	
pump	751/tcp	
pump	751/udp	
qrh	752/tcp	
qrh	752/udp	
rrh	753/tcp	
rrh	753/udp	
tell	754/tcp	send
tell	754/udp	send
nlogin	758/tcp	
nlogin	758/udp	
con	759/tcp	
con	759/udp	
ns	760/tcp	
ns	760/udp	
rxe	761/tcp	
rxe	761/udp	
quotad	762/tcp	
quotad	762/udp	
cycleserv	763/tcp	

Table C.1 *Port Assignments (Cont'd)*

Keyword	Decimal	Description
cycleserv	763/udp	
omserv	764/tcp	
omserv	764/udp	
webster	765/tcp	
webster	765/udp	
phonebook	767/tcp	phone
phonebook	767/udp	phone
vid	769/tcp	
vid	769/udp	
cadlock	770/tcp	
cadlock	770/udp	
rtip	771/tcp	
rtip	771/udp	
cycleserv2	772/tcp	
cycleserv2	772/udp	
submit	773/tcp	
notify	773/udp	
rpasswd	774/tcp	
acmaint_dbd	774/udp	
entomb	775/tcp	
acmaint_transd	775/udp	
wpages	776/tcp	
wpages	776/udp	
wpgs	780/tcp	

Table C.1 *Port Assignments (Cont'd)*

Keyword	Decimal	Description
wpgs	780/udp	
concert	786/tcp	Concert
concert	786/udp	Concert
mdbs_daemon	800/tcp	
mdbs_daemon	800/udp	
device	801/tcp	
device	801/udp	
xtreelic	996/tcp	Central Point Software
xtreelic	996/udp	Central Point Software
maitrd	997/tcp	
maitrd	997/udp	
busboy	998/tcp	
puparp	998/udp	
garcon	999/tcp	
applix	999/udp	Applix ac
puprouter	999/tcp	
puprouter	999/udp	
cadlock	1000/tcp	
ock	1000/udp	

The GNU General Public License

Many of the programs and tools covered in this book are covered by the Free Software Foundation's "copyleft" license, which provides for free re-use and modification. It's provided here as an example of how to license free software and as a formal accompaniment to the GNU-licensed tools provided on the CD-ROM. The license includes a Preamble, which provides background, the Terms, and a final section, which demonstrates how the Terms can be used by programmers.

The GNU General Public License—Version 2, June 1991

Copyright © 1989, 1991 Free Software Foundation, Inc. 59 Temple Place, Suite 330, Boston, MA 02111-1307 USA Everyone is permitted to copy and distribute verbatim copies of this license document, but changing it is not allowed.[1]

Preamble

The licenses for most software are designed to take away your freedom to share and change it. By contrast, the GNU General Public License is intended to guarantee your freedom to share and change free software—to make sure the software is free for all its users. This General Public License applies to most of the Free Software Foundation's software and to any other program whose authors commit to using it. (Some other Free Software Foundation software is covered by the GNU Library General Public License instead.) You can apply it to your programs, too.

When we speak of free software, we are referring to freedom, not price. Our General Public Licenses are designed to make sure that you have the freedom to distribute copies of free software (and charge for this service if you wish), that you receive source code or can get it if you want it, that you can change the software or use pieces of it in new free programs; and that you know you can do these things.

To protect your rights, we need to make restrictions that forbid anyone to deny you these rights or to ask you to surrender the rights. These restrictions translate to certain responsibilities for you if you distribute copies of the software, or if you modify it.

For example, if you distribute copies of such a program, whether gratis or for a fee, you must give the recipients all the rights that you have. You must make sure that they, too, receive or can get the source code. And you must show them these terms so they know their rights.

---

1. Minor typographical adjustments were made to this document in June 1999. An HTML version can be found at
http://www.gnu.org/copyleft/gpl.html

We protect your rights with two steps: (1) copyright the software, and (2) offer you this license which gives you legal permission to copy, distribute and/or modify the software.

Also, for each author's protection and ours, we want to make certain that everyone understands that there is no warranty for this free software. If the software is modified by someone else and passed on, we want its recipients to know that what they have is not the original, so that any problems introduced by others will not reflect on the original authors' reputations.

Finally, any free program is threatened constantly by software patents. We wish to avoid the danger that redistributors of a free program will individually obtain patent licenses, in effect making the program proprietary. To prevent this, we have made it clear that any patent must be licensed for everyone's free use or not licensed at all.

The precise terms and conditions for copying, distribution and modification follow.

GNU GENERAL PUBLIC LICENSE TERMS AND CONDITIONS FOR COPYING, DISTRIBUTION AND MODIFICATION

0. This License applies to any program or other work which contains a notice placed by the copyright holder saying it may be distributed under the terms of this General Public License. The "Program," below, refers to any such program or work, and a "work based on the Program" means either the Program or any derivative work under copyright law: that is to say, a work containing the Program or a portion of it, either verbatim or with modifications and/or translated into another language. (Hereinafter, translation is included without limitation in the term "modification.") Each licensee is addressed as "you."

Activities other than copying, distribution and modification are not covered by this License; they are outside its scope. The act of running the Program is not restricted, and the output from the Program is covered only if its contents constitute a work based on the Program (independent of having been made by running the Program). Whether that is true depends on what the Program does.

1. You may copy and distribute verbatim copies of the Program's source code as you receive it, in any medium, provided that you conspicuously and appropriately publish on each copy an appropriate copyright notice and disclaimer of warranty;

keep intact all the notices that refer to this License and to the absence of any warranty; and give any other recipients of the Program a copy of this License along with the Program.

You may charge a fee for the physical act of transferring a copy, and you may at your option offer warranty protection in exchange for a fee.

2. You may modify your copy or copies of the Program or any portion of it, thus forming a work based on the Program, and copy and distribute such modifications or work under the terms of Section 1 above, provided that you also meet all of these conditions:

a) You must cause the modified files to carry prominent notices stating that you changed the files and the date of any change.

b) You must cause any work that you distribute or publish, that in whole or in part contains or is derived from the Program or any part thereof, to be licensed as a whole at no charge to all third parties under the terms of this License.

c) If the modified program normally reads commands interactively when run, you must cause it, when started running for such interactive use in the most ordinary way, to print or display an announcement including an appropriate copyright notice and a notice that there is no warranty (or else, saying that you provide a warranty) and that users may redistribute the program under these conditions, and telling the user how to view a copy of this License. (Exception: if the Program itself is interactive but does not normally print such an announcement, your work based on the Program is not required to print an announcement.)

These requirements apply to the modified work as a whole. If identifiable sections of that work are not derived from the Program, and can be reasonably considered independent and separate works in themselves, then this License, and its terms, do not apply to those sections when you distribute them as separate works. But when you distribute the same sections as part of a whole which is a work based on the Program, the distribution of the whole must be on the terms of this License, whose permissions for other licensees extend to the entire whole, and thus to each and every part regardless of who wrote it.

Thus, it is not the intent of this section to claim rights or contest your rights to work written entirely by you; rather, the intent is to exercise the right to control the distribution of derivative or collective works based on the Program.

In addition, mere aggregation of another work not based on the Program with the Program (or with a work based on the Program) on a volume of a storage or distribution medium does not bring the other work under the scope of this License.

3. You may copy and distribute the Program (or a work based on it, under Section 2) in object code or executable form under the terms of Sections 1 and 2 above provided that you also do one of the following:

a) Accompany it with the complete corresponding machine-readable source code, which must be distributed under the terms of Sections 1 and 2 above on a medium customarily used for software interchange; or,

b) Accompany it with a written offer, valid for at least three years, to give any third party, for a charge no more than your cost of physically performing source distribution, a complete machine-readable copy of the corresponding source code, to be distributed under the terms of Sections 1 and 2 above on a medium customarily used for software interchange; or,

c) Accompany it with the information you received as to the offer to distribute corresponding source code. (This alternative is allowed only for noncommercial distribution and only if you received the program in object code or executable form with such an offer, in accord with Subsection b above.)

The source code for a work means the preferred form of the work for making modifications to it. For an executable work, complete source code means all the source code for all modules it contains, plus any associated interface definition files, plus the scripts used to control compilation and installation of the executable. However, as a special exception, the source code distributed need not include anything that is normally distributed (in either source or binary form) with the major components (compiler, kernel, and so on) of the operating system on which the executable runs, unless that component itself accompanies the executable.

If distribution of executable or object code is made by offering access to copy from a designated place, then offering equivalent access to copy the source code from the same place counts as distribution of the source code, even though third parties are not compelled to copy the source along with the object code.

4. You may not copy, modify, sublicense, or distribute the Program except as expressly provided under this License. Any attempt otherwise to copy, modify, sublicense or distribute the Program is void, and will automatically terminate your rights

under this License. However, parties who have received copies,
or rights, from you under this License will not have their licenses
terminated so long as such parties remain in full compliance.

5. You are not required to accept this License, since you have
not signed it. However, nothing else grants you permission to
modify or distribute the Program or its derivative works. These
actions are prohibited by law if you do not accept this License.
Therefore, by modifying or distributing the Program (or any
work based on the Program), you indicate your acceptance of
this License to do so, and all its terms and conditions for copying, distributing or modifying the Program or works based on it.

6. Each time you redistribute the Program (or any work based
on the Program), the recipient automatically receives a license
from the original licensor to copy, distribute or modify the Program subject to these terms and conditions. You may not impose
any further restrictions on the recipients' exercise of the rights
granted herein. You are not responsible for enforcing compliance by third parties to this License.

7. If, as a consequence of a court judgment or allegation of
patent infringement or for any other reason (not limited to
patent issues), conditions are imposed on you (whether by court
order, agreement or otherwise) that contradict the conditions of
this License, they do not excuse you from the conditions of this
License. If you cannot distribute so as to satisfy simultaneously
your obligations under this License and any other pertinent obligations, then as a consequence you may not distribute the Program at all. For example, if a patent license would not permit
royalty-free redistribution of the Program by all those who
receive copies directly or indirectly through you, then the only
way you could satisfy both it and this License would be to
refrain entirely from distribution of the Program.

If any portion of this section is held invalid or unenforceable
under any particular circumstance, the balance of the section is
intended to apply and the section as a whole is intended to apply
in other circumstances.

It is not the purpose of this section to induce you to infringe any
patents or other property right claims or to contest validity of
any such claims; this section has the sole purpose of protecting
the integrity of the free software distribution system, which is
implemented by public license practices. Many people have
made generous contributions to the wide range of software distributed through that system in reliance on consistent application of that system; it is up to the author/donor to decide if he or
she is willing to distribute software through any other system
and a licensee cannot impose that choice.

This section is intended to make thoroughly clear what is believed to be a consequence of the rest of this License.

8. If the distribution and/or use of the Program is restricted in certain countries either by patents or by copyrighted interfaces, the original copyright holder who places the Program under this License may add an explicit geographical distribution limitation excluding those countries, so that distribution is permitted only in or among countries not thus excluded. In such case, this License incorporates the limitation as if written in the body of this License.

9. The Free Software Foundation may publish revised and/or new versions of the General Public License from time to time. Such new versions will be similar in spirit to the present version, but may differ in detail to address new problems or concerns.

Each version is given a distinguishing version number. If the Program specifies a version number of this License which applies to it and "any later version," you have the option of following the terms and conditions either of that version or of any later version published by the Free Software Foundation. If the Program does not specify a version number of this License, you may choose any version ever published by the Free Software Foundation.

10. If you wish to incorporate parts of the Program into other free programs whose distribution conditions are different, write to the author to ask for permission. For software which is copyrighted by the Free Software Foundation, write to the Free Software Foundation; we sometimes make exceptions for this. Our decision will be guided by the two goals of preserving the free status of all derivatives of our free software and of promoting the sharing and reuse of software generally.

NO WARRANTY

11. BECAUSE THE PROGRAM IS LICENSED FREE OF CHARGE, THERE IS NO WARRANTY FOR THE PROGRAM, TO THE EXTENT PERMITTED BY APPLICABLE LAW. EXCEPT WHEN OTHERWISE STATED IN WRITING THE COPYRIGHT HOLDERS AND/OR OTHER PARTIES PROVIDE THE PROGRAM "AS IS" WITHOUT WARRANTY OF ANY KIND, EITHER EXPRESSED OR IMPLIED, INCLUDING, BUT NOT LIMITED TO, THE IMPLIED WARRANTIES OF MERCHANTABILITY AND FITNESS FOR A PARTICULAR PURPOSE. THE ENTIRE RISK AS TO THE QUALITY AND PERFORMANCE OF THE PROGRAM IS WITH YOU. SHOULD THE PROGRAM PROVE DEFECTIVE, YOU ASSUME THE COST OF ALL NECESSARY SERVICING, REPAIR OR CORRECTION.

12. IN NO EVENT UNLESS REQUIRED BY APPLICABLE LAW OR AGREED TO IN WRITING WILL ANY COPYRIGHT HOLDER, OR ANY OTHER PARTY WHO MAY MODIFY AND/OR REDISTRIBUTE THE PROGRAM AS PERMITTED ABOVE, BE LIABLE TO YOU FOR DAMAGES, INCLUDING ANY GENERAL, SPECIAL, INCIDENTAL OR CONSEQUENTIAL DAMAGES ARISING OUT OF THE USE OR INABILITY TO USE THE PROGRAM (INCLUDING BUT NOT LIMITED TO LOSS OF DATA OR DATA BEING RENDERED INACCURATE OR LOSSES SUSTAINED BY YOU OR THIRD PARTIES OR A FAILURE OF THE PROGRAM TO OPERATE WITH ANY OTHER PROGRAMS), EVEN IF SUCH HOLDER OR OTHER PARTY HAS BEEN ADVISED OF THE POSSIBILITY OF SUCH DAMAGES.

END OF TERMS AND CONDITIONS

How to Apply These Terms to Your New Programs

If you develop a new program, and you want it to be of the greatest possible use to the public, the best way to achieve this is to make it free software which everyone can redistribute and change under these terms.

To do so, attach the following notices to the program. It is safest to attach them to the start of each source file to most effectively convey the exclusion of warranty; and each file should have at least the "copyright" line and a pointer to where the full notice is found.

<one line to give the program's name and a brief idea of what it does.> Copyright (C) 19yy <name of author>

This program is free software; you can redistribute it and/or modify it under the terms of the GNU General Public License as published by the Free Software Foundation; either version 2 of the License, or (at your option) any later version.

This program is distributed in the hope that it will be useful, but WITHOUT ANY WARRANTY; without even the implied warranty of MERCHANTABILITY or FITNESS FOR A PARTICULAR PURPOSE. See the GNU General Public License for more details.

You should have received a copy of the GNU General Public License along with this program; if not, write to the Free Software Foundation, Inc., 59 Temple Place, Suite 330, Boston, MA 02111-1307 USA

Also add information on how to contact you by electronic and paper mail.

> If the program is interactive, make it output a short notice like this when it starts in an interactive mode:
>
> Gnomovision version 69, Copyright (C) 19yy name of author Gnomovision comes with ABSOLUTELY NO WARRANTY; for details type 'show w'. This is free software, and you are welcome to redistribute it under certain conditions; type 'show c' for details.

The hypothetical commands 'show w' and 'show c' should show the appropriate parts of the General Public License. Of course, the commands you use may be called something other than 'show w' and 'show c'; they could even be mouse-clicks or menu items—whatever suits your program.

You should also get your employer (if you work as a programmer) or your school, if any, to sign a "copyright disclaimer" for the program, if necessary. Here is a sample; alter the names:

> Yoyodyne, Inc., hereby disclaims all copyright interest in the program 'Gnomovision' (which makes passes at compilers) written by James Hacker.
>
> <signature of Ty Coon>, 1 April 1989 Ty Coon, President of Vice

This General Public License does not permit incorporating your program into proprietary programs. If your program is a subroutine library, you may consider it more useful to permit linking proprietary applications with the library. If this is what you want to do, use the GNU Library General Public License instead of this License.

Glossary

This small corpus of UNIX, security, and Internet-related technical terms is intended for the general reader. More terms and definitions can be found at

`http:/www.netdictionary.com`

A

Acceptable Use Policy

Abbreviated AUP. A formal set of rules that governs how a network may be used. For example, the original NSFnet Acceptable Use Policy forbade non-research use by commercial organizations. AUPs sometimes restrict the type of material that can be made publicly available; many AUPs ban the transmission of pornographic material. The enforcement of AUPs has historically been very uneven. This was true of the NSFnet AUP: its limitations on commercial activity were so widely ignored that it was finally abandoned in 1994, enabling the development of today's commercial Internet. See also *Netiquette*.

access control

Ensuring that users access only those resources and services that they are entitled to access.

active attack

An attack which results in an unauthorized state change, such as the manipulation of files, or the adding of unauthorized files.

asymmetric cipher

See *public-key cipher*.

attack

An attempt to bypass security controls on a computer. The attack may alter, release, or deny access to data.

audit

The independent examination of records and activities to ensure compliance with established controls, policy, and operational procedures, and to recommend any indicated changes in controls, policy, or procedures.

audit trail

In computer security systems, a chronological record of system resource usage. This includes user login, file access, various other activities, and whether any actual or attempted security violations occurred.

authentication

Ensuring that users are the persons they claim to be; the verification of the identity of a person or process.

availability

Ensuring that a system is operational and functional at a given moment, usually through redundancy. Loss of availability is often referred to as *denial of service*.

B

back door

A hole in the security of a computer system deliberately left in place by designers or maintainers. Synonymous with *trap door*; a hidden software or hardware mechanism used to circumvent security controls.

baud

1. An obsolete term for the speed of a modem. Specifically, baud refers to the number of times per second a communications channel changes the carrier signal it sends on the phone line. A 2400-baud modem changes the signal 2400 times a second. Baud is often confused with bits per second (bps) even though they are technically different measurements.

2. Originally, a unit of telegraph signalling speed. Set at one Morse code dot per second, it was named after J.M.E. Baudot (1845-1903), the French engineer who constructed the first successful teleprinter.

Blowfish

A block cipher developed by Bruce Schneier in 1993 as a general replacement for DES.

bomb

A malicious piece of code hidden in a program that remains dormant until it is triggered. A *logic bomb* is triggered by a user action or event; a *time bomb* is triggered either after a set amount of time has elapsed or once a specific date is reached.

brute force

A programming style that relies on the computer's raw processing power rather than intelligent design and implementation decisions on the part of the programmer. An example of brute force is a password-cracking routine that feeds the target system all the words from a dictionary.

BSD

Abbreviation for Berkeley Software Distribution. A family of UNIX versions developed by Bill Joy and others at University of California Berkeley starting in 1980. BSD versions 4.1, 4.2 and 4.3 featured paged virtual memory, TCP/IP networking enhancements, and other features that were widely implemented in commercial UNIX systems from Sun Microsystems and others. The current version is 4.4; it's implemented in FreeBSD, OpenBSD, and NetBSD. BSD is sometimes compared to and contrasted with AT&T UNIX.

bug

A problem with computer software or hardware that causes it to malfunction or crash.

C

Certificate Authority

Abbreviated CA. An entity that attests to the identity of a person or organization for the purposes of network security.

checksum

A mathematical calculation applied to the contents of a packet or file before and after it is transmitted. If the "before" calculation does not match the "after" calculation, there were errors in the transmission.

cipher

See *cryptography*.

circuit switching

The signal switching traditionally used by telephone companies to create a continuous physical connection between a caller and a called party. Contrast *packet switching*.

confidentiality
Ensuring that information is not accessed by unauthorized persons.

connect-time logging
Performed by various programs that write records into */var/log/ wtmp* (or */var/adm/wtmp*), and */var/run/utmp* (or */etc/utmp*). Programs such as login update the *wtmp* and *utmp* files so that sysadmins can keep track of who was logged into the system and when that user was logged in.

cookies
Electronic identifiers that enable web servers to record and track user movements through a site. Cookies are small files designed to support shopping cart applications; when a user returns to a site, a cookie is used to recall the items that were placed in the cart during their last session. Cookies are also used to help advertisers deliver new banner ads to repeat visitors and to store user names and passwords so they don't have to be re-entered each time a secure site is visited. Invented by Lou Montulli while at Netscape, cookies raise controversial privacy and security concerns. A proposed Internet standard (RFC 2109) would give users the power not only to disable all cookies but to detect when a site is tracking a user. It would also allow users to accept cookies based on individual preferences.

cracker
A malicious hacker who breaks (or cracks) the security of computer systems in order to access, steal, or destroy sensitive information. "Hacker" is often incorrectly used instead of cracker, especially by the media. Contrast *hacker.*

crypt
The original UNIX encryption program based on the WWWII-era Enigma machine.

cryptography

The art and science of keeping files and messages secure. It
works by mathematically transforming a *plaintext* (or
cleartext) message into a disguised *ciphertext*, a process known
as *encryption*. *Decryption* involves turning the ciphertext back
into plaintext. The mathematical function used for encryption
and decryption is called a *cryptographic algorithm* or *cipher*.

cyberspace

1. The place where computer networking hardware, network
software, and people using them converge. First coined by
William Gibson in his novel, *Neuromancer*. Defined by author
Bruce Sterling as the place where a telephone call appears to
occur: "Not inside your actual phone, the plastic device on
your desk. Not inside the other person's phone, in some other
city. *The place between* the phones. The indefinite place *out
there,* where the two of you, two human beings, actually meet
and communicate." John Perry Barlow first adopted the term
as a synonym for the nexus of computer and
telecommunications networks. Barlow maintains that
cyberspace should be regarded as a qualitatively new world, a
frontier governed by new sets of rules and behaviors.

2. The prefix *cyber* is often combined with other words, as in
cyberpunk.

cybotage

To willfully and maliciously destroy or impede the automatic
control processes of computers. To deliberately disrupt a
network.

D

daemon

In UNIX, a background process that lies dormant waiting to
perform some useful task. The sendmail daemon, for example,
continually runs but becomes active only when email is sent or
received.

dark-side hacker

A malicious or criminal hacker; a cracker; one who breaks into computer systems for evil purposes. From George Lucas' *Star Wars* movie—those seduced by the "Dark Side of the Force" are opposed by elite Jedi Knights.

Data Encryption Standard

Abbreviated DES. Developed by NIST (National Institute of Standards and Technology) in the 1970s; it remains a worldwide standard. This symmetric cipher uses a 56-bit key. A modified form is used in the UNIX password encoding system. In general, the use of DES is deprecated due to the availability of "DES cracker" machines. DES should no longer be considered "secure."

denial of service

A form of attack that prevents authorized users from accessing an information resource by making spurious requests. This term should be hyphenated when used as an adjective, as in "denial-of-service attack."

DES

See *Data Encryption Standard*.

digital signature

Extra data appended to a message which identifies and authenticates the sender and message data using public-key cryptography.

E

Electronic Frontier Foundation

Abbreviated EFF. To quote its mission statement, "The Electronic Frontier Foundation is a non-profit civil liberties organization working in the public interest to protect privacy, free expression, and access to public resources and information online, as well as to promote responsibility in new media." See http://www.eff.org

encryption

A procedure that renders the contents of a message or file unintelligible to anyone not authorized to read it. PGP (Pretty Good Privacy) is a commonly-used encryption program. See also *cryptography*.

error logging

Performed by the *syslogd(8)* daemon. Various system daemons, user programs, and the kernel report noteworthy conditions via the *syslog(3)* function to the file, */var/log/syslog*.

F

FAQ

Acronym for Frequently Asked Questions. A reference document created for particular topic or group that answers to common beginners' questions. It is considered poor Netiquette to ask a question without first reading the FAQ.

finger

A UNIX utility that reports information about other users who have UNIX accounts. Finger can tell you, for example, where and when a person last logged in to the system. It can also be used on a single host or across the Internet.

firewall

A component or set of components that restricts access between a protected network and the Internet or between other sets of networks. A firewall can be hardware in the form of a router or computer, software running on a gateway system, or some combination.

free

Many UNIX security tools are "free" both in the sense of not costing money and in the sense that you're free to deploy them without strict licensing or other restrictions. Be forewarned: None of them are free in terms of the time needed to find, understand, implement, and run them. To paraphrase Richard Stallman: Think "free speech" rather than "free beer." See "The GNU General Public License" on page 397.

G

gateway
A special purpose, dedicated computer that attaches to two or more networks and routes packets from one to the other.

GID
Group ID; a user's primary group membership.

H

hacker
An expert programmer who likes to spend a lot of time figuring out the finer details of computer systems or networks, as opposed to those who learn only the minimum necessary. Contrast *cracker*.

home directory
The initial working directory when a user logs in.

hypertext
Text that includes links or shortcuts to other documents, allowing the reader to easily jump from one text to related texts, and consequentially from one idea to another, in a non-linear fashion. Coined by Ted Nelson in 1965.

I

IDEA
See *International Data Encryption Algorithm*.

identity hacking
Posing as someone else. Posting anonymously or pseudonymously, usually with the intent to deceive.

International Data Encryption Algorithm
Abbreviated IDEA. First developed by Xuejia Lai and James Massey in 1990. IDEA is a block cipher that operates on 64-bit plaintext blocks; the key is 128 bits long. IDEA is implemented in Pretty Good Privacy (PGP), a widely-used crypto program.

integrity

Ensuring that information is not altered by unauthorized persons in a way that is not detectable by authorized users.

Internet

A worldwide network of networks that all use the TCP/IP communications protocol and share a common address space. First incarnated as the ARPANET in 1969, the Internet has metamorphosed from a military internetwork first to an academic research internetwork and then to the current commercial internetwork. It commonly supports services such as email, the World Wide Web, file transfer, and Internet Relay Chat. The Internet is experiencing tremendous growth in the number of users, hosts, and domain names. It is gradually subsuming other media, such as proprietary computer networks, newspapers, books, television, and the telephone.

internet

Any collection of packet-switching networks interconnected by gateways and sharing protocols that allow them to function as a single, large, virtual network. The uppercase Internet is the most prominent example of an internet.

Internet Protocol

Abbreviated IP. The part of the TCP/IP suite that defines packets as the basic unit of information on an internetwork. IP lies at the core of the Internet and many of its component networks. It defines the header of each packet, a structured collection of bytes that identifies the sender as well as the destination. The header is followed by the packet's contents, a larger block of arbitrary data that is reassembled at the receiving end.

Internet Worm

In November 1988, Robert Tappan Morris released the infamous worm that corrupted thousands of net-connected machines overnight. Morris, the son of a security official, brought issues of UNIX security to the forefront of the world's attention. The worm exposed a Pandora's Box of vulnerabilities in UNIX, including bugs in the venerable sendmail and finger programs.

IP

See *Internet Protocol*.

IP address

A string of four numbers separated by periods used to represent a computer on the Internet, such as 207.44.147.151 (hostname www.albion.com). The format of the address is specified by the Internet Protocol in RFC 791. When a PC accesses the Internet through an ISP, it may receive a temporary IP address.

K

kernel

The essential core of UNIX and other operating systems responsible for resource allocation, low-level hardware interfaces, and security.

key

A string of characters used to mathematically encode a message so that it can only be read by someone in possession of that key or another related key (depending on whether the encryption method being used is symmetric or asymmetric). Most cryptosystems rely on a key, which can be one of a large number of values (the *keyspace*). In general, the security of a cipher lies in the key.

kluge

A quick fix to a problem that places expediency over elegance. Pronounced *klooge*. Variant spelling is *kludge*.

M

mailbombing

The act of sending massive amounts of email to a single address with the malicious intent of disrupting the system of the recipient. Mailbombing is considered a serious breach of Netiquette and is probably illegal.

N

Netiquette

Network etiquette, or the set of informal rules of behavior that have evolved in cyberspace, including the Internet and online services. See `http://www.albion/netiquette`

network security

Concerned with protecting network and telecommunications equipment, protecting network servers and transmissions, combatting eavesdropping, controlling access from untrusted networks, building firewalls, and detecting intrusions.

nonrepudiation

Ensuring that the originators of messages cannot deny that they in fact sent the messages.

O

one-time passwords

Passwords that work once and once only. In a one-time password (OTP) system, users are provided with a list of passwords. After using a password to log in, the user crosses off it off the list, and subsequently uses the next one on the list for the next login.

one-way hash function

A hash function that is difficult to reverse—given a hash value, it should be hard to compute the message it was generated from. In addition, it should be hard to find two random messages that hash to the same value. A one-way hash function works on a message of arbitrary length and returns a fixed-length hash value (say, 128 bits).

operational/procedural security
Concerned with everything from managerial policy decisions to reporting hierarchies.

P

packet
A unit of data sent across a network. When a large block of data is to be sent over a network, it is broken up into a number of packets, sent, and the reassembled at the other end. Packets often include checksum codes to detect transmission errors. The exact layout of an individual packet is determined by the protocol being used.

packet sniffing
The intentional and usually illegal act of intercepting packets of data being transmitted over a network (or the Internet) and searching them for information (like passwords).

packet switching
A data transmission technique whereby user information is segmented and routed in discrete data envelopes called packets, each with its own appended control information for routing, sequencing, and error checking. This technique allows a communications channel to be shared by many users, each using the circuit only for the time required to transmit a single packet. Packet switching networks revolutionized the data transmission industry and made possible massive information networks like the Internet and its World Wide Web. Contrast *circuit switching*.

passive attack
An attack that does not result in an unauthorized state change, such as one that only monitors and/or records data.

password

A unique character string held by each user, a copy of which is also stored in the system in encoded form. During login, the authentication process requires that the password a user enters matches the stored value. Since passwords are shared secrets, they need to chosen and handled with care. See also *one-time passwords*, *password aging*, and *shadow passwords*.

password aging

A scheme for keeping track of how long passwords have been in effect and forcing users to change their passwords with some frequency.

patch

Interim code designed to fix a problem or problems with the released version of a software package. See also *bug*.

permissions

In UNIX, the ownership and access controls assigned to files and directories. They determine who can do what to a file. There are settings that determine whether the owner (set by user ID), the group (a predetermined set of user), or the world (anyone) can read (r) a file, write (w) to a file, or execute (x) a file. For example, a setting of "-rw-r--r--" means the owner can read or write to the file, the group can only read the file, and the world can only read the file.

personnel security

Concerned with hiring employees, background screening, training, security briefings, monitoring, and handling departures.

physical security

Controlling the comings and goings of people and materials as well as protection against the elements and natural disasters.

piracy

The unauthorized use or distribution of a computer program, compact disk, or other intellectual property. This term is most often used to describe the theft of commercial software programs, which are routinely cracked by either hobbyists, who distribute it over the Internet as warez, or by organized crime triads that resell the software on the black market.

Pretty Good Privacy

Abbreviated PGP. A program, developed by Phil Zimmerman, that uses cryptography to protect files and electronic mail from being read by others. PGP also includes a feature which allows users to digitally "sign" a document or message, in order to provide non-forgeable proof of authorship.

privacy

Ensuring that individuals maintain the right to control what information is collected about them and how it is used as well as to know who has used it, who maintains it, and what purpose it is used for.

process accounting

Process accounting's main purpose is to provide command usage statistics for billing. Upon termination of a process, one record per process is written to a file, often */var/adm/pacct*.

protocol

A series of rules and conventions that allow different kinds of computers and applications to communicate over a network.

public-key ciphers

An encryption method that uses different keys for encryption and decryption. In other words, a stranger can use your public key to encrypt a message that only you, holder of your private key, can decrypt.

R

Realtime Blackhole List

Abbreviated RBL. A list of networks that are known to be friendly or neutral to spammers who use these networks to send unsolicited commercial email. See `http://maps.vix.com/rbl`

README file

1. A text file included with an application that contains important (and often last minute) information about installing and using the application.

2. A text file on an FTP site that provides valuable information about the context of site.

3. Any text file that you are supposed to read before proceeding.

relay spam

The unethical and possibly illegal use of third party mail relays to send spam. By default, many email servers will relay or forward mail from any source to any destination. Spammers use this trust to save computational horsepower and bandwidth at the expense of innocent relay operators, who often must deal with the fall-out.

replay attack

A type of attack that defeats an authentication system by recording and replaying previously sent messages. The attacker records a username/password combination, for example, and then later uses the data to forge messages that appear to be authentic.

RFC

Abbreviation for Request for Comment. One of a long-established series of informal informational documents and standards that guide the development of the Internet. The most famous is RFC 822, the Internet mail standard drafted by David Crocker.

root

The administrative user account on a UNIX system that can bypass security controls. Sysadmins will log in as root when they need to perform tasks such as modifying system files, creating new user accounts, or setting up new services. The root account is also known as the superuser account. Root passwords are closely guarded and changed frequently by security-conscious sysadmins. See also *sysadmin*.

route

The path that network traffic takes from its source to its destination. In a TCP/IP internet, each IP datagram is routed separately. The route a datagram follows may include many gateways and many physical networks.

router

A computer that directs traffic and moves packets between networks. Any machine responsible for making decisions about which of several paths network traffic will flow. When used with TCP/IP, this term refers specifically to an IP gateway that routes datagrams using IP destination addresses.

RSA Algorithm

RSA is an abbreviation of Rivest-Shamir-Aldeman. This widely-implemented public-key cryptographic algorithm hinges on the assumption that the factoring of the product of two large primes is difficult.

S

security

Ensuring that private information remains private and uncompromised in an atmosphere where all other information is free. Security techniques such as encryption, passwords, and firewalls are designed to prevent unauthorized access to information, to protect the integrity of computing resources, and to limit the potential damage that can be caused by attackers and intruders. The notion of a "secure computer" is relative though: the only truly secure computer is one powered down in a locked facility that no one has access to.

seven-layer reference model

The standard model for communications protocols that is formally approved by ISO and CCITT. The ISO model identifies seven separate layers: the Physical Layer, the Data Link Layer, the Network Layer, the Transport Layer, the Session Layer, the Presentation Layer, and the Application Layer. The layers are organized conceptually so that the "lowest" layer represents the physical link between two systems and the "highest" layer represents user applications. In order for two systems to communicate, both should support an implementation of each layer. Each layer is referred to as a *protocol stack*.

shadow passwords

A system that stores passwords in a protected "shadow" file instead of */etc/passwd*.

shell

A command interpreter that's executed and presented when a user logs in. There are several popular shells, including the Bourne shell (*/bin/sh*), the C shell (*/bin/csh*), the Korn shell (*/bin/ksh*), and the Bash shell (*/bin/bash*).

smurfing

A denial-of-service attack that floods the target system with ping packets, causing network congestion and outages.

socket

An abstraction that allows an application to access the TCP/IP protocols. An application opens a socket, specifies the service desired, binds the socket to a specific destination, and then sends or receives data. Sockets were originally implemented in Berkeley UNIX (BSD).

social engineering

A cracking method that relies on deceit or trickery to overcome impediments posed by information security measures.

spam

To send a message (usually an advertisement) to many
discussion groups (bulletin boards, mailing lists, and/or
newsgroups) or to thousands or even millions of random email
addresses, without regard for topical relevance, ethics, or
legality. The act of spamming was pioneered in 1994 by Canter
& Siegel, the immigration lawyers who sent an advertisement
for their services to every USENET newsgroup and received a
whole lot of flamage in return. Since then, the net has been
flooded with fraudulent spam offers including get-rich-quick
scams, bogus work-at-home businesses, illegal multi-level
marketing and Ponzi schemes, solicitations for porn sites, and
sales pitches that are too good to be true. Spammers have
gotten more and more sophisticated in their methods of attack.
The technology behind spamming has been advanced by the
development of bulk email programs that can steal millions of
email addresses from the web and commercial online services
and mailbomb them all at once. A typical spam message is a
study in the art of fraud; spammers frequently forge the reply-
to header field of their outgoing mail (from
"anyuser@anywhere.com") so that enraged recipients have no
way to directly respond. They also often exploit open mail
relays in order to hide the message path. Spam companies
appear overnight, blast the net with millions or billions of
messages, and then disappear. Spam is widely frowned-upon in
cyberspace: no legitimate business spams the net or conducts
business with spam companies. Aside from using the mail filters
that are supported by many mail programs, the best response to
spam is to delete it. Responding to spam or responding to
offers to be "taken off the list" often only serve to confirm to
the spammer that an address is valid, resulting in more spam.
See also *Realtime Blackhole List*.

spoofing

A deliberate attempt to induce a user or resource to do the
wrong thing by pretending to be someone or something else.

superuser account

See *root*.

SUID/SGID

In UNIX, the set user-id (SUID) and set group-id (SGID) bits are part of the permissions associated with an executable file. If set, these bits allow a user to assume the effective identity of the file's owner (SUID) and/or group (SGID) with respect to the process while it is running. A potential security risk, these permissions should be carefully monitored by sysadmins and are detected by a number of security tools.

symmetric ciphers

Symmetric ciphers use the same key for encryption and decryption (as opposed to public-key or asymmetric ciphers). Symmetric ciphers fall into two broad classes: *stream ciphers*, which work on plaintext one bit at a time, and *block ciphers*, which work on groups of bits (blocks).

sysadmin

The system administrator of a UNIX machine, or someone who maintains UNIX systems. See also *root*.

system security

Concerned with user access and authentication controls, assignment of privilege, maintaining file and filesystem integrity, backups, monitoring processes, log-keeping, and auditing.

T

TCP

See *Transmission Control Program*.

TCP/IP

Abbrev. for Transmission Control Protocol/Internet Protocol. A collection of protocols that define the basic workings and features of the Internet.

Telnet

A protocol which allows a user to log onto a remote UNIX computer as if directly connected to it. Telnet usually requires a user ID and password combination that is recognized by the remote system.

terminal hijacking
An attack that takes over control of a terminal session. The attacker can send and receive terminal I/O while a user is on the terminal.

threat
Any action that has the potential to breach information security.

tiger team
A group of professional hackers that attempts to break into computer systems in order to test security measures. This term derives from US military jargon.

Transmission Control Program
Abbreviated TCP. The TCP/IP standard transport level protocol that provides the reliable, full duplex, stream service on which many network tools and services depend. It is connection-oriented in the sense that before transmitting data, participants must establish a connection.

Trojan horse
An insidious and usually illegal computer program that masquerades as a program that is useful, fun, or otherwise desirable for users to download. Once the program is run, it performs a destructive act. This usage is derived from the wooden horse in which, according to legend, the Greeks hid and gained access to Troy.

U

UDP
See *User Datagram Protocol.*

uebercracker
A highly-skilled and determined cracker that has gone beyond simple cookbook methods of breaking into systems. Motivated by personal gain, the uebercracker picks specific targets for specific reasons (as opposed to *hackers*, who are often motivated by intellectual curiosity).

UID

User ID; a user's unique identification number.

umask

A mask (i.e., a numeric string that blocks bits in a pattern) that determines the default permissions to be assigned to files and directories created by the associated user.

UNIX

A set of enabling technologies first developed at AT&T that have been incorporated into several legally distinct but closely related operating systems, each of which can be considered to be a "UNIX system." If it looks like UNIX, operates like UNIX, runs common UNIX utilities and programs, and is developed with UNIX as a model, it's UNIX.

USENET

The most available distribution of newsgroups is USENET, which contains over ten thousand unique newsgroups covering practically every topic and human proclivity. It is not part of the Internet, but can be reached through most Internet service providers. USENET was originally implemented in 1979-80 by Steve Bellovin, Jim Ellis, Tom Truscott, and Steve Daniel at Duke University. The names of newsgroups are comprised of a string of words separated by periods, such as "rec.humor.funny" or "misc.jobs.offered". The first word (i.e., "rec" or "misc") represents the top level category of newsgroups. The second word (in these examples "humor" and "jobs") represents a subcategory of the first level, and the third word a subcategory of the second.

User Datagram Protocol

Abbreviated UDP. The TCP/IP standard protocol that allows an application program on one machine to communicate with an application program on another machine. UDP includes a protocol port number that allows the sender to distinguish among multiple applications on the receiving machine.

UUCP

Abbrev. for Unix-to-Unix Copy. UNIX software that allows email and news messages to be exchanged on a store-and-forward basis between remote computers. Before the rise of the Internet, this was the main way that remote UNIX machines were networked. It is no longer in wide use.

V

virus

An insidious piece of computer code written to damage systems. Viruses can be hidden in executable program files posted online.

vulnerability

Any mechanism that could lead to a breach of the security of a system in the presence of a threat.

W

wetware

Hacker slang for the human central nervous system, especially the brain. Most computing systems have three essential components: software, hardware, and wetware.

worm

An insidious and usually illegal computer program that is designed to replicate itself over a network for the purpose of causing harm and/or destruction. While a virus is designed to attack a single program or system, a worm is designed to attack a network. The most infamous worm was created by Robert Tappan Morris in November 1988; it infiltrated over 6,000 network systems around the globe.

Z

zombie

A UNIX process that has died but remains listed as a running process.

Bibliography

Most of the citations in this work are contained in footnotes. This bibliography is designed to allow the reader to readily locate book sources as well as books germane to UNIX security. It's divided into five sections: "UNIX Security Books" on page 432, "Computer Security Books" on page 432, "UNIX Books" on page 433, "Books About Hackers" on page 434, and "Miscellaneous Books" on page 434. See also "Internet Resources" on page 345.

UNIX Security Books

- Braun, Christoph. *UNIX System Security Essentials.* Wokingham, England: Addison-Wesley, 1994, ISBN 0-201-42775-3.
  A good overview of UNIX security even though the title's reference system is SINIX, a somewhat obscure UNIX implementation from Siemens Nixdorf.

- Curry, David A. *UNIX System Security: A Guide for Users and System Administrators.* Reading, MA: Addison-Wesley, 1994, ISBN 0-201-56327-4.
  This hardcover book covers all the bases.

- Farrow, Rik. *UNIX System Security.* Reading, MA: Addison-Wesley, 1991, ISBN 0-201-57030-0.
  A solid if somewhat dated overview of practical UNIX security.

- Ferbrache, David, and Gavin Shearer. *UNIX Installation, Security & Integrity.* Englewood Cliffs, NJ: Prentice Hall, 1993, ISBN 0-13-015389-3.
  A decent overview of UNIX security that's particularly strong on programming for security.

- Garfinkel, Simson, and Gene Spafford. *Practical UNIX and Internet Security.* Sebastopol, CA: O'Reilly & Associates, 1996, ISBN 1-56592-148-8.
  This is the "bible" of practical UNIX security, the one security book you'd want if you could only have one.

- R&D Books. *UNIX Security: Sys Admin Essential Reference Series.* Lawrence, KS: R&D Books, 1997, ISBN 0-87930-471-5.

Computer Security Books

- Parker, Donn B. *Computer Security Management.* Reston, VA: Reston Publishing Company, Inc., 1981, ISBN 0-8359-0905-0.

- Norman, Adrian R.D. *Computer Insecurity.* New York, NY: Chapman and Hall Ltd., 1983, ISBN 0-412-22310-4.

- Baker, Richard H. *Computer Security Handbook*. Blue Ridge Summit, PA: TAB Books, 1991, ISBN 0-8306-3592-0.

- Garfinkel, Simson, and Eugene Spafford. *Web Security & Commerce*. Sebastopol, CA: O'Reilly & Associates, Inc., 1997, ISBN 1-56592-269-7.

- Garfinkel, Simson. *PGP: Pretty Good Privacy*. Sebastopol, CA: O'Reilly & Associates, Inc., 1995, ISBN 1-56592-098-8.

- Hemphill, Charles F. Jr., and John M. Hemphill. *Security Procedures for Computer Systems*. Homewood, IL: Dow Jones-Irwin, 1973, ISBN 0-87094-058-9.

- Schneier, Bruce. *Applied Cryptography: Second Edition*. New York, NY: John Wiley & Sons, Inc., 1996, ISBN 0-471-12845-7.

- Summers, Rita C. *Secure Computing*. New York, NY: McGraw-Hill, 1997, ISBN 0-07-069419-2.

UNIX Books

- Frisch, Aeleen. *Essential System Administration, Second Edition*. Sebastopol, CA: O'Reilly & Associates, Inc., 1995, ISBN 1-56592-127-5.

- Levine, John R., and Margaret Levine Young. *UNIX For Dummies*. San Mateo, CA: IDG Books, 1993, ISBN 1-878058-58-4 (4th Edition, ISBN 0-7645-0419-3).

- Maxwell, Steven. *UNIX Network Management Tools*. New York, NY: McGraw-Hill, 1999, ISBN 0-07-913782-2.

- Medinets, David. *UNIX Shell Programming Tools*. New York, NY: McGraw-Hill, 1999, ISBN 0-07-913790-3.

- Peek, Jerry, Tim O'Reilly, Mike Loukides, and others. *UNIX Power Tools*. Sebastopol CA: O'Reilly & Associates, Inc., 1997, ISBN 1-56592-260-3.

Books About Hackers

- Sterling, Bruce. *The Hacker Crackdown: Law and Disorder on the Electronic Frontier.* New York, NY: Bantam, 1992, ISBN 0-553-08058-X (paperback ISBN 0-553-56370-X).
  Covers the "hacker crackdowns" of 1990, including a number of UNIX hacks.

- Hafner, Katie, and John Markoff. *Cyberpunk: Outlaws and Hackers on the Computer Frontier.* New York, NY: Simon and Schuster, 1991, ISBN 0-671-68322-5 (paperback ISBN 0-684-81862-0).
  A tightly-written account of three hackers: Kevin Mitnick, Pengo, and Robert T. Morris.

- Levy, Steven. *Hackers: Heroes of the Computer Revolution.* New York, NY: Dell, 1984, ISBN 0-385-19195-2 (paperback ISBN 0-385-31210-5).
  A classic about the origins of the computer industry.

- Stoll, Cliff. *The Cuckoo's Egg: Tracking a Spy Through the Maze of Computer Espionage.* Garden City, NY: Doubleday, 1989, ISBN 0-385-24946-2 (paperback ISBN 0-671-72688-9).
  A general interest title that contains many nuggets of wisdom about UNIX security.

Miscellaneous Books

- Comer, Douglas E. *Internetworking With TCP/IP, Vol. 1: Principles, Protocols, and Architecture, Third Edition.* Englewood Cliffs, NJ: Prentice-Hall, Inc., 1995, ISBN 0-13-216987-8.

- Laurie, Ben, and Peter Laurie. *Apache: The Definitive Guide.* Sebastopol, CA: O'Reilly & Associates, Inc., 1997, ISBN 1-56592-250-6.

- Oxford. *Dictionary of Computing, Fourth Edition.* Oxford, England: Oxford University Press, 1996, ISBN 0-19-853855-3.

- Bryan Pfaffenberger, *Webster's New World Dictionary of Computing Terms, Sixth Edition*. New York: Simon and Schuster, 1997, ISBN 0-02-861890-4.

- Raymond, Eric S. *The New Hacker's Dictionary, Third Edition*. Cambridge, MA: The MIT Press, 1996, ISBN 0-262-68092-0.

- Red Hat Software, Inc. *Red Hat Linux 5.0: The Official Red Hat Linux Installation Guide*. Research Triangle, NC: Red Hat Software Inc., 1997, ISBN 1-888172-97-5.

Index

About the Author

Seth T. Ross has been working on UNIX security issues since 1990 when he launched one of the first Internet businesses, Albion.com. His writing credits include *Taking the Next Step: The Buyers' Guide to NeXTSTEP Computing* and Netdictionary (www.netdictionary.com), as well as numerous UNIX software and hardware reviews completed as a Contributing Editor to *NeXTWORLD* magazine. A graduate of Brown University, Seth has lived and worked in the San Francisco Bay Area for thirteen years.

Software and Information License

The software and information on this diskette (collectively referred to as the "Product") are the property of The McGraw-Hill Companies, Inc. ("McGraw-Hill") and are protected by both United States copyright law and international copyright treaty provision. You must treat this Product just like a book, expect that you may copy it into a computer to be used and you may make archival copies of the Products for the sole purpose of backing up your software and protecting your investment from loss.

By saying "just like a book," McGraw-Hill means, for example, that the Product may be used by any number of people and may be freely moved from one computer location to another, so long as there is no possibility of the Product (or any part of the Product) being used at one location or on one computer while it is being used at another. Just as a book cannot be read by two different people in two different places at the same time, neither can the Product be used in two different places at the same time (unless, of course, McGraw-Hill's rights are being violated).

McGraw-Hill reserves the right to alter or modify the contents of the Product at any time.

This agreement is effective until terminated. The Agreement will terminate automatically without notice if you fail to comply with any provisions of this Agreement. In the event of termination by reason of your breach, you will destroy or erase all copies of the Product installed on any computer system or made for backup purposes and shall expunge the Product from your data storage facilities.

Limited Warranty

McGraw-Hill warrants the physical diskette(s) enclosed herein to be free of defects in materials and workmanship for a period of sixty days from the purchase date. If McGraw-Hill receives written notification within the warranty period of defects in materials or workmanship, and such notification is determined by McGraw-Hill to be correct, McGraw-Hill will replace the defective diskette(s). Send request to:

Customer Service
McGraw-Hill
Gahanna Industrial Park
860 Taylor Station Road
Blacklick, Ohio 43004-9615

The entire and exclusive liability and remedy for breach of this Limited Warranty shall be limited to replacement of defective diskette(s) and shall not include or extend any claim for or right to cover any other damages, including but not limited to loss of profit, data, or use of the software, or special, incidental, or consequential damages or other similar claims, even if McGraw-Hill has been specifically advised as to the possibility of such damages. In no event will McGraw-Hill's liability for any damages to you or any other person ever exceed the lower of suggested list price or actual price paid for the license to use the Product, regardless of any form of the claim.

The McGraw-Hill Companies, Inc. specifically disclaims all other warranties, express or implied, including but not limited to, any implied warranty of merchantability or fitness for a particular purpose. Specifically, McGraw-Hill makes no representation or warranty that the Product is fit for any particular purpose and any implied warranty of merchantability is limited to the sixty day duration of the Limited Warranty covering the physical diskette(s) only (and not the software or information) and is otherwise expressly and specifically disclaimed.

This Limited Warranty gives you specific legal rights; you may have others which may vary from state to state. Some states do not allow the exclusion of incidental or consequential damages, or the limitation on how long an implied warranty lasts, so some of the above may not apply to you.

This agreement constitutes the entire agreement between the parties relating to use of the Product. The terms of any purchase order shall have no effect on the terms of this Agreement. Failure of McGraw-Hill to insist at any time on strict compliance with this Agreement shall not constitute a waiver of any rights under this Agreement. This Agreement shall be construed and governed in accordance with the laws of New York. If any provision of this Agreement is held to be contrary to law, that provision will be enforced to the maximum extent permissible and the remaining provisions will remain in force and effect.